The Message of Social Psychology

Perspectives on Mind in Society

Edited by Craig McGarty and
S. Alexander Haslam
Australian National University

First published 1997

2 4 6 8 10 9 7 5 3 1

Blackwell Publishers Inc.
238 Main Street
Cambridge, Massachusetts 02142
USA

Blackwell Publishers Ltd
108 Cowley Road
Oxford OX4 1JF
UK

Library of Congress Cataloging-in-Publication Data

The message of social psychology: perspectives on mind in society / edited by Craig McGarty and S. Alexander Haslam.
p. cm.
Includes bibliographical references and index.
ISBN 0-631-19779-6 (alk. paper). – ISBN 0-631-19781-8 (pbk.: alk. paper)
1. Social psychology. I. McGarty, Craig. II. Haslam, S. Alexander.
HM251.M45326 1997
302 – dc20 96-16494
CIP

British Library Cataloging in Publication Data

A CIP catalogue record for this book is available from the British Library.

Commissioning Editor: Alison Mudditt
Desk Editor: Hilary Scannell
Production Controller: Lisa Eaton

Typeset in 10½ on 12 pt Ehrhardt
by Best-set Typesetter Ltd., Hong Kong
Printed in Great Britain by T.J. Press Ltd, Padstow, Cornwall

This book is printed on acid-free paper

Contents

Figures

Tables

Contributors

Elliot Aronson University of California, Santa Cruz, USA
Michael Billig University of Loughborough, UK
Marilynn B. Brewer Ohio State University, USA
Willem Doise Université de Genève, Switzerland
Martin Fishbein University of Illinois at Urbana-Champaign, USA
Susan T. Fiske University of Massachusetts at Amherst, USA
Kenneth J. Gergen Swarthmore College, USA
Rom Harré University of Oxford, UK
O. J. Harvey University of Colorado, USA
Miles Hewstone University of Wales, Cardiff, UK
E. Tory Higgins Columbia University, USA
Bibb Latané Florida Atlantic University, USA
Jacques-Philippe Leyens Université Catholique de Louvain, Belgium
Diane M. Mackie University of California, Santa Barbara, USA
William J. McGuire Yale University, USA
Antony S. R. Manstead University of Amsterdam, The Netherlands
Penelope J. Oakes The Australian National University, Australia
Albert Pepitone University of Pennsylvania, USA
Richard E. Petty Ohio State University, USA
Gün R. Semin Kurt Lewin Institute, Free University of Amsterdam, The Netherlands
Eliot R. Smith Purdue University, USA
Sheldon Stryker Indiana University, USA
Peter Suedfeld University of British Columbia, Canada
Harry C. Triandis University of Illinois at Urbana-Champaign, USA
John C. Turner The Australian National University, Australia

The Editors

Craig McGarty was educated at the University of Adelaide and Macquarie University, receiving his doctorate from Macquarie University in 1991 (where he was a tutor from 1985 to 1989). His doctorate (supervised by John Turner) was on categorization and the social psychology of judgment. He spent 1990 as a lecturer in social psychology/social interaction at the University of Western Sydney, Nepean. In 1991 he moved to the Australian National University as a research associate and was appointed to a lectureship there in 1993. He has worked on a wide variety of topics in experimental social psychology, approached from the perspective of self-categorization theory. His recent work has focused on categorization, social stereotyping and the perception of minorities, social influence, and persuasion.

Alex Haslam received an M.A. in psychology from the University of St Andrews in 1985. He then spent a year at Emory University as a Jones Scholar before completing his doctorate (1991) as a Commonwealth Scholar at Macquarie University under the supervision of John Turner. After lecturing in the Faculty of Health Sciences at the University of Sydney, he was a post-doctoral researcher at the Australian National University where he is now a lecturer in social psychology. He is the co-author of *Stereotyping and Social Reality* (Oakes, Haslam, & Turner, 1994) and the co-editor of *The Social Psychology of Stereotyping and Group Life* (Spears, Oakes, Ellemers, & Haslam, 1996).

Preface

The idea for this book originated in 1990 shortly after we were appointed to our first jobs as lecturers. In our respective posts at different institutions we had to give some courses in social psychology to students whose primary academic interests lay in other fields: media studies, mass communication, organizational behavior, and nursing – to name just four. We both found this responsibility quite challenging and often discussed the problems we were facing in trying to explain to students what social psychology was about, why it was relevant to them, and what it had to offer. In order to clarify our thoughts we came up with the idea of each writing concluding lectures in which we tried to state as precisely as possible what "take-home messages" were offered by our respective courses. Many students remarked that they found these lectures the most useful that we gave. Many also stated that they would have liked to have heard the lectures at the beginning rather than the end of the course in order to contextualize later material and to make it clear exactly why they should devote time and effort to studying social psychology.

This reaction led to two additional observations on our part. First, we were motivated to speculate about the lectures that would be given by prominent social psychologists if they had to summarize their own visions. Second, in reflecting on this point, we noted that there was no existing text containing analyses of the sort which we were attempting; no source to which we could refer students that presented a range of diverse perspectives on the field as a whole. The more we discussed these observations, the more we argued and the more we saw the need for a book of this sort. It was this process which has led, some six years later, to the present volume.

Details about the precise brief which authors were given are presented in the introductory chapter, but broadly speaking this is the same as that which we set ourselves in those initial lectures: to seek to explain to a broad audience comprised of readers both uninitiated and well-versed in social psychology exactly what research in this field is about and what can be learned from exposure to it.

These questions seemed to us to be essential and timely for the discipline; and so we were extremely pleased at the response which our invitations to contribute to the volume received, and heartened by the enthusiasm and creativity with which the contributors set about their task. As a number of them note, it is not an easy one and it presents a number of frustrations. But in spite – or perhaps because – of this, in our role as editors we found the contributions to be insightful, thought-provoking and, above all, compelling reading. For that we would like to thank all the authors. We would like too to thank our partners, Fiona and Catherine, for their support as well as our colleagues and Alison Mudditt at Blackwell's for encouraging us to pursue the project to its conclusion. This book though, is dedicated to our parents: the first people to teach us the need for argument and the value of disagreement.

Craig McGarty and *Alex Haslam*, Canberra, 1996

1 Introduction and a Short History of Social Psychology

Craig McGarty and S. Alexander Haslam

The Purpose of this Book

> The department of psychology that is of primary importance for the social sciences is that which deals with the springs of human action, the impulses and motives that sustain mental and bodily activity and regulate conduct; and this, of all the departments of psychology, is the one that has remained in the most backward state, in which the greatest obscurity, vagueness, and confusion still reign. (McDougall, 1908/1910, p. 3)

William McDougall, writing at the start of the century, saw social psychology as part of this "department of psychology." In the same work he went on to state what he saw as the fundamental problem for social psychology to address:

> Social psychology has to show how, given the native propensities and capacities of the individual human mind, all the complex mental life of societies is shaped by them and in turn reacts upon the course of their development and operation in the individual. (p. 18)

As we come to the end of this century, it is appropriate to ask how far we have moved beyond the "backward state" that McDougall identified, and how much progress we have made in solving this fundamental problem or in addressing new ones.

It is obvious that, after getting under way around the turn of the century, modern social psychology is a large and very active field, and has been so for at least the last fifty years. Psychology itself is a huge discipline which encompasses many different fields, and social psychology is one of its major divisions. Psychology is often seen to be a particularly important science because it stands between the biological sciences (like biology, genetics, and medicine) and the social sciences (like sociology and economics). In fact, some psychologists regard themselves as social scientists and some regard themselves as biological scientists. The importance of social psychology is in part, as McDougall pointed out, that it is the section of psychology which is closest to, and most relevant for, the social sciences.

However, it is also true that social psychologists have not been completely successful in explaining the nature and functions of their work to non-specialists. Without going into the question of whether social psychology is less well understood than other comparable areas, it certainly is true that the subject matter of social psychology is of interest to people outside the field, and that many people feel a need for social psychology to make itself clearer.

In large part the external interest in social psychology stems from the fact that *to a greater extent than any other field*, it studies the events and processes that comprise people's everyday lives. Social psychologists study feeling and thinking, belief and disbelief, truth and beauty, love and hate, conflict and cooperation, communication and deception, pride and prejudice, and an endless list of other things which impact on people's lives in the most direct way. It is true that each of these things is studied by other scientists, but no field of any science can claim to study *all* of them.

Of course, other sciences are relevant to everybody as well. We all live on the same planet so the study of the earth's ecology is relevant to us all. We all live in the same universe, so the science of cosmology can also be said to be relevant to all of us. However, one difference is that all of the abstract concepts in the brief list above become deeply and personally relevant to all functioning members of the human race at some point. Our continued existence as people requires us to understand these things. We all have minds and we all live in contact with other people. It follows that all people are social-psychologically active, and can even be said to be amateur social psychologists (in that all people need to have some understanding of social-psychological processes). People can also be amateur cognitive psychologists, or cell biologists or astronomers, but not everybody is required, in the same way, to be such an amateur expert on these fields. Thus, an understanding of biochemistry might be extremely useful to have in the latter part of the twentieth century, but it is not essential for all people. However, everybody on the planet has to have some sort of explanation (no matter how rudimentary) as to why, for example, other people like or dislike them. A world where people did not seek to explain the most important events of their everyday lives is difficult to imagine.

Furthermore, it is even the case that the ways in which other scientists might seek to make the relevance of their science apparent to the wider community are, first and foremost, social-psychological endeavors. If, for example, environmental scientists wanted to make people aware of information about global warming in order to get those people to behave in a more environmentally responsible manner, then they would be engaged in a process of persuasion – an important part of social psychology. Nevertheless, to accept the rationale for this book, you need not be convinced that the subject matter of social psychology is more basic than that of other disciplines. You only need accept that it is about as basic as that studied by other sciences.

Despite the staggering breadth of the subject matter of the field it would be wrong to suggest that social psychology has provided the answers to all, or even most, of the questions that can be asked about these topics. On the contrary, we have only pointed to the extent of the subject matter to show the scope and diversity of social psychology, and to suggest the potential importance of this field of study. It is because of this diversity that we decided to edit this book – partly to give social psychologists the opportunity to explain their field to people outside it, but just as importantly, to provide in one volume the contrasting views of many different social psychologists about their subject. It is a fact that, perhaps as a result of the enormous richness and variety of the subject matter (or perhaps for other reasons), social psychology is characterized by a large number of contrasting perspectives. There is even reasonably widespread disagreement within social psychology about what it is, and what it should be (though such disagreements are by no means uncommon in science).

Fundamental questions about the nature of social psychology might be addressed in two ways. We could ask what progress social psychology has made in developing concepts which would be useful for the other social sciences (the concern about "the backward state" expressed by McDougall all those years ago). However, this question is best addressed by social scientists who are not social psychologists. The people who are best placed to judge the impact of social psychology on other social sciences are the historians of those sciences.

However, there are fundamental questions about social psychology which social psychologists can address fruitfully, and this is the task with which we are concerned here. In short, this book is our attempt to bring together answers to the question "What are the principal lessons to be learned from social psychology?" As even the most cursory glance at the field reveals, this is an enormously complex question which has many answers, and therefore it may be well beyond the ability of any single writer to do it justice. For this reason, we have sought to provide answers by inviting a range of social psychologists to offer their views. Thus this book is a collection of writings by important social psychologists on social psychology. The best model for this type of book is the *Festschrift* (German for "celebratory writing") written in recognition of distinguished scholars towards the end of their careers. If anything, this book is a *Festschrift* for social psychology *as a whole*. We believe, however, that some of the contributions may be somewhat more critical than those commonly found in *Festschrifts*, and we at least hope that social psychology is not approaching the end of its career!

Our approach of inviting a large number of social psychologists to submit their views is an entirely reasonable strategy, because, as those readers who are already familiar with social psychology will be aware, the contributors to this volume have done much to make social psychology what it is today. If anyone is to account for the current nature and form of social psychology, then collectively, the contributors to this volume should be well placed to do so. For the reasons outlined above we hoped to produce a book that would be useful both for nonspecialists who wished to find out more about the field, and for social psychologists who wished to compare and contrast approaches to the field and to have a consolidated source of the views of many of their colleagues.

Nevertheless, it is essential to make clear that the contributors to this book should not be seen as simply the best, or even the most eminent, contemporary social psychologists. Instead, they are a selection of those people who the editors thought would provide views which you, the reader, would be interested in. All of the contributors have had a substantial impact on social psychology, but they were invited to contribute on the basis of three criteria. These criteria were that the contributors should be:

1. eminent social psychologists who have been of major historical significance in the development of social psychology;
2. leading exponents of mainstream theoretical trends or approaches to social psychology which are currently having a major impact on social psychology;
3. people who were likely to express unique and interesting views because they are leading exponents of alternative theoretical perspectives, or because they have a demonstrated interest in the history of social psychology, or the status of the science.

By applying these criteria we hoped to obtain a wide range of views to encompass the diversity of social psychology (though it is worth noting that certain views and traditions are underrepresented – not least because not everyone took up our invitation to contribute). We would have come up with quite a different list of people to invite had we focused on simply the most eminent or influential social psychologists (though the decisions involved in creating these lists would have been just as difficult for us as editors).

We wished to present a wide range of answers from eminent social psychologists to the question we had posed. They were to be presented in a format with minimal academic editing or commentary, so that readers could compare and contrast them for themselves. It is largely for this reason that the chapters are simply ordered alphabetically by their first author.

After absorbing these twenty-two contrasting viewpoints, the reader may not be able to make up his or her own mind about what social psychology is, or even what lessons it is important to learn from social-psychological inquiry. We do, however, hope that the book serves to highlight material which will help readers make sense of a range of potential approaches to research in an ever-burgeoning field. In this sense, the book may not provide definitive answers; but it is hoped it will provide signposts to enable readers to develop their own.

The substantive content of the contributions that you are about to read has been edited only very minimally and the editors did not pass on any details to contributors about the content of other chapters until all had been completed. This means that the authors have been able to present their views to you independently and in as pure a form as possible. You can assume, therefore, that these essays express what their authors really think.

We asked the contributors to write their essays in a form appropriate for undergraduate students of social psychology. They were asked to address the following question: "What are the principal lessons to be learned from the study of social psychology?" The contributors were under no compulsion whatsoever to adhere to any format, providing that they addressed the message of social psychology in their essays. They were told that they could address metatheory (i.e. issues of broad approach to social psychology), theory (i.e. actual explanations of social psychological phenomena), empirical findings of research, or any combination of these three. The contributors were asked to provide an essay about 5,000 words long and to make reference to issues and advances in their own areas of expertise.

Before we get to these contributions though, by way of an introduction to social psychology for those readers who may be new to it, we will present some of the classic definitions of social psychology and also note some of the major historical trends in its investigation.

What is Social Psychology?

Of course, answering this question is largely what this book is all about, and we do not intend to try to answer it in great detail here. What we hope to do in this section, however, is to cover some of the classic definitions of social psychology. The point of this is to provide a sketchy introduction for those who might be coming to social psychology for the first time (though we should not be surprised if we find the contributors introducing new or different definitions).

Social psychology, for the purpose of this book at least, is a branch of psychology. It is thus concerned with those aspects of mental life which relate to social interaction and social phenomena in general. It is important to distinguish from the outset this type of social psychology (which is a branch of psychology) from another important and continuing tradition of social psychology which is a branch of sociology. This is really a separate tradition that approaches similar topics from a different direction. Sociological social psychology has its own textbooks and journals. The contributors to this book tend to come from the psychological tradition.

Within this psychological tradition, one social psychologist who was influential in many ways, but who has been particularly influential in providing long-lasting definitions of social psychological concepts, is Gordon W. Allport. It is entirely appropriate that we start with his definition of social psychology:

> With few exceptions, social psychologists regard their discipline as an attempt to understand and explain how the thought, feeling and behaviour of individuals is influenced by the actual, imagined or implied presence of others. The term "implied presence" refers to the many activities the individual carries out because of his position (role) in a complex social structure and because of his membership in a cultural group. (1954/1968, p. 3)

This definition is very much based on the idea of social psychology as the study of social influence. The idea here is that the central task of social psychology is to explain the ways in which interaction between people affects the way they think and behave. Social influence therefore encapsulates some of the major areas of social psychology such as persuasion, attitude change, conformity, and so on.

Clearly, though, social psychology is broader than just social influence (important as this may be). It is helpful perhaps to consider the diagram below showing the three broad domains of social psychology: social perception, social influence, and social interaction. Social perception and judgment concern how we see other social objects (i.e. people and things associated with them). Social interaction relates to social behavior, that is, behavior relating to people (and includes areas like cooperation and conflict, interpersonal relationships and many others). As we have already discussed, social influence has the central status of providing the links between the two broad domains. The links can be in both directions: social influence can involve the influence of perceptions on behavior, or the influence of behavior on perception.

One thing that we must make completely clear is that these domains are not separate bodies of inquiry. It is almost impossible to consider social interaction

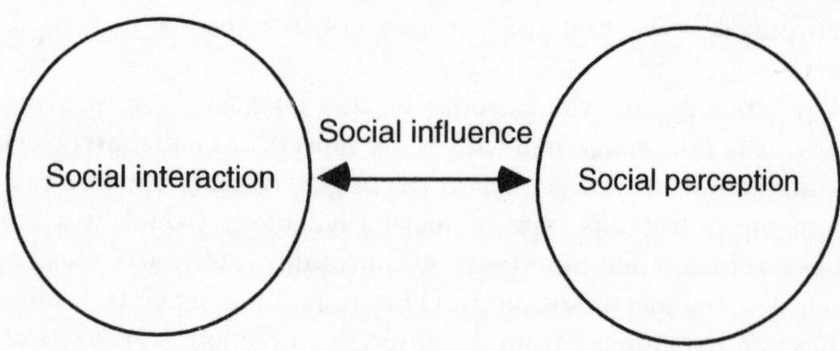

separately from social influence or social perception, and this is the point to note from the diagram. What we are trying to convey in the diagram is not that social psychology is made up of three *separate* domains, but that the domains of social psychology are *inextricably bound together*.

Up to this point we have skirted around the meaning of the word "social." This is a word that is used in very many senses by social psychologists and others. For example, social psychologists may define "social" as:

1. relating to interaction between people;
2. of, or pertaining to, society or culture;
3. of, or pertaining to, groups of people (where the terms "societal" and "cultural" are reserved for definition (2));
4. relating to problems affecting large numbers of people;
5. involving more than one person (this minimal definition usually carries with it ideas associated with definition (1)).

Definitions of social psychology tend to be associated with different preferred uses of this term. For example, a definition based on usage (2) above might define social psychology as the science of mind and society, whereas one based on definition (4) might define social psychology as the science devoted to the solution of social problems. Many of these definitions are necessarily prescriptive; they tell us what the writer thinks social psychology should be, rather than what it is, or has become.

A major tension apparent in any definition of social psychology is between the individual mind and the broader social context. The sort of definition of social psychology one comes up with depends upon the importance the writer attaches to these two elements. If one sees the broader social context as of critical importance then the definition will reflect this. If one sees the social context as being of somewhat less importance then this also will be borne out in the definitions proposed or accepted. Often this is presented as a conflict between social psychology as a psychological science and social psychology as a social science. As we will see, this tension has continued from the very outset of modern social psychology. To some extent, then, the difficulty in reaching agreement on what social psychology is, relates to variations in the meaning of the term "social." This is one reason why Allport's definition continues to be quoted – it works well as a compromise definition.

One solution, which is commonly adopted in science, when scientists cannot agree on what their science *should be*, is to opt for a *descriptive* definition. For example, we could try to define social psychology (rather trivially) as that area of academic inquiry which is conducted by people who call themselves social psychologists. Better still, we could define social psychology as the study of social interaction, social influence, and social perception. Thus, we might try to define social psychology in terms of a set of research practices (the methodology of social psychology). Again, this is not as easy as it sounds. To explain why, we really need to review briefly the history of social psychology. This should make clear the enormous diversity of social psychology, and also help the reader understand why it is not easy to define social psychology as a set of research practices.

A Short Historical Overview of Social Psychology

The purpose of this historical overview is to highlight some of the most important developments in social psychology this century. In developing this historical view we have tried to stick to describing what has happened, rather than explaining why these changes have come about. However, there can never be a true dividing line between these two types of history. Any history is necessarily selective and reflects the viewpoint and concerns of the writer. (On the other hand, in trying to write a nonpartisan history which accommodates many views one is always in danger of pleasing nobody.)

The foundations of modern social psychology can be traced to two developments in European psychology and social theory in the nineteenth century: German *Völkerpsychologie* and French and Italian writings on the psychology of the crowd (Graumann, 1988, provides a discussion on which the present treatment of early social psychology is based). *Völkerpsychologie* (literally: psychology of peoples) was an academic study of aspects of collective thinking. The approach was very much tied up with the political movement towards German unification (i.e. creating one state from the many small kingdoms and principalities which made up Germany for most of its history). In fact, the theorists were mainly interested in establishing the common aspects of the German mind, so that they could identify a distinctively German national character. Wilhelm Wundt, the famous **introspectionist** founder of modern experimental psychology, was also a leading figure of *Völkerpsychologie*. Nevertheless, the concerns of *Völkerpsychologie* were not carried on by later social psychologists. The movement basically died out but has recently been rediscovered.

Crowd psychology had a longer-lasting impact. Crowd psychology developed from the work of French and Italian writers in the late nineteenth century, and was based on observations of social upheaval in Europe around that time. Most of the groundwork had been done when Gustave Le Bon published his book *Crowd psychology* in 1895 which included many of the ideas of previous scholars. This work by Le Bon was extremely influential.

A central idea in crowd psychology was the group mind thesis. This was the idea that crowds and other groups took on mental properties which were similar to those of living organisms. In other words, group mind theorists either believed that the crowd was an organism with a mind of its own, or that it could be treated as if it were such an organism. Different forms of the thesis were held by Le Bon, William McDougall, and Sigmund Freud.

At the end of the nineteenth century the first social psychological experiments were performed. The earliest experiment has often been attributed to Triplett (1898). He had noticed that cyclists tended to go faster when there was someone else on the track even if they were not in a race with the other person. He tested this phenomenon in the laboratory where he had children wind fishing reels either alone, or in the presence of other people performing the same task. This was the start of the study of the phenomenon of **social facilitation**. It has been pointed out by Haines and Vaughan (1979) that earlier experiments were performed by Binet and his co-workers in the early 1890s on **suggestibility** (i.e. as in hypnosis), a hypothesized form of social influence.

The establishment of the date of the first experiment in social psychology has been considered important because, as we will see, the experimental method soon came to dominate the subject, and has continued to be dominant until the present day. Some people would argue that it is only possible to identify the origins of social psychology when we find evidence of research which uses social-psychological methods.

A next step in the development of social psychology was the publication in 1908 of the first textbooks in English, by two social psychologists, one of whom, McDougall, came from the psychological tradition that we are primarily concerned with here; the other, E. A. Ross, came from a sociological tradition, and was concerned with the structure of society.

McDougall's work was entirely based on the concept of **instinct**. His thinking had been influenced by Charles Darwin's concept of evolution which had revolutionized much of late nineteenth-century thinking in the life sciences. Darwin argued that organisms had inherited characteristics which are selected over many generations to adapt the organism for survival. McDougall's text book, *An introduction to social psychology*, is devoted to a consideration of how certain innate characteristics of the human mind (such as instincts for gregariousness, pugnacity, acquisition, and so on, and their links to corresponding emotions) are the basis of social life. Over time, instinct has been replaced by other motivational constructs as psychologists realized that to argue (for example) that humans were sociable because they had instincts to be sociable, was *renaming* rather than *explaining* the behavior. Nevertheless, instinct theories were necessary steps on the path to more sophisticated motivational explanations.

In the period immediately after World War 1, a backlash against the introspectionism of Wundt and the instinct-based psychology of McDougall and others took the form of **behaviorism**. Behaviorists argued that the subject matter of psychology must be firmly grounded in observed human behavior rather than in unobservable mental constructs. This approach suggested completely new theoretical structures and empirical approaches. Behaviorism was largely an American phenomenon, and its dominance led to the field being centered in the United States ever since. The most famous early behaviorist social psychologist was Floyd Allport (elder brother of Gordon). His textbook *Social psychology* appeared in 1924.

Allport, like other behaviorists, argued that a scientific psychology must be based, to the greatest possible extent, on observable behavior. That is, there was no point in seeking to describe unobservable phenomena such as groups. Furthermore, it was obvious to the behaviorists that whatever groups might be, they were not organisms, and they did not have minds. There could be no strong role for unobservable phenomena as explanatory tools in a science of behavior. That is, they considered a concept like "group" as a convenient analytical abstraction that could be used to summarize the properties of individuals, but which could be nothing more than the sum of those properties. In other words, behaviourist social psychology was strongly **individualist** (in that it focused on individuals) and **reductionist** (in that it sought to reduce complex systems into their constituent parts in order to explain them).

Explanations in terms of mental phenomena had a strictly circumscribed role in behaviorist social psychology. That is, the focus of explanation was on behavior rather than cognition. A number of important influences converged to change this state of affairs.

One important event was the development of a technology of attitude measurement by Thurstone and his co-workers in the 1920s. The concept of attitude had been developed in nineteenth-century psychology to refer to a predisposition to respond towards some social object. Although not originally seen as a mental construct, it came to be considered as one. Thurstone and colleagues sought to measure psychological constructs in a manner they considered analogous to the measurement of physical quantities. An important part of this work was the attempt to measure attitudes as mental phenomena of individuals which were related to some group (for example, the attitudes of whites towards African-Americans).

Another important event was the development of the work of the *Gestalt*-inspired psychologists such as Sherif, Lewin, and Asch. These theorists built on the *Gestalt* concept in the (mostly German) tradition of the psychology of perception. This work had been concerned with the idea that whole objects (or sums of individual particles) could have emergent properties which were more than the sum of their individual parts. For example, an orchestra can be considered as making a sound which is a property of the whole, and cannot be described simply as a property of the various individual musical instruments.

Social psychologists such as Asch, Lewin, and Sherif saw this idea as compelling when applied to social behavior. Here the individual particles are individual people and, tantalizingly, the prospect emerged that aggregations of individuals could be more than the convenient summaries that individualists had said they were. In fact, groups could have real consequences for social life

– in ways which were not explainable in terms of the properties of individuals. Thus, these *Gestalt* psychologists rejected in the same breath both the mental properties attributed to the group by the group mind theorists, and the individualist stand of the behaviorists that groups were not real in themselves.

This view was put most clearly by Asch (1952). He challenged the plausibility of the world envisaged by individualists where the most central aspects of social life (i.e. groups and institutions) were nothing more than fictions. He observed that the social environment is made up not only of things, but of relations between things, and he claimed that the latter have important psychological implications.

The *Gestalt* tradition in social psychology therefore promoted a concern with groups as real social entities, and the tradition of research on group processes and group dynamics can be traced quite directly to the influence of Kurt Lewin on North American social psychology. It also stimulated interest in mental phenomena as a topic of study (in fact, areas of social psychology acted as a sort of haven for the study of cognition during the years when general psychology was almost completely dominated by behaviorism). Another effect of the *Gestalt* tradition was to reinforce a strongly experimental approach in social psychology that had been evident in behaviorist work. However, the research conducted was of much wider scope, and was applied to a much wider range of phenomena. Effectively, the *Gestalt* tradition, and the continuing but opposed behaviorist influence, defined the theoretical orthodoxies of social psychology.

The tradition of work on group dynamics that was founded by Lewin and his junior colleagues and students became enormously influential. The best evidence of this came from the work of Festinger who in the 1950s proposed a series of theories which were unlike previous theories in that they were immediately relevant for all social psychologists. The theories of **informal social communication** (1950), **social comparison processes** (1954), and **cognitive dissonance** (1957) advanced the understanding of intragroup processes, interpersonal interaction, and social influence to new levels. Moreover, these theories were presented in a testable form, and the empirical tests proceeded rapidly, in particular through a series of ingenious experiments designed by Schachter and his colleagues.

These theories helped to establish and formalize traditions of research on social influence and **conformity**, social comparison, cognitive consistency, and intergroup conflict which represent an orthodoxy which has provided a centerpiece of social psychology (this tradition is reviewed by Jones, 1985). This tradition, which is sometimes called the **interdependence** approach (at least by people working outside it), provided one of two pillars of the edifice of mainstream social psychology (the other one being provided, consecutively, by attitude research and attribution theory) in the 1950s and 1960s. In particular, research on social influence and related topics revealed a variety of intriguing findings, in a series of important experiments. Many of these experiments (such as those by Asch on conformity and by Milgram on obedience) became the classic studies which provided the core of social psychology courses for successive generations.

This immediate post-war period was also notable for other trends. World War II had created political pressure for applied social research, which was designed to help achieve the war-fighting objectives of the allied powers. It became very important, for example, to understand persuasion and social cooperation in societies at war. After the war, research into prejudice and racial intolerance recommenced in earnest. This had been an important topic earlier, but the need to understand how seemingly normal people, in seemingly civilized societies, could behave in such inhumane ways to their fellow human beings, was now much greater. Post-war explanations for the negative behavior and attitudes that people displayed towards **outgroups** was in terms of **personality types**. The most famous example of this type of explanation was the massive project that led to the book *The authoritarian personality* by Adorno, Frenkel-Brunswik, Levinson, & Sanford (1950). Broadly, the personality explanations of prejudice argued that particular types of people were likely to develop negative attitudes, and show negative behaviors, towards groups of people different from themselves. However, nonpersonality-based explanations of prejudice also started to appear in the work of writers like Gordon Allport and Joshua Fishman in the 1950s.

World War II had also promoted interest in attitudes and attitude change. After the war the concept of attitude rose to become the most important single concept in social psychology. This research (led by Hovland) centered around Yale University, and those who attempted to understand the variables which led to successful attitude change were referred to as the Yale School. The interest in attitude change was generated by socio-political pressures which are beyond the scope of this overview. Suffice it to say, that by the mid-1960s, when it seemed that there were problems with the ability of attitudes to predict observed behavior, the importance of the attitude concept declined rapidly.

Three other trends occurred at about the same time as the attitude concept was waning in importance. One of these was that the behaviorist paradigm in general psychology was breaking down, especially as psychologists started to look to digital computers as metaphors for human information processing. The trend to include mental constructs in psychological theories helped to break down the behaviorist heritage of social psychology (although there had always been a strong cognitive element in social psychology).

Secondly, the 1960s saw the start of what has come to be referred to as the crisis in social psychology. The crisis stemmed from attempts to apply the methods of social psychology to an examination of social psychological research. This application was highly successful in that it demonstrated many problems with the ways that research had been conducted up to that time. At a deeper level, though, it also led many people to question the utility of social psychology and the validity of the very enterprise of social psychological research. The crisis was associated with a fractionating of the sub-discipline into new areas and a trend for new critical perspectives to arise, which suggested that social psychology should start anew. The most central of these criticisms was that social psychology took insufficient account of social context.

Another major occurrence in the late 1960s was the rise in stature of European social psychology. By and large the tradition of social psychology in Europe expressed the concern with social context that was emerging again in America. That is, many European social psychologists wondered aloud whether the dominant North American tradition of social psychology was too dry and artificial, and whether it paid too little attention to enduring aspects of social structure. The two most important figures in European social psychology at this time were Henri Tajfel and Serge Moscovici.

Tajfel brought to the study of group processes and social perception the **intergroup perspective** and the concept of **social identity**. Like Muzafer Sherif before him, he argued that to understand groups one needed to understand the relations between those groups, as well as the distinctive contribution that group life made to the cognitive processes of the individual. Tajfel also brought to his social psychology a strong cognitive tradition (being influenced by the New Look tradition in perception which had demonstrated the roles of need and value in organizing perception). As a result of his work the process of **categorization** (classifying stimuli into groups) became a central concern in social psychology and was applied directly to the explanation of **stereotyping** (which, with the rise of social cognition, has become one of the most important single topics in social psychology). Overall, this tradition is best seen as an intellectual descendant of the original *Gestalt*-inspired work on group processes and cognition (as is also the interdependence tradition). The intergroup perspective in social psychology is now a major part of the science in Europe and elsewhere.

Moscovici's influence on European social psychology was also very wide ranging. He challenged the orthodoxy in social influence research that had been developed from the group dynamics influence. In particular, he argued that social psychology had focused on influence that was related to conformity in behavior and attitudes. This was missing much of the story because, Moscovici argued, social psychology needed to explain **innovation** and social change achieved by minorities (the concept of **minority influence**). Moscovici was also influential in popularizing the concept of **social representations**. This was an extension of the idea of collective representations that had been developed by the sociologist Emile Durkheim in the late nineteenth century. Social representations are broad ways of understanding and experiencing the world that are shared by particular communities. An example of a social representation is psychoanalysis in Western culture. This is seen to be a widely shared pattern of experience which is used, by people who have access to it, to make sense of aspects of the world. The social representations tradition, then, was an attempt to grapple with the existence of broad social consensuses. In other words, it attempts to explain how it is that different people can understand the same things in the same way.

The most important implication of the rise of social psychology in Europe was the fact that, for the first time, social psychology was established broadly in more than one culture at one time (though cross-cultural social psychology itself has always been an important part of the sub-discipline). Early social psychology had been predominantly European. From about the 1920s it had been conducted primarily in the United States (though heavily influenced by immigrants and refugees from Europe). Now it was apparent that social psychology was becoming well established worldwide, though the center remained in the United States.

The third major trend that was occurring in the 1960s, with the breakdown of the dominance of the attitude concept, was the rise of **attribution theory**. The groundwork was laid by Heider's (1958) book *The psychology of interpersonal relations*, but during the 1960s attribution theories were also proposed by Jones and Davis (1965) and Kelley (1967). Attribution theory was concerned with people's explanations of behavior, that is, how people in their everyday lives understand the causes of other people's actions. Attribution theories were explicitly cognitive in that they were attempting to explain mental constructs (attributions, which are perceived causes of behavior). Thus whereas attitude research had had behaviorist (technically, neo-behaviorist) antecedents, attribution theory built on the cognitive revolution in psychology, and the tradition of cognitive consistency in social psychology (mainly from the work of Heider and Festinger). Attribution was for most of the 1970s the dominant concern in social psychology, and its domination was very nearly as complete as the previous reigns of group dynamics and attitude research.

During the 1970s critical traditions emerged from the crisis in social psychology. Important trends included the **social constructionism** of Gergen and others and the **ethogenics** of Harré and Secord. These and other critical traditions called for social psychology to be reformed in a new paradigm which was not dominated by the laboratory experiment. At the same time, social psychology was rapidly splintering. Many people who had formally defined themselves as social psychologists began to define themselves as working in different fields such as organizational or environmental psychology. Furthermore, workers in other sub-disciplines of psychology such as developmental psychology, psycholinguistics, and educational psychology were conducting more research that would have previously been considered to be social psychological. On the whole, this work has occurred with relatively little connection to mainstream social psychology.

It was in this setting that the most recent mainstream trend in social psychology developed in the mid-1970s, and has continued to be dominant to this day. Although the information processing revolution had had some influence on attribution theory, it was fair to say that the rise of attribution theory could be understood entirely within the context of social psychology. **Social cognition**, however, represented the explicit translation from cognitive psychology of the idea that human beings could be considered as information processing devices (like computers). Its novelty lay not in that it was cognitive as such (as social psychology had a long history of investigating mental constructs), but in the approach to cognition that it adopted. The mainstream approach was best exemplified in the work of Susan Fiske, Shelley Taylor, and their colleagues. They argued that people are faulty information processors (an idea which stems from work on attribution theories in the 1970s). That is, because of a **limited information processing capacity**, people take cognitive shortcuts, which lead them to make mistakes. This idea has been developed most extensively in the study of stereotyping and impression formation, but has impacted on every aspect of social psychology.

Without the benefit of hindsight it is difficult to be sure, but social cognition appears to enjoy a similar level of dominance to that of any of the previous majority trends. It is certainly the case, however, that there is a continuing critique of the mainstream approach to social cognition by researchers approaching the area from the European-inspired intergroup perspective, and by social psychologists concerned that mainstream social cognition is not social in that it does not relate to society, culture, or groups (usages (2) and (3) of the term "social" above – it is even sometimes claimed that social cognition does not relate well to interaction between people).

As we suggested above, social cognition really takes mainstream social psychology up to the present day. There are but two other trends which we will note here, though neither is anything like a majority trend. One important trend is the increased emphasis on language and rhetoric in social psychology, in particular the **discourse analysis** movement which is dominant in social psychology in the United Kingdom (but has had more limited impact elsewhere). This work is inspired by twentieth-century linguistic philosophy and European work on literary criticism (particularly, poststructuralism and deconstructionism).

Secondly, if the trend of importing ideas from cognitive psychology continues (with a lag of five to ten years), we may expect that social cognition will be influenced by models of cognitive architecture based on connectionism, parallel-distributed processing, and models of behaviors of systems based on chaos theory. Evidence of this work, currently a minority interest in social psychology, is increasing.

Conclusion

What should be most apparent from this overview is that social psychology has been structured by a series of revolutions that typically have lasted between ten and twenty years. Thus at one time it seemed that the majority of social psychologists (at least in North America) were behaviorists, then *Gestalt*-inspired group dynamicists, then attitude researchers, then attribution theorists, then social cognitivists. The clearest exception to this is the simultaneous dominance of the interdependence tradition (developing out of group dynamics) which remained part of the mainstream orthodoxy while attribution replaced attitude as a key concept.

However, none of the revolutions was ever completely dominant. The revolutions reflect the concentration of high-profile intellectual energy at particular times, as evidenced by publications that are seen as influential in hindsight. It is not the case, for example, that the vast majority of social psychologists were working on attitudes in 1960; but that is what the intellectual leaders of the field were to be found doing. All of the other traditions remained alive throughout the entire period up to the present day. Thus, with the exception of the group mind thesis and instinct theories, it is the case that all of the intellectual traditions mentioned above are still being actively researched. This is one reason why we have canvassed the opinions of so many people for this book. Secondly, it is apparent that sometimes the revolutions appear to involve a change of theoretical approach and at other times they involved a change in content area. In fact, both of these sorts of changes often go hand in hand. It is true both that the social cognitivists of the late 1970s approached social psychology in different ways to the attitude or attribution theorists (although many social cognition researchers had earlier been, and continued to be, attribution theorists) and also that they tended to focus on different social phenomena.

This historical overview has necessarily been cursory. We have not attempted to provide a unified commentary on a field which is characterized by enormous breadth and diversity. We believe that it is much better that you hear more about social psychology from distinguished proponents of various approaches to the field.

Glossary of Technical Terms Used in this Chapter (as marked in bold above)

The following definitions are intended to be as jargon free as possible. It should also be noted that many definitions are themselves the subject of considerable controversy.

attribution theory A approach developed to explain how people infer cause and effect in social interaction (e.g. whether they perceive an individual's behavior to reflect properties of the person or the situation)

behaviorism The doctrine which asserts that human behavior can be understood in terms of stimulus–response relationships without necessarily referring to underlying mental states

categorization The process of grouping stimuli (typically people or things) together and treating them as in some sense equivalent

cognitive dissonance Psychological discomfort, produced by having attitudes inconsistent with behavior, which creates pressures to change those attitudes

conformity The process through which individuals change their opinions or behavior so as to bring them into line with those of other people

discourse analysis A research methodology based on detailed analysis of all forms of language. No recourse need be made to explanations in terms of underlying mental states

empirical findings The results which emerge from any given piece of research

ethogenics A means of studying human behavior which does not seek to identify "causes" as such, but which seeks to identify those things in a given culture (typically shared representations and rules) which make certain forms of behaviour possible

individualism (a) A doctrine which proposes that the subject matter of social psychology consists of, and can be explained purely with reference to, individual people. (b) An ideology or cultural value which favors or stresses the importance of the individual and individual action and is often contrasted with collectivism or communalism

informal social communication A theory concerned with the manner in which individuals reach consensus through interaction with other group members

innovation The process by which individuals come to embrace new ideas (typically ideas different from those of a majority)

instinct Behavior that arises as a consequence of innate (inherited) pressures

interdependence A property of human relations pertaining to individuals' mutual reliance on each other (e.g. for the satisfaction of needs and the provision of rewards)

intergroup perspective An approach to social psychology which maintains that significant aspects of individual behavior and psychology arise from group life and relations between groups

introspectionism The doctrine which asserts that through a process of self-reflection individuals can gain access to their own psychological states

limited information processing capacity The notion that human psychological resources (e.g. memory and attention) are finite and hence that the nature of psychological processes is partly dictated by the need to conserve them

metatheory The overarching perspective or approach which underpins and guides research (but which is often not articulated explicitly)

minority influence The process through which a relatively small group impacts upon the views and behavior of a larger one or society in general

outgroups Those groups of which a person in not a member (as distinct from ingroups)

personality types Distinctions between different sorts of individuals on the basis of underlying predispositions to think and behave in certain ways

reductionism The doctrine which asserts that because complex things (e.g. society) are made up of simpler things (e.g. individuals) the complex things can be explained in terms of the simpler things

social cognition Like the term "social psychology," this has multiple meanings. Most commonly, it refers either (a) to mental processes associated with the processing of information about people (rather than things) or (b) to mental processes that are associated with, or affected by, social interaction, or (c) to the study of (a) or (b)

social comparison The process through which people compare themselves with others (typically in order to obtain information about their own abilities and opinions)

social constructionism The doctrine which suggests that all that we take to be true (objective) and good (moral) about the world and self, is a byproduct of social interaction. The languages that construct our worlds are both fashioned by and themselves sustain communal ways of life

social facilitation The process through which the presence of other people enhances individual performance

social identity That part of a person's self-concept which derives from their group membership (as distinct from "personal identity" which relates to that part of the self-concept relating to their uniqueness)

social influence The process by which people bring about change in the opinions and behavior of others

social psychology This has multiple meanings most of which relate either (a) to the study of psychological processes (e.g. thinking and feeling) associated with social interaction or (b) to those processes themselves (as in "the social psychology of crowd behavior")

social representations Understandings of social phenomena (e.g. "class" and "mental illness") that are widely shared in a given culture or community and which provide the basis for a common interpretation of things relating to those phenomena (e.g. "poverty" and "madness")

stereotyping The process of perceiving people in terms of their group membership (e.g. as students or women) rather than as individuals

symbolic interactionism A social psychological/sociological theory developed by Mead which suggests, among other things, that a person's sense of self develops reflexively through interaction with others. This interaction is seen to require the development and use of shared symbols with shared meaning

suggestibility An individual's readiness to be led (without the experience of voluntary choice) to behave in a particular way as a result of social interaction

theory A system of explanation used to make sense of, and integrate, a range of empirical findings

Völkerpsychologie A branch of psychology developed in Germany in the nineteenth century which advocated a historical and comparative approach to the study of cultural aspects of behavior

References

Adorno, T. W., Frenkel-Brunswik, E., Levinson, D. J., & Sanford, R. N. (1950). *The authoritarian personality*. New York: Harper.

Allport, F. H. (1924). *Social psychology*. Boston, MA: Houghton Mifflin.

Allport, G. W. (1954). *The nature of prejudice*. Reading, MA: Addison-Wesley.

Allport, G. W. (1968). The historical background of modern social psychology. In G. Lindzey & E. Aronson (Eds.), *The handbook of social psychology* (2nd ed., Vol. 1). Reading, MA: Addison-Wesley.

Asch, S. E. (1952). *Social psychology*. Englewood Cliffs, NJ: Prentice Hall.

Festinger, L. (1950). Informal social communication. *Psychological Review*, *57*, 271–282.

Festinger, L. (1954). A theory of social comparison processes. *Human Relations*, *7*, 117–140.

Festinger, L. (1957). *A theory of cognitive dissonance*. Evanston, IL: Row, Peterson.

Graumann, C. F. (1988). Introduction to a history of social psychology. In M. Hewstone, W. Stroebe, J.-P. Codol, & G. M. Stephenson (Eds.), *Introduction to social psychology* (pp. 3–19). Oxford and New York: Blackwell.

Heider, F. (1958). *The psychology of interpersonal relations*. New York: Wiley.

Haines, H., & Vaughan, G. M. (1979). Was 1898 a "great date" in the history of experimental social psychology? *Journal of the History of the Behavioural Sciences*, *15*, 323–332.

Jones, E. (1985). Major developments in social psychology during the past five decades. In G. Lindzey & E. Aronson (Eds.), *The handbook of social psychology* (3rd ed., Vol. 1, pp. 47–107). New York: Random House.

Jones, E. E., & Davis, K. E. (1965). From acts to dispositions: The attribution process in person perception. In L. Berkowitz (Ed.), *Advances in experimental social psychology* (Vol. 2). New York: Academic Press.

Kelley, H. H. (1967). Attribution theory in social psychology. In D. Levine (Ed.), *Nebraska Symposium on motivation* (Vol. 15). Lincoln, NE: University of Nebraska Press.

Le Bon, G. (1895/1947). *The crowd: A study of the popular mind*. London: Benn.

McDougall, W. (1908/1910). *Introduction to social psychology* (3rd ed.). London: Methuen.

Ross, E. A. (1908). *Social psychology*. New York: Macmillan.

Triplett, N. D. (1898). The dynamogenic factor in pacemaking and competition. *American Journal of Psychology*, *9*, 507–533.

2

The Theory of Cognitive Dissonance: The Evolution and Vicissitudes of an Idea

Elliot Aronson

Elliot Aronson was born in 1932. He received his doctorate from Stanford in 1959, where he worked with Leon Festinger. He has written or edited 16 books and over 120 research articles. He has won numerous national awards for teaching, research, writing, and public service. These include the American Association for the Advancement of Science award for distinguished research in social psychology (1970), the National Media Award of the American Psychological Association (APA) for his book, *The social animal* (1973), the Gordon Allport prize for contributions to prejudice reduction (1981). In 1980 he received (simultaneously) the distinguished teaching award and the Campbell distinguished research award from APA. In 1992 he was inducted into the American Academy of Arts and Sciences.

He has been elected President of the Western Psychological Association and President of the Society of Personality and Social Psychology. In 1995 he was given the Distinguished Senior Scientist Award by the Society of Experimental Social Psychology. In 1993, the University of California Alumni Association named him its favorite teacher.

In 1957, Festinger's theory of cognitive dissonance, a deft blend of motivational and cognitive constructs, burst on the scene. The theory revitalized social psychology, inspiring an extraordinary amount of exciting research producing a burgeoning of knowledge about human social behavior. Perhaps its most dramatic accomplishment involved challenging the long-standing dominance of reinforcement theory as an all-purpose explanation of social-psychological

I would like to thank Dr Ruth Thibodeau for her many insightful contributions to this essay.

phenomena. By the mid-1970s, however, the appeal of dissonance theory declined as interest in the entire topic of motivation faded and the journals were all but overwhelmed by purely cognitive approaches to social psychology. Recently, social psychologists seem to have rediscovered motivation, and several mini-theories have emerged blending cognition with motivation – in much the same way Festinger did some forty years ago.

In this chapter, I will analyze these developments, beginning with the emergence of dissonance theory and its early substantive and methodological impact on the field as well of the evolution and refinement of the theory. I will then discuss the changing fortunes of the theory, from its decline in the mid-1970s to its recent reappearance in the form of several mini-theories that combine cognitive and motivational perspectives with a central emphasis on the self. Finally, I briefly address the merits of a synthetic approach to theory and research, one that calls for an integration of these newer, conceptually related models with the dissonance research of the late 1950s and early 1960s.

The Historical Context of Dissonance Theory

When I entered graduate school in the mid-1950s, social psychology was in the doldrums – and seemed pretty boring to me. The "hot" item at the time was the Yale research on communication and persuasion which, among other things, demonstrated that people are more persuaded by a message delivered by a trustworthy source than by a less reputable one. For example, if you present subjects with a message indicating that nuclear submarines are feasible, it is more effective if you attribute it to a respected physicist than if you attribute it to an unreliable source, such as the Soviet newspaper *Pravda* (Hovland & Weiss, 1951). In retrospect, I can see that this research was important, but at the time it seemed so obvious that it hardly seemed necessary to perform an elaborate experiment to demonstrate that it was true.

In those days, almost everything done in the field was inspired by a rather simplistic derivation from reinforcement theory. Indeed, the name of the game was, "Let's find the external reward." If a person does something, there must be a reason, and that reason had to be the gaining of an identifiable reward such as food, money, or praise, or the removing of an unpleasant state of affairs such as pain, fear, or anxiety. If food will induce a hungry rat to press the lever of a Skinner box or turn left in a Y-maze, surely similar rewards can induce a person to hold a given opinion (see Miller & Dollard, 1941). Thus, in the above example, it was argued that people tend to be more easily persuaded by a credible source because it is clearly more rewarding (in the sense that it is more likely that one's opinions will be correct) to be in agreement with a trustworthy expert than to be in agreement with a biased newspaper run by a totalitarian government.

Even classic experiments that were not specifically inspired by reinforcement theory could easily be recast and explained by it. Consider Solomon Asch's (1951) well-known experiment in which a unanimous majority apparently disagrees with the individual subject on a simple, unambiguous perceptual judgment. Here people who would otherwise have made almost no errors in judging the length of a given line did so consistently because they reproduced the incorrect responses of other participants in the experiment (who were in league with the experimenter). Why do so many people conform to this kind of group pressure about something as trivial and as obvious as the size of lines? Reinforcement theorists suggested that it makes people anxious to be alone against a unanimous majority.

While research that could be explained by the reinforcement approach was reasonably clear and replicable, the effects did not seem very powerful or long lasting. For example, in the classic experiment by Hovland and Weiss (1951) it was found that, while subjects tended to believe the distinguished physicist J. Robert Oppenheimer when he allegedly wrote that atomic submarines were feasible, the effects of his credibility faded rather rapidly – one month later, there was virtually no difference between the effectiveness of the highly credible source and a source having low credibility.

Most experimental social psychologists seemed sanguine about their inability to produce long-lasting changes in attitudes and apparently were content with reward/reinforcement theory as an explanation for social influence. Of course, it goes without saying that there are many situations where reinforcement works well as a way of increasing the frequency of a response; but is that all there is to social behavior? One suspected that the human heart and mind were more interesting than that – but, if they were, it didn't seem to be reflected in the bulk of the research that was being done by American social psychologists in the 1940s and 1950s.

Then, in 1959, a startling experiment demonstrated a more exciting approach to persuasion. Picture the following scene. A young man performs a monotonous, tedious task as part of an experiment. After completing it, he is informed that his participation as a subject is over. The experimenter then appeals to him for help. He states that his research assistant was unable to be there and asks the subject if he would help run the experiment. Specifically, the experimenter explains that he is investigating the effect of people's preconceptions on their performance of a task – specifically, he wants to see if a person's performance is influenced by whether he's told either good things about the task (in advance), bad things about the task (in advance), or nothing at all about the task. The next participant, who is about to arrive, is assigned to be in the "favorable information condition." The experimenter asks the subject if he would tell the incoming participant that he had just completed the task (which is true) and that he found it to be an exceedingly enjoyable one (which is not true, according to the subject's own experience). The subject is offered either $1 or $20 for telling this lie and for remaining on call in case the regular assistant cannot show up in the future.

This is the scenario of the classic experiment by Festinger and Carlsmith (1959). The results were striking. The subjects who said that they found the task enjoyable in order to earn a paltry $1 came to believe that it actually *was* enjoyable to a far greater extent than those who said it for $20. The experiment was, of course, derived from the theory of cognitive dissonance. Briefly, as originally stated, the theory held that people strive for consistency among their cognitions regarding their actions, beliefs, past experiences, and so forth. Accordingly, when faced with cognitions that are psychologically inconsistent, the individual experiences dissonance, an uncomfortable motivational state similar to hunger or thirst. Once dissonance is aroused, the individual becomes motivated to reduce it, either by changing one or both cognitions to make them more consonant or by adding a third cognition which will render the original cognitions less inconsistent with one another.

Thus, if I were a subject in the Festinger–Carlsmith experiment, my cognition that the task I performed was boring is dissonant with the fact that I informed another person that it was enjoyable. If I were paid $20 for making that statement, this cognition would provide ample external justification for my action. However, if I were paid only $1, I would lack sufficient external justification for having made the statement. This discrepancy produces dissonance. One way to reduce dissonance would be for me to convince myself that the task was somewhat more interesting than it seemed at first. In effect, I would convince myself that my statement to the other student was not a great lie, in the process persuading myself that the task was actually interesting.

Dissonance-generated attitude change is not limited to such trivial judgments as the dullness of a boring task. It has been extended to much more important opinions, such as a reassessment of the dangers of smoking marijuana among students at the University of Texas (Nel, Helmreich, & Aronson, 1969), and the softening of Yale students' attitudes toward the alleged anti-student brutality of the New Haven police (Cohen, 1962). It has also been extended to include important changes in behavior like the conservation of water and energy (Dickerson, Thibodeau, Aronson, & Miller, 1992), and increases in condom use among sexually active teenagers (Aronson, 1991; Stone, Aronson, Crain, Winslow, & Fried, 1994). I have suggested (Aronson, 1968, 1969, 1980) that the persuasive effects in these experiments are more powerful and will last longer than those resulting from advertising, and other "direct" persuasion attempts – as in the Hovland and Weiss experiment – because the arousal of dissonance always entails relatively high levels of *personal involvement*, and therefore the reduction of dissonance always requires some form of *self-justification*. Let me elaborate on that assertion.

Dissonance and the Self: The Power of Self-Persuasion

After working with dissonance theory for a few years, I began to believe that Festinger's original formulation might be a little too vague. Several situations arose where it wasn't entirely clear what the theory would predict. Accordingly, I began to confront the vagueness of the theory by drawing attention to the underlying importance of clear expectancies in arousing dissonance, particularly expectancies regarding the self (Aronson, 1960). Specifically, I proposed a modification of the theory arguing that dissonance theory makes its clearest predictions when an important element of the self-concept is threatened – that is, when an individual performs a behavior that is inconsistent with his or her sense of self.

My modification was a modest one; it retained the core notion of inconsistency but shifted the emphasis to the self-concept. This modification increased the predictive power of the theory without seriously limiting its scope. In a subsequent article, Merrill Carlsmith and I (Aronson & Carlsmith, 1962) argued that Festinger's original statement – and all of the early experiments – rested on the implicit assumption that individuals have a reasonably positive self-concept. But, if an individual considered himself to be a "schnook," he might expect himself to do schnooky things – like go through a severe initiation in order to get into a group, or say things that he didn't quite believe. For such individuals, dissonance would not be aroused under the same conditions as for persons with a favorable view of themselves. Rather, we argued, dissonance would occur when negative self-expectancies were violated – that is, when the person with a poor self-concept engages in a behavior that reflects positively on the self.

A few years later, I carried this reasoning a step further (Aronson, 1968; Aronson, Chase, Helmreich, & Ruhnke, 1974), elaborating on the centrality of the self-concept in dissonance processes and suggesting that, in this regard, people generally strive to maintain a sense of self that is both consistent *and* positive. That is, because most people have relatively favorable views of themselves, preserving a stable, consistent self-concept will also involve maintaining a positive self-concept – broadly speaking, a sense of self that is competent and morally good. As a result, such acts as lying, advocating a position contrary to one's true beliefs, or otherwise acting against one's principles – the stock in trade of countless dissonance experiments – will arouse dissonance for most individuals.

In sum, efforts to reduce dissonance involve a process of self-justification because, in most instances, dissonance is experienced after engaging in an action that leaves one feeling stupid or immoral (see Aronson et al., 1974). Moreover, the greater the personal commitment or self-involvement implied by the action and the smaller the *external* justification for that action, the greater the dissonance and, therefore, the more powerful the attitude change. Thus, in the Festinger–Carlsmith experiment, the act of deceiving another person would make one feel immoral or guilty. In order to reduce that dissonance, one must convince oneself that little or no deception was involved – in other words, that the task *was*, in fact, a rather interesting activity. By justifying one's actions in this fashion, one is able to restore a sense of self as morally good.

Compare this active process of cognitive change – or *self-persuasion* – with a typical study of the effects of persuasive campaigns (e.g. Hovland & Weiss, 1951). Here, the reason I'm changing my opinion is that someone smart and trustworthy thinks that something is true. Very little of me is invested. Conversely, when dissonance is involved, the individual's self-concept is deeply engaged in the process of self-justification. Therefore, it is expected that, if an individual's opinions on important matters can be changed, these changes can be of a substantial magnitude and more or less permanent.

There are some solid data on the permanence of dissonance-induced opinion change. For example, Freedman (1965) conducted a conceptual replication of Aronson and Carlsmith's (1963) "forbidden toy" experiment, in which children were threatened with either severe or mild punishment if they played with an attractive toy. As predicted, Aronson and Carlsmith's experiment revealed that children complying in the face of mild threats subsequently convinced themselves that the forbidden toy was *less* attractive than did those children who were confronted with severe threats. The derivation from Festinger's theory should be clear to the reader. If I am a child eager to play with a particularly attractive toy and an authority figure threatens to break my arm if I play with it, I will not play with the toy and I will experience no dissonance. The cognition that you will break my arm is more than ample justification for my abstinence. But what if you issued a mild threat – one just barely sufficient to induce short-term compliance but was not a superabundant justification? Here, my not playing with the toy would be dissonant with the attractiveness of the toy. In this case, I would seek additional justification for my abstinence – by convincing myself, for example, that the toy wasn't all that attractive.

Freedman conceptually replicated these results. The experimenter admonished children (either with mild or severe threats) not to play with an extraordinarily attractive toy (a battery-powered robot). Several weeks later, a different person visited the school and, in a totally unrelated activity, administered a test to the students in the same room where the toy study had been conducted. The toys were casually scattered about the room. The visitor administered a written test to each child and, while grading it, suggested that the child might want to spend some time playing with those toys that "someone must have left here." The results were striking. Children who previously had been in the severe-threat condition showed a greater tendency to play with the forbidden toy. After all, why not? The person who had threatened them was no longer around; compliance was no longer necessary. On the other hand, the children in the mild-threat condition had little external justification for this restraint; as a result, they had a much stronger need for *self*-justification. In other words, they needed to convince themselves that they weren't playing with the toy because they really didn't want to – and they didn't really want to because they didn't like the toy.

As predicted, this cognitive activity had an enduring impact, reflecting a deep-seated, *internalized* attitude change rather than mere compliance due to fear of punishment. Indeed, up to nine weeks after the initial experiment, the overwhelming majority of the children in the mild-threat condition refrained from playing with the previously forbidden toy. As Freedman's experiment demonstrates, the power of self-justification *does* produce important, long-lasting changes in attitudes.

Impact on the Field

For students of the 1990s, the results of early experiments on cognitive dissonance may seem boring and obvious. Nonetheless, at the time of their publication, they startled the social-psychological community. The findings departed from the general orientation accepted either tacitly or explicitly by most social psychologists in the 1950s: it seemed logical for high incentives (not *low* incentives) to produce greater learning, greater conformity, greater performance, greater satisfaction, greater persuasion, and so on.

These results generated enthusiasm for many social psychologists because, at the time, they represented a striking and convincing act of liberation from the dominance of a general reward-reinforcement theory. The findings of these early experiments demonstrated dramatically that, at least under certain conditions, reward theory was inadequate. In doing so, dissonance research sounded a clarion call to cognitively oriented social psychologists, proclaiming that human beings *think* – engaging in all kinds of cognitive gymnastics aimed at justifying their own behavior; they do not always behave in a mechanistic manner.

Perhaps most important, dissonance theory inspired an enormous number and variety of hypotheses which were specific to the theory and could be tested in the laboratory. The wide array of research that dissonance theory has inspired has been truly astonishing. Dissonance research runs the gamut from decision making to the socialization of children; from interpersonal attraction to the antecedents of hunger and thirst; from color preference to selective informational exposure; from the proselytizing behavior of religious zealots to the behavior of gamblers at a race track, from shower-taking behavior to the practice of safer sex.

The impact of dissonance theory went even beyond the generation of new and exciting knowledge. Given the nature of the hypotheses we were testing, dissonance researchers were forced to develop a new experimental methodology; a powerful, high impact set of procedures that allowed us to ask truly important questions in a very precise manner. As we all know, the laboratory tends to be an artificial environment. But dissonance research made it necessary to overcome that artificiality by developing a methodology that would enmesh subjects in a set of events – a drama, if you will – which made it impossible for them to avoid taking these events seriously.

In my writing on research methods (Aronson & Carlsmith, 1968; Aronson, Ellsworth, Carlsmith, & Gonzales, 1990) I've called this tactic "experimental reality" where, within the admittedly phoney confines of the lab, real things are happening to real people. Because of the nature of our hypotheses, we could not afford the luxury – so common in contemporary research – of having subjects passively look at a video tape of events happening to someone else and then make judgments about them. Rather, our research questions required the construction of an elaborate scenario in which subjects became immersed. Thus, what dissonance research brought into focus more clearly than any other body of work is the fact that the social psychological laboratory, with all of its contrivances and complex scenarios, can produce clear, powerful effects which are conceptually replicable in both the laboratory and in the real world.

Eclipse and Re-emergence

Waning of interest

Dissonance theory proved to be an extraordinarily fruitful and powerful explanatory concept, both in and out of the laboratory. From the late 1950s to the mid-1970s, dissonance research dominated the journals of social psychology. The theory inspired hundreds of experiments, many yielding nonobvious insights into otherwise perplexing aspects of the human condition. Moreover, by the mid-1970s the theory had transcended the boundaries of academic social psychology and was widely cited in journals in a variety of disciplines including economics, philosophy, law, political science, and anthropology. The concept also managed to seep into the popular culture, being featured in articles in the *New York Times*, *Newsweek*, *Playboy* and, alas, the *National Enquirer*.[1] It even found its way into daytime soap operas. Ironically, however, just as a wide range of intellectuals and the general public were beginning to embrace the notion of cognitive dissonance, interest in the theory among social psychologists began to wane. Indeed, by the end of the 1970s, dissonance experiments had all but disappeared from the social-psychological literature.

How did this come about? There are a number of interrelated reasons, which I have explored in greater detail elsewhere (Aronson, 1992). One of the most important reasons for the theory's decline, however, lies in a larger historical trend involving the shifting fortunes of research interests in social psychology, wherein certain topics and perspectives fall out of fashion, as others ascend to claim their moment in the sun (e.g. see Jones, 1985; Aronson, 1992). In particular, the dwindling interest in dissonance theory coincided with a growing fascination with information processing approaches to social-psychological phenomena, imported from cognitive psychology. Eventually, under the sway of the cognitive revolution, motivational perspectives in general – and dissonance theory, in particular – fell out of favor (Aronson, 1989, 1992; Berkowitz & Devine, 1989).

In his influential paper on the intuitive psychologist and his shortcomings, Lee Ross (1977) suggested that it might be a good idea to temporarily abandon motivational constructs altogether in order to concentrate on the purely cognitive influences on attributional judgments. This was a useful temporary strategy; but it was also a convenient fiction – one with unintended, and unfortunate, consequences. One of them was that we tended to forget that it *was* simply a convenient fiction – and nothing more.

Once the cognitive perspective gained ascendancy, researchers not only lost interest in the concept of motivation, they seemed to forget it existed. Interestingly enough, a great many social psychologists began to reinvent experiments to test cognitive notions that could have easily been done under the rubric of dissonance theory; but now there were different, nonmotivational explanations for the processes under investigation. Most important, the connection between this new body of research and the older research was not noted, and therefore, was severed.

There are dozens of examples of this phenomenon in the literature; I'll discuss only one. It is a particularly cogent example because it was a fine piece of research done by people I respect a great deal (Lord, Ross, & Lepper, 1979). Let me quote from the abstract of that article:

> People who hold strong opinions on complex social issues are likely to examine relevant empirical evidence in a biased manner. They are apt to accept "confirming" evidence at face value while subjecting "disconfirming" evidence to critical evaluation, and as a result to draw undue support for their initial positions from mixed or random empirical findings.

This experiment is directly derivable from dissonance theory. Indeed, here is what Festinger (1957) predicted would happen if a person were forced to read a persuasive communication which went against a strong belief, in this case about the hazards of smoking:

> One might expect to observe such things as . . . erroneous interpretation or perception of the material. . . . [for example], it is only among smokers [not non-smokers] that one would expect to find skepticism concerning the reported research findings [linking smoking to cancer].

Although the wording of these two passages is almost identical, the article by Lord et al. contains thirty-two references – but not one to dissonance theory or any of the dissonance experiments. That is, the authors were content with a purely cognitive-heuristic explanation for their results. But just because it is possible to explain those results without recourse to motivational constructs does not mean that a motivational explanation is incorrect.

I want to make it clear that I am not accusing Lord et al. of shoddy scholarship – far from it. I single them out precisely because they are such irreproachably *good* scholars. I use this experiment solely as an illustration of what happens when artificial barriers are erected and related theories get insulated from each other: We decrease our ability to forge vital syntheses – and, consequently, our discipline becomes unnecessarily fragmented and disjointed.

Dissonance by any other name

The above example illustrates how, as dissonance theory faded from the minds of mainstream social psychologists, new data that were highly compatible with the theory were attributed to non-motivational processes. During the past several years, however, many of the researchers who had been enthralled by social cognition in the 1970s and early 1980s have apparently come to the realization that pure cognition can only carry us so far. Accordingly, several social psychologists seem to have rediscovered the idea of motivation and have come to the conclusion that it might be interesting to try to combine cognition with motivation – in other words, exactly the strategy Leon Festinger employed so brilliantly in 1957.

Thus, in recent years a plethora of mini-theories has sprung up, all of which are strikingly reminiscent of dissonance theory in uniting cognitive and motivational perspectives, along with a central emphasis on the self-concept. These conceptual efforts include self-affirmation theory (e.g. Steele, 1988), symbolic self-completion theory (e.g. Wicklund & Gollwitzer, 1982), motivating reasoning (e.g. Kunda, 1990), self-evaluation maintenance theory (e.g. Tesser, 1988), self-discrepancy theory (Higgins, 1989), and self-verification theory (e.g. Swann, 1984).

Each of these theories is a worthy and interesting effort. All of them, in one way or another, share a central concern with how people cope with threats to the self-concept. Yet each of these theories has a limited scope and a fairly narrow domain of application. What's more, every one of them, in my judgment, has the potential to be integrated within the broader conceptual framework of dissonance theory, once the central role of the self-concept is acknowledged (Aronson, 1968, 1992; Thibodeau & Aronson, 1992). This is not meant to imply that each of these narrow-range theories fails to offer something important. They do. Rather, the concern I would raise is this: it does not advance the science when we have a half-dozen or more theories doing the work of one.

Why do I think it's better to have one big theory rather than seven or eight little ones? Is it simply a matter of esthetics or what? No, it is much more than that. As Berkowitz and Devine (1989) have cogently argued, social psychologists have been much more prone toward analysis than synthesis in their approach to theory and research. By analysis, they refer to the careful delineation and differentiation of the theoretical concepts and propositions which lead to the prediction of different outcomes. By synthesis, Berkowitz and Devine refer to the integration of apparently disparate observations under a common theoretical umbrella. It goes without saying that both orientations are vitally important to any discipline. But, in my view, a problem has arisen in social psychology because there seems to be a much greater professional payoff for analysis than for synthesis – a good analysis simply seems more original and creative than a good synthesis. Among other things, this has led to a huge imbalance in the analysis/synthesis ratio during the past several years, resulting in a plethora of small theories with hardly anyone taking the trouble to try to find the common ground among them.

As Berkowitz and Devine have observed, the emphasis on analysis has been costly. There are great advantages to synthesis in terms of economy of thought and connectivity among approaches, including allowing us to discover the full meaning of any given theory. Let me give you a few examples, from dissonance theory, to illustrate why I think synthesis might be particularly important here.

In the early 1960s, Merrill Carlsmith and I conducted a piece of research that was inspired by the self-concept revision of dissonance theory, as mentioned earlier. In this experiment, we found that under certain conditions, college students would rather cling to their ability to predict and confirm their own behavior, even if it meant setting themselves up for failure. Specifically, we found that students who had developed negative self-expectancies regarding their performance on a task showed evidence of dissonance arousal when faced with success on that task. That is, after repeated failure at the task, subjects who later achieved a successful performance actually changed their responses from accurate to inaccurate ones, in order to preserve a consistent, though negative, self-concept (Aronson & Carlsmith, 1962).

Working from Swann's self-verification theory some twenty-five years later, Swann and Pelham (1988) found that people prefer to remain in close relationships with friends and room mates whose evaluations of their abilities are consonant with their own self-evaluations – even when those evaluations are highly negative. In other words, people prefer to be close to someone whose evaluations of them are consonant with their self-concept, as opposed to someone whose evaluations of them are more positive than their own self-views.

I see this as not merely an interesting new finding; in fact, these results assume great importance precisely because of their linkage to and extensions of the earlier findings of Aronson and Carlsmith (1962) described above. That is, when theorists and researchers build on previous theory and data, it enhances our discipline by highlighting its continuity. What these two pieces of research have in common was identified in some of our earliest thinking within the dissonance tradition – the need people have to form a stable self-concept and to predict their own behavior. Thus, individuals will try to behave in predictable ways (as Carlsmith and I found in 1962), and they will be most comfortable around people who neither expect too much nor too little from them (as Swann and Pelham found in 1988). Twenty-six years is a long time in social psychology. Given our field's proclivity to avoid synthesis, it is little wonder that Swann and Pelham failed to recognize the full meaning of this connection.

To take another example, consider the work of Steele and his colleagues (e.g. Steele, 1988; Steele & Liu, 1983) on self-affirmation theory. Briefly, Steele reinterprets dissonance as involving a threat to the global integrity of the self. This threat, in the typical dissonance experiment, is provoked when subjects engage in a counter-attitudinal behavior. By changing their attitudes, Steele argues, subjects in these experiments are not trying to resolve a particular inconsistency between a given attitude and behavior. Rather, they are simply attempting to re-establish a positive sense of self.

Steele and his associates have produced a considerable body of data showing that, after affirming an aspect of the self-concept that is irrelevant to an experimentally induced inconsistency, subjects no longer reduce dissonance via attitude change (see Steele, 1988, for a review). For example, in a study by Steele and Liu (1983), subjects who held strong esthetic values were allowed to affirm these values after writing a counter-attitudinal essay opposing funds for the handicapped. Unlike subjects for whom esthetic values were unimportant, subjects who had this opportunity to "self-affirm" did not reduce dissonance by changing their attitudes in the direction of their essays. According to self-affirmation theory, these results suggest that people are much more resilient in the face of cognitive inconsistencies than Festinger had envisioned. Dissonance reduction, in this view, is merely a strategy for restoring the individual's larger sense of integrity and self-worth; bringing one's attitudes into a more consistent relationship with one's behavior is simply one way of achieving this goal. As a result, Steele and Liu's self-affirming subjects had no need to rationalize their inconsistent behavior via attitude change. The opportunity to self-affirm had already re-established their positive self-conceptions.

As is apparent, the core ideas of self-affirmation theory are largely compatible with the self-concept revision of dissonance (Aronson, 1960, 1968). Both perspectives embrace the general notion that, after engaging in a behavior that threatens the self-concept, people are motivated to reduce that threat. In addition, both downplay the importance of resolving a lower-order inconsistency arising from a specific counter-attitudinal behavior – such as saying a boring task is interesting, when one knows it is, in fact, extremely dull (Festinger & Carlsmith, 1959).

Do Steele's findings require a new and separate theory? In my view, they do not. Rather, the notion that unrelated self-affirming cognitions are, at least in some circumstances, successful in reducing dissonance would seem to constitute an important extension of the self-concept position. Thus, the innovative contribution of self-affirmation theory lies in its discovery that routes to dissonance reduction are far more flexible than previously assumed.

Conclusion

I want to make it clear that I am not simply saying that there is nothing new under the sun. I don't believe that. Moreover, I hope it is obvious that I don't believe that dissonance theory does or should account for everything. Far from it. I see the scope of dissonance theory as being limited to a clearly defined set of psychological situations (see Aronson, 1969). But where there *are* related phenomena, it can be of great value to view them under the same rubric – at least until their similarities and differences can be empirically explored.

As I have argued, the findings of the newer theories are interesting and important – but I do not think that we need a new framework to account for them. Rather, it is precisely by keeping conceptually related sets of findings under the same roof that we can fully appreciate their interrelatedness and begin to overcome the current state of fragmentation in the field.

In this sense, then, dissonance theory *is* making a comeback – but under a variety of different names. I think the time has arrived for a synthesis. Now that social psychology has rediscovered the richness in the hypotheses to be generated by combining the cognitive with the motivational, I believe that it would be a serious mistake to continue to diffuse that energy into a series of unconnected mini-theories. I believe that it is appropriate to reach back into our fertile past to achieve continuity as we continue to discover new and interesting things.

Note

1. The *National Enquirer* is a tabloid famous for publishing gossipy stories about celebrities or space ships landing on earth. While some stories have a grain of truth, most are huge distortions. Most sentient people hold it in very low repute.

Further Reading

Aronson, E. (1978). The theory of cognitive dissonance: A current perspective. In L. Berkowitz (Ed.), *Cognitive theories in social psychology* (pp. 215–220). New York: Academic Press. An attempt to recast dissonance theory as a theory of self-consistency and self-justification.

Aronson, E. (1980). Persuasion via self-justification: Large commitments for small rewards. In L. Festinger (Ed.), *Four decades of social psychology*. New York: Oxford University Press. A brief summary of the classic research inspired by the theory of cognitive dissonance.

Aronson, E. (1989). Analysis, synthesis, and the treasuring of the old. *Personality and Social Psychology Bulletin*, *15*, 508–512. An impassioned plea for the value and beauty of appreciating and utilizing the shoulders on which we scientists are standing.

Aronson, E. (1992). The return of the repressed: Dissonance theory makes a comeback. *Psychological Inquiry*, *3*, 303–311. An attempt to bring dissonance theory up to date by discussing current research being inspired by the theory and relating it to a wide range contemporary research in social psychology.

Aronson, E. (1995). *The social animal*. San Fransisco, CA: Freeman. A very readable treatment of social psychology – in which the theory of cognitive dissonance plays a central role.

Festinger, L. (1957). *A theory of cognitive dissonance*. Evanston, IL: Row, Peterson. The original statement of the theory by one of social psychology's most original thinkers and most graceful writers. Almost forty years after its publication, it is still an awfully good read.

References

Aronson, E. (1960). *The cognitive and behavioral consequences of the confirmation and disconfirmation of expectancies*. Grant proposal submitted to the National Science Foundation. Harvard University.

Aronson, E. (1968). Dissonance theory: Progress and problems. In R. P. Abelson, E. Aronson, W. J. McGuire, T. M. Newcomb, M. J. Rosenberg, & P. H. Tannenbaum (Eds.), *Theories of cognitive consistency: A sourcebook*. Skokie, IL: Rand-McNally.

Aronson, E. (1969). A theory of cognitive dissonance: A current perspective. In L. Berkowitz (Ed.), *Advances in experimental social psychology* (Vol. 4, pp. 1–34). New York: Academic Press.

Aronson, E. (1989). Analysis, synthesis, and the treasuring of the old. *Personality and Social Psychology Bulletin*, *15*, 508–512.

Aronson, E. (1992). The return of the repressed: Dissonance theory makes a comeback. *Psychological Inquiry*, *3*, 303–311.

Aronson, E., & Carlsmith, J. M. (1962). Performance expectancy as a determinant of actual performance. *Journal of Abnormal and Social Psychology*, *65*, 178–182.

Aronson, E., & Carlsmith, J. M. (1963). Effect of severity of threat on the valuation of forbidden behavior. *Journal of Abnormal and Social Psychology*, *66*, 584–588.

Aronson, E., & Carlsmith, J. M. (1968). Experimentation in social psychology. In G. Lindzey & E. Aronson (Eds.), *The handbook of social psychology* (2nd ed.). Reading, MA: Addison-Wesley.

Aronson, E., Chase, T., Helmreich, R., & Ruhnke, R. (1974). A two-factor theory of dissonance reduction: The effect of feeling stupid or feeling awful on opinion change. *International Journal for Research and Communication*, *3*, 59–74.

Aronson, E., Ellsworth, P., Carlsmith, J. M., & Gonzales, M. H. (1990). *Methods of research in social psychology*. New York: McGraw Hill.

Aronson, E., Fried, C. B., & Stone, J. (1991). Overcoming denial and increasing the intention to use condoms through the induction of hypocrisy. *American Journal of Public Health*, *81*, 1636–1637.

Asch, S. E. (1951). Effects of group pressure upon the modification and distortion of judgments. In H. Guetzkow (Ed.),

Groups, leadership and men (pp. 177–190). Pittsburg, PA: Carnegie Press.

Berkowitz, L., & Devine, P. G. (1989). Research tradition, analysis, and synthesis in social psychological theories: The case of dissonance theory. *Personality and Social Psychology Bulletin*, *15*, 493–507.

Cohen, A. R. (1962). An experiment on small rewards for discrepant compliance and attitude change. In J. W. Brehm & A. R. Cohen (Eds.), *Explorations in cognitive dissonance* (pp. 73–78). New York: Wiley.

Dickerson, C., Thibodeau, R., Aronson, E., & Miller, D. (1992). Using cognitive dissonance to encourage water conservation. *Journal of Applied Social Psychology*, *22*, 841–854.

Festinger, L. (1957). *A theory of cognitive dissonance*. Evanston, IL: Row, Peterson.

Festinger, L., & Carlsmith, J. M. (1959). Cognitive consequences of forced compliance. *Journal of Abnormal and Social Psychology*, *58*, 203–211.

Freedman, J. (1965). Long term behavioral effects of cognitive dissonance. *Journal of Experimental Social Psychology*, *1*, 145–155.

Higgins, E. T. (1989). Self-discrepancy theory: What patterns of self-beliefs cause people to suffer? In L. Berkowitz (Ed.), *Advances in experimental social psychology* (Vol. 22, pp. 93–136). Orlando, FL: Academic Press.

Hovland, C. I., & Weiss, W. (1951). The influence of source credibility on communication effectiveness. *Public Opinion Quarterly*, *15*, 635–650.

Jones, E. (1985). Major developments in social psychology during the past five decades. In G. Lindzey and E. Aronson (Eds.), *The handbook of social psychology* (Vol. 1, pp. 47–107). New York: Random House.

Kunda, Z. (1990). The case for motivated reasoning. *Psychological Bulletin*, *108*, 480–498.

Lord, C. G., Ross, L., & Lepper, M. R. (1979). Biased assimilation and attitude polarization: The effects of prior theories on subsequently considered evidence. *Journal of Personality and Social Psychology*, *37*, 2098–2109.

Miller, N. E., & Dollard, J. (1941). *Social learning and imitation*. New Haven: Yale University Press.

Nel, E., Helmreich, R., & Aronson, E. (1969). Opinion change in the advocate as a function of the persuasibility of the audience: A clarification of the meaning of dissonance. *Journal of Personality and Social Psychology*, *12*, 117–124.

Ross, L. (1977). The intuitive psychologist and his shortcomings: Distortions in the attribution process. In L. Berkowitz (Ed.), *Advances in experimental social psychology* (Vol. 10, pp. 174–221). Orlando, FL: Academic Press.

Steele, C. M. (1988). The psychology of self-affirmation: Sustaining the integrity of the self. In L. Berkowitz (Ed.), *Advances in experimental social psychology* (Vol. 21, pp. 261–302). New York: Academic Press.

Steele, C. M., & Liu, T. J. (1983). Dissonance processes as self-affirmation. *Journal of Personality and Social Psychology*, *45*, 5–19.

Stone, J., Aronson, E., Crain, A. L., Winslow, M. P., & Fried, C. B. (1994). Inducing hypocrisy as a means for encouraging young adults to use condoms. *Personality and Social Psychology Bulletin*, *20*, 116–128.

Swann, W. B., Jr. (1984). Quest for accuracy in person perception: A matter of pragmatics. *Psychological Review*, *91*, 457–477.

Swann, W. B., Jr. & Pelham, B. W. (1988). *The social construction of identity: Self-verification through friend and intimate selection*. Unpublished manuscript, University of Texas-Austin.

Tesser, A. (1988). Toward a self-evaluation maintenance model of social behavior. In L. Berkowitz (Ed.), *Advances in experimental social psychology* (Vol. 21, pp. 181–227). Orlando, FL: Academic Press.

Thibodeau, R., & Aronson, E. (1992). Taking a closer look: Reasserting the role of the self-concept in dissonance theory. *Personality and Social Psychology Bulletin*, *18*, 591–602.

Wicklund, R. A., & Gollwitzer, P. M. (1982). *Symbolic self-completion.* Hillsdale, NJ: Lawrence Erlbaum.

3

Discursive, Rhetorical, and Ideological Messages

Michael Billig

Michael Billig was born in 1947. He studied as an undergraduate at Bristol University and continued there as a postgraduate, researching on the social psychology of intergroup relations under the supervision of the late Henri Tajfel. His first publication was as joint author to the study reporting the first minimal intergroup experiment: Tajfel, Billig, Bundy, and Flament (1971) in the *European Journal of Social Psychology*. He was awarded his doctorate in 1972. In 1973 he was appointed Lecturer in Psychology at University of Birmingham and he moved to Loughborough University in 1985 as Professor of Social Sciences. He has investigated ideology and nationalism, and was a founder member of the Loughborough Discourse and Rhetoric Group, which has been developing new forms of social psychology based on the study of language. His books include *Arguing and thinking* (1987), *Ideology and opinions* (1991), *Talking of the Royal Family* (1992) and *Banal nationalism* (1995).

How is it possible to call oneself a social psychologist, but to read few of the main social-psychological journals and, indeed, to feel alienated from much of their content? Surely there is a contradiction: to be a social psychologist should mean affiliating oneself with the main bodies of work bearing the label of "social psychology." Nevertheless, an increasing number of academics, especially in the United Kingdom, are finding themselves in this contradictory position. They call themselves social psychologists; they claim to be interested in social-psychological problems; yet they believe that mainstream social psychology has taken a number of wrong turnings. In consequence, such academics are involved in alternative, critical social psychologies.

This chapter discusses the discursive and rhetorical approaches to social psychology, which are being developed out of this critical movement. This work is expressed in a growing volume of publications (see, for example, Billig, 1987, 1991; Potter & Wetherell, 1987; Edwards & Potter, 1992, 1993; Harré & Gillett, 1994). One of the key texts for this critical movement was *The explanation of social behaviour*, written by Rom Harré and Paul Secord and published in 1972. Harré and Secord argued that social psychologists needed to take linguistic philosophy seriously. Their critique went beyond methodological complaints; the problem was not that social psychologists were using the wrong techniques of investigation or were misanalyzing their results. The critique charged that social psychologists were misunderstanding the very nature of social-psychological phenomena. Because of this misunderstanding, social psychologists, or so it was alleged, were looking in the wrong places for the subject matter of social psychology.

The discursive/rhetorical approaches, discussed in this chapter, have derived from the sort of deep-rooted critique which Harré and Secord made. They also possess their own particular features. The discursive dimension takes insights and methodological techniques from the sort of conversation analysis which has been developed by micro-sociologists. The rhetorical dimension stresses the importance of argumentation in social life and self-consciously draws from the ancient tradition of rhetoric which dates back to ancient Greece. In addition, there is also an emphasis upon situating social-psychological phenomena in their historical and ideological context. This point was stressed by Kenneth Gergen (1973) in a key critical paper published in the year after *Explanation of social behaviour*. Individuals do not merely voice a particular set of opinions because of their own individual personalities. Each person lives in a particular age and is located within a network of social relations. His or her views will bear the ideological traces of his or her age and social location. In this sense, the individual's social-psychological make up is itself a social, historical, and ideological creation.

By considering such issues, the new emerging discursive and rhetorical social psychologies are taking on a very different complexion from mainstream social psychology. They tend to be linked more closely with other social sciences – with sociology, anthropology, practical linguistics, cultural studies, and so on – than with individual psychology. Orthodox social psychologists may find these emerging critical social psychologies strange; they may even reject them out of hand without inquiring about the nature of their strangeness. Nevertheless, as will be argued, the critical social psychologies have, despite their appearance of novelty and strangeness, deep philosophical and intellectual heritages.

Locating the Topics of Social Psychology

Discursive social psychologists engage in very different sorts of research methodologies than do orthodox social psychologists. Whereas orthodox social psychologists tend to conduct experiments whose results are statistically analyzed, discursive psychology is much more interpretative. Pieces of ordinary conversation or of printed texts are analytically interpreted. Given that the two sorts of social psychology have such different methodologies, it might be thought that methodological considerations lie at the root of their divide. However, the methodological differences reflect more basic philosophical differences. These concern disagreement about the nature of the phenomena which constitute the very subject matter of social psychology.

By and large, conventional social psychologists assume that the subject matter of social psychology comprises internal states or processes, which are themselves unobservable but which have to be inferred from outward behavior. For example, social psychologists, who study attitudes, might assume that their goal is to discover the "attitudinal systems" of individuals and to outline what effect such systems have on outward behavior. An "attitudinal-system" does not, and cannot, exist in the way that a table or chair might exist. One cannot claim to touch or see an "attitudinal system." It is presumed to be hidden within the individual's head, governing the way that the individual organizes thoughts, experiences, and reactions. By studying systematically the individual's reactions, the psychologist hopes to construct a picture of the hidden "attitudinal system." What the social psychologist cannot do is to study the "system" directly, because it is unobservable, like all the cognitive structures which are assumed to intervene between stimuli and response. Thus, much of social psychology, especially cognitive social psychology, has objects of study, whether "attitude-systems," "social identities," or "cognitive schemata," which are presumed to be internal processes and, as such, hidden from view. These objects are the focus of considerable social-psychological investigation, but are ghostly essences, lying behind and supposedly controlling what can be directly observed.

Discursive and rhetorical psychology does not take these hidden essences as its object of study. Instead, discursive social psychologists claim that the phenomena of social psychology are constituted through social interaction, especially discursive interaction. Thus, social psychologists should study that interaction, examining in particular the ways that language is used in practice by participants. In so doing, they will be able to observe directly what now appears to be hidden and secret.

In itself, this is not novel. Seventy years ago the great Russian linguist and philosopher, Mikhail Bakhtin, was saying similar things. In *Marxism and the philosophy of language*, which he published for political reasons under the name of Volosinov, Bakhtin criticized the idea that the objects of social psychology were inner states (or "within" the individual):

> Social psychology in fact is not located anywhere within (in the "souls" of communicating subjects) but entirely and completely *without* – in the words, the gesture, the act.

There is nothing left unexpressed in it, nothing "inner" about it – it is wholly on the outside, wholly brought out in exchanges, wholly taken up in material, above all in the material of the world. (Volosinov, 1973, p. 19; emphasis in original)

In Bakhtin's vision of social psychology, prime importance should be paid to the study of language as it is actually used in practice. Often linguists have considered language as some sort of abstract system of grammatical rules, whereas Bakhtin proposed a practical linguistics to examine language in action. Thus, Bakhtin/Volosinov continued: "Social psychology is first and foremost an atmosphere made up of multifarious *speech performances*" and, as such, "social psychology exists primarily in a wide variety of forms of 'utterance' of little *speech genres* of internal and external kinds" (Volosinov, 1973, pp. 19–20, emphases in original).

Bakhtin was suggesting that psychological states, as commonly understood, are formed in interaction, especially interaction involving the use of language. If one wishes to study such states, then one should study interaction and utterances. Similar points were made by the philosopher Wittgenstein, who has provided the intellectual inspiration for important strands of critical social psychology, as John Shotter's (1993a, 1993b) scholarly and important analyses make clear. Wittgenstein, in his later philosophy, advocated that close attention should be paid to the use of language. Philosophers, Wittgenstein argued, are prone to muddle if they do not understand the customary practices of language, or what he called "language-games." Given that language is socially shared, there must be public criteria for the use of words. We learn how to use words such as "table" and "chair" by observing how these words are used: in this way, we learn to play the appropriate language-games, in which such words are used. One of Wittgenstein's great insights was to claim that precisely the same happens with the use of psychological words, such as "remember," "feel," or "see." These words are used in various "language-games" and their sense must be understood in terms of the practices of their usage. Wittgenstein warned against assuming that such psychological words stand for internal processes, which provide their criteria of usage. Children learn to use language such as "I remember" or "I have a pain" in the same way that they learn other concepts; and they can be corrected if their usage is incorrect. The criteria for using such words cannot be internal, private states. As Wittgenstein stated in *Philosophical investigations*, "an 'inner process' stands in need of outward criteria" (1953, remark 580).

In consequence, if we wish to study "memory," "perception," "emotion," we should not be searching for the hidden inner processes which are assumed to stand behind the use of these words. To search for such entities is a mistake. As Wittgenstein wrote, it is a "misleading parallel" to say that "psychology treats of processes in the psychical sphere, as does physics in the physical" (1953, remark 571). Seeing, hearing, thinking, and feeling are not "the subject of psychology *in the same sense*" as the physical movements are the subject matter of physics; physicists see, hear, think about and inform us about the subjects of their research, whereas "the psychologist observes the *external reactions* (the behavior) of the subject" (Wittgenstein, 1953, remark 571, emphasis in original).

The implication is that we should study memory, perception or emotion by investigating the relevant "language-games," or what Bakhtin called the "genres of utterance." Attention should be paid to the ways in which people talk about their memories, perceptions, and emotions. In so doing, we will discover the outward criteria for the social usage of these words. These criteria will be rooted in social practices. As will be suggested, more is involved. By taking seriously the idea that psychology is constituted in language, it will then become possible to study directly the processes of thinking.

Collective Memory

The insights of Bakhtin and Wittgenstein can be used to construct a very different sort of empirical social psychology than that which is conventionally practiced. This can be illustrated briefly with respect to two topics, which have long been important in the conventional study of social psychology: memory and attitudes. Both topics have also been studied in detail by discursive/rhetorical psychologists. And on both topics, Wittgenstein made important remarks in *Philosophical investigations*.

Psychologists often discuss the topic of memory in terms of the storing and retrieving of stimulus information. Much effort has been devoted to discovering whether the processes of storage and retrieval differ when stimulus information is accurately, as opposed to inaccurately, remembered. In these investigations, the retrieval and storage "systems" cannot be observed directly: they have to be inferred from the tasks which subjects are instructed to perform under experimental conditions. For example, cognitive psychologists might talk about "memory organization packets" or MOPs (Stevenson, 1993); but these are not physical packets, which can be put under the microscope as neurones can be. No one can claim to see a MOP, although MOPs are presumed to determine the business of remembering.

Because psychologists are searching for unknowable entities, they tend to pay little attention to the social activity which is occurring when remembering is taking place both naturally and in the psychological laboratory. That this activity – which typically is glossed over in the descriptions of procedure in the experimental reports – may be crucial is implied by one of Wittgenstein's remarks in *Philosophical investigations* (remark 305). Wittgenstein was discussing the supposed role of "inner processes" in memory. He suggested that the issue is not whether "inner processes" occur, when people claim to remember things; the point was to specify what it means to claim that such inner processes occur. He stressed that the activity of remembering should not be understood as an inner process (for example, the hidden MOPs locked away in the individual's head). Wittgenstein states that he does not deny that there might be "inner processes." Quite the contrary:

> What we deny is that the picture of the inner process gives us the correct idea of the use of the word "to remember." We say that this picture with its ramifications stands in the way of our seeing the use of the word as it is. (Wittgenstein, 1953, p. 102)

For Wittgenstein, to understand "remembering" one must investigate how the word "remember" is used, when people are said to be "remembering."

Wittgenstein, in common with other linguistic philosophers, tended to analyze hypothetical examples. However, his insights lead the way to the empirical analysis of word use in actual social interaction. Conversation analysts have developed techniques and theoretical concepts for the micro-analysis of conversational data (Heritage, 1984; Antaki, 1994). Much of the intellectual impetus for such work was derived from the pioneering work of Harvey Sacks (e.g. Sacks, 1972a, 1972b). Conversation analysts have revealed the enormous complexity of the most trivial-seeming exchanges. Even greetings can be delicate interchanges of meaning (Brown & Levinson, 1987; Nofsinger, 1991). The exact timing with which a reply follows a question, or the presence of a voiced hesitation, can be shown to be discursively important.

Many of the techniques of conversation analysis were developed initially for the analysis of routine exchanges rather than for discourse, which uses psychological words. Discursive psychologists have been able to show how these techniques could be applied to talk about psychological phenomena, such as claims to remember things. When such talk is analyzed then psychological phenomena, such as remembering, are not seen to be located in hidden mental entities, but are rooted in social and discursive activity.

Edwards and Middleton (1986) observed mothers looking at photo albums with their young children. As they talked, the mothers were telling the children about memory. Not only were they recalling the events of the past, and providing memory stories for the children to repeat, but they were also communicating the sorts of things which should be remembered, or considered memorable. In so doing they were instructing the children how the events of the past should be remembered and, thus, what it means "to remember." In this way, remembering is not an individual psychological process, which happens spontaneously; it is a social activity, which, like other social activities, has to be learnt in order to be performed proficiently.

Discursive psychologists are particularly interested in observing what people are doing when they make memory claims. In conversations, people's claims about memory do not suddenly pop up, as if out of the blue. Often memory claims are made when matters are in dispute. In this sense, the business of remembering can be a highly rhetorical or controversial business, so that the memory claims might be accomplishing a variety of interactive business (Potter & Edwards, 1990; Edwards & Potter, 1992).

Billig (in press) and Billig and Edwards (1994) have analyzed part of a conversation in which a British family are talking about the Royal Family (the incident is taken from a wider project, reported in Billig, 1992). The details cannot be given here, for that would involve looking at the transcript of the original conversation. However, the gist can be outlined. The father was dismissing royal weddings as something which would only interest women: he had not bothered, so he said, to watch the televised proceedings. His daughter-in-law, a keen royalist, declares that she will never forget the wedding of Prince Charles and Princess Diana. As she and her mother-in-law start reminiscing about the wedding, which they had watched on television, they start arguing about the identity of one of the singers, who had participated in the service. In the event, it is the father-in-law who supplies the name, which the others accept as being the correct one.

Such conversations, which are typical of countless family exchanges, are revealing. In an obvious sense the conversation was about memory, but, in another sense, the claims about memory concerned much more than the recall of information. The daughter-in-law, in claiming that she would never forget the service, was making a statement about the importance of the occasion for her. She and her mother-in-law were conducting family business. They were overtly pursuing what had been branded as the womanly business of watching royal weddings. In this, they were countering the father-in-law's dismissive views about the wedding and gender. He, of course, was "doing masculinity" by making such remarks. Unless the daughter-in-law's remarks about never forgetting the wedding are understood in this wider context, then it is not possible to understand why her failure to remember details of the singer did not occasion astonishment or accusation. Again, her father-in-law's ability to remember what he had not personally experienced did not evoke surprise.

The episode illustrates an important point about memory. The social activity of remembering is not tied to the recall of directly experienced stimuli for we can, and continually do, claim to remember events at which we were not personally present. Thus, a present generation can "remember" a previous generation's sacrifice. Such memories can be passed across time, rather as the mothers, talking about family photographs with their children, were transmitting the family memories across time. In this sense, memory is not to be located within the individual's head in hypothetical MOPs. As Maurice Halbwachs wrote many years ago, memory is "collective" rather than individual (Halbwachs, 1980; see also Middleton & Edwards, 1990). It is something which is shared and the activity of remembering can also be collectively and discursively accomplished. As such, remembering is pre-eminently a social-psychological topic, especially if social psychology is understood to be the analysis of collective activity, rather than the search for internal processes which are hidden within the individual.

Attitudes and Arguments

The conversation about remembering the singer at the royal wedding illustrates how the activity of jointly remembering involves more than remembering. As the family remembered, so they discussed, argued, and pursued the complex business of family relations. In their discussions, they were displaying what social psychologists loosely call "attitudes." The daughter-in-law and mother were showing their keen royalist "attitudes." The father was countering with his cooler views on royalty. They were all linking these "attitudes" to gender and, in so doing, they were outwardly "performing gender" within the family.

Just as the activity of remembering deserves close social-psychological attention so does the business of giving opinions. Again, a turn from the internal to the external is called for. Social psychologists have traditionally viewed attitudes as internal states of mind or feeling. By contrast, the discursive approach analyzes the giving of opinions in terms of discursive action. In this, a particular form of discourse is involved – rhetorical discourse. Rhetoric refers to discourse which is argumentative and which seeks to persuade; as such the activities of criticism and justification are central to rhetorical discourse (Antaki, 1994; Billig, 1987; Edwards & Potter, 1992). Attitudes, far from being mysterious inner events, are constituted within the business of justification and criticism.

The same general points, which were made about memory, can be applied to attitudes. Wittgenstein, in discussing what it means to have an opinion, suggested that we should ask what "do we regard as criteria for someone's being of such-and-such opinion" (1953, remark 573). We should investigate the conditions under which people are said to alter their opinion or to come to an opinion. We should not seek to depict an internal state, but to discover "what gets treated grammatically as a *state* here." Again, the focus is shifted to outwardly observable, social activity – in this case, the business of talking about opinions.

Discursive psychologists, who have studied the circumstances in which people give opinions in conversation, stress the rhetorical nature of opinion-giving (e.g. Billig, 1989, 1991; Edwards & Potter, 1992). Rarely, if ever, is the giving of an opinion merely a spontaneous report of an internal state. If someone says "I feel that capital punishment is wrong" they are unlikely to be making a claim to be reporting a particular internal state of feeling, which only occurs when the topic of capital punishment arises and which is attached to no other topic. Their utterance is likely to be part of a conversation and its meaning should be analyzed in terms of the conversational context.

Bakhtin (1986) claimed that all utterances are dialogic in that they are responses to other utterances and their meaning has to be understood in relation to these other utterances. This is particularly relevant for attitude statements. Rather than being simple reports of internal states, attitude statements tend to be uttered as stances in matters of public controversy. Thus, people generally are not said to have "attitudes" on issues which are seen to be beyond public doubt. For example, McGuire (1964), in a classic social psychological study, investigated "cultural truisms," or beliefs which no one in a given culture seriously doubted (for example, the belief in contemporary Western society that one should clean one's teeth). These beliefs tend not to be termed "attitudes," unless they are challenged. As soon as someone doubts the value of cleaning teeth, then the issue becomes one on which attitudes can be expressed (Billig, 1987).

That being so, attitude statements will typically bear a rhetorical meaning, which must be understood in terms of the contexts of their utterance. A statement in favor of capital punishment is not merely a report about the speaker's self-positioning on the issue. Nor is it merely a statement about what the speaker supports. It is also a positioning against counter-positions, for instance against the abolitionists. More than this, it represents an intervention in the argument against the abolitionists. When people give their opinion in dialogue, they give typically arguments, justifying their own views and criticizing counter-views. In this sense, the statement of an opinion often indicates a readiness to argue on a matter of controversy (Billig, 1989, 1991).

Traditional social psychology has tended to assume that "attitudes" are systematized schemas of response. The implication is that the more strongly an individual holds an attitude the more fully worked out the schema of response. In consequence, the individual with strongly held attitudes will tend to respond in predictable ways, his or her responses being determined by a personal elaborated schema. However, the business of giving views in conversation is complex. In conversations people do not repeat themselves exactly, but they formulate utterances which, at least in their detail, are novel. Even persons with strong views do this. In fact, they may do so with greater frequency than those with not so strong commitments: they are concerned with a particular issue and will talk about it frequently. If arguing about their hobby-horse, they might be confronted with new counter-statements, which will demand novel dialogic responses (Billig, 1989).

Discursive psychologists have examined how people, in discussion, are continually making utterances which fit the rhetorical demands of the moment (Potter & Wetherell, 1987; Wetherell & Potter, 1992). In the conversational thrust and counter-thrust, novel remarks are made. In analyzing such conversations, social psychologists are not merely studying the processes of conversation; they are studying directly the traditional topic of cognitive psychology: the processes of thought (Billig, 1991). Cognitive psychologists have assumed that thinking is a mysterious process, lying behind outward behavior. However, the response and counter-response of conversation is too quick for it to be the outward manifestation of the "real" processes of thought. The remarks are the thoughts: one need not search for something extra, as if there is always something lying behind the words, which we should call the "thought." Wittgenstein put the point graphically: "When I think in language, there aren't 'meanings' going through my mind in addition to the verbal expressions: the language is itself the vehicle of thought" (1953, remark 329).

When the language is spoken out loud, the thinking can, quite literally, be heard. And, if one wished to differentiate between a speaker, who might be said to be speaking thoughtfully and one who is not, then "I could *certainly not* say that the difference lay in something that goes on or fails to go on while he is speaking" (Wittgenstein, 1967, remark 93). In short, to discover what is being thought, when words are uttered, the observer should analyze the rhetorical complexity of the utterances themselves. Thus, discussions, in which people are responding rapidly to new dialogic challenges and are in their turn creating such challenges, offer the psychologist a royal road to examining thinking in action.

This is not to deny that silent, solitary thinking does occur. However, the rhetorical position stresses that such thinking is typically modeled on outer dialogue. It is, to use the phrase of Bakhtin, "inner speech." When we think about a matter, we often are debating silently with ourselves, weighing up the pros and cons. This is only possible if this sort of thinking is publicly observable in dialogue. If thinking were locked mysteriously and unobservably within the brain, then we could never learn, or be taught, to think: it would be something which occurs unstoppably and unalterably (Billig, 1987). The Eleatic Stranger, in Plato's dialogue *The sophist*, expressed an important insight: "Thought and speech are the same: only the former, which is a silent inner conversation of the soul with itself, has been given the special name of thought" (Plato, 1948, 263e). In consequence, dialogic conversation can offer the social psychologist a direct glimpse at the social processes of thought.

Action, Words, and Discrimination

So far, it might be thought that the discursive approach represents a turn from the study of behavior to the study of talk. Discursive psychologists might be suspected of only taking words into account and not actions. However, that is not so, for the criticism assumes that in social behavior there is a clear distinction between words and action. This is contested by "speech-act theory," which is a philosophical position underlying much work of conversation analysis (Potter & Wetherell, 1987). According to speech-act theory, making an utterances is itself an action; also, many actions are performed through utterances. Conversation analysts, in studying the words of speakers, must ask themselves what are the speakers doing in making their utterances. The young woman, talking about never forgetting the royal wedding, was doing more than uttering words about memory: she was arguing, discussing, interacting, and performing family business by her discursive actions.

It is easy to exaggerate the difference between words and actions, as if the latter were more "real" than the former. In social life words are rarely "mere words." Many important social actions are performed through utterances. This can be illustrated briefly by considering the topics of intergroup prejudice and discrimination, which have long formed a key part of social-psychological research. It is easy to assume that prejudice is basically a matter of words, such as the verbal repetition of stereotypes, while discrimination involves behavior, or the putting of prejudiced words into practice. However, if acts of discrimination are examined in detail, one can see that the distinction between words and actions soon collapses.

Philomena Essed (1988) examined how white male employers in the Dutch civil service discriminate against black female job seekers. The processes involve subtle and often unconscious details of interaction. In interviews, the employer might ask the sort of question, which implies that the black female has a pattern of behavior which fits prevailing stereotypes and which is inappropriate for a high level job. She, in turn, is discomfited and responds tensely. In consequence, the white male deems the interview unsatisfactory and offers the position elsewhere. All this is performed through utterances. Moreover, the very act of discrimination – the refusal to offer employment to the black female – is accomplished through words. Successful and unsuccessful candidates have to be informed; papers have to be signed, telephone calls made. All these verbal activities – written and spoken utterances – perform the discrimination. In our language-saturated society, actions such as racial and sexual discrimination do not exist apart from utterances. They are performed through complex sequences of utterances, including, typically, utterances which deny that discrimination and prejudice is taking place (Billig, 1991; van Dijk, 1992, 1993; Wetherell & Potter, 1992).

The importance of utterances, and their comparative neglect in conventional social psychology, can be seen by looking at one of the famous studies in social psychology. The Sherif boys' camp experiments (Sherif & Sherif, 1953; Sherif, 1966; Sherif, 1981) are recognized to be classic studies of intergroup relations (see, for example, the tributes by Taylor and Moghaddam, 1994; Cherry, 1994). These studies observed intergroup behavior *in situ*, as Muzafer and Carolyn Sherif divided the boys in a summer camp into two separate groups, organized competitions between the groups and observed the growth of intergroup hostilities and prejudices. The experiment is usually regarded as showing how prejudiced mental structures (such as group stereotypes) develop within the group members and, also how intergroup behavior (such as pushing and shoving) occurs. A quick glance at Muzafer Sherif's description of events illustrates the importance of language.

At a crucial stage in the camp's activities, the boys were divided into two groups. This was accomplished by the camp authorities giving verbal instructions. Sherif (1981) reports how the groups developed. Words and speech were vital to the development of group identity:

> As the group became an organization, the boys coined nicknames . . . Each group developed its own jargon, special jokes, secrets and special ways of performing tasks. One group, after killing a snake near a place where it had gone to swim, named the place "Moccasin Creek" and thereafter preferred this swimming hole to any other, though there were better ones nearby. (p. 321)

Sherif does not describe the killing of the snake in detail. One can imagine how the boys called to each other to coordinate their activities, how they talked about it, and how it became a mythic event in the history of the group. We do hear that the event becomes mythologized in a place name, although we are not provided with the transcripts of the conversations which made this possible. It makes no sense to ask whether the boys invented these names because they had internal feelings of identity, as if the real causes were hidden from view. The invention of the names – the performance of the group rituals – was the way of accomplishing and demonstrating the group loyalty (see also Widdicombe & Wooffitt, 1995).

Similarly, the intergroup hostilities were not set apart from utterances and rhetoric. Sherif recounts how the good sporting spirit of the tournament soon degenerated. Language was involved:

> The members of members of each group began to call their rival "stinkers," "sneaks" and "cheaters" . . . The rival groups made threatening posters, and planned raids, collecting hoards of green apples for ammunition . . . name-calling scuffles and raids were the rule of the day. (p. 324)

Of course, the actual throwing of the ammunition itself is not a verbal act, but the planning, the interpretation, the coordinating, the mythologizing of the apple throwing are all accomplished through utterances, as was the name calling. Without such utterances, the activities could not have had their intergroup significance. The Sherif experiments can be interpreted in many ways. In an obvious sense, the Sherifs had provided a metaphor for warfare, showing how easily group loyalties can be created and brought into conflict with each other. If language is necessary for all this, then a further moral can be drawn. It is no coincidence that the only species which possesses the ability of language (or what Pinker, 1994, has called "the language instinct") is a species which engages in organized warfare. Utterance is necessary to kill and die for the honor of the group.

History and Ideology

The stress on examining language in practice may give the impression that discursive/rhetorical psychology is primarily concerned with interpersonal dynamics, as if all comes down to investigating what speakers are doing when they make utterances. Certainly much conversation analysis is focused on the details of interpersonal communication, looking, for example, at ways of making or refusing requests, or opening and closing exchanges and so on (Nofsinger, 1991). These matters can form an important part of discursive psychology (Edwards & Potter, 1992, 1993). However, more can be said about language, as the focus is shifted from the interpersonal to the historical and ideological. When the shift is made, the discursive/rhetorical approach shares a similar aim to Serge Moscovici's theory of social representations in making social psychology "historical and anthropological" (Moscovici, 1984, p. 948).

Individuals, when they speak, do not create their own language, but they use terms which are culturally, historically, and ideologically available. Each act of utterance, although in itself novel, carries an ideological history. As Bakhtin stressed in *Marxism and the philosophy of language* social psychologists, by investigating acts of utterance, should be studying ideology. An ideology comprises the ways of thinking and behaving within a given society which make the ways of that society seem "natural" or unquestioned to its members (Eagleton, 1991). In this way, ideology is the common sense of the society. Through ideology, the inequalities of that society will appear as "natural" or "inevitable." Thus, ideology comprises the habits of belief, which, for example, in former terms made it appear "natural" that women should not be full citizens, or which, in our day, make it appear obvious that the street sweeper be paid a fraction of the company director's remuneration. These ideological habits can be deeply rooted into language, and, thereby, into consciousness.

There is an important implication for the study of social psychology. If social-psychological states are constituted within language and if languages are historical and ideological creations, then so are the topics of social psychology. It should then be possible to examine, through the study of utterance, how ideology creates the subjects of psychology. A number of discursive investigators have examined explicitly ideological themes, relating to social inequality. For example, several have investigated racist discourse (Billig, 1991; Wetherell & Potter, 1992; van Dijk, 1991, 1992, 1993) and also sexist discourse (Edley & Wetherell, 1995). The examples of families talking about the British Royal Family were taken from a project, which used the topic of monarchy to see how ideological notions of nationhood and inequality are diffused in contemporary British common sense. In such studies, investigators show how speakers use themes, which they take to be common sense, but how, in using such themes, speakers are making ideological utterances about themselves and society.

Often the utterances of ideology are not straightforward, but are "dilemmatic" (Billig, Condor, Edwards, Gane, Middleton, & Radley, 1988). It is the nature of common sense that it contains contrary themes – for example there are maxims praising both caution and risk taking, or praising both firmness and mercy. If ideologies did not contain contrary themes, they would not provide the resources for common sense thinking, for thinking involves dialogic discussion, or the counter-positioning of contrary themes, which can both appear in their way to be reasonable. In discussions, one can hear people jostling with the contrary themes of common sense. This is particularly so when the topics are explicitly ideological. Thus, those making racist remarks often assert their own lack of prejudice, even as they make their racist utterances. Or English speakers claim to want the Royal Family both to be ordinary and not ordinary, thereby simultaneously articulating themes in favor of both equality and inequality. Investigators, studying such discussions from a discursive/rhetorical perspective, are not aiming to describe the "attitude system" of each speaker, as if all speakers must possess a clearly demarcated internal system, before they speak. Rather the aim is to see how the themes of ideology are instantiated in ordinary talk, and how speakers are part of, and are continuing, the ideological history of the discursive themes which they are using.

This involves paying greater attention to the meaning of categories than social psychology has tended to do. For example, much cognitive social psychology, especially that concerned with intergroup relations, has been concerned with the process of categorization. It has been asserted that categorization is crucial for the development of group identity (i.e. Turner, Hogg, Oakes, Reicher, & Wetherell 1987; Tajfel, 1981; Abrams & Hogg, 1990). Such investigators tend to treat categorization as if it were a universal process. They search for the common psychological factors involved in categorization. In consequence, different forms of group categories are treated as being similar and as exemplifying the supposed general processes of categorization. What is forgotten in such studies is that categories, as Edwards (1991) has written, are "for talking": they should be studied in their discursive and rhetorical contexts. Moreover, categories carry meanings and not all categories – certainly not all group categories – carry identical meanings. A social psychology which seeks to study how ideological forces shape psychological states cannot afford to ignore these meanings.

The point can be illustrated by the example of national identity. National identities depend upon the creation and maintenance of national categories, such as "French," "German," or "Bolivian." In this respect, national identity resembles other group identities, including those formed by the young boys in the Sherif experiments. However, the national category also carries particular meanings, which relate to the historically particular ways in which nation states have been created in the past two hundred and fifty years. The era of nation states has seen national communities being "imagined" in particular ways, which, for example, are very different from the ways communities were "imagined" in the Middle Ages (Anderson, 1983; Gellner, 1983; Billig, 1995). When groups declare themselves to be national groups, they are making particular political statements, evoking an ideological history of entitlements and rights. For example, when Palestinians declare themselves to have a national identity, they are doing more than claiming a psychological feeling of commonality: they are making a claim about the rights to statehood and national territory, which follow from a group defining itself as a "national group," rather than any other sort of group.

In the modern age, the notion of national identity has been bound up with the notion of the nation state. Today, these notions appear commonplace and solid, so that it is difficult to imagine that in previous ages communities were not imagined in this way. The assumptions of nationhood have seeped through contemporary consciousness, so that the nation state appears as a "natural" form of community. In established nation states, such as the USA, the United Kingdom, or France, there is what can be called a "banal" form of nationalism (Billig, 1995). The link between people and soil, which was once articulated in mystical terms, has now become banal, even unnoticed. In routine ways, citizens of the state are reminded that they live in a nation within a world of nation states. This reminding – or "flagging" of the nation – takes place, for the most part, in taken for granted, unnoticed ways. The metaphor of the flag illustrates the banality of this nationalism. The political nationalist, who seeks to establish a new nation state, might wave the national flag vigorously and self-consciously; by contrast, the citizen of the nation state daily walks past, without a second glance, the flag flying outside the public building. Millions of such barely glanced at flags are on display each day. All these unmindful reminders are necessary for the continuation of the nation state and for its members' sense of belonging. In consequence, those who wish to study nationalism and "national identity" in contemporary states should pay attention to the banal forms by which those states are reproduced (for details of "banal nationalism," see Billig, 1995).

One might argue that the behavior of the boys in the Sherif experiment was only possible in a world suffused with the assumptions of nationalism, where the nation state has provided the common sense model of "society." The assumptions of this model have permeated forms of life and thinking, which, at first sight, seem remote from the formal structures of the nation state. The boys in the Sherifs' camp were, without self-consciousness, creating mini-simulacra of states, equipped with their territorial markers and flags. Similarly, the national model can be seen in the behavior of American male, urban teenage gangs, marking out their territories, fighting their street wars and appealing to a sort of "patriotism" which takes its rhetoric directly from discourses of nationalism (Conquergood, 1995).

By examining these sorts of issues, the scope of social psychology will be widened. The traditional topics of social psychology are to be studied in terms of discursive utterances and language games. However, the analysis does not stop there. Discourses are not merely to be investigated in terms of their particular uses and immediate contexts. The ideological history of the discourses is to be sketched, in order to see how this history shapes and is continued by the local practices. In examining ideology – and the history of ideology – the analyst is decoding what is being taken for granted as common sense, for ideology embraces the common sense of each social period. Historical and anthropological dimensions can be directly added by making comparisons with other ages and with other types of community. By noting anthropological and historical differences in the use of psychological language, the analyst can show how social psychological phenomena differ according to place and period (Harré & Gillett, 1994).

In addition, the rhetorical analysis of argumentation can be used to investigate patterns of ideology, for it can reveal what is being taken for granted as common sense. The analyst, in examining patterns of discussion and argument, observes not merely what issues are being overtly challenged by speakers and how these challenges are being discursively effected; the analyst can also note what is being left unchallenged or what is being presented as if unchallengeable. Commonly in discussions, speakers will attempt to justify their particular stances by appealing to common values (or rhetorical "topoi"), which they will assume are acceptable to all (Billig, 1987, 1991). These appeals to what Perelman and Olbrechts-Tyteca (1971) called the "universal audience" contain clues about the ideological common sense of the times. In addition, the analyst should be alert to gaps. In investigating ideologies one is looking, not merely for the themes which are presented as "common sense," but also for what is commonsensically left unsaid and what is assumed to be beyond controversy.

If social psychologists take seriously the project to investigate ideology, then the nature of social psychology will be dramatically transformed. Not merely will such a social psychology have very different methodological procedures, but, more importantly, its intellectual reach will be expanded. By incorporating historical, anthropological, and linguistic insights, this social psychology will draw closer to other social scientific investigations. In so doing, it will be addressing some of the most important issues in the contemporary social sciences.

References

(Those marked * are recommended for further reading.)

Abrams, D., & Hogg, M. A. (Eds.) (1990). *Social identity theory*. New York: Springer Verlag.

Anderson, B. (1983). *Imagined communities*. London: Verso.

Antaki, C. (1994). *Explaining and arguing*. London: Sage.

Bakhtin, M. M. (1986). *Speech genres and other late essays*. Austin, TX: University of Texas.

*Billig, M. (1987/1996). *Arguing and thinking* (Rev. ed.). Cambridge: Cambridge University Press.

Billig, M. (1989). The argumentative nature of holding strong views: A case study. *European Journal of Social Psychology*, *19*, 203–222.

Billig, M. (1991). *Ideology and opinions*. London: Sage.

Billig, M. (1992). *Talking of the Royal Family*. London: Routledge.

*Billig, M. (1995). *Banal nationalism*. London: Sage.

Billig, M. (in press). Rhetorical and discursive analysis: How families talk about the Royal Family. In N. Hayes (Ed.), *Introduction to qualitative methods*. Sussex: Lawrence Erlbaum.

*Billig, M., Condor, S., Edwards, D., Gane, M., Middleton, D., & Radley, A. R. (1988). *Ideological dilemmas: A social psychology of everyday thinking*. London: Sage.

Billig, M., & Edwards, D. (1994). La construction sociale de la mémoire. *La Recherche*, *25*, 742–745.

Brown, P., & Levinson, S. C. (1987). *Politeness: Some universals in language use*. Cambridge: Cambridge University Press.

Cherry, F. (1994). *The stubborn particularities of social psychology*. London: Routledge.

Conquergood, D. (1995). For the nation! How street gangs problematize patriotism. In H. Simons, & M. Billig (Eds.), *After postmodernism*. London: Sage.

Eagleton, T. (1991). *Ideology: An introduction*. London: Verso.

Edley, N., & Wetherell, M. (1995). *Men in perspective*. London: Prentice Hall.

Edwards, D. (1991). Categories are for talking. *Theory and Psychology*, *1*, 515–542.

Edwards, D., & Middleton, D. (1986). Conversational remembering and family relationships: How children learn to remember. *Journal of Social and Personal Relationships*, *5*, 3–25.

*Edwards, D., & Potter, J. (1992). *Discursive psychology*. London: Sage.

Edwards, D., & Potter, J. (1993). Language and causation: A discursive action model of description and attribution. *Psychological Review*, *100*, 23–41.

Essed, P. (1988). Understanding verbal accounts of racism: Politics and the heuristics of reality constructions. *Text*, *8*, 5–40.

Gellner, E. (1983). *Nations and nationalism*. Blackwell: Oxford.

Gergen, K. J. (1973). Social psychology as history. *Journal of Personality and Social Psychology*, *26*, 309–320.

Halbwachs, M. (1980). *The collective memory*. Harper and Row: New York.

Harré, R., & Gillett, G. (1994). *The discursive mind*. London: Sage.

Harré, R., & Secord, P. F. (1972). *The explanation of social behaviour*. Oxford: Blackwell.

Heritage, J. (1984). *Garfinkel and ethnomethodology*. Cambridge: Polity Press.

McGuire, W. J. (1964). Inducing resistance to persuasion: Some contemporary approaches. In L. Berkowitz (Ed.), *Advances in experimental social psychology* (Vol. 1). New York: Academic Press.

Middleton, D., & Edwards, D. (Eds.) (1990). *Collective remembering*. London: Sage.

Moscovici, S. (1984). The myth of the lonely paradigm: A rejoinder. *Social Research*, *51*, 939–967.

Nofsinger, R. E. (1991). *Everyday conversation*. Newbury Park, CA: Sage.

Perelman, C., & Olbrechts-Tyteca, L. (1971). *The new rhetoric*. Indiana: University of Notre Dame Press.

Pinker, S. (1994). *The language instinct*. Harmondsworth: Penguin.

Plato (1948). *The sophist*. London: Loeb Classical Library.

Potter, J., & Edwards, D. (1990). Nigel Lawson's tent: Attribution theory, discourse analysis and the social psychology of factual discourse. *European Journal of Social Psychology*, *20*, 405–424.

*Potter, J., & Wetherell, M. (1987). *Discourse and social psychology*. London: Sage.

Sacks, H. (1972a). An initial investigation of the usability of conversational data for doing sociology. In D. Sudnow (Ed.), *Studies in social interaction*. New York: Free Press.

Sacks, H. (1972b). Notes on police assessment of moral character. In D. Sudnow (Ed.), *Studies in social interaction*. New York: Free Press.

Sherif, M. (1966). *Group conflict and co-operation*. London: Routledge and Kegan Paul.

Sherif, M. (1981). Experiments in group conflict. In E. Aronson (Ed.), *Readings about the social animal*. New York: Freeman.

Sherif, M., & Sherif, C. W. (1953). *Groups in harmony and tension*. New York: Harper.

Shotter, J. (1993a). *The cultural politics of everyday life*. Milton Keynes: Open University.

Shotter, J. (1993b). *Conversational realities: Studies in social constructionism*. London: Sage.

Stevenson, R. J. (1993). *Language, thought and representation*. Chichester: John Wiley.

Tajfel, H. (1981). *Human groups and social categories*. Cambridge University Press: Cambridge.

Taylor, D. M., & Moghaddam, F. M. (1994). *Theories of intergroup relations*. Westport: Praeger.

Turner, J. C., Hogg, M. A., Oakes, P. J., Reicher, S. D., & Wetherell, M. (1987). *Rediscovering the social group*. Oxford: Blackwell.

van Dijk, T. A. (1991). *Racism and the press*. London: Routledge.

van Dijk, T. A. (1992). Discourse and the denial of racism. *Discourse and Society*, *3*, 87–118.

van Dijk, T. A. (1993). *Elite discourse and racism*. Newbury Park, CA: Sage.

Volosinov, V. N. (1973). *Marxism and the philosophy of language*. New York: Seminar Press.

*Wetherell, M., & Potter, J. (1992). *Mapping the language of racism*. Hemel Hempstead: Harvester/Wheatsheaf.

Widdicombe, S., & Wooffitt, R. (1995). *The language of youth subcultures*. Hemel Hempstead: Harvester/Wheatsheaf.

Wittgenstein, L. (1953). *Philosophical investigations*. Oxford: Blackwell.

Wittgenstein, L. (1967). *Zettel*. Oxford: Blackwell.

4

On the Social Origins of Human Nature

Marilynn B. Brewer

Marilynn Brewer is Ohio State Regents Professor of Social Psychology at the Ohio State University. Since completing her doctorate in social psychology at Northwestern University in 1968, she was written numerous books and research articles on the social psychology of person perception, stereotyping, and intergroup relations. Her books include two volumes on intergroup relations co-authored with Norman Miller: *Groups in contact: The psychology of desegregation* (1984) and *Intergroup relations* (1996). Brewer was recipient of the 1992 Donald T. Campbell Award for Distinguished Research in Social Psychology, and the 1995 Kurt Lewin Award from the Society for the Psychological Study of Social Issues. In 1993 she was elected President of the American Psychological Society and has also served as President of the Society for Personality and Social Psychology in the USA.

The founders of modern social psychology in the 1930s and 1940s took it for granted that there was something special about the social level of analysis – that social phenomena were not derivative or reducible to mechanisms at lower levels of organization. But over the years, the process of legitimizing social psychology as a sub-field of the discipline of psychology has led us to focus almost exclusively on the cognitive, motivational, and affective *underpinnings* of social behavior – treating these individual level processes as the "building blocks" of social processes. This emphasis has had the unintended consequence of "colonializing" social psychology, which has been viewed – from inside

Thanks to Donald T. Campbell and Linnda R. Caporael for inspiring the ideas expressed in this chapter and for valuable comments on an earlier draft.

and out – as a branch of learning theory, cognitive psychology, or psychophysiology.

The purpose of this essay is to try to reverse this colonial image of social psychology and to pursue a more imperialistic agenda – to gain recognition for the idea that the so-called building blocks of human perception, cognition, and motivation have been shaped by and derived from the requirements of social living.

Group Selection and Human Sociality

For the most part, social psychologists have not incorporated evolutionary models into their theories of social behavior. In general, we have either denied the relevance of evolutionary processes for human social life, or accepted the imperialism of biological or genetic determinism. Most versions of what is called "evolutionary psychology" place an inordinate emphasis on reproductive behaviors – primarily mating and parenting – as the essence of selective adaptation (e.g. Buss, 1995; Kenrick, 1994). But this view represents a rather impoverished notion of human social life. Certainly mating and parenting are major life tasks for adult humans; but these functions are embedded in a rich social mosaic of relationships and obligations to extended family, peer groups, authority structures, and other social networks. In human societies, being married and becoming parents are as much a matter of taking one's position in a social order as they are reproductive activities.

I advocate a view of the evolutionary history of human beings that starts from the premise that coordinated group living is the primary survival strategy of the species (Leakey, 1978). At some point between *homo erectus* and *homo sapiens*, social organization at the level of the extended band became the *modus operandi* for continuation of the species. The social group, in effect, provided a buffer between the individual organism and the exigencies of the physical environment. As a consequence, the requirements of group living define the immediate selection environment for human evolution. In effect, then, the exigencies of the physical environment exercise only indirect selective force on human adaptation, while the requirements of social living constitute the immediate selective environment.

For a truly social species, interdependence at the group level is obligatory (Caporael & Brewer, 1995). That is, all individuals' chances for survival are affected not only by their own skills, abilities, and efforts, but by the efforts and behaviors of others within a bounded social community. Coordination and exchange within such a system are not based merely on voluntary exchange relationships, to be entered into or withdrawn from as immediate costs and benefits dictate. Commitment to and acceptance of interdependence among all members of the social unit is a requirement of group living. Within a social community, individuals are invested in the children of other individuals – not because of genetic relatedness but because the survival of one's own offspring is dependent on the continuity of the group as a whole.

Cooperative groups must meet certain structural requirements in order to exist, just as organisms must have certain structural properties in order to be viable. For groups these organizational imperatives include mobilization and coordination of individual effort, communication, internal differentiation, optimal group size, and boundary definition. The benefits *to individuals* of cooperative arrangements cannot be achieved unless prior conditions have been satisfied that make the behavior of other individuals predictable and coordinated. Group survival depends on successful solution to these problems of *internal* organization and coordination, quite independent of *inter*group competition.

What I am talking about here is what Campbell (1974, 1990) called "downward causation" across system levels. Downward causation operates whenever structural requirements at higher levels of organization determine some aspects of structure and function at lower levels (a kind of reverse reductionism). A particularly good illustration of a causal relationship between social and biological levels of organization is the phenomenon of synchrony of lutenizing hormone (LH) cycles that has been documented in rodents, primates, and humans (McClintock, 1987). A group of females living in close proximity over a period of time exhibit synchronized LH cycles. This synchrony makes possible near-simultaneous conceptions and births and paves the way for cooperative rearing of offspring. This phenomenon is an illustration of social regulation of biology (downward causation) in that group living arrangements shape hormonal activity at the individual level.

The notion of downward causation is consistent with recent hierarchical models in evolutionary biology (e.g. L. Buss, 1987; Brandon, 1990; Maynard Smith & Szathmary, 1995; Wilson & Sober, 1995). Such models recognize that the concept of "fit" must be hierarchically organized. Genes, as one level of organization, must fit the environment of their cellular machinery; cells must fit the environment of the individual organism; and individual organisms must fit the next higher level of organization within which they function.

For human beings, as for other social species, this hierarchical organization continues beyond the individual organism to various levels of group structure. Caporael (1995) has proposed that there are four basic levels of organization that have been present throughout the evolution of human social life. These four basic configurations are (1) *dyads*, two-person units such as the parent-child relationship; (2) *teams*, family or work groups of three to seven people; (3) *bands*, face-to-face interacting communities of approximately thirty to fifty people; and (4) *tribes*, macrobands characterized by shared identity and informational interdependence without continual face to face interaction. Each of these levels of organization exists to serve different survival functions, and each entails different problems of coordination and regulation. Collectively, these forms of group organization define the selection environment within which human beings evolved.

Recognizing the social group as selection environment sheds new light on the question of what humans have been adapted for. Individuals whose cognitive and motivational capacities are well suited for coordinated group life have a better chance of survival in that environment. Coordination at the group level of organization requires shared perceptions and distributed cognition which are now being recognized as primary shapers of many cognitive processes and associated neurological structures (Levine, Resnick, & Higgins, 1993). The capacity for language is no doubt the product of downward causation originating in the intensity of coordination and interdependence within groups. Further, interdependence means that humans have developed cognitive mechanisms that are highly tuned to the implications of *other* individuals' behavior (Campbell, 1982). As group members, individuals will gain advantage if they selectively avoid, reject, or eliminate other individuals whose behaviors are disruptive to group organization.

However arbitrary the "rules" of a group may be, failure to adhere to those rules is a cue to social pathology and subject to selection pressures. To be rejected by the group precludes or significantly reduces the chances for individual survival, with ultimate consequences for the distribution of genotypes in the population. Thus, social interdependence is the basis for integrality of the biological and social aspects of the human phenotype. As Oyama (1991) put it, "nature is a product of nurture." Biology is as much a product of culture as culture a product of biology.

Ambivalent Sociality

Under this evolutionary scenario, the species characteristics that we would expect to be biologically "built in" would be those associated with human sociality (Campbell, 1983; Caporael, Dawes, Orbell, & van de Kragt, 1989). Sociality encompasses those propensities most associated with group identity – cooperativeness, group loyalty, adherence to socially learned norms, and fear of social exclusion (Baumeister & Tice, 1990). However, sociality does not imply noncontingent altruism or self-sacrifice. Human beings are clearly vested with self-interest, but this view of evolutionary history contends that self-interest is naturally mitigated by identification with groups.

Since individual self-interest and collective interests do not always coincide perfectly, the necessities of group living require coordination not only between individuals but *within* individuals, to meet competing demands from different levels of organization. Human social life can be characterized as a perpetual juggling act – maintaining the integrity of individual identity, interpersonal relationships, and collective interests simultaneously. Humans are not driven either by unmitigated individual selfishness or by noncontingent altruism, but instead show the capacity for variable motivation and behavior patterns contingent on the state of the environment.

When individual self-interest and collective interests are placed in opposition, the innate ambivalences in human nature are revealed. "Social dilemmas" constitute a special set of interdependence problems in which individual and collective interests are at odds. The dilemma arises whenever individuals acting in their own rational self-interest would engage in behaviors that cumulatively disadvantage everyone. In the modern world, social dilemmas include problems of maintaining scarce collective resources such as water and rainforests, preserving public goods such as parks and public television, and preventing pollution and destruction of the environment. The self-interests of each individual are best served by taking advantage of the benefits of collective resources without contributing to their maintenance, but the cumulative effect of such self-interested actions would be that everyone pays the cost of resource depletion and environmental damage. To the extent that social life is characterized by these types of interdependencies, some mechanisms for balancing individual interests and collective welfare must be achieved.

Experimental research on social dilemmas such as public goods problems and resource conservation demonstrate how individuals behave when they must choose between immediate self-interest and group-interest (Caporael et al., 1989; Kramer & Brewer, 1984). In these choice situations, individuals do not behave consistently selfishly or unselfishly; a great deal depends on the group context in which the decision is made. When a collective social identification is not available, individuals tend to respond to the depletion of a collective resource by increasing their own resource use, at the cost of long-term availability. However, when a symbolic collective identity has been made salient, individuals respond to a resource crisis by dramatically reducing their own resource use (Kramer & Brewer, 1984). Further, when a public goods decision is preceded by even a brief period of group discussion, the rate of cooperative choice (when decisions are made individually and anonymously) is almost 100 percent (Caporael et al., 1989). This level of cooperative responding suggests that, under appropriate conditions, group welfare is just as "natural" as self-gratification as a rule for individual decision making. Situational cues, cultural indoctrination, and behavior of others determine which predisposition will dominate on any particular occasion.

Human Nature and Ethnocentrism

The necessity for meeting demands of existence at the individual, interpersonal, and collective levels of organization suggests that human social life is regulated not by single social motives but by the complex effects of multiple, competing motivational systems. Brewer's (1991) model of "optimal distinctiveness" provides one illustration of how such competing motivational systems might work. The model posits that humans are characterized by two opposing needs that govern the relationship between the self-concept and membership in social groups. The first is a need for *assimilation and inclusion*, a desire for belonging that motivates immersion in social groups. The second is a need for *differentiation* from others that operates in opposition to the need for immersion. As group membership becomes more and more inclusive, the need for inclusion is satisfied but the need for differentiation is activated; conversely, as inclusiveness decreases, the differentiation need is reduced but the need for assimilation is activated. These competing drives assure that interests at one level are not consistently sacrificed to interests at the other. According to the model, the two opposing motives produce an emergent characteristic – the capacity for social identification with distinctive groups that satisfy both needs simultaneously.

Social identification involves a blurring of the distinction between self and others in the formation of a self-concept. In effect, social identities are an extension of the cognitive representation of the self to include others who share a common category membership (Turner et al., 1987). The process of social identification represents the perceptual, affective, and cognitive mechanisms that support the development and maintenance of group membership and collective behavior. But there is a downside to this capacity for self-extension. The same process that generates social cooperation and sacrifice for the collective welfare also begets ethnocentrism and in-group bias.

The term "ethnocentrism" was coined by William Graham Sumner in his book *Folkways* (1906). The concept was driven by the observation that human social arrangements are universally characterized by differentiation into in-groups and out-groups – the we–they distinctions that demarcate boundaries of loyalty and cooperation among individuals. Attitudes and values are shaped by this in-group–out-group distinction in that individuals view all others from the perspective of the in-group. In Sumner's words, ethnocentrism

> is . . . the view of things in which one's own group is the center of everything, and all others are scaled and rated with reference to it . . . Each group nourishes its own pride and vanity, boasts itself superior, exalts its own divinities, and looks with contempt on outsiders. Each group thinks its own folkways the only right ones . . . (E)thnocentrism leads a people to exaggerate and intensify everything in their own folkways which is peculiar and which differentiates them from others. (Sumner, 1906, pp. 12–13)

In a further analysis of the ethnocentrism concept, LeVine and Campbell (1972) identified twenty-three facets of culture that differentiate attitudes, perceptions, and behaviors toward the in-group from those directed toward out-groups (e.g. viewing "us" as virtuous and superior, "them" as immoral and inferior; "us" as peace loving and cooperative, "them" as treacherous and untrustworthy; loyalty, respect, and obedience toward in-group authority, contempt for out-group authority; differential sanctions for acts of aggression toward in-group as opposed to out-group members, etc.). During the early 1970s, LeVine and Campbell undertook an ambitious collaborative effort to test cross-culturally the universality of ethnocentric perception. The Cross-Cultural Study of Ethnocentrism (CCSE) project introduced a novel method of data collection designed to blend ethnographic case study and structured interview techniques. Experienced ethnographers in field sites in Africa, New Guinea, North America, and Asia were commissioned to use their best local informants to obtain information on precolonial in-group organization and intergroup attitudes, using a structured, open-ended interview format. Both qualitative and quantitative analyses of coded interview responses confirm the robustness of the tendency to differentiate the social environment in terms of in-group–out-group distinctions and to value in-group characteristics over those of other groups (Brewer, 1972, 1986; Brewer & Campbell, 1976).

Contemporaneously with the CCSE project, Henri Tajfel's social psychology research group in Bristol, UK, was developing a very different paradigm for studying in-group bias and intergroup discrimination in the laboratory. In a laboratory setting, experiments with the so-called "minimal intergroup situation" (Tajfel, 1970) provided a powerful demonstration that merely classifying individuals into arbitrary distinct social categories was sufficient to produce in-group–out-group discrimination and bias, even in the absence of any interactions with fellow group members or any history of competition or conflict between the groups.

Remarkably, results of the cross-cultural field research and these laboratory studies converged in confirming the power of we–they distinctions to produce differential evaluation, liking, and treatment of other persons depending on whether they are identified as members of the in-group category or not. Further, the laboratory experiments with the minimal intergroup situation demonstrated that ethnocentric loyalty and bias clearly do not depend on kinship or an extensive history of interpersonal relationships among group members, but can apparently be engaged readily by symbolic manipulations that imply shared attributes or common fate. What appears to be critical for in-group attachment is that there be a basis for *distinctive* identification of who is "us" and who is "them" – a rule of exclusion as well as inclusion.

In evolutionary terms, ethnocentrism can be understood as the consequence of an extension of the idea of "reciprocal altruism" (Trivers, 1971). The benefits of sharing and other forms of cooperative altruism can be gained if individuals extend their altruistic behavior contingently – only to those who can be expected to reciprocate. An in-group can be considered an "altruist pact," where members are expected to extend benefits to all other members of the group and can, in turn, expect to receive benefits from all others who share that group identity (Brewer, 1981). This "depersonalized altruism," however, extends only to the boundary of the in-group and not to members of out-groups.

The structural requirements of coordinated activity and mutual interdependence depend on a psychology of trust and obligation toward fellow group members. In effect, in-groups represent bounded communities of reciprocal trust and cooperation. Within those boundaries, individuals can legitimately expect to receive (and to give) positive regard, aid, and predictability in the form of adherence to shared social norms and rules – expectations that are not extended to those outside the boundary. Within such a bounded system, it is not surprising that we learn to think of our own in-groups as more virtuous than out-groups. This gives rise to what Campbell (1982) called "clique selfishness" – where the capacity for selflessness on behalf of in-groups is matched by the most selfish extremes of greed and hostility when in-group interests are pitted against those of out-groups.

Although ethnocentric loyalty can give rise to out-group hostility and intergroup conflict, the important point about an evolutionary analysis of in-group bias is that it derives not from xenophobia but from the requirements of adaptation to in-group living. Although the in-group positivity component of ethnocentrism appears to be universal, attitudes toward relevant out-groups vary tremendously in different social contexts – from cautious hospitality, to indifference, contempt, or disdain, to hostility and fear. There is no universal out-group hostility that corresponds to the universality of in-group positivity. In-group identification is perhaps a necessary but not sufficient cause of intergroup conflict.

The accumulated findings from research on in-group bias are consistent with the idea that it was not the *inter*group environment but the exigencies of *intra*group coordination and structure that shaped the evolution of human cognition, emotion, and physiology. In this view, sociality is not simply the product of biology – human biology is the product of social organization.

References

(Those marked * are recommended for further reading.)

Baumeister, R. F., & Tice, D. M. (1990). Anxiety and social exclusion. *Journal of Social and Clinical Psychology*, 9, 165–195.

Brandon, R. N. (1990). *Adaptation and environment*. Princeton, NJ: Princeton University Press.

Brewer, M. B. (Series Ed.) (1972). *HRAFlex Ethnocentrism Interview Series*. New Haven, CN: Human Relations Area Files.

Brewer, M. B. (1981). Ethnocentrism and its role in interpersonal trust. In M. Brewer & B. Collins (Eds.), *Scientific inquiry and the social sciences* (pp. 345–360). San Francisco, CA: Jossey-Bass.

Brewer, M. B. (1986). The role of ethnocentrism in intergroup conflict. In S. Worchel & W. G. Austin (Eds.), *Psychology of intergroup relations* (pp. 82–102). Chicago, IL: Nelson-Hall.

*Brewer, M. B. (1991). The social self: On being the same and different at the same time. *Personality and Social Psychology Bulletin*, *17*, 475–482.

Brewer, M. B., & Campbell, D. T. (1976). *Ethnocentrism and intergroup attitudes: East African evidence*. Beverly Hills, CA: Sage.

Buss, D. M. (1995). Evolutionary psychology: A new paradigm for psychological sciences. *Psychological Inquiry*, *6*, 1–30.

Buss, L. W. (1987). *The evolution of individuality*. Princeton, NJ: Princeton University Press.

Campbell, D. T. (1974). "Downward causation" in hierarchically organised biological systems. In F. Ayala & T. Dobzhansky (Eds.), *Studies in the philosophy of biology* (pp. 179–186). London: Macmillan.

Campbell, D. T. (1982). Legal and primary social controls. *Journal of Social and Biological Structures*, *5*, 431–438.

*Campbell, D. T. (1983). Two distinct routes beyond kin selection to ultrasociality: Implications for the humanities and social sciences. In D. Bridgeman (Ed.), *The nature of prosocial development: Theories and strategies* (pp. 11–41). New York: Academic Press.

Campbell, D. T. (1990). Levels of organization, downward causation, and the selection-theory approach to evolutionary epistemology. In G. Greenberg & E. Tobach (Eds.), *Theories of the evolution of knowing* (pp. 1–17). Hillsdale, NJ: Lawrence Erlbaum.

Caporael, L. R. (1995). Sociality: Coordinating bodies, mind, and groups. *Psycolloquy*, 95.6.01 [on-line serial].

Caporael, L. R., & Brewer, M. B. (1995). Hierarchical evolutionary theory: There is an alternative, and it's not creationism. *Psychological Inquiry*, *6*, 31–34.

Caporael, L. R., Dawes, R. M., Orbell, J. M., & van de Kragt, A. (1989). Selfishness examined: Cooperation in the absence of egoistic incentives. *Behavioral and Brain Sciences*, *12*, 683–739.

Kenrick, D. T. (1994). Evolutionary social psychology: From sexual selection to social cognition. In M. Zanna (Ed.), *Advances in experimental social psychology* (Vol. 26, pp. 75–121). New York: Academic Press.

Kramer, R. M., & Brewer, M. B. (1984). Effects of group identity on resource use in a simulated commons dilemma. *Journal of Personality and Social Psychology*, *46*, 1044–1057.

*Leakey, R. E. (1978). *People of the lake: Mankind and its beginnings*. New York: Avon.

Levine, J. M., Resnick, L. B., & Higgins, E. T. (1993). Social foundations of cognition. *Annual Review of Psychology*, *44*, 585–612.

*LeVine, R. A., & Campbell, D. T. (1972). *Ethnocentrism: Theories of conflict, ethnic attitudes and group behavior*. New York: Wiley.

Maynard Smith, J., & Szathmary, E. (1995). *The major transitions in evolution*. Oxford: W. H. Freeman.

McClintock, M. K. (1987). A functional approach to the behavioral endocrinology of rodents. In D. Crews (Ed.), *Psychobiology of reproductive behavior: An evolutionary perspective* (pp. 176–203). Englewood Cliffs, NJ: Prentice-Hall.

Oyama, S. (1991). Bodies and minds: Dualism in evolutionary theory. *Journal of Social Issues*, *47*(3), 27–42.

Sumner, W. G. (1906). *Folkways*. New York: Ginn.

Tajfel, H. (1970). Experiments in intergroup discrimination. *Scientific American*, *223*(2), 96–102.

Trivers, R. L. (1971). The evolution of reciprocal altruism. *The Quarterly Review of Biology*, *46*(4), 35–57.

Turner, J. C., Hogg, M., Oakes, P., Reicher, S., & Wetherell, M. (1987). *Rediscovering the social group: A self-categorization theory*. Oxford: Basil Blackwell.

*Wilson, D. S., & Sober, E. (1995). Reintroducing group selection to the human behavioral sciences. *Behavioral and Brain Sciences*, *17*, 585–608.

5 Organizing Social-psychological Explanations

Willem Doise

Willem Doise was born in Flanders, Belgium, in 1935 and received his doctorate (supervised by Otto Klineberg) in social psychology at the Sorbonne, Paris, in 1967. He was a researcher at the CNRS in Paris between 1967 and 1972 and has been Professor of experimental social psychology at the University of Geneva since 1972. His first publication in French appeared in 1968, his first in English in 1969. He was a member of the executive committee of the European Association of Experimental Social Psychology from 1975 to 1981 and President of that association from 1978 to 1981. He has been a visiting professor at the Universities of Brussels, Auckland, Tilburg, Bologna, Rome, Leuven, Belgrano, Otago, Liège, Savoie, and Provence. His main research interests are in intergroup relations, social identity, socio-cognitive development, social representations, and explanations in social psychology.

Introduction

In social psychology, the enormous mass of ideas which accumulate each year in various journals, edited books, and monographs is widely disparate. Interesting ideas are developed, they stimulate research, but in most cases research trends remain juxtaposed and no attempt at integration is achieved. The following still remains a fair description of the scattered reality of contemporary social psychology:

> The topics in social psychology read more like a Sears and Roebuck catalogue than like a novel. They provide a listing of items of possible interest to the reader rather than a story with a plot, development of characters and so on. Our work is like that of mining

engineers, who find a vein of valuable material and dig it out, and not like the work of geologists, who identify various features of the earth, describe their interrelations, and explain their origins. (Kelley, 1983, p. 8)

However, interrelations between explanatory principles used by social psychologists exist. This contribution will describe (1) some general organizing themes which occur in many superficially unrelated explanations; (2) how research traditions are anchored in common historical lineages relating to major problems in the history of philosophy; and (3) a method for studying interrelationships between research traditions by means of the articulation of levels of analyses.

Organizing Themes

In social psychology, several fragmented notions, illustrated by apparently unrelated experiments, are the expression of more general explanatory notions, based on the themes of integration and differentiation, of autonomy and interdependence. The structure of our manual of experimental social psychology (Doise, Deschamps, & Mugny, 1978/1991, and for a fuller version, Doise, Deschamps, & Mugny, 1980) is organized around these general themes.

How are these themes organized? A first major series of theoretical concepts in social psychology bear upon collective dynamics, that is, on the processes through which individuals introduce divergences within and between social groups and integrate themselves into groups. In such studies, bipolarity appears: some are clearly more concerned with clarifying dynamics of differentiation and deal, for instance, with processes of categorization, deviance, and minority influence. Other studies attempt to clarify dynamics of integration such as normalization, polarization, or social identity. Although bipolarity clearly appears in explanatory approaches aimed at accounting either for dynamics of convergence and similarity or for dynamics of divergence and heterogeneity, nevertheless these approaches can be considered complementary. So, to account for effects of integration into a group, differentiation from other groups should be analyzed, and vice versa. Such a complementarity is exemplified in Sherif's (1966) studies on intergroup competition. A more complex relationship between integration and differentiation is envisaged by Lorenzi-Cioldi (1988), who distinguishes between groups whose members are characterized by their differences and originality (collections – such as groups of artists) and groups whose members are defined by their homogeneity (aggregates – usually dominated groups).

A second series of theoretical concepts analyses human social behavior in terms of dependence on others (e.g. social comparison, reactance, group work) and autonomy (e.g. cognitive development, dissonance reduction, attributions). Again, these different processes of interdependent and of autonomous functioning are considered to be complementary. The study of autonomous individual functioning necessitates the study of interdependence and vice versa. Such a conception was the guiding idea of our studies on the social development of intelligence (Doise & Mugny, 1984). In these studies the individual was seen as mastering schemas, regulations of actions, and behavioral repertoires enabling him or her to participate in social interactions. In the course of these interactions, individual principles of organization are integrated within complex social regulations which can produce new individual capacities for more complex coordinations. These new competencies then allow the individual to benefit from more complex social coordinations, and so on. This conception was based on the notion of a spiral of causality: a given state of the individual makes possible participation in certain social interactions which give rise to new individual states. Of course, at a certain level of generality it is arbitrary to begin the process with an individual state or a social interaction, since there is a continuous interdependence between the two.

However, interdependence and autonomy, just like differentiation and integration, are too often used as unrelated notions without analyzing their complementarity. Such one-sidedness was also denounced by Kelley (1983, p. 23):

> One polar tendency is studied at a time, without consideration of its opposites and of relevant contingencies. Explicit attention to the polarities will give us a more comprehensive understanding of the basic dilemmas of life . . .

Anchoring in Historical Lineages

It seems obvious that the organizing principles of explanations used by social psychologists share a common origin: major problems of the history of philosophy. Wilhelm Wundt, social psychologist but also founder of the first laboratory of experimental psychology, wanted to continue a philosophical tradition while transforming it. He therefore gave the name *Philosophische Studien* to the psychological journal he founded and whose aim was also to report on experimental research.

James Baldwin (1913), in his history of psychology, credited Fichte, Schelling, and Hegel with introducing the principal categories of functionalist theories in psychology: cognition, volition, and affect. But he challenged the Hegelian concept of knowledge that explained the development of thought by the laws immanent within it: "Once acknowledged that, whatever may happen, thought is realising itself by an inner dialectical law of its own nature – and anything may happen!" (Baldwin, 1913, p. 42). In order to avoid the arbitrariness of ideas about dialectics purely internal to thinking he resorted to social psychology: "Psychology should be a science in which the material is, so to speak, social rather than individual" (ibid., 1913, p. 35). According to him: "The need became apparent for a genetic and social psychology which would reveal the state of the individual mind given social conditions; the relation, that is, between individual and collective 'representation', to extend somewhat the phraseology of the French writers referred to in the discussion of primitive thought" (ibid., p. 106).

I have described elsewhere how Cattaneo (1864) had already advocated half a century before Baldwin the same approach to the study of the philosophical concept of antithesis (see Doise, 1987). In a lecture at the Royal Lombardic Institute of Sciences, Letters and Arts he recommended in its title "Antithesis as a method for social psychology." Social psychology is defined as a "Psicologia delle menti associate" and has to study "how the most eminent performances of science and ethics are obtained in agreements and disagreements between men in close interaction" (Cattaneo, 1864, p. 264). The main mechanism formulated by Cattaneo to explain the difference between the achievements of collective and single minds is conflict, and he describes how in the course of some conflicts the negation of an idea can lead to the elaboration of a new one "which arises from the conflict between different minds and would not arise in agreeing minds or in a single mind" (ibid., p. 265).

Nowadays, the works of philosophers on the theory of communicative action (Habermas, 1979) show how alive the links between philosophy and social psychology still are. This is further proof of the importance of the ideation work done in social psychology. The apparently very limited scope of explanatory contexts used in research on attribution, social influence, or social interaction in cognitive development are in keeping with philosophical theses on the nature of freedom, of knowledge, and of morality. Very fragmentary-looking socio-psychological analyses thus have more general relevance, to which many research reports virtually never refer. Researchers in social psychology use theoretical tools that they do not link to the philosophical traditions that forged these instruments. They therefore miss opportunities to have an impact on these traditions.

One of the most interesting questions social psychologists have to answer was raised by Durkheim (1902) in the preface to the second edition of *The division of labor in society*:

> As to the question which gave rise to this work it is that of the relations between the individual personality and social solidarity. What explain the fact that, while becoming more autonomous, the individual becomes more closely dependent on society? How can he simultaneously be more personally developed and more socially dependent? For it is undeniable that these two developments, however contradictory they may seem, are equally in evidence. That is the problem which we have set ourselves. What has seemed to us to resolve this apparent antinomy is a transformation of social solidarity due to the steadily growing development of the division of labour. (Durkheim, 1902, pp. xliii–xliv)

As is well known, Durkheim described two prototypes of society. One, the society based on mechanical solidarity, is essentially characterized by its homogeneity, with individual states of consciousness being common to all members of a social segment so that there can be no question of individual and collective consciousness coming into conflict. By contrast, society with organic solidarity is characterized by its variety, with different individuals having their own individual consciousness. Collective consciousness loses importance and morality becomes more rational and open to discussion, and is not seen to be transcendent since it is ultimately founded in the rights of the individual.

The Genevan developmental psychologist Piaget (1932, p. 336) espouses the famous opposition of the sociologist:

> As Durkheim himself has pointed out, one cannot explain the passage from the forced conformity of "segmented" societies to the organic solidarity of differentiated societies without invoking the diminished supervision of the group over the individual as a fundamental psychological factor. The "denser" the community, the sooner will the adolescent escape from the direct constraint of his relations and, coming under a number of fresh influences, acquire his spiritual independence by comparing them with one another. The more complex the society, the more autonomous is the personality and the more important are the relations of cooperation between equal individuals.

In his book on moral judgment Piaget places much emphasis on the difference between relations of constraint and relations of cooperation. I consider the child psychologist's position between constraint and cooperation as a social-psychological version of Durkheim's theory, since relations of constraint are supposed to hinder cognitive development. I quote again Piaget, from a paper first published in 1928 in a philosophical review, but republished in 1976: "In a society where the generations thus heavily weigh upon each other, none of the conditions required to eliminate childish mentality can be met. There is no discussion, no exchange of view" (Piaget, 1976, p. 76). Thus only social relations based on cooperation can lead to a liberation of rational thought:

> Cooperation opposes both autism and constraint. It progressively reduces autistic or egocentric processes of thought . . . Discussion generates inner reflection. Mutual control generates the need for proof and objectivity. The exchange of thought implies adopting the principles of contradiction and identity as discourse regulators. As regard constraint, cooperation destroys it whenever differentiation and free discussion between individuals develop. (Piaget, 1976, p. 77)

An important issue for my present argument is to find out if there exist important causal links between patterns of social relations and the development of moral or cognitive competence in the individual.

According to contemporary sociologists and psychologists such links do exist. Bernstein's (1973) distinction between elaborated and restricted speech styles implies, according to me, differences in cognitive functioning – which does not mean differences in competences – and these differences in functioning are related to differences in social relationships. The more actors in a situation have characteristics in common, the more they share, so to speak, mechanical solidarity, the more they share meanings which need not be made explicit on every occasion. This results in a special "restricted" discourse, which cannot be understood outside the situation. Other kinds of situation may be characterized by differences between the actors: in the situation of more organic solidarity meanings must be made more explicit. The code in this case will be more "universalistic" or "elaborated" so as to permit expression of the special experience of each individual.

I consider Bernstein's theory to be a socio-psychological theory which explains how patterns of mechanical and of organic solidarity can coexist in our society. His distinction between "positional families" and "person-oriented families" has been further elaborated by the psychologists Bearison and Cassel (1975). Such a typological opposition of patterns should not prevent us from conceiving that they coexist to some extent in the same family. Such typological distinctions seem only useful insofar as they clarify complex concrete situations in which the two types of relationships are in fact intimately intermingled.

The idea of combining two fundamental processes, one more concerned with the transmission of a common heritage and an opposed one more related to challenging common truths, is important. Consider again the classical conception defended by Baldwin (1913, p. 35):

> The material of self is, in its origin, collective, not individual. The immature child thinks of the self as a term in a social situation, as part of a larger whole. If this is true, the science of mind must be one in which the concept of an isolated individual mental life is used as a logical abstraction, as an instrument of method rather than as a truth of analysis and explanation.

Such a conception defining society as "a mass of mental and moral states and values, which perpetuates itself in individual persons" (ibid., p. 108) has to be complemented by an analysis of how individuals construct their autonomy. When such analyses are neglected, metaphors describing the individual as a "new cell in the social tissue" (ibid., p. 107) can easily be exploited by fascist ideologies. Indeed, the social psychology of Orano (1902) became one of Mussolini's main sources of ideological inspiration (see Doise, 1986b).

Durkheim's ideas have operated in the manner of a grand theory – that is, they have pointed to general directions for research which have allowed other scholars to investigate more specific areas. In order to explain cognitive development, the Durkheimian orientation refers to the prior structuring of the social environment, which means the norms, rules, or – to use more up-to-date concepts – the scenarios or scripts which govern the social interactions in which children may participate. But another idea, equally important, is the idea of socio-cognitive conflict leading to innovation and progress. As we have mentioned, this idea was already very strongly defended by Cattaneo in 1864. According to him merely raising an idea may be sufficient to create an opposition, and even if the resulting conflict can be considered as affective, it also involves cognitive coordinations:

> Each objection asks for an answer; each reasoning asks for a reasoning which is logically complementary and which forces opposed ideas into an inseparable whole. In regard to passion, people who discuss are fighters, in regard to the world of ideas they are smiths hammering the same iron-piece; they are blind instruments of a common undertaking. Each new effort adds a link to the chain which tows both parties into the vortex of truth. (Ibid., p. 268)

Nowadays processes of transmission of competences, also based on Vygotsky's (1962, 1978) ideas, and processes of innovation or construction are integrated in theories of development (see for instance Winnykamen, 1990). Doise and Mugny's (1984) work on the role of social marking and socio-cognitive conflict in cognitive development is an attempt to integrate ideas about transmission of culturally transmitted regulations with ideas about the construction of new coordinations.

The investigation of the Geneva team on the social development of the intellect ascribes an important explanatory function to cognitive conflict that is socially produced. Such conflict is considered to be an important motor of cognitive progress. A special instance of such socio-cognitive conflict occurs when the incorrect cognitive solutions of a task involving specific objects contradicts the social norms mediated through the use of these objects. Such conflicts were, for instance, studied in conservation of liquid tasks. Children of 5 to 6 years usually think that equal amounts of liquid contained in two equal glasses do not remain equal when they are poured in glasses of different shapes. The setting changes drastically when this apparent inequality contradicts a norm of equal sharing: in such a "socially marked" situation children acquire conservation of equality and generalize their new skill to tasks that are less socially relevant. For other examples and an elaborated theoretical explanation of these results see Doise and Mugny (1984) and to De Paolis, Doise, and Mugny (1987).

Other authors, not necessarily using the same theoretical premises, stress the constructive role of cognitive conflicts that are socially produced in educational settings (e.g. Johnson & Johnson, 1983). Oser (1986, p. 922), a Swiss educational psychologist, describes in the following way the main characteristics of interactional situations which should promote and stimulate moral development through socio-cognitive conflict:

> 1. Presentation of the subjective truth completely and exhaustively . . . as conceived by the participants in the conflict; 2. Absence of an authority presenting an outside or

observer's point of view of the "right" answer; 3. Creation of a disequilibrium by presenting different arguments and different opinions to stimulate development of moral judgment on increasingly complex grounds; 4. Interaction among students (discussants) coordinated in such a way that everyone reacts openly and fairly to one another's point of view (positive climate and transactional discourse); 5. Linking of the principles of discourse to the principles of justice.

These characteristics are similar to those described by Doise and Mugny (1984) in their work on the social development of the intellect. They are confrontation and coordination of viewpoints; avoidance of compliance; socio-cognitive conflict; articulation of organizing social principles with more abstract cognitive principles (for the social construction of the intellect) or with fundamental justice principles (for social construction of ethics). And interestingly enough, these conditions are also homologous to some of those that, according to Janis (1972), should prevent "groupthink" from exerting its often disastrous effects in collective political decision making. This homology could be considered as an illustration of the relevance of ideas conceived in one area of psychology for other areas of social sciences, but in our view such cross-fertilization is possible because different research traditions are in fact grounded in the same philosophical traditions.

Articulation of Levels of Analysis

Another way of organizing the vast amount of research in social psychology takes into account the nature of the explanatory principles involved: these are the principles which relate to an individual's organizational processes, to interpersonal dynamics, to asymmetrical social positioning and to the impact of social norms and representations. I want to illustrate how important this distinction of levels of analysis is if we wish to introduce a theoretical organization in the area of intergroup relations studies (see also Doise, 1984; Lorenzi-Cioldi & Doise, 1990).

Paradoxically, the first-level models used by social psychologists for studying intergroup relations do not seem to involve social explanations because they focus on the study of intraindividual processes. The models used deal with the way individuals organize their experience of the environment. Many investigations deal with categorization models. In an article published in 1959 (pp. 20–21), Tajfel formulates six experimental predictions concerning the effects of links between, on the one hand, accentuation of contrasts in quantitative judgments, and on the other hand, variations in value and/or differences in category membership of a series of stimuli. Elsewhere, I have related in detail how each of these predictions has been experimentally validated (Doise, 1978). Although initially Tajfel's model concerned accentuation of differences between members of different categories, Tajfel and Wilkes (1963) extended the model in an important way by adding that predicted differentiation between categories goes together with accentuation of similarity within categories.

A second level of explanation describes interindividual and situational processes. At this level of analysis, individuals are often considered interchangeable, and it is their interactional systems that provide the explanatory principles typical of this level. Sherif's (1966) intergroup theory was based on analyses at this level. Individuals who through their interdependent actions pursue a common goal become a group. When two groups pursue goals that are negatively interdependent (i.e. when a group can only achieve its goal providing the other does not), intergroup hostility and discrimination arise. Intergroup hostility is reduced by the introduction of superordinate goals, involving all members of both groups in an interdependent activity necessary to achieve an important common goal. This explanation in terms of relations between goals is typically at the interindividual level. It relates to the dynamics of interaction between individuals, who are treated at the outset as occupying interchangeable positions but whose subsequent relations are linked to shared or opposed affiliations which the experimenter introduces in the situation.

A third level of analysis takes account of the different positions which social actors occupy in the fabric of relations typical of a society. Analyses of power and status relationships between groups are located at this level. According to Lorenzi-Cioldi (1988), members of high status groups appear to bolster interpersonal distinctiveness, whereas members of low status groups strengthen more a sense of group cohesiveness. It is hypothesized that such variations in patterns of differentiation depend on individuals' positions in a network of asymmetrical intergroup relations. Members of dominating groups consider themselves individually as the point of reference in relation to which other people are defined; they perceive themselves as unique individuals and do not seek self-definition in terms of group membership. Members of dominated groups define themselves, and are also defined by others, more in terms of social categorizations imposed on them.

A fourth level of analysis resorts to systems of social beliefs, representations, evaluations, and norms. They are cultural and ideological productions typical of a society or of some special groups that not only give a meaning to the behaviors of individuals but also create or maintain social differentiations in the name of general principles such as equity. One can hardly think of an investigation on intergroup relations that does not involve analyses of this level. Indeed, the phenomena of categorical differentiation, of cooperative and competitive interaction between groups, of different social identities, all presuppose the existence of values diffused in a society which determine the dimensions on which groups define themselves in relation to one another. Such dimensions can be interrelated in complex ways, allowing different status groups in the same society to define positive identities on complementary dimensions (see for instance Peabody, 1985).

Distinguishing four levels of analysis not only serves classificatory purposes but it furthers articulation of analyses. Too often, articulation between explanatory models of different levels remains implicit and is thwarted by a modeling approach that, by definition, tries to disregard heterogeneous factors in order to describe "pure" processes. In my view, it is experimentation that remains the best method for a fuller study of these processes by demonstrating the intervention of factors of other levels in intergroup dynamics that are supposed to take place at one of these four levels. Such experimentation prompts researchers to better describe a process conceptualized at one of the levels, while making clearer its functioning conditions that always involve other levels of analysis as well. For instance, Lorenzi-Cioldi and Doise (1990) show this to be the case for the analysis of the asymmetry in perceptions of homogeneity in an in-group and an out-group. Although cognitive factors (such as familiarity) are often invoked for explaining perception of more variety in the in-group, status differences between groups can inverse this asymmetry leading to a perception of higher variety in a higher status out-group.

Intraindividual and social explanations often appear to be located at opposite poles in social-psychological, but also in sociological theories (see Doise & Lorenzi-Cioldi, 1989). They are weighted differently by different groups of researchers. However, the distinction of four levels of analysis and of their articulation shows that such an opposition between a more psychological and a more sociological social psychology does not necessarily reflect the complexities and intricacies of social-psychological explanations used by researchers (see Doise, 1980). Articulating analyses of different levels is an essential aspect of social psychologists' scientific endeavor. Complementing explanations located at one level of analysis by explanations at another level does not only extend the validity of socio-psychological analyses, it also produces a more cumulative science by integrating findings obtained by models at different levels.

Conclusion

Generally, a researcher in social psychology works with a specific model and tries to create experimentally, or to observe systematically, the optimal conditions for this model to function. This research practice, whose legitimacy is widely recognized, has made it possible to elaborate many models in social sciences. Often, competition has developed among researchers in order to elaborate explanatory models which are more powerful than those of colleagues and especially to show that the facts explained by a given model also included phenomena apparently explained by rival models. This is only normal in the struggle for survival in the scientific community whose laws were described by Lemaine (1979; Lemaine, Matalon, & Provansal, 1969).

If that is so for the researcher, it is otherwise for the practitioner involved in ever-changing and many-sided experiences. S/he cannot delimit the social world according to the outlines of a situation ideally relevant to the illustration of a model, and the unexplained residue may well appear to him or her in the form of beings in the flesh demanding their due.

Often, an intervention program has only little chance of succeeding, if it rests on a single theory for interpreting a social situation. A whole body of knowledge, not based on one and the same theory, is often necessary for solving a problem. To organize this knowledge, one must come up with approaches that combine lessons of different relevant theories to account for all of the dynamics that characterize a situation.

But one should not exaggerate the differences between basic and applied research. Indeed, many researchers, while involved in formalizing cognitive processes of an intraindividual type, are nevertheless conceptualizing the intervention of dynamics from other levels (see, for instance, Hewstone, 1989). They consider that each reasoning process is always a complex social dynamic, and they study it while taking account of the social purposes that animate it, and analyze the social conditions necessary for its actualization.

For a specific reason, the question of explanation in social psychology is now asked with renewed acuteness. If I have repeatedly tried to answer this question (Doise, 1980, 1984, 1986a; Doise, Deschamps, & Mugny, 1978, 1991), the renewed acuteness stems from the contemporary predominance of cognitive psychology in which the work of modeling and formalization seems more advanced than it appears at first sight in most sectors of social psychology. But this is a mere façade, at least if one accepts the possibility of several forms of modeling.

In social psychology, the most heuristic models resort often to a propositional or topological logic describing relational properties and relations of order. This was, for instance, the case for the dissonance studies: the definition of dissonance itself concerned relationships between cognitions and in most studies experimental conditions could only be ordered according to degrees of dissonance. In many other experiments, as in those on causal explanations of behavior, the relative importance of independent variables cannot, or are not necessarily, measured in interval scales. This does not rule out a high degree of sophistication in the use of statistical operations of verifying hypotheses and modeling relationships (see Doise, Clémence, & Lorenzi-Cioldi, 1993), and this does not imply that social psychology would be a sort of soft discipline that would not produce strong explanatory models and would only supplement work already done mostly within the theoretical framework of other disciplines.

True, social psychology is a science at the junction of explanatory systems. The junction can be particularly crowded with many roads leading to it.

Researchers in different disciplines may converge while thinking that they move in different spaces. Showing that these spaces have at least common intersections is one of the main tasks of social psychologists.

They would not be able to accomplish this work, if they had no organizing principles, no awareness of historical research traditions and of thematic ideas that cross the borders of different disciplines in social sciences. In my view, there is no area in social psychology in which such perspective taking does not become quickly profitable.

Further Reading

Breakwell, G. M., & Rowett, C. (1982). *Social work: The social psychological approach*. Wokingham: Van Nostrand Reinhold. Levels of analysis in applied social psychology.

Durkin, K. (1995). *Developmental social psychology: From infancy to old age*. Oxford, Blackwell. A synthesis of the social psychological contributions to the study of lifespan development.

Emler, N., & Reicher, S. (1995). *Adolescence and delinquency*. Oxford, Blackwell. A relevant socio-psychological analysis of a sociological phenomenon.

Fiske, S. T., Bersoff, D. N., Borgida, E., Deaux, K., & Heilman, M. E. (1991). Social science research on trial: Use of sex stereotyping research in *Price Westerhouse* v. *Hopkins*. *American Psychologist*, *46*, 1049–1060. An illustration of the societal meaning of experimental social psychology.

McGuire, W. J. (1983). A contextualist theory of knowledge: Its implications for innovation and reform in psychological research. In L. Berkowitz (Ed.), *Advances in experimental social psychology* (Vol. 16, pp. 1–47). New York: Academic Press. A skilled and well-founded argument in favor of theoretical eclecticism.

Moscovici, S. (1993). *The invention of society: Psychological explanations for social phenomena*. Oxford: Polity Press. A demonstration of how the core ideas of founding fathers of sociology (Durkheim, Simmel, Weber) are based on psychological ideas.

References

Baldwin, J. M. (1913). *History of psychology: From John Locke to the present time* (Vol. 2). London: Watts.

Bearison, D. J., & Cassel, T. Z. (1975). Cognitive decentration and social codes: Communicative effectiveness in young children from differing family contexts. *Developmental Psychology*, *11*, 29–36.

Bernstein, B. (1973). *Class, codes and control*. St Albans: Paladin.

Cattaneo, C. (1864). Dell' antitesi come metodo di psicologia sociale. *Il Politecnico*, *20*, 262–270.

De Paolis, P., Doise, W., & Mugny, G. (1987). Social marking in cognitive operations. In W. Doise & S. Moscovici (Eds.), *Current issues in European social psychology* (Vol. II, pp. 1–45). Cambridge, Cambridge University Press.

Doise, W. (1978). *Groups and individuals: Explanations in social psychology*. Cambridge: Cambridge University Press.

Doise, W. (1980). Levels of explanation in the *European Journal of Social Psychology*. *European Journal of Social Psychology*, *10*, 213–231.

Doise, W. (1984). Social representations, inter-group experiments and levels of analysis. In R. M. Farr & S. Moscovici (Eds.), *Social representations* (pp. 255–268). Cambridge/Paris: Cambridge University Press/Maison des Sciences de l'Homme.

Doise, W. (1986a). *Levels of explanation in social psychology*. Cambridge/Paris: Cambridge University Press/Maison des Sciences de l'Homme (originally published as *L'explication en psychologie sociale*. Paris: Presses Universitaires de France, 1982).

Doise, W. (1986b). Mass psychology, social psychology and the politics of Mussolini. In C. F. Graumann & S. Moscovici (Eds.), *Changing conceptions of crowd mind and behavior* (pp. 69–82). New York: Springer Verlag.

Doise, W. (1987). Idées nouvelles et notions anciennes. In J. L. Beauvois, R. V. Joule, & J. M. Monteil (Eds.), *Perspectives cognitives et conduites sociales*. Cousset: Del Val.

Doise, W., & Lorenzi-Cioldi, F. (1980). Socioloques et psychologie sociale. *Revue Européenne des Sciences Sociales*, *27*, 147–196.

Doise, W., & Mugny, G. (1984). *The social development of the intellect*. Oxford: Pergamon Press.

Doise, W., Clémence, A., & Lorenzi-Cioldi, F. (1993). *The quantitative analysis of social representations*. Hemel Hempstead: Harvester Wheatsheaf.

Doise, W., Deschamps, J. C., & Mugny, G. (1978/1991). *Psychologie sociale expérimentale* (2nd ed.). Paris: A. Colin.

Doise, W., Deschamps, J. C., & Mugny, G. (1980). *Psicologia sociale*. Bologna: Zanichelli.

Durkheim, E. (1902). *De la division du travail social* (2nd ed.). Paris: Alcan.

Habermas, J. (1979). *Communication and the evolution of society*. Boston, MA: Beacon Press.

Hewstone, M. (1989). *Casual attribution*. Oxford: Blackwell.

Janis, I. L. (1972). *Victims of groupthink*. Boston, MA: Houghton Mifflin.

Johnson, D. W., & Johnson, R. T. (1983). The socialization and achievement crisis: Are cooperative learning experiences the solution? In L. Bickman (Ed.), *Applied social psychology* (Annual 4). Beverly Hills, CA: Sage.

Kelley, H. H. (1983). The situational origins of human tendencies: A further reason for the formal analysis of structures. *Personality and Social Psychology Bulletin*, *9*, 8–30.

Lemaine, G. (1979). Différentiation sociale et originalité sociale. In W. Doise (Ed.), *Expériences entre groupes*. Paris: Mouton.

Lemaine, G., Matalon, B., & Provansal, B. (1969). La lutte pour la vie dans la cité scientifique. *Revue française de sociologie*, *10*, 139–165.

Lorenzi-Cioldi, F. (1988). *Individus dominants et groupes dominés. Images masculines et féminines*. Grenoble: Presses Universitaires de France.

Lorenzi-Cioldi, F., & Doise, W. (1990). Levels of analysis and social identity. In D. Abrams & M. A. Hogg (Eds.), *Social identity theory: Constructive and critical advances* (pp. 72–88). London: Harvester Wheatsheaf.

Orano, P. (1902). *Psicologia sociale*. Bari: Gius, Laterza & Figli.

Oser, F. K. (1986). Moral education and values education: The moral discourse perspective. In M. C. Wittrock (Ed.), *Handbook of Research on Teaching* (3rd ed.). New York: Macmillan.

Peabody, D. (1985). *National characteristics*. Cambridge: Cambridge University Press.

Piaget, J. (1932). *The moral judgment of the child*. London: Routledge and Kegan.

Piaget, J. (1976). Logique génétique et sociologie. In G. Busino (Ed.), *Les sciences sociales avec et apres Jean Piaget*. Geneva: Droz.

Sherif, M. (1966). *In common predicament*. New York: Houghton Mifflin.

Tajfel, H. (1959). Quantitative judgment in

social perception. *British Journal of Psychology*, *50*, 16–29.

Tajfel, H., & Wilkes, A. L. (1963). Classification and quantitative judgment. *British Journal of Psychology*, *54*, 101–114.

Vygotsky, L. S. (1962). *Thought and language*. Cambridge, MA: MIT Press.

Vygotsky, L. S. (1978). *Mind in society*. Cambridge, MA: Harvard University Press.

Winnykamen, F. (1990). *Apprendre en imitant*. Paris: Presses Universitaires de France.

6

Predicting, Understanding, and Changing Socially Relevant Behaviors: Lessons Learned

Martin Fishbein

Martin Fishbein received his B.A. from Reed College in 1957 and his doctorate (in psychology) from UCLA in 1961. Since that time he has been at the University of Illinois at Urbana-Champaign, where he is currently Professor of Psychology and Research Professor, Institute of Communications Research. Since 1992 he has also been a guest researcher at the Centers for Disease Control and Prevention, where he now serves as Acting Chief, Behavioral Intervention and Research Branch, Division of STD Prevention. He is past-president of the Society for Consumer Psychology (Division 23 of the APA) and of the Interamerican Psychological Society.

He is in the American Marketing Association's Attitude Research Hall of Fame, and has received the Paul D. Converse Award for "distinguished contributions to theory and science in marketing," the National Association of Recording Merchandisers Special Recognition Award for "his contribution to the development of market research in the recorded music industry," the Interamcrican Psychology Society's prize for "distinguished contributions to psychology as a science and as a profession," and the Society for Consumer Psychology's Distinguished Scientific Contribution Award.

In their introduction to this volume, the editors suggested that this book be viewed as a *Festschrift* to social psychology. They hoped, however, that such a celebratory volume would not be taken as an indication that social psychology was approaching the end of its career. Unfortunately, social psychology may be doing just that if it continues to largely ignore the fundamental question of why people behave the way they do and if it continues to place relatively little value on applied research concerned with important societal issues.

Although psychology is best defined as the scientific study of human *behavior*, contemporary social psychology has, in practice, largely ignored behavior and real-world problems. Indeed, it would appear that social psychology has been paying less and less attention to understanding the factors underlying people's decisions to perform or not perform relevant behaviors, while spending more and more time investigating cognitive and judgmental processes without ever worrying about how, or whether, these processes or judgments impact upon behavior. Unfortunately, one cannot know whether different types of cognitive processing impact upon behavior unless one assesses behavior, and my guess is that less than 10 percent of "social psychological studies" have an observed or self-reported behavior as their dependent variable.

If social psychology is to survive as a viable science, social psychologists will have to stop assuming that real-world problems are beneath them and they will have to start paying more attention to understanding why people *behave* the way they do. This is particularly important given that social psychology emerged as a separate discipline within psychology primarily because it was going to provide new insights into human behavior by scientifically studying attitudes (which were assumed to be behavioral dispositions). In fact, many early theorists virtually defined the field of social psychology as the scientific study of attitudes (e.g. Thomas & Znaniecki, 1918; Watson, 1925).

Most of the early evidence for a link between attitude and behavior came from cross-sectional studies showing that people who behaved favorably with respect to some object or group also held favorable attitudes toward that object or group. But when social psychologists went beyond known group comparisons and tried to predict who, in a given group of people, did or did not perform a given behavior, or when they went beyond cross-sectional studies and conducted prospective studies attempting to predict behaviors at time 2 from attitudes assessed at time 1, they quickly found that their measures of attitude appeared to have relatively little to do with behavior (for a review see Wicker, 1969). But rather than questioning the attitude–behavior linkage, most social psychologists questioned the definition of attitude. And so, from a relatively simple unidimensional construct that referred to "the amount of affect for or against an object" (Thurstone, 1931), attitude became a complex multidimensional construct containing cognitive, affective, and conative (or behavioral) components (see e.g. Rosenberg & Hovland, 1960).

While the conception of attitude changed, its operationalization did not. All of the standard attitude measurement instruments (i.e. Thurstone, Likert, Guttman, and semantic differential scales) continued to arrive at a single score that indexed an individual's favorableness or unfavorableness with respect to a given person, group, or object.

And as Thurstone (1931) had pointed out, this index of a person's favorableness or unfavorableness with respect to a given object should not have been expected to be related to any given behavior with respect to that object. Indeed, Thurstone argued that it was perfectly reasonable for two people with the same attitude toward some object to behave quite differently toward it. The overall pattern of their behaviors with respect to that object, however, should indicate the same degree of favorableness (or unfavorableness) toward that object. According to Thurstone, there are many different ways of expressing a favorable (or unfavorable) attitude, and it is unreasonable to assume that different people will express their favorableness (or unfavorableness) in exactly the same ways.

While the transition from a simple unidimensional concept to a complex multidimensional concept did not help our understanding of the attitude–behavior relationship, it did lay the groundwork for examining the relationship between cognition and affect. Analyses of this relationship provided strong evidence to support the hypothesis that a person's overall feeling of favorableness or unfavorableness with respect to a given object (i.e. his or her attitude toward that object) was based upon his or her beliefs about (or cognitions concerning) that object. Generally speaking, the more one believed that a given object possessed or was associated with positive characteristics, qualities, and attributes, the more one felt favorable toward that object. Similarly, the more one believed that the object possessed or was associated with negative characteristics, qualities, and attributes, the more one disliked or felt unfavorable toward the object. While this belief-based (or expectancy-value) model of attitude gained wide acceptance in the 1960s and 1970s, the 1980s saw a new movement arguing for nonbelief-based determinants of attitude (see e.g. Petty & Caccioppo, 1986; Chaiken & Stangor, 1987). There is, however, a real question of whether findings supporting such nonbelief-based determinants of attitude are anything more than methodological artifacts resulting from the use of inappropriate belief-based measures and/or inappropriate attitudinal criteria (see Fishbein & Middlestadt, 1995). Indeed, when appropriate belief-based measures are used to predict appropriate attitudinal measures, there appears to be little evidence that nonbelief-based factors contribute to our understanding of why people like or dislike a given individual, group, or object.

To summarize briefly, then, attitude is a relatively simple construct that refers to a person's overall favorableness or unfavorableness with respect to an object. Although there are increasing claims for noncognitive determinants of attitude, it would appear that, in general, attitudes toward an object are primarily based upon one's beliefs about it. The more one associates the object with positive characteristics, qualities, and attributes the more favorable is one's attitude toward the object. Similarly, the more one associates the object with negative characteristics, qualities, and attributes, the less favorable is one's attitude toward the object. Although one's attitude toward an object does seem to have a strong and significant influence on the pattern of behaviors one engages in *vis-à-vis* the object, it rarely determines any specific behavior with respect to the object.

Unfortunately, if one is really concerned with solving social problems, one usually wants to change specific behaviors. For example, we might want to increase the likelihood that someone will vote in a given election, use condoms, wear seatbelts, or attend an aerobic exercise class. So what does social psychology have to tell us about behavior and behavior change?

Lessons Learned – Understanding and Predicting Behavior

Behavior is a complex construct defined by four elements: action, target, context and time

If, for example, one is interested in consumer behavior, one does not simply observe "buying" (the action). Instead, all one can directly observe is someone buying (the action) a given product (the target), in a given location (the context) at a given point in time. Variations in any one of these four elements changes the definition of the behavior being considered. Although it is possible to define each of the elements at a very general or at a very specific level, the way in which we conduct our behavioral observations defines the behavior we are studying.

For example, although I may be interested in whether someone does or does not buy (action) toothpaste (target; context and time unspecified), what I may actually observe is someone buying or not buying (a given brand of) toothpaste in a particular location (e.g. a given store) at a given point in time. If all I observe is whether shoppers at the 6th Street Supermarket do or do not buy toothpaste, and if I only record this behavior between 6 p.m. and 10 p.m. on Friday night, then the behavior I'm observing is "buying (action) toothpaste (target) at the 6th Street Supermarket (context) between 6 p.m. and 10 p.m. on Friday night (time)". Clearly, this is a very different behavior than "buying toothpaste." And trying to understand why someone did or did not buy toothpaste at the 6th Street Supermarket between 6 p.m. and 10 p.m. on Friday night, is very different than trying to understand why someone did or did not buy toothpaste. Clearly, if an investigator is trying to directly observe whether a respondent does or does not buy Crest toothpaste in the next three months, the investigator (or someone working with the investigator) will either have to follow the respondent around (day and night) for the next three months (or until the person does buy Crest) or he or she will have to rely upon the respondent's self-report (i.e. three months later the respondent can be asked,

"Did you buy Crest toothpaste in the last three months?"). Selecting and assessing a behavioral criterion is often the most difficult part of any behavioral study.

It is important to distinguish between behavior, behavioral categories, and goals

All too often, studies of behavior have assessed goals (e.g. losing weight, getting an A on an exam, staying healthy, getting pregnant, avoiding AIDS) or behavioral categories (e.g. dieting, exercising, studying, practicing safe sex) rather than behaviors. Unfortunately, this distinction between behaviors, behavioral categories, and goals is not always obvious or easy. For example, while use of the male condom is a behavior for heterosexual men, it is a goal for women and for gay and bisexual men when they are in the role of the receptive partner. Even among heterosexual men, however, condom use is not a specific behavior, but a behavioral category. That is, one does not just "use a condom." Instead, condoms are used for given sexual activities with specific partners, and using a condom for vaginal sex with one's main partner or spouse, for example, is a very different behavior than using a condom for vaginal sex with an occasional partner, or using a condom for anal sex with one's main partner. More important, a variable that predicts one of these behaviors may be unrelated to the other two behaviors.

The single best predictor of whether a person will or will not engage in a given behavior is that person's intention to perform that behavior

The intention, however, must correspond to the behavior in question in terms of all four elements. Thus, if one is going to observe whether or not a person buys toothpaste at the Sixth Street Supermarket on Friday between 6 p.m. and 10 p.m., one must measure intentions to "buy toothpaste at the 6th Street Supermarket on Friday between 6 p.m. and 10 p.m." Similarly, if someone is going to obtain a self-report of whether or not respondents bought Crest toothpaste in the past three months, the corresponding intention is the intention "to buy Crest toothpaste in the next three months." Although intentions to perform a given behavior are quite accurate predictors of whether or not the behavior will be performed, the lack of necessary skills and abilities and/or the presence of environmental constraints may prevent the respondent from carrying out his or her intention. Generally speaking, however, people are very good predictors of their own behavior and most people do not form intentions to perform behaviors that are beyond their abilities or that they cannot carry out because of environmental constraints. Nevertheless, people can overestimate their skills and abilities or they may be unaware of environmental constraints. But when a person has formed a strong intention to perform some behavior, has the necessary skills and abilities to perform that behavior, and when there are no environmental constraints to prevent the person from carrying out his or her intention, the probability is close to 1 that the behavior will be performed.

It is important to note that while behavioral intentions are quite accurate predictors of corresponding behaviors, intentions to engage in a class of behavior or to reach a given goal are usually poor predictors of engaging in objectively defined behavioral categories or of goal attainment. With respect to behavioral categories, the problem is mainly one of definition. That is, the respondent and the investigator may have different definitions of the behavioral category. For example, what a respondent means by "safer sex" may not correspond to what an investigator means by "safer sex" and thus while a respondent may perform what she thinks are safer sex behaviors (e.g. avoiding sex with gay men and injecting drug users) she may not perform any of the behaviors the investigator is assessing (e.g. always using a condom with all sexual partners, reducing the number of sexual partners). With respect to goal attainment, the problem is very different and primarily has to do with questions of control. That is, whether one does or does not achieve a given goal often depends less upon behavioral performance than upon factors outside of one's control. For example, although two people trying to lose weight may eat the same foods, and follow the same exercise regimen, metabolic and other biomedical factors may allow one person to lose weight while the other person does not.

There are relatively few variables that serve as the immediate determinants of intention (and behavior)

For example, according to the theory of reasoned action (Ajzen & Fishbein, 1980; Fishbein, 1980; Fishbein & Ajzen, 1975), there are only two primary determinants of intention: the attitude toward performing the behavior and the subjective norm concerning the behavior. More specifically, the more one is favorable toward performing the behavior in question and/or the more one perceives social pressure to perform the behavior, the more likely one is to form an intention to perform that behavior. For accurate prediction, however, both the attitude and the subjective norm must correspond to the intention in terms of action, target, context, and time. Thus for example, if one is interested in predicting whether a male intends to "always (time) use (action) a condom (target) for vaginal sex with occasional partners (context)," one must measure the attitude toward, and the subjective norm with respect to, "my always using a condom for vaginal sex with my occasional partners."

The attitude toward performing a given behavior is viewed as a function of the person's beliefs that performing the behavior in question will lead to certain outcomes or consequences and the person's evaluation of those consequences. Thus, if one believes that performing a given behavior is more likely to lead to "good" than to "bad" consequences, the person should hold a positive attitude toward performing the behavior. On the other hand, if the person believes that performing the behavior will lead to more "negative" than "positive" outcomes, the person should hold a negative attitude toward his or her performing the behavior. Once again, for accurate prediction (and for a better understanding of why people are favorable or unfavorable toward performing the behavior in question) these behavioral beliefs must correspond to the attitude in terms of action, target, context, and time.

The subjective norm is also based on beliefs, but here we are concerned with beliefs about the normative proscriptions of specific significant others and the respondent's motivation to comply with those others. The more people believe that specific others (with whom they are motivated to comply) think they should perform the behavior, the more they should feel social pressure to perform the behavior. On the other hand, the more they believe that specific others (with whom they are motivated to comply) think they should not perform the behavior, the more they should feel social pressure not to engage in the behavior. Here, too, the normative beliefs should correspond to the subjective norm with respect to action, target, context, and time.

Other theories have also suggested only a relatively small number of behavioral determinants. For example, according to social cognitive theory (Bandura, 1986, 1992) there are also two major factors influencing the likelihood that a person will engage in a given behavior. First, similar to the concept of behavioral beliefs underlying attitude in the theory of reasoned action, the person must believe that the benefits of performing the behavior outweigh the costs (i.e. a person should have more positive than negative outcome expectancies). Second, and perhaps most important, the person must have a sense of personal agency, or self-efficacy, with respect to performing the behavior. That is, the person must believe that he or she has the skills and abilities necessary for performing the behavior under a variety of circumstances.

It is interesting to note that Ajzen (1988) has utilized all of the above variables in his theory of planned behavior. According to this theory, intentions to perform a given behavior are primarily determined by: (1) the attitude toward performing the behavior (which is based on behavioral beliefs [or outcome expectancies]); (2) the subjective norm concerning the behavior (which is based on normative beliefs); and (3) perceived behavioral control (which is based upon control beliefs that are very similar to the barriers that represent the different circumstances affecting self-efficacy). Indeed, Ajzen originally viewed perceived behavioral control as being very similar to self-efficacy. However, in more recent operationalizations (e.g. Ajzen, 1991), perceived behavioral control appears to be more a measure of whether performing the behavior would be "easy or difficult," than a measure of whether the person could perform the behavior if he or she "really wanted to."

Unfortunately, this conceptual shift makes perceived behavioral control very similar to an attitude measure. That is, "easy/difficult" is highly correlated with other attitude measurement items such as "pleasant/unpleasant" and "enjoyable/unenjoyable." For this reason, I am not yet ready to accept perceived behavioral control (as presently defined) as an independent determinant of behavior. And although I believe that a self-efficacy type construct may prove to be an additional determinant of intentions (and behavior), I also have concerns about the concept of self-efficacy, particularly as it is operationalized by Bandura (see Fishbein et al., in press). More specifically, self-efficacy is measured by asking people how certain they are that they *could* or *can* perform the behavior in question under a number of different circumstances (that typically vary in terms of difficulty). While this is theoretically different from asking them how certain they are that they *would* or that they *will* perform the behavior, it is not at all clear that respondents make this distinction. Thus, it is possible that the measure of self-efficacy essentially sums (or averages) a person's intentions to perform the behavior in question under a number of different circumstances, and this score may best be seen as an alternative measure of the "general" intention to perform the behavior in question.

For example, I could ask a respondent to indicate the likelihood that he will "always use a condom for vaginal sex with his main partner." I could also ask him how certain he was that he will perform this behavior "when he was drunk or high," "when his partner was drunk or high," "when he didn't feel like using a condom," "when his partner didn't want him to use a condom," "when he was feeling lonely or depressed," etc. Summing or averaging responses to these individual intention items should lead to a score that would be highly correlated with the more general intention measure. The question that remains is whether substituting the word "could" or "can" for "will" makes any difference. Until this question is answered, I am reluctant to view self-efficacy as an independent determinant of either intention or behavior.

Be that as it may, other investigators may wish to add self-efficacy and/or perceived behavioral control, to a "shortlist" of possible behavioral determinants. Although space precludes a detailed analysis, at least two other variables also seem worthy of further consideration: emotional reactions and self-image. According to Triandis's (1977) *Theory of subjective culture and interpersonal relations*, intentions are viewed as a function of perceived consequences of performing the behavior (i.e. outcome expectancies or behavioral beliefs), social influences (including norms, roles, and the self-concept) and emotions. Thus, in addition to considering outcome expectancies (or attitude) and perceived norms, people are most likely to form an intention to perform a given behavior if their emotional reaction to performing the behavior is more positive than negative and if they perceive performance of the behavior to be more consistent than inconsistent with their self-image (i.e. if the person sees himself or herself as "the type of person who would perform" the behavior in question. Although these two variables deserve further attention, I'm not convinced that emotions can be empirically distinguished from attitudes. In addition, I think that the measure of self-image may simply be another alternative (or indirect) measure of intention. That is, it seems likely that a person who sees himself or herself as "the type of person who would perform behavior X," would also state that it is quite likely that he or she will perform behavior X.

To summarize briefly, although there may be as many as eight variables that serve as key determinants of behavior (i.e. intentions, skills and abilities, environmental constraints, attitudes, norms, self-efficacy, self-image, and emotional reactions [see Fishbein et al., in press]), I believe that there are only three immediate determinants of behavior (intentions, skills and abilities, and environmental constraints) and only two (but possibly three) major determinants of intentions (attitudes, norms, and possibly self-efficacy). I would suggest, however, that people interested in predicting and understanding behavior should, whenever possible, assess all eight variables and study their interrelationships as well as their relationships to behavior. I think studies of this type, particularly when the behavior is socially significant, will go a long way in re-establishing social psychology as a dynamic and behaviorally relevant field.

The relative importance of attitudes and norms as determinants of intentions (and behaviors), depends upon both the behavior under consideration and upon the population being considered

While some intentions may be primarily influenced by attitudinal considerations, others may be primarily influenced by norms, and still others may be strongly influenced by both variables. Similarly, a given behavior may be primarily under attitudinal control in one population but be primarily under normative control in another.

For example, while attitudes were found to be the primary determinant of intentions to use seatbelts under relatively safe driving conditions (e.g. a short trip on dry roads in daylight), norms were found to be most important under dangerous conditions (e.g. a long trip on icy roads at night) (Stasson & Fishbein, 1990). Similarly, while normative considerations were found to be most important in determining condom-use intentions among a sample of sexually experienced male college students in the USA, these same intentions were primarily under attitudinal influence among a comparable sample of sexually experienced male college students in Mexico City (Fishbein, 1990).

The substantive content of the beliefs underlying attitudes and norms also varies as a function of both the behavior and population being considered

This helps to explain why it is necessary to define behavior in terms of action, target, context, and time. Changing any one of the four elements can increase or decrease the relevance of a given referent and often leads to very different outcomes. For example, the relevant referents and perceived consequences of always using a condom for vaginal sex with one's spouse may be very different from those associated with always using a condom for vaginal sex with an occasional partner. Perhaps even more important, different populations (or different segments of a given population) may have different referents and/or may perceive very different outcomes for the same behavior. In order to fully understand why members of a given population do or do not perform a given behavior, it is necessary to identify the referents and outcomes that are salient for that population *vis-à-vis* the behavior in question.

Lessons Learned – Behavior Change

While the above six "lessons" are primarily directed at predicting and understanding why an individual may or may not perform a given behavior, they also have important implications for behavior change and for developing interventions to produce behavior change. Research on behavior change has taught us the following lessons.

Behaviors that were assumed to be difficult (if not impossible) to change, can be changed and changed radically

For example, as a result of the AIDS epidemic, we have witnessed major changes in various sexual practices among at least some segments of the gay community as well as major changes in needle-use behavior (both cleaning and sharing) among some injecting drug users. Although social psychologists cannot take credit for most of the early risk reduction in these populations, there is growing evidence that well designed, theoretically based interventions can be effective in producing such change (see e.g. Jemmot, Jemmot, & Fong, 1992; Fishbein et al., in press).

Information in and of itself can *produce behavior change*

Despite the oft repeated statement that "information in and of itself cannot produce behavior change," there is abundant evidence to the contrary (e.g. Lhotka, 1964; Ball-Rokeach, Rokeach, & Grube, 1984; Fishbein, Ajzen, &

McArdle, 1980). Although it is true that providing people with some types of information (e.g. about a disease and how it is spread) will have little or no effect on their behavior, it is also true that other types of information (e.g. about the consequences of performing the behavior, about groups who support behavioral performance, and/or about ways to overcome barriers to behavioral performance) can be effective. Indeed, what social psychology has to offer to behavior change programs is an understanding of the types of information necessary to change or maintain a given behavior.

Prior to developing any behavior change program, it is first necessary to determine whether the failure to perform the behavior in question is due to a lack of intention, the absence of skills and abilities, or to the presence of environmental constraints

Clearly, very different intervention programs will be necessary if people have already formed strong intentions to perform a given behavior but are unable to act upon that intention, than if people have not yet formed an intention to perform the behavior.

The most effective interventions will be those directed at changing specific behaviors

Different behaviors may require different skills and abilities and the presence or absence of environmental constraints will also depend upon the behavior under consideration. Perhaps more important, and as indicated above, changing peoples intentions to reach goals or to engage in a category of behaviors does not ensure change in any specific behavior. In contrast, changing someone's intention to perform (or not perform) a specific behavior will usually be followed by a change in that behavior.

If we are going to try to change a behavioral intention, we must first learn whether that intention is primarily determined by attitudinal or normative (or perhaps self-efficacy) considerations

Clearly, if a behavior (or behavioral intention) is primarily determined by attitudinal considerations, little will be accomplished by attempting to change perceived norms. Similarly, if a behavior (or behavioral intention) is primarily determined by normative considerations, little will be gained by trying to change attitudes toward performing the behavior.

If attitudes are most strongly related to intention, then one should try to identify behavioral beliefs (or outcome expectancies) that distinguish between those who have and have not formed intentions to perform the behavior. For example, one might find that those who intend to always use condoms for vaginal intercourse with their spouse believed that this "was the responsible thing to do," while those who did not intend to use condoms did not hold this belief. Similarly, those who intend to use condoms might believe that "Always using a condom when I have vaginal intercourse with my spouse will protect me from AIDS" while those not intending to use condoms might believe that "Always using a condom when I have vaginal intercourse with my spouse will NOT protect me from AIDS." If this were the case, a theoretically based intervention would stress responsibility and the health consequences of always using a condom.

On the other hand, if norms were most highly correlated with intention, one should try to identify differences in perceived norms between those who have and have not formed intentions to perform the behavior. For example, one might find that those who intended always to use a condom for vaginal sex with their spouse perceived that their spouses thought they should use a condom, while those who did not hold this intention believed that their spouses were opposed to condom use. Similarly, one might find that those who intended to use condoms believed that their doctors thought they should always use condoms with their spouses, while those without this intention perceived that their doctors thought that consistent condom use with their spouses was unnecessary. In this case, the intervention should focus on providing information designed to change perceptions about the expectations of spouses and doctors.

Just as one does not "throw together" a vaccine, one cannot just "throw together" an intervention

It must be realized that behavior change interventions, like vaccines, take time to develop. Unlike vaccines, however, effective interventions must be tailored to both the behavior and the population being considered.

Based upon data obtained from formative qualitative and quantitative research, one can determine not only which variables need to be addressed in the intervention, but more importantly, one should also be able to identify the particular outcome expectancies, normative beliefs (and perceived barriers) that need to be addressed to produce changes in intentions and behavior. One must then develop interventions to produce these changes. That is, one must develop interventions that provide the target population with the information necessary to produce these changes. One must also determine the most effective ways of delivering this information to the population in question (i.e. via mass media, small media, in-groups, or in one-on-one interactions). In addition, one must determine where the intervention will be delivered (e.g. in clinics, community based organizations, other fixed-location sites, or "on the streets" by, for example, volunteers or outreach workers). Determining "how" and "where" to deliver the intervention should also be guided by findings from formative (often ethnographic) research.

In evaluating or testing an intervention, it must be given time to have an effect

Behavioral interventions cannot be looked at as a "quick fix." Behavior change is not an all-or-nothing, immediately occurring phenomenon. We must become more realistic in our expectations about the amount of behavioral change one can expect a given intervention to produce in a given time period.

Some Concluding Comments

In the past seventy-five years, social psychology has contributed greatly to our understanding of behavior and behavior change. Although there is much more to be learned, what we have learned thus far makes it possible for us to produce effective, theory-based, culturally sensitive, population, and behavior-specific interventions. Unfortunately, with relatively few exceptions, social psychologists have not become involved in either furthering our understanding of behavior and behavior change or in developing and evaluating interventions to change socially relevant behaviors. To a large extent, the growing fields of community psychology, consumer psychology, environmental psychology, and health psychology all bear witness to social psychology's apparent unwillingness to deal with such socially relevant behaviors. If we don't quickly mend our ways, this volume will, in fact, be a *Festschrift* to a field approaching the end of its career.

Further Reading

Ajzen, I., & Fishbein, M. (1980). *Understanding attitudes and predicting social behavior*. Englewood Cliffs, NJ: Prentice Hall. This is still the best source for an overview of the theory of reasoned action and illustrations of how it can be applied in a variety of content areas.

Fishbein, M., & Ajzen, I. (1975). Prediction of behavior. In *Belief, attitude, intention and behavior: An introduction to theory and research* (Chapter 8). Boston, MA: Addison-Wesley. This chapter considers different types of behavioral criteria and defines behavior in terms of the four elements of action, target, context, and time. It also shows how the principle of correspondence effects behavioral prediction.

Fishbein, M., Triandis, H. C., Kanfer, F. H., Becker, M. H., Middlestadt, S. E., & Eichler, A. (in press). Factors influencing behavior and behavior change. In A. Baum, T. Revenson, & J. Singer (Eds.), *Handbook of Health Psychology*. NJ: Lawrence Erlbaum. This chapter identifies similarities and differences among five leading theories of behavioral prediction and behavior change and identifies (and operationally defines) a limited set of variables that should be taken into consideration in attempts to understand and influence social behavior.

Fishbein, M., Guenther-Grey, C., Johnson, W., Wolitski, R. J., McAlister, A., Rietmeijer, C. A., O'Reilly, K., and the AIDS Community Demonstration Projects (in press). Using a theory-based community intervention to reduce AIDS risk behaviors: The CDC's AIDS community demonstration projects. In S. Oskamp & S. Thompson, *Understanding and preventing HIV risk behavior*. Thousand Oaks, CA: Sage. An example of how theory can be used to guide the development of behavior change interventions. This chapter illustrates many of the lessons referred to in this essay.

Fishbein, M., & Middlestadt, S. E. (1995). Non-cognitive effects on attitude formation and change: fact or artifact? *Journal of Consumer Psychology*, *4*(2), 181–202. Many investigators are now questioning the belief-based (or expectancy-value) view of attitude. This paper suggests that many of the findings supporting nonbelief-based influences may be methodological artifacts resulting from the use of inappropriate predictors or criteria.

Thurstone, L. L. (1931). The measurement of attitudes. *Journal of Abnormal and Social Psychology*, *26*, 249–269. Everybody should read at least one original Thurstone article. Had we paid more attention to his insights about attitudes and the attitude–behavior relationship, the field would probably have moved ahead much more quickly.

References

Ajzen, I. (1988). *Attitudes, personality, and behavior*. Chicago, IL: Dorsey Press.

Ajzen, I. (1991). The theory of planned behavior. *Organizational Behavior and Human Decision Processes*, *50*, 179–211.

Ajzen, I., & Fishbein, M. (1980). *Understanding attitudes and predicting social behavior*. Englewood Cliffs, NJ: Prentice Hall.

Ball-Rokeach, S. J., Rokeach, M., & Grube, J. W. (1984). *The great American values test: Influencing behavior and belief through television*. New York: The Free Press.

Bandura, A. (1986). *Social foundations of thought and action: A social cognitive theory*. Englewood Cliffs, NJ: Prentice Hall.

Bandura, A. (1992). Exercise of personal agency through the self-efficacy mechanism. In R. Schwarzer (Ed.), *Self-efficacy: Thought control of action* (pp. 3–38) Washington, DC: Hemisphere.

Chaiken, S., & Stangor, C. (1987). Attitudes and attitude change. *Annual Review of Psychology*, *38*, 575–630.

Fishbein, M. (1980). A theory of reasoned action: Some applications and implications. In H. Howe & M. Page (Eds.), *Nebraska Symposium on Motivation* (pp. 65–116). Lincoln: University of Nebraska Press.

Fishbein, M. (1990). Aids and behavior change: An analysis based on the theory of reasoned action. *Interamerican Journal of Psychology*, *24*(1), 37–56.

Fishbein, M., & Ajzen, I. (1975). *Belief, attitude, intention and behavior: An introduction to theory and research* (p. 587). Boston, MA: Addison-Wesley.

Fishbein, M., Ajzen, I., & McArdle, J. (1980). Changing the behavior of alcoholics: Effects of persuasive communication. In I. Ajzen & M. Fishbein (Eds.), *Understanding attitudes and predicting social behavior* (pp. 217–242). Englewood Cliffs, NJ: Prentice-Hall.

Fishbein, M., Triandis, H. C., Kanfer, F. H., Becker, M. H., Middlestadt, S. E., & Eichler, A. (in press). Factors influencing behavior and behavior change. In A.

Baum, T. Revenson, & J. Singer (Eds.), *Handbook of Health Psychology*. Hillsdale, NJ: Lawrence Erlbaum.

Fishbein, M., Guenther-Grey, C., Johnson, W., Wolitski, R. J., McAlister, A., Rietmeijer, C. A., O'Reilly, K., and the AIDS Community Demonstration Projects (in press). Using a theory-based community intervention to reduce AIDS risk behaviors: The CDC's AIDS community demonstration projects. In S. Oskamp & S. Thompson, *Understanding and preventing HIV risk behavior*. Thousand Oaks, CA: Sage.

Fishbein, M., & Middlestadt, S. E. (1995). Non-cognitive effects on attitude formation and change: Fact or artifact? *Journal of Consumer Psychology*, *4*(2), 181–202.

Jemmot, J. B., Jemmot, L. S., & Fong, G. T. (1992). Reductions in HIV risk-associated sexual behaviors among black male adolescents: Effects of an AIDS prevention intervention. *American Journal of Public Health*, *82*, 372–377.

Lhotka, D. C. (1964). The seat belt story. *Traffic Safety*, *64*, 22–35.

Petty, R. E., & Caccioppo, J. T. (1986). *Communication and persuasion: Central and peripheral routes to attitude change.* New York: Springer-Verlag.

Rosenberg, M. J., & Hovland, C. I. (1960). Cognitive, affective, and behavioral components of attitudes. In C. I. Hovland & M. J. Rosenberg (Eds.), *Attitude organization and change: An analysis of consistency among attitude components* (pp. 1–14). New Haven, CT: Yale University Press.

Stasson, M., & Fishbein, M. (1990). The relation between perceived risk and preventive action: A within subject analysis of perceived driving risk and intentions to wear seatbelts. *Journal of Applied Social Psychology*, *20*(19), 1541–1557.

Thomas, W. I., & Znaniecki, F. (1918). *The Polish peasant in Europe and America* (Vol. 1). Boston, MA: Badger.

Thurstone, L. L. (1931). The measurement of attitudes. *Journal of Abnormal and Social Psychology*, *26*, 249–269.

Triandis, H. C. (1977). *Interpersonal behavior*. Monterey, CA: Brooks-Cole.

Watson, J. B. (1925). *Behaviorism*. New York: W. W. Norton.

Wicker, A. W. (1969). Attitude versus actions: The relationship of verbal and overt behavioral responses to attitude objects. *Journal of Social Issues*, *25*(4), 41–78.

7

Let Social Psychology be Faddish or, at Least, Heterogeneous

Susan T. Fiske and Jacques-Philippe Leyens

Susan T. Fiske is Distinguished University Professor of Psychology, University of Massachusetts at Amherst. A Harvard Ph.D., she received an honorary doctorate in 1995 from the Catholic University of Louvain, Louvain-la-Neuve, Belgium. Her federally funded social cognition research focuses on social structure, motivation, and stereotyping, which led to expert testimony cited by the US Supreme Court. The broader context was set by Fiske and Taylor's *Social cognition* (1984/1991). Fiske won the 1991 American Psychological Association Award for Distinguished Contributions to Psychology in the Public Interest, Early Career; was 1994 President of the Society for Personality and Social Psychology; and edits, with Gilbert and Lindzey, the *Handbook of social psychology* (4th ed., in press).

Jacques-Philippe Leyens is Professor of Social Psychology at the Catholic University of Louvain (Louvain-la-Neuve) where he received his Ph.D. Former editor of the *European Journal of Social Psychology*, he has been a staff member of Summer Schools organized by the European Association of Experimental Social Psychology. He is also a member of the Society of Experimental Social Psychology and has held visiting positions in several European and American universities. For a long time, he studied the effects of filmed violence, and he is now interested in social perception. He counts ex-Ph.D. students in ten countries and friends in many more.

The writing of this chapter was supported by an exchange agreement between our two universities, as well as by a Belgian National Science Foundation research grant to Leyens and a US National Science Foundation research grant to Fiske. This chapter is based largely on ideas presented by Leyens at Touloise, May 1995, further developed in collaboration with Fiske, who as always is grateful for his provocative insights.

Fads and fashions dominate psychology in general, and social psychology in particular. People have usually spoken disparagingly of the rise and fall of theoretical perspectives on the social being. Instead, we will defend the idea that a healthy, and prosperous, social psychology should welcome simultaneously several approaches – or fads. We shall base our reasoning on looking at the history of recent social psychology along two dimensions. First, to what extent has social psychology taken into account the subjects' situation, that is, the social context? Second, to what extent has social psychology adopted an objective anchor for the human mind, "outside an individual, in external objective phenomena whose properties are reconstructed by a subject in a cognitive act?" Alternatively, to what extent has it adopted a subjective anchor, "within the subject and his or her capacity to construct subjective conceptions of the world" (Lewicka, 1988, p. 285, italics omitted)?

These two dimensions – a focus on social context and a focus on subjectivity – are logically independent, yet we will argue that they have been negatively correlated in the history of social psychology. Certain periods have privileged context, at the expense of subjectivity, whereas others have privileged subjectivity, at the expense of context. In each period, however, a minority viewpoint has sustained the neglected perspective.

Showy Demonstration Studies over Intimate Studies: A High for Context and a Low for Subjectivity

Around the 1960s, social context was not neglected by social psychology. Research was immersed in social context, and this is probably why social psychology attracted so many students. At that time, experimenting meant running big showy demonstration studies. Think of Sherif's experiments in summer camps, Festinger's students and their dissonance set ups, Milgram's obedience studies, Schachter's experiments on affiliation and on emotions, Bandura's and Berkowitz's respective studies on aggression, Darley and Latané's emergency situations, Berscheid and Walster (Hatfield)'s investigations of romantic love, Zimbardo's simulation of prisons, and so on.

To caricature just a little, one could say that the observed effects in these treasures of our field were almost entirely contained in the context. The explanation was in danger of tautology because it merely described the situations that were supposed to drive the effects. For instance, antagonism between groups was due to the competition for scarce resources, that is, to the antagonism created by the scarcity of resources. It is easy to recognize a behaviorist influence in this power of situations, even if researchers did not adhere to behaviorism and often opposed it. This is also the period when Mischel (1968) wrote at book that glorified situations, while discouraging personality research for a least a decade.

If one accepts this view, Tajfel's (1972) criticism of social psychology is paradoxical. Indeed, Tajfel accused social psychologists of working in a "social vacuum" and made them responsible for the crisis that hurt social psychology in the 1970s. Does this criticism mean that Tajfel thought that social psychologists did not take situations into account? We believe that Tajfel's point dealt with the then-current anchor that was essentially objective; the situation was part of an objective reality that had to correspond to what experimenters meant it to be. That is, subjective construals by the research participant had little relevance; the experimenter specified the objective reality of the situation, which then provoked the subject's unexpected, counter-intuitive responses. Part of the lasting marvel of these studies was how such a small change in the objective situation could create such a large change in the subjects' behavior. But the subjects' experience of the situation was not examined with any enthusiasm. Context was loud; subjectivity was quiet.

In a minority contrast to these studies were Heider's ideas about cognitive balance and attribution, as well as Asch's (1946) studies on impression formation, in which subjectivity was focal. Even Asch's studies on conformity – which are usually thought to show how easily people are swayed by their peers and how they can be independent of social pressure – even these studies initially were designed to show the limits of how people subjectively construct an object of judgment. That is, Asch was interested in showing how an objective perceptual judgment could limit the conformity observed for the totally subjective stimuli provided by Sherif's use of the autokinetic effect and by the famous quotations used in earlier work on prestige suggestion. This is the meaning of Asch's phrase to describe subjectivity in operation: "a change in the object of judgment, rather than a change in the judgment of the object." The originality, or anachronism, of the Heider and Asch studies was that the subject, rather than the situation, was their focus; in that sense, they were intimate with the subject, and the anchor was clearly subjective. Context was (relatively) neglected.

The 1960s thus saw a majority of showy demonstration studies, with an objective anchor, whose explanations were often restricted to a description of their situation, and a minority of studies in which the subject was focal, context was neglected, and the anchor subjective.

Reasons for the Shift

Our distinction admittedly constitutes something of a didactic caricature. Indeed, the most celebrated demonstration studies (e.g. cognitive dissonance, altruism, obedience, labeling of emotions) were not entirely anchored in the object. Most likely, they are still celebrated today because the situation by itself is insufficient to explain them, and their results are unexpected. Take, for instance, the "weapons effect." Few people would predict that the mere situation of viewing a weapon is sufficient to make aroused people more aggressive. It is therefore not so surprising that these studies on the "weapons effect" led to a new conceptual view about aggression, more anchored in the subject than had been the case before (Berkowitz, 1993; C. W. Turner & Leyens, 1992).

For similar reasons, a shift occurred in the balance of studies during the 1970s and 1980s; the majority became a minority, and the previous minority became a considerable majority. Here are some of the reasons (Leyens & Yzerbyt, 1992). (1) More and more situational studies integrated cognitive mediational variables. See, for instance, Bandura's (1965) model of imitation that stresses attentional and memory variables before proposing the concept of self-efficacy. (2) As they grew theoretically more sophisticated, researchers became uncomfortable with the huge variability introduced by the showy demonstration studies. Zajonc is a paragon of this orientation. At some point, he preferred to work with animals such as cockroaches, rather than with humans, precisely to avoid the variability induced by demonstration studies. (3) Conferring all the explanatory power on situations was theoretically unsatisfactory. As noted, this explanation is often tautological. If the expected effect is observed, all the better, and the explanation is attributed to the situation. If, however, the situation does not lead to the anticipated effect, the situation is supposed not to be good enough (see Aronson & Carlsmith's original 1968 *Handbook* chapter on experimentation in social psychology). (4) As demonstration research went on, experimental scenarios became increasingly lavish. Deceiving subjects through confederates had constituted methodological progress, but some researchers put their talent into deceiving subjects about more vital and potentially damaging issues. The Vietnam War and US civil rights movement brought ethical principles to the forefront; talent was no longer measured by the daring of the deception. (5) Finally, cognitivism overflowed social psychology, with paper-and-pencil experiments, without behavior, and with a zest for minimal deception.

The shift in research was twofold. On the one hand, the social context has been increasingly neglected. Researchers have been interested in universal processes that take place in subjects' minds, irrespective of the specific situations in which they arise. On the other hand, processes of impression formation and of attribution that were first investigated with a subjective anchor were now approached from an objective viewpoint. Hypothetical models that were descriptive (Heider, 1958) became prescriptive (Nisbett & Ross, 1980). The common view has been that people are "cognitive misers" (Fiske & Taylor, 1984) who stupidly resort to heuristics. These heuristics replaced situations as explaining every phenomenon. This substitution is not necessarily a great theoretical improvement. The explanation again is in danger of tautology: people err in their judgments because they use heuristics, and they use heuristics because they are cognitive misers.

The Social Cognition Research Hegemony

We will now briefly present the "new majority research," that is, the first wave of social cognition research. We present it in somewhat more detail than the previous two fads because it is the one with which we are most associated, and we hope that it will change with the times. We will also comment upon the lens that it used for looking at society; indeed, explicating metatheories is often useful to understand why some questions, rather than others, have been asked.

By the expression "social cognition research," we understand a series of approaches to social psychology that are best epitomized by two definitions. According to Hamilton, social cognition research includes "a consideration of all factors influencing the acquisition, representation, and retrieval of person information, as well as the relationship of these processes to judgments made by the perceiver" (1981, p. 136). Fiske and Taylor, on the other hand, define social cognition research as the study of "how ordinary people think about people and how they think they think about people" (1984, p. 1).

As stated by Stroebe and Insko (1989), social cognition research adopts a nonconflictual view of society from the perspective of the individual. That is, it ignores group conflicts and group membership and concentrates on the essentially asocietal individual. We would add that this individual is a nonstigmatized White male member of the silent majority. In other words, this person has no reason to believe that anyone worth considering differs from himself in any important ways. The ideal society to which this individual belongs is composed only of individuals like him, and it is bad taste to encapsulate people in specific groups because supposedly everyone is essentially the same if one looks hard enough. Just as some nations (such as France and the USA) only take into account the rights of individuals supposed to be equal, they also hold that the majority's rule is necessarily dominant and hardly questioned.

Such an asocietal viewpoint has obvious implications. First, it means that an accurate perception of a given person must necessarily be "individualized." Indeed, everybody should be part of the majority, and no boundaries are to exist. Decategorization is an imperative, especially when the "enclaves" are socially "touchy." The color-blind perspective in the USA exemplifies this view. Second, it means that the investigated groups will be innocuous (extroverts, diurnals, etc.) or only those disturbing groups (Blacks, Hispanics, females, etc.) about whom the majority feels guilty. In the former case, group membership has no other implication than an aseptic theoretical test; in the latter case, theory is potentially marred with moral concerns because when the individuals are treated in terms of their stigmatized group, categorizing is judged not moral, whereas when they are treated in terms of the unique person, this corresponds to the adequate moral stance. Third, the asocietal viewpoint means that the mishaps of treating persons as category members are considered the result of prejudice, error, ignorance, or laziness. The solution is therefore to outlaw prejudice, to inform, to teach, and to supply incentives. Finally, in a society supposedly without conflict, because individuals are defined as equal in rights and obligations, identical exposure to information should allow perception of a unique and correct reality, provided that the information is processed in an identical way. To the same extent that equal opportunities in terms of information prevent seeing reality without blinders, they allow seeing this reality without categorical boundaries. Processing information and the variables likely to affect it (amount and type of information, attention, ability, and incentives) will therefore be of paramount importance. It follows that the explanation of perception will tend to be restricted to mental (essentially memory) models. An accurate perception is individualized.

In conclusion, the first wave of social cognition research adopted an objective anchor. External reality and normative (prescriptive) models dictated accuracy. Also, this first wave of social cognition research ignored context, except to the extent it considered a single context. This context resembled an office with a computer to solve social problems as if they were intellectual ones. Like Sherlock Holmes or Mr Spock, the ideal performer finds the solutions of the most intricate cases by interrogating his tremendous memory, noticing all the details provided by the computer, and always making the correct inferences.

The Social Identity Theory Challenge

Social cognition research's view of society has been challenged by social identity theory (SIT; Tajfel & Turner, 1979), to which we now turn. Here again, we make explicit some assumptions that underlie SIT's view of society.

In contrast to the breadth of the social cognition research approaches, SIT constitutes a narrower theoretical path that is carefully fenced by its proponents. However,

> Strictly speaking, there are now in fact two social identity theories: the original intergroup theory, which is an analysis of intergroup conflict and social change and focuses on individuals' need to maintain and enhance the positively valued distinctiveness of their ingroups compared to outgroups to achieve a positive social identity . . . and the more recent self-categorization theory . . . which represents a general theory of group processes based on the idea that shared social identity depersonalizes individual self-perception and action. (Turner, 1988, p. xx)

The viewpoint adopted by SIT is completely at odds with the one of first-wave social cognition research. Where social cognition research has been low context and high objectivity, SIT has been high on context and (apparently) total subjectivity. For SIT, society is composed of groups, rather than of individuals, that are overtly in conflict. Individuals mainly think of themselves as group members, and the different groups are not equal in resources or in status. The appropriate target of investigation is the minority that has to strive for a positive social identity because, being at a disadvantage, they are most painfully aware of their group membership and its social consequences. Here again, many implications are obvious. First, perceptions by groups will be privileged over perceptions by individuals. The psychological validity of these perceptions will not be questioned; because they are perceptions, they are psychologically valid. Second, attention will be focused on the conditions that sustain or modify the boundaries between groups. For instance, the status and power of the different groups, the legitimacy of these variables, and the permeability of boundaries between groups will rank among the favorite factors investigated by SIT theorists. Third, because society is composed of different groups that are in a continuing dynamic state of alliance or conflict, and because individuals think of themselves in terms of group memberships that may vary, social context is of utmost importance for SIT. Context will dictate whether, at a given moment, people consider themselves as members of a specific group, and consider this group as opposed to other groups. In this sense, also, context will determine whether people belong to a majority or a minority, have a negative or positive social identity, and whether change is possible.

Contrary to social cognition research, SIT, and especially self-categorization theory (SCT), thus affords a great importance to the context, which is approached in cognitive-perceptual terms. For instance, context will be manipulated by having a Belgian person judge either French and Flemish targets, or French and American targets. In these two cases, the French targets are not identical because the context of judgment has changed (*pace* Asch!). In a recent article, Turner, Oakes, Haslam, and McGarty (1994) remind us that judgment is a function of the relative accessibility of a category and of the normative and comparative fits between the category and the reality. Context obviously affects accessibility and comparative fit, which, in turn, determine the final judgment.

It follows from this reasoning that, for SIT and SCT, the anchor is as objective as it is for social cognition research. What seemed highly subjective is actually evaluated according to objective standards. Correct or good answers are to be found in external reality. However, whereas stereotypes are errors for social cognition approaches because they do not correspond to an individuated entity, they are not errors for SCT. For SCT (Oakes & Turner, 1990), stereotypes depend on a multitude of contexts that may drastically vary from time to time. Thus, social cognition research and SIT essentially differ in the subjective reality that is considered relevant, individuals versus groups. They also have essentially differed on exploiting a single and rigid context versus numerous and ever-variable contexts.

The Ingredients of the Message

Most people would agree that social cognition research revitalized the field of social psychology (for a collection of appreciations, see Devine, Hamilton, & Ostrom, 1994). It addressed new questions to old problems. Its focus on information processing brought new methodologies. Its finesse at approaching processes is yet unchallenged in social psychology. By contrast, its view of societal context – the larger world – may have been narrow minded. A society without conflict, with no sub-groups but only equal citizens, may be a dream for constitutional lawyers, but it is hardly a reality for social psychologists. Often, individuals do not act as individuals but as members of groups, with special goals. These aspects were often neglected in social cognition research. Take something as well known as the "restaurant script," which assumes that first people are seated, then choose from a menu, eat, are fed, pay, and leave (Abelson, 1981); it contains typically middle-class knowledge, alien to less privileged people. Would a very poorly dressed person even be admitted in the restaurant and its script?

In a similar way, in their time, SIT and SCT brought fresh air, especially in so-called European social psychology. The right of group differences was recognized. Social contexts, and conflicts, were taken into consideration. Compared to social cognition research, these are not only theoretical but mostly societal differences. Does that mean that our perception of people varies constantly with context? To a Belgian, Americans, for instance, are in-groupers if compared to Iraqis, but out-groupers if compared to Belgians. Without denying the role of context, the shortcoming of SIT/SCT is that it does not make sense that we are forever fluctuating in our perception of ourselves and of others. To the same extent that, in adaptation-level experiments, a croquet ball may seem lighter after lifting a bowling ball but is not confused with a ping-pong ball, people's perceptions may be somewhat altered by the context, but they will rarely be turned upside down.

Certainly nobody with common sense would deny that both social cognition's information processing and SIT/SCT's context are important. However, the simple fact that some apparently believe that social perception can be totally explained by either is an invitation to consider both perspectives, at least as a possibility, as well as to remain open to still other avenues.

Social cognition research and SIT are asking different questions. The appropriateness of these questions is a matter of taste. Social cognition research and SIT are looking at different realities. Both of these realities exist. Asking one set of questions does not make the other set superfluous, and looking at one type of reality does not make the other nonexistent. Rather than simply pleading for a *rapprochement* of the two approaches, as we have presented them, we would like to argue that both social cognition research and SIT should also consider the possibility of a subjective anchor, returning to the minority viewpoint of Heider and Asch.

In a brilliant chapter, Lewicka (1988, p. 287) hypothesizes

> That human beings are both realists and constructivists, but that they are rarely both at the same time. Hence cognitive acts performed by an individual are either anchored in the cognized object, thus leading to realistic assessment of its properties, or in the subject, favoring freedom in construction of its diverse interpretations.

She then defends the idea that the objective anchor corresponds to an observer viewpoint; in contrast, the subjective anchor corresponds to an actor viewpoint. Our question is what triggers one or the other viewpoint.

The first ingredient of our "message" is to vary subjective vs. objective anchors through interaction goals. As noted, social cognition research has tended to imprison subjects into a single context, which evokes a certain interaction goal ("the get to know" situation according to Snyder (1992), and the "assessment set" according to J. Hilton & Darley, 1989): judging another person as, for instance, a chemist would analyze the elements of a given substance, that is, by processing as correctly (normatively) as possible all the available information about this person. Maybe this is what a professional psychologist is supposed to do but this is certainly not what is expected by most of us most of the time. Suppose your romantic partner asks you if he or she is the most attractive person of all your relationships. What would you reply: the truth or something that will keep harmony in your relationship (provided that this is what you want)?

Lewicka (1988) elaborates the contrasting viewpoints, suggesting that the external observer viewpoint activates a necessity-oriented rule of reasoning, and therefore, we would note, a concern with disconfirming cases; the subjective actor viewpoint activates a sufficiency-oriented rule, which we would note allows a focus on confirming cases. We suggest that this creates a goal-based motivational dichotomy, a "socially useful–useless" one, in terms of necessity and sufficiency (see Table 7.1).

First, the sufficiency-oriented rule corresponds to a subject's privileged search for characteristics that confirm the category. If this rule applies, the hypothesis is deemed correct as soon as a reasonable number of confirming

Table 7.1 Different approaches to reality in person perception

Viewpoint	*Anchor*	*Assessment*	*Rule*	*Focus*
Observer	Object	Realistic	Necessity	Disconfirmatory
Actor	Subject	Constructivist	Sufficiency	Confirmatory

features have been identified. When disconfirming information is encountered, the perceivers keep on searching for additional confirming features. Under the second strategy, the necessity-oriented rule, subjects are alert to disconfirmation. More specifically, information that runs counter to one's hypothesis will have a larger influence than confirming information.

The most appropriate response for subjects is to use both strategies. Most of the time, however, people restrict themselves to one single strategy, and they favor the sufficiency-oriented rule. They do it most likely for pragmatic reasons (Fiske, 1992, 1993; Leyens, Yzerbyt, & Schadron, 1994). When you invite an American for dinner, you don't prepare organ meats such as brains (even if you are an American host); you instead restrict yourself to confirmation through a sufficiency-oriented rule. Usually, it works better than testing for disconfirmation. Obviously, it is simpler to test one rather than two strategies. This does not mean, however, that the sufficiency-oriented rule is, by definition, a lazier strategy than the necessity one. People can go to great lengths to confirm their initial hypothesis (e.g. Kunda, 1990). In a study conducted by Yzerbyt, Rocher, and Coull (1995), for instance, subjects were provided with information about a target that consisted in his/her category (computer scientist) and a mixture of behaviors that were consistent (reflecting introversion), inconsistent (reflecting extroversion) and neutral (e.g. married) regarding the category. When having to judge the category ("the computer scientists"), subjects did not alter their stereotype in the light of the somewhat atypical target, and they used the neutral information to reconcile the inconsistent behaviors with the category (e.g. the spouse is extroverted and influenced him/her). However, subjects did alter their stereotype when they had been cognitively busy during the presentation of the target; apparently, the lack of cognitive resources interfered with the reconciliation work. This demonstrates that even a sufficiency-oriented rule, the apparent default, requires some work.

Several theoretical orientations are usefully extended by the necessity- and sufficiency-oriented rules. According to the social judgeability theory of Leyens and his colleagues (Leyens, 1993; Leyens et al., 1994), a judgment about someone is deemed adequate when it takes into account the information (i.e. the data, the reality), respects social rules (i.e. theories about judgments), provides an explanation of the target's behavior (i.e. a theory about the data), and protects the integrity of the self or of the in-group (i.e. personal or social identity). The motivational part of the judgment is most obvious in the integrity element, as indicated when subjects have to decide whether a target belongs to their group rather than to a threatening out-group, they need more information before feeling confident about their decision (Leyens & Yzerbyt, 1992; Yzerbyt, Leyens, & Bellour, 1995).

We suggest that interactions leading to a possibly threatening judgment or outcome for the self or the in-group will trigger disconfirmation and a necessity-oriented rule. Working from the continuum model of impression formation (Fiske & Neuberg, 1990), one assumes that people start with category membership as a default mode of impressions and only go beyond depending on the pragmatics of the social situation (Fiske, 1992, 1993b). For example, when subjects are outcome dependent, that is, need another person in order not to lose an important prize, they spend much time examining information about that person that disconfirms their expectations (Erber & Fiske, 1984; Neuberg & Fiske, 1987; Ruscher & Fiske, 1990; Ruscher, Fiske, Miki, & Van Manen, 1991). When subjects are under someone else's power and the personal threat is increased, however, they may abandon necessity and disconfirmation, in favor of the comfort of believing the best about the other person (Stevens & Fiske, 1995).

When subjects have power over another person, they are under the least threat, so they apparently rely on the sufficiency-oriented rule, attending most to confirming information, and not at all to disconfirming information (Fiske, 1993a; Goodwin & Fiske, 1995; Goodwin, Fiske, & Yzerbyt, 1995). As in the Yzerbyt, Rocher, and Coull (1995) study, the sufficiency rule requires effort beyond the ordinary default of inattention to detailed information about the other.

Other studies similarly indicate that certain kinds of social threat invoke the necessity rule: For example, when subjects learn that they are ill, they ask for much more information than if they learn they are healthy (Ditto & Lopez, 1992). When subjects are warned that their judgment will be evaluated by experts, they take the disconfirming information more into account than if they know that the judgment task is a mere exercise (Kruglanski & Mayseless, 1988; Tetlock, 1992). An accuracy goal can be threatening by itself. Indeed, inducing such a goal means for subjects that there is a correct answer to be found if they do not want to appear fools (see the work of Trope, 1986, on diagnosticity, for instance). Finally, the relative homogeneity of in-groups versus out-groups can be considered along the same lines. People feel threatened (or, at least, they dislike) to be exactly similar to the other members of their group, except if the very existence of this group is justified by a strong homogeneity (e.g. stigmatized or politically extreme groups) (Codol, 1987; Leyens, Yzerbyt, & Rogier, 1995). It is therefore no wonder that people usually judge their in-group as more heterogeneous than an out-group, except when they belong to a minority, and especially to a stigmatized one (Simon, 1992).

The processes at work in these different interaction contexts have previously been subsumed under two competing motivations: the cost of being wrong vs. the cost of being indecisive (Fiske & Taylor, 1991) and high vs. low need for closure (Kruglanski, 1990). Perhaps the cost of being wrong just describes the more stringent focus of using disconfirming information under the necessity orientation, whereas the cost being indecisive fits the good-enough, sufficiency-oriented focus on default confirmatory cues. The necessity–sufficiency dichotomy, however, makes salient the impact of the objective–subjective anchor, itself a function of social context.

The link between the necessity–sufficiency dichotomy and threat also allows us to view the role of motivation in a more diversified way than used to be the case. Indeed, motivation was traditionally presumed to lead to more "exact" judgments, that is, to judgments that considered consistent as well as inconsistent information. Think now of you and your American guest; you really want to please this visitor. Will you therefore try and prepare sheep brains – and risk ruining the visit? What we suggest is that motivation may lead to more confirmation than no motivation when subjects are sure of themselves or when the potential outcome is safe (you will prepare a Chateaubriand, with a lot a different salads and cheeses, in case s/he is vegetarian). The Goodwin et al. (1995) research on power exemplifies certainty and safety. That is, people motivated to maintain power, for example, make an effort to attend to information that confirms their stereotypes. Moreover, the varied effects of motivation may be why differential inducements of motivation did not bring different results in Snyder, Campbell, and Preston's (1982; see also Snyder, 1984) experiments on hypothesis confirmation; to the extent participants felt sure of themselves, different "educational interventions" may simply have reinforced their feelings of confidence, leading to more hypothesis confirmation.

The reasoning applies to domains that, at first sight, seem alien to person perception. We borrow the following example from Hilton and Kemmelmaier (1995) and adapt it for our purpose. Imagine you were presented with four cards with a single digit or letter (E, K, 4, and 7) printed on each, and you were asked to verify the rule that "If a card has a vowel on one side, then it has an even number on the other." Which cards would you turn over? Readers familiar with Wason and Johnson-Laird's (1965) famous "if p then q" task will know to turn over the E (examining the proposition, p) and 7 (examining the complement of the conclusion, i.e. not-q). There can, however, be other rational choices. Let us take the following statement used by Hilton and Kemmelmaier: "if you see an enemy submarine 'blip' then launch depth charges." This statement can be understood as "be sure to get any enemy submarine" or as "be sure to launch the charges only if it is an enemy submarine." In the first case, one is testing sufficiency (p, not-q), and in the second case, necessity (not-p, q). Which strategy is adopted depends on which outcome is seen as more threatening (letting an enemy submarine get through unscathed or launching depth charges in response to a false alarm).

In person perception, similarly, the same conclusion can be threatening to one person, and safe for another one. If this is so, the two persons should adopt a different strategy to test the same problem. In threatening situations, people will tend to adopt a necessity strategy, and in nonthreatening situations, they will adopt a sufficiency strategy. For instance, do you think that a French person and a Belgian will react identically to the sentence: "If he eats *frites* ('French' fries) then he is Belgian?" For the French person, who is always quick to judge a Belgian out-grouper, it is sufficient to eat *frites* in order to be Belgian. Judging someone to be Belgian is not threatening, so sufficiency will do. For the Belgian, it is more threatening to mistakenly judge a stranger as Belgian (especially knowing the food is as good in Belgium as in France), so the person will follow a necessity rule. For that person, it will be necessary to show that non-Belgians never eat *frites*, before classifying a particular *frite*-eater as Belgian.

Obviously, the presence of intergroup conflicts arouses special goals. Their consideration in terms of necessity/sufficiency could lead to new questions and bring order to seemingly chaotic results. Let us take as an example the complexity–extremity model of Linville (Linville & Jones, 1980; Linville, 1982) and the "black sheep" effect (Marques, Yzerbyt, & Leyens, 1988; Marques & Paez, 1994). According to Linville, people have more nuanced perceptions for in-group than for out-group members because they are more familiar with the former than the latter and thus have more complex views about the in-group than the out-group. Marques and colleagues, on the other hand, have repeatedly obtained opposite results. That is, people are more favorable to a good in-group member than to an equally good out-group member, showing thereby an in-group favoritism bias; they are also less favorable to a bad in-group member than to an equally bad out-group member, presumably to preserve their positive social identity that is threatened by the "black sheep." How is it possible to reconcile these two different sets of data? Presumably, it is the presence of conflict that distinguishes when people will conform to Linville's or to Marques's results. Branscombe, Wann, Noel, and Coleman (1993) have recently shown that, in case of conflict between in-group and out-group, those people who strongly identify with the in-group reveal the "black sheep" effect whereas those who do not care about the conflict obey the complexity–extremity model. Does this mean that people follow a rule of familiarity in the absence of threat and that they follow a completely different rule when there is conflict? Is it not more economical to suggest that people follow a rule of necessity in the case of threat and a rule of sufficiency in the case of serenity? Indeed, when threatened in their identity, subjects focus on the potential disconfirmation of their expectancies about in-groupers; in the absence of conflict, it is sufficient to account for the characteristics of the out-group.

What about victims of prejudice? Except for relative deprivation theorists, few researchers have specifically considered what discriminated persons think of their discriminators (Eberhardt & Fiske, 1996). Such neglect explains why Ostrom and Sedikides (1992) found so few studies that measured reciprocal perception of in-group and out-group; much more numerous were the experiments that considered the unilateral view of one group by another. In terms of necessity- and sufficiency-oriented rules, one should also find differences between prejudiced and prejudged people. The contrast between the necessity-oriented rules of the powerless (Stevens & Fiske, 1995) and the sufficiency-oriented rules of the powerful (Goodwin & Fiske, 1995; Goodwin et al., 1995) is surely a case in point.

In conclusion, we believe that interaction goals, stemming from social context, should be much more focal than they presently are. We suggest that goals may be linked to subjective and objective anchors through sufficiency- or necessity-oriented rules of reasoning. We illustrated our points with research and proposed new hypotheses along these lines. All these remarks are speculative, and it is precisely why research is needed. Such investigations would also have the advantage of making a rapprochement between various research traditions. Heterogeneity, the acceptance of all the fads, would be brought to the fore by looking at social interaction goals. Is that not logical from a psychological viewpoint?

Perception is (for) action. The second ingredient of our message concerns behavior; context and anchors are relevant here, too. Social cognition research and SIT (or, more precisely, SCT) increasingly relied on words as independent and dependent variables (de la Haye, 1991; Fiske, 1995). Let us be honest. Social psychologists, even attitude researchers, are not interested in verbal judgments *per se*. We study them with the hope that they will inform us about behaviors. Now, the discrepancy between words and acts is theoretically interesting in itself. But this interest should not be our ultimate goal or else social psychology might lose its attraction for young people. When starting medical school, students are not interested in the fact that some people get cancer and others not; they are probably not interested in why some get cancer and others not; they are interested because they may cure cancer. Researchers know that the "why" question is important, but it should not be enough. Researchers who concentrate only on the "why" question may be able to speak to colleagues in the field, but not to the society at large. Society, especially students, rightly expect that the "why" question answers the question "how will we be able to change something?"

There is another reason – theoretical this time – to focus more on behavior. Perceiving other people is an (inter)action in that it has immediate consequences upon the target, who is also a perceiver (for a discussion, see Fiske & Taylor, 1991; for an empirical example, see Gilbert & Jones, 1986). Interacting directly with someone rather than via a sheet of paper or a computer screen brings into the situation new elements that may also affect the perception process. Theoretically and socially important contexts carry different implications than do aseptic "contexts" that do not represent social reality.

Social psychologists know very well that people do not necessarily behave as they think they would (e.g. Milgram, 1974), or for the reasons they believe they do (e.g. Nisbett & Wilson, 1977). Such a discrepancy is particularly intriguing in the case of social perception. Why would I indeed judge Ronald incompetent but behave towards him as if he were intelligent? Concern for social desirability is not an adequate answer because I am sometimes ready to let my unfavorable judgment be known to the target.

It is probably a small jump to say that judging via a computer corresponds to an observer viewpoint and that interacting with someone corresponds to an actor viewpoint. To take a greater leap, Lewicka would also venture the possibility that the observer viewpoint corresponds to a necessity-oriented rule and that the actor viewpoint corresponds to a sufficiency-oriented rule. Let us make both jumps.

Consider the classic LaPiere (1934) study. When asked by letter, hotel managers said that they would refuse Chinese clients. Yet, when a Chinese couple presented themselves with an American friend to each of several hotels, they were almost always accepted. This study is especially cited in the attitude area presumably because it reveals the gap between attitude (measured by the letters) and behavior (measured at the hotel desk). Henry (1991) conducted a very similar study in Canada in 1984 and in 1989. In one condition, accomplices with a foreign (for instance, Antillan) or an English Canadian accent applied by phone to advertised jobs. Discrimination occurred in both years. In another condition, Black-Antillan or English-Canadian accomplices presented themselves directly to firms in order to be hired. Their competence was equal. Discrimination against the Black-Antillan accomplices was evident in 1984 but disappeared in 1989 although the job market had not changed. Thus, in both LaPiere's and Henry's studies, less discrimination occurred when there was an encounter between the protagonists than when no "real (inter)action" was at stake.

Is this outcome simply the result of a difference between attitude and behavior? Can't it be explained as the observer viewpoint (by phone or by letter) and as the actor viewpoint (the real encounter), each determined by social context? Again, real social context seems to determine objective and subjective anchors.

Let us take a final example from our own research (Leyens, 1989; Leyens, Dardenne, & Fiske, 1995). When people have to formulate questions before an interview, they ask only diagnostic questions, that is, questions that do not presuppose a given answer on the part of the interviewee. However, when people formulate questions during the interview, not only do they ask diagnostic questions, but they also ask questions leading toward a given answer. In other words, people adopt a "diagnostic" position before the interview but show their biases in the course of the interaction. Again, can't the difference be explained by the difference of viewpoints, that is, an observer's objective anchor before the interview but an actor's subjective anchor once inside the interview context? We also believe that these two sets of studies are interesting because they show that stereotyping, or discrimination, is not restricted to a specific viewpoint.

In conclusion, our proposal in this second set of ingredients to our message is not to abandon verbal statements as independent and dependent variables. It is not to find ways (e.g. reaction times) that would be closer to behaviors and more representative of them than written responses on a scale (Fiske, 1995). This would actually be a pledge for the homogeneity of a single fad. Our proposal is to add behaviors to our studies, both at the level of the experimental scenario and at the level of the dependent variable. In Aronson and Carlsmith's terms (1968), "experimental realism" and "mundane realism" should cohabit in our studies because neither of the two contains the very truth. Our proposal is also to study the influence of verbal statements upon behaviors and vice versa, and to examine the social contexts that affect both. Such a shift would really show that perception is action and is for action. In brief, we invite more creativity in our designs by way of the heterogeneity of multiple simultaneous "fads."

Conclusions

Writing an invited chapter of this form allows more speculation than a technical paper. Let us benefit from this fortunate opportunity.

In Belgium, currently, many Flemish people complain because Walloons contribute less to and spend more of the social security budget than they do. This imbalance arises because there are more elderly and unemployed people in the Wallonian south than in the Flemish north of Belgium. Up to now, Belgian social security has been a federal matter. This situation has not been changed, mainly because of "solidarity between groups" (and, maybe, because some specialists foresee a reversal of the tide in a few decades). If one believes most Flemish newspapers, the imbalance of the social security budget reveals that this is due to the lazy, exploitative, and irresponsible nature of Walloons. The connections that link these stereotypic attributes together and explain them as a whole, we can call a naive theory. Assume now that the social security budget is regionalized and that a Flemish couple who moved to work in Wallonia must depend on the poor Walloon system rather than on the richer Flemish one. It is likely that this couple will explain the Walloon budget by the individualistic, chaotic, and disorganized nature of the Walloons. It is unlikely, however, that this couple will change their behavior toward Walloons. In other words, the change of subsidizing of the budget has brought a change in the naive theory or beliefs about Walloons but not in the behaviors towards Walloons. This is so because linguistic groups are an accepted social division in Belgium. The societal context acknowledges group membership.

Suppose that the next president of the USA is a Black person. Apparently, behavior changed in this fictional example: votes went to a Black candidate rather than to a white one. Would that change the naive theories held by white Americans about Black people? We doubt it and, in fact, we speculate that if it occurs the behavior will be addressed to an individual (e.g. someone whose race is not an overt part of his identity, such as Colin Powell) and not to a member of a minority group (e.g. someone whose race is an explicit center of his identity, such as Jesse Jackson). This is so because acceptance of groups, rather than of individuals, is considered bad in the USA (and thus we felt obliged to use the term "Black people" and not Blacks as a single noun, the way we did for the Flemish or Walloons).

What we want to say here is that naive theories may change at least superficially without concomitant behavioral change. Innovations may not affect behavior, but they may need different justifications for the same behavior. It is well known that the worsening of the economic situation changes views about minority groups such as delinquent, poor, or immigrant people; curiously enough, what becomes responsible for the status of these groups is not the bad economy but their genes (see the recent success of "The Bell Curve" and of Rushton's 1994 book, not to mention the budget spent on finding the violent gene). Thus, changes in theories do not necessarily imply changes of behaviors. It is much more difficult to imagine a change of behavior that would not be preceded or followed by a change of naive theory. We believe that a change of behavior necessitates a change of theory. In our American example, if the president had been elected precisely because he was a Black person, it is hard to think that theories about Black people had remained unchanged (before and after the election).

Voting for a certain person or using stereotypes are not only that. They are the expression of a meaning and, social psychologists should be more interested in the meaning than in the expression. There is something of a hermeneutic flavor in experimental work but researchers tend to forget it; it is not (yet) faddish. Social psychologists have come a long away towards opening the "black box" of subjects' minds but are not yet ready to show the same tolerance for their own approach as experimentalists.

At a time when cross-cultural concerns attract an increasing number of adherents, the study of meaning production, of differences of or shifts in meaning, should be of particular interest. Whatever the reason for "judging" another person, there are not many ways to do it if researchers stick to traditional methods (using written statements): most of the time, the perceptual judgment consists of a list of attributes. Pondering, summing, averaging, remembering, or imagining these attributes will not help much in finding the meaning. Looking at the behavior of people when they are engaged in different types of interaction contexts will. And it will be even more helpful if researchers look at the phenomena from many different viewpoints.

References

(Those marked * are recommended for further reading.)

Abelson, R. P. (1981). The psychological status of the script concept, *American Psychologist*, *36*, 715–729.

Aronson, E., & Carlsmith, J. M. (1968). Experimentation in social psychology. In G. Lindzey & E. Aronson (Eds.), *The handbook of social psychology* (Vol. 2, pp. 1–79). Reading, MA: Addison-Wesley.

Asch, S. E. (1946). Forming impressions of personality. *Journal of Abnormal and Social Psychology*, *41*, 1230–1240.

Bandura, A. (1965). Vicarious processes: A case of no-trial learning. In L. Berkowitz (Ed.), *Advances in experimental social psychology* (Vol. 2, pp. 1–55). New York: Academic Press.

Berkowitz, L. (1993). *Aggression: Its causes, consequences, and control.* New York: McGraw Hill.

Branscombe, N. R., Wann, D. L., Noel, J. G., & Coleman, J. (1993). In-group or out-group extremity: Importance of threatened social identity. *Personality and Social Psychology Bulletin*, *19*, 381–388.

Codol, J. P. (1987). Comparability and incomparability between oneself and others: Means of differentiation and comparison reference points. *Cahiers de psychologie cognitive/European Bulletin of Cognitive Psychology*, *7*, 87–105.

Darley, J. M., & Fazio, R. H. (1980). Expectancy confirmation processes arising in the social interaction sequence. *American Psychologist*, *35*, 867–881.

*Devine, P. G., Hamilton, D. L., & Ostrom, T. M. (Eds.) (1994). *Social cognition: Contributions to classic issues in social psychology*. New York: Springer Verlag.

Ditto, P. H., & Lopez, D. F. (1992). Motivated skepticism: Use of differential decision criteria for preferred and nonpreferred conclusions. *Journal of Personality and Social Psychology*, *63*, 568–584.

Eberhardt, J., & Fiske, S. T. (1996). Motivating individuals to change: What is a target to do? In N. Macrae, M. Hewstone, & C. Stangor (Eds.), Foundations of stereotypes and stereotyping (pp. 369–415). New York: Guilford.

Erber, R., & Fiske, S. T. (1984). Outcome dependency and attention to inconsistent information. *Journal of Personality and Social Psychology*, *47*, 709–726.

Fiske, S. T. (1992). Thinking is for doing: Portraits of social cognition from daguerreotype to laserphoto. *Journal of Personality and Social Psychology*, *63*, 877–889.

Fiske, S. T. (1993a). Controlling other people: The impact of power on stereotyping. *American Psychologist*, *48*, 621–628.

*Fiske, S. T. (1993b). Social cognition and social perception. In M. R. Rosenzweig & L. W. Porter (Eds.), *Annual review of psychology* (Vol. 44, pp. 155–194). Palo Alto, CA: Annual Reviews Inc.

Fiske, S. T. (1995). Words! Words! Words! Confronting the problem of observer and self reports. In P. E. Shrout and S. T. Fiske (Eds.), Personality research, methods and theory: A festschrift honoring Donald W. Fiske (pp. 231–340). Hillsdale, NJ: Lawrence Erlbaum.

Fiske, S. T., & Neuberg, S. L. (1990). A continuum model of impression formation, from category-based to individuating processes. Influence of information and motivation on attention and interpretation. In M. P. Zanna (Ed.), *Advances in experimental social psychology* (Vol. 23, pp. 1–74). New York: Academic Press.

Fiske, S. T., & Taylor, S. E. (1984). *Social cognition*. New York: Random House.

Fiske, S. T., & Taylor, S. E. (1991). *Social cognition* (2nd ed.). New York: McGraw Hill.

Gilbert, D. T., & Jones, E. E. (1986). Perceiver-induced constraint: Interpretations of self-generated reality. *Journal of Personality and Social Psychology*, *50*, 269–280.

Goodwin, S. A., & Fiske, S. T. (1995). *Power and motivated impression formation: How powerholders stereotype by default and by design*. Manuscript submitted for publication.

Goodwin, S. A., Fiske, S. T., & Yzerbyt, V. Y. (1995, August). *Social judgment in power relations: A judgment monitoring perspective*. Poster session presented at the annual meeting of the American Psychological Association, New York.

Hamilton, D. L. (Ed.) (1981). *Cognitive processes in stereotyping and intergroup behavior*. Hillsdale, NJ: Lawrence Erlbaum.

Haye, A.-M. de la. (1991). Problems and procedures: A typology of paradigms in interpersonal cognition. *European Bulletin of Cognitive Psychology*, *11*, 279–304.

Heider, F. (1958). *The psychology of interpersonal relations*. New York: Wiley.

Henry, E. (1991). Préjugée et tolérance an Canada. In *Le nouvean visage du Canada. Incidence économique et sociale de l'immigration*. Ottawa: Conseil Economique du Canada.

Hilton, D., & Kemmelmaier, M. (1995). *A pragmatic theory of conditionals: Communication, interpretation and hypothesis-testing*. Unpublished manuscript.

Hilton, J. L., & Darley, J. M. (1989). The effect of interaction goals on person perception. In M. P. Zanna (Ed.), *Advances in Experimental Social Psychology* (Vol. 24, pp. 235–267). San Diego, CA: Academic Press.

Kruglanski, A. W. (1990). Motivations for judging and knowing: Implications for causal attribution. In E. T. Higgins & R. M. Sorrentino (Eds.), *Handbook of motivation and cognition: Foundations of social behavior* (Vol. 2, pp. 13–37). New York: Guilford Press.

Kruglanski, A. W., & Mayseless, O. (1988). Contextual effects in hypothesis testing: The role of competing alternatives and epistemic motivations. *Social Cognition*, *6*, 1–20.

Kunda, Z. (1990). The case for motivated reasoning. *Psychology Bulletin*, *108*, 80–98.

LaPiere, R. T. (1934). Attitudes versus actions. *Social Forces*, *13*, 230–237.

*Lewicka, M. (1988). On objective and subjective anchoring of cognitive acts: How behavioral valence modifies reasoning schemata. In W. J. Baker, L. P. Mos, H. V. Rappard, & H. J. Stam (Eds.), *Recent trends in theoretical psychology* (pp. 285–301). New York: Springer Verlag.

Leyens, J.-Ph. (1989). Another look at confirmatory strategies during a real interview. *European Journal of Social Psychology*, *19*, 255–262.

Leyens, J.-Ph. (1993). Qu'est-ce qu'un bon jugement social? [What is an adequate social judgment?] In J. L. Beauvois, R. V. Joule, & J. M. Monteil (Eds.), *Perspectives cognitives et conduites sociales. IV. Jugements sociaux et changement des attitudes* [Cognitives perspectives and social behaviors. IV. Social judgments and attitude change]. Lausanne: Delachaux et Niestlé.

Leyens, J.-Ph., & Yzerbyt, V. Y. (1989). La cognition sociale. D'où vient-elle et où pourrait elle aller? [Social cognition: Where does it come from and where could it go?] *Bulletin de Psychologie*, *42*, 255–262.

Leyens, J.-Ph., & Yzerbyt. V. Y. (1992). The in-group overexclusion effect: Impact of valence and confirmation on stereotypical information search. *European Journal of Social Psychology*, *22*, 549–570.

Leyens, J.-Ph., Dardenne B., & Fiske, S. T. (1995). Is there a useful bias in hypothesis? Unpublished manuscript, University of Louvain, at Louvain-la-Neuve.

*Leyens, J.-Ph., Yzerbyt, V. Y., & Rogier, A. (1995). *Differences are preferred to similarities: Empirical evidence from memory data*. Manuscript submitted for publication.

Leyens, J.-Ph., Yzerbyt, V. Y., & Schadron, G. (1994). *Stereotypes and social cognition*. London: Sage.

Linville, P. W. (1982). The complexity-extremity effect and age-based stereotyping. *Journal of Personality and Social Psychology*, *42*, 193–211.

Linville, P. W., & Jones, E. E. (1980). Polarized appraisals of out-group members. *Journal of Personality and Social Psychology*, *38*, 689–703.

Marques, J. M., & Paez, D. (1994). The "black sheep effect": Social categorization, rejection of in-group deviates, and perception of group variability. In W. Stroebe & M. Hewstone (Eds.), *European Review of Social Psychology* (Vol. 5, pp. 37–68). Chichester: Wiley.

Marques, J. M., Yzerbyt, V. Y., & Leyens, J.-Ph. (1988). The "black sheep effect": Extremity of judgments towards in-group members as a function of group identification. *European Journal of Social Psychology*, *18*, 1–16.

Milgram, S. (1974). *Obedience to authority*. New York: Harper & Row.

Mischel, W. (1968). *Personality and assessment*. New York: Wiley.

Neuberg, S. L., & Fiske, S. T. (1987). Motivational influences on impression formation: Outcome dependency, accuracy-driven attention, and individuating processes. *Journal of Personality and Social Psychology*, *53*, 431–444.

*Nisbett, R. E., & Ross, L. (1980). *Human inference: Strategies and shortcomings of social judgment*. Englewood Cliffs, NJ: Prentice-Hall.

Nisbett, R. E., & Wilson, T. D. (1977). Telling more than we can know: Verbal reports on mental processes. *Psychological Review*, *84*, 231–259.

Oakes, P. J., & Turner, J. C. (1990). Is limited information processing capacity the cause of social stereotyping? In W. Stroebe & M. Hewstone (Eds.), *European Review of Social Psychology* (Vol. 1, pp. 111–135). Chichester: Wiley.

Ostrom, T. M., & Sedikides, C. (1992). Out-group homogeneity effect in natural and minimal groups. *Psychological Bulletin*, *112*, 536–552.

Ruscher, J. B., & Fiske, S. T. (1990). Interpersonal competition can cause individuating processes. *Journal of Personality and Social Psychology*, *58*, 832–843.

Ruscher, J. B., Fiske, S. T., Miki, H., & Van Manen, S. (1991). Individuating processes in competition: Interpersonal versus intergroup. *Personality and Social Psychology Bulletin*, *17*, 595–605.

Rushton, J. P. (1994). *Race, evolution, and behavior*. New Brunswick, NJ: Transaction Publishers.

Simon, B. (1992). The perception of in-group and out-group homogeneity: Reintroducing the intergroup context. *European Review of Social Psychology* (Vol. 3, pp. 1–30). Chichester: Wiley.

Snyder, M. (1984). When belief creates reality. In L. Berkowitz (Ed.), *Advances in experimental social psychology* (Vol. 18, pp. 248–306). San Diego, CA: Academic Press.

Snyder, M. (1992). Motivational foundations of behavioral confirmation. In M. P. Zanna (Ed.), *Advances in experimental social psychology* (Vol. 25, pp. 67–114). San Diego, CA: Academic Press.

Snyder, M., Campbell, B. H., & Preston, E. (1982). Testing hypotheses about human nature: Assessing the accuracy of social stereotypes. *Social Cognition*, *1*, 256–272.

Stevens, L. E., & Fiske, S. T. (1995). Forming motivated impressions of a powerholder: Accuracy under task dependency and misperception under evaluation dependency. Unpublished manuscript, University of Massachusetts at Amherst.

Stroebe, W., & Insko, C. A. (1989). Stereotypes, prejudice, and discrimination: Changing conceptions in theory and research. In D. Bar-Tal, C. F. Graumann, A. W. Kruglanski, & W. Stroebe (Eds.), *Stereotypes and prejudice: Changing conceptions* (pp. 3–34). New York: Springer Verlag.

Tajfel, H. (1972). Social categorization [English ms. of La categorization sociale]. In S. Moscovici (Ed.), *Introduction à la psychologie sociale* (Vol. 1, pp. 272–302). Paris: Larousse.

Tajfel, H., & Turner, J. C. (1979). An integrative theory of intergroup conflict. In S. C. Worchel & W. G. Austin (Eds.), *Psychology of intergroup relations*. Monterey, CA: Brooks-Cole.

Tetlock, P. E. (1992). The impact of accountability on judgment and choice: Toward a social contingency model. In M. P. Zanna (Ed.), *Advances in experimental social psychology* (Vol. 25). New York: Academic Press.

Trope, Y. (1986). Identification and inferential processes in dispositional attribution. *Psychological Review*, *93*, 239–257.

Turner, C. W., & Leyens, J.-Ph. (1992). The weapons effect revisited: The effects of firearms on aggressive behavior. In P. Suedfeld & P. E. Tetlock (Eds.), *Psychology and social policy*. New York: Hemisphere Publishing Corporation.

Turner, J. C. (1988). Preface. In M. A. Hogg & D. Abrams, *Social identification: A social psychology of intergroup relations and group processes* (pp. x–xi). London: Routledge.

Turner, J. C., Oakes, P. J., Haslam, S. A., & McGarty, C. (1994). Self and collective: Cognition and social context. *Personality and Social Psychology Bulletin*, *20*, 454–463.

Wason, P. C., & Johnson-Laird, P. N. (1965). Psychology of reasoning: Structure and content. London: Batsford.

Yzerbyt, V. Y., Leyens, J.-Ph., & Bellour, F. (1995). The in-group overexclusion effect: Identity concerns in decisions about group membership. *European Journal of Social Psychology*, *25*, 1–16.

Yzerbyt, V. Y., Rocher, S., & Coull, A. (1995). Unpublished data.

8

Social Psychology as Social Construction: The Emerging Vision

Kenneth J. Gergen

Kenneth Gergen is the Mustin Professor of Psychology at Swarthmore College. His current teaching, writing, and public lecturing address such diverse topics as social construction, relational theory and practice, technology and the self, performative psychology, therapeutic process, and cultural politics. He is also a co-founder of The Taos Institute, an organization attempting to wed social constructionist ideas to practices of therapy, organizational development, and education. Among his best-known books are *Toward transformation in social knowledge*, *The saturated self*, and *Realities and relationships*.

My commitment to social-psychological inquiry has now exceeded three decades; the commitment has been a passionate one throughout. However, the nature of this passion – the sense of the inquiry and its significance – has changed substantially over this period. The "message" of the discipline, as it initially kindled my excitement, now seems deeply mistaken – in certain respects even injurious to the society. Because the various assumptions that grounded this message were (and continue to be) the assumptions of the vast majority of the discipline, my evolving writings drew strong criticism. For some the emerging writings seemed anti-science, anti-psychological, and even nihilistic. Yet, while I no longer find the traditional views of science and psychology compelling, I am far from pessimistic about the future of the discipline. In light of critical reflection and continuing dialogue within various sectors of the field and within the social sciences more generally, I find myself more excited by the prospects for social psychology than ever before. For present purposes, then, it is propitious to proceed autobiographically. I shall proceed to lay out some of the traditional assumptions and reasons for my abandonment of them. More importantly, I shall explore the contemporary vision of the field growing from this soil of discontent, and describe some of its special promises. These promises can be placed under the more general rubric of social constructionism.

Progress in Perpetuity: The Experimental Paradigm

In my university years I was struck by what seemed to be two obvious facts: first, the greatest contributions to human betterment of the preceding century were those emanating from the natural sciences, and second, that we continued to remain ignorant of the wellsprings of human behavior. The discipline of psychology seemed not only to recognize both these facts, but held the promise that if we could but generate scientific knowledge of human behavior, society would be able to solve many of its severest problems – problems of aggression, exploitation, prejudice, class conflict, immorality, abnormality, and the common suffering of daily life among them.

These inviting possibilities also furnished me with an individual *raison d'être*. As a trained scientist, I could establish experimental settings in which precise causal linkages could be traced – the effects of various stimulus conditions (as they are called) on the psychological processes of individual subjects and the effects of these psychological processes on subjects' behavior toward each other. Observations of these causal sequences could also be evaluated statistically so as to ensure their broad generality. I could then make these findings available to my colleagues for further study, and as weaknesses and limitations were discovered in this work, further research would be invited. Over time, aided by my participation, the field would generate highly sophisticated and well-tested theoretical accounts (principles and explanations) of broad generality. These accounts would not be biased by any particular ideology, political position, or ethical commitment. In effect, these accounts could be made available to all people, so that policy makers, organizational decision makers, community leaders – indeed, any private citizen – could benefit in their attempts to improve the human condition.

These various beliefs were scarcely my own; indeed they are major suppositions within what is generally called *empirical* or *experimental social psychology*. To illustrate these assumptions in action, let me draw from early research of my own, on a topic that continues to fascinate me even today, namely the self. Joining with my many colleagues in psychology, I believed that any proper understanding of individual action must take into account various psychological processes – such as perception, motivation, emotion, memory and the like. However, I was particularly struck by the possible impact on human behavior of the individual's conception of self and others. Our moment-to-moment decisions, it seemed, depend on what we think of ourselves (our concept of self, self-esteem, and the like) and others (their personality, expectations, etc.). In contrast to many personality theorists, I was also impressed by what seemed to me a profound lability in self-conception. We don't seem to have a single, stable conception of ourselves, it seemed to me, but to have the capacity for infinite fluctuation. Further, to extend George Herbert Mead's (1934) insights, these fluctuations seem directly connected to others' behavior toward us. As I reasoned, then, an individual's self-esteem can be shaped from moment to moment by others' expressions of esteem for them.

This sort of reasoning invited an experimental study in which I attempted to trace the systematic effects of one's person's evaluations on the self-esteem of another. Within the context of a very elaborate study, with many variables and measures, I thus had subjects (college sophomores) interviewed by a graduate student (stimulus person). During the interview the subjects were asked to make a series of self-evaluations. In an experimental group, the interviewer subtly agreed with the subject each time she evaluated herself positively, and was silent or disagreed when she evaluated herself negatively. As I found, the self-ratings of the subjects increased steadily throughout the interview. They did not do so in a control group who were not exposed to this form of feedback. In a subsequent test of self-esteem, administered privately, the experimental subjects demonstrated statistically higher ratings than control group subjects. The positive feedback, in effect, seemed to carry past the interview itself. These and other results were subsequently published for my professional colleagues (Gergen, 1965), and I derived a certain satisfaction from the sense of having contributed to a growing body of research that would eventually inform us of the nature of self-conception, and which could be used by therapists, educators, parents, and all of us concerned with each others' welfare.

To summarize, the message of social psychology inherent in the prevailing *Zeitgeist* was that empirical research can furnish an unbiased and systematic description and explanation of social behavior, that the accuracy and generality of these theoretical accounts are subject to continuous improvement through research, and that there is nothing so practical for society as an accurate, empirically supported theory. In effect, scientists can offer society enormous riches in terms of principles of human interaction, and with these principles society can improve itself. With respect to our understanding of selves, progress in knowledge is interminable.

The Early Impasse: Social Psychology as History

The preceding pages were difficult to write, much like attempting to reignite the naive idealisms of adolescence. No, I don't wish to abandon all the premises, and certainly not the optimistic sense of potential for the discipline. However, it was essential to squarely face the foolishness if some sort of salvaging was to take place. For me, the first step in critical self-reflection was the growing realization of the historical perishability of social-psychological knowledge. Much of the above enthusiasm depends on the belief that knowledge accumulates: each experiment can add to the previous and the accretion of findings gives us an improved fix on the realities of social life. But what if social life is not itself stable; what if social patterns are in a state of continuous and possibly chaotic transformation? To the extent this is so, then the science does not accumulate knowledge; its knowledge represents no more than a small, and perhaps not very important history of college student behavior in artificial laboratory settings.

These doubts began to arise even in the design of the above described research on self-evaluation. In an additional part of the study I argued that in order for the feedback of others' to affect one's level of self-esteem, this feedback would have to appear authentic. If one believed the feedback was insincere, not intended to be an accurate expression of feeling, then the feedback would have little effect. Indeed, I tested this hunch by running a group of subjects under the same conditions as above, with the exception of telling them that the interviewer would be practicing a set of interview techniques. The results confirmed my hypothesis. However, in moments of repose, it also struck me that none of the feedback in any of the conditions was truly sincere; all of it was experimentally arranged. This meant that it was not what the interviewer actually did in the interchange that mattered, but the interpretation that was placed on it. Yet, if interpretations come and go across cultural history, and there is virtually no limit on the ways events can be interpreted, then what are we to make of these results? There was widespread belief at one time in people's souls, and in demon possession; such interpretations are no longer favored. In the sixteenth century, states of melancholy were detected everywhere; early in the present century, people suffered from "nervous breakdowns." These interpretations are now little evidenced. My results seemed, then, to be reflections of the present cultural conditions.

To think about the way "nervous breakdowns" disappeared from view, and concepts like "identity crisis," and "anomie" came and went in more recent years, added an additional wrinkle to the gathering doubt. There are many ways in which psychology is a creative discipline. It is continuously developing new terminologies, new explanations, and novel insights into the wellsprings of human conduct. Aren't these efforts all adventures in interpretation? And if they are, don't they contribute to the interpretive mix within the society? Aren't they pressing our interpretations in new directions, and thus affecting our actions toward each other? In effect, to the extent that social psychological theories enter society, they have the capacity to alter social patterns. In effect, the field itself contributes to the very transience in social patterning that invalidates its faith in cumulative knowledge.

The plot thickens: consider again my little study on self-conception. My theoretical reasoning seems compelling enough, some might say that it reflects general common sense. But let us consider where my assumptions about selves differ from common sense. For most of Western culture, we are each endowed with capacities for autonomous choice. We are fundamentally free to chose one path of action as opposed to another. Indeed, it is just such a commitment to individual choice that undergirds our beliefs in democracy, law, and the kind of everyday morality in which we hold each other responsible for our actions. Yet the self I portray in my experiment has no voluntary agency. One's sense of self, in this context, is determined by social feedback; I am simply the repository of others' attitudes toward me. In this sense I suppress or negate the common cultural wisdom, and subtly undermine the rationale for the cultural institutions of democracy, legal responsibility, and so on. If I extend my theoretical assumption, I even destroy the assumption of authentic or sincere feedback, as all feedback from others would equally well be the outcome of social programming.

The upshot of this line of reasoning is that the discipline of psychology not only stirs the pot of social meaning, but that it is value saturated. That is, in spite of its attempt to be value neutral, the interpretations of the discipline subtly lend themselves to certain kinds of action and discredit others. The tradition's best-known research, for example, discredits conformity, obedience, and succumbing to attitude change pressures. In this way the discipline subtly champions independence, autonomy, and self-containment; cooperation, collaboration, and empathic integration of the other are all suppressed. So not only does the field operate to change (or sustain) interpretations, it also functions unwittingly as a moral and political advocate. The hope of a value-neutral science is deeply misguided.

Most of these arguments were published in an early article, "Social psychology as history" (Gergen, 1973). The effects were startling. Broad controversy ensued; my arguments were rejected as counter-productive philosophy by some, pilloried by others, and for a few, there was a sense of "at last, vindication of long silent doubts." This article, combined with a range of additional critique (Harré & Secord, 1972; Ring, 1967; McGuire, 1973) produced what was called the "crisis in social psychology" (see, for example, Strickland, 1976). Yet, within a few years the crisis subsided; the experimentalists returned to business as usual; self-reflection largely disappeared from the pages of the major journals. At the same time, for a small number of beleaguered but undaunted souls, there loomed but dimly the vision of a reconstructed social psychology.

The Emergence of Social Construction

For me, exploration of this vision grew importantly from attempts to defend my initial criticisms. This was not only true in the general sense that for purposes of defense it was essential that I broaden my acquaintance with relevant work in philosophy, sociology, history, and other relevant fields. However, the possibility of a positive alternative to the traditional view of the field was also invited more specifically by what seemed to me the most powerful attack on my thesis of social psychology as history. To paraphrase this interesting line of argument: my thesis was altogether too concerned with public activity. To be sure, social patterns were in constant flux; styles, ideologies, public opinion, and customs are subject to historical shifts, and psychologists (to the extent they are read or understood), might affect these proclivities. However, social psychology is not interested in exterior ephemera. Its task is to lay bear the psychological bases of these patterns – how it is that basic processes of cognition, motivation, prejudice, and the like function in human organisms. These processes are not unstable; they are inherent in human nature. Only their expressions are mutable.

This defense did seem a little awkward, inasmuch as the field was ostensibly dedicated to predicting and understanding social behavior, in effect, patterns that are inherently unstable. However, there were few means by which I could be certain that the underlying processes were not both stable and universal. But why the uncertainty; and how could the critic be so certain that there were such enduring phenomena? How could we judge whether the internal processes were indeed ephemeral or universal? This question continued to haunt me until ultimately a rebuttal was forthcoming. And it was this rebuttal that furnished the critical turning point toward a new, constructionist social psychology. The important reading for me was Gadamer's (1975) classic work *Truth and method*. Gadamer was grappling with the question that had plagued hermeneutic scholars for several centuries: how is it that we can understand the meaning within a text – what the author is attempting to say? The question had never yielded a satisfactory answer within the hermeneutic tradition, a fact that was very interesting to me indeed. For the problem of how readers understand the meaning within texts is essentially equivalent to how it is psychologists comprehend the psychological processes giving rise to overt action. For me, the pivotal concept in Gadamer's work is the "horizon of understanding." As he argued, a reader approaches a text with a forestructure of understanding in place, essentially a range of interpretive tendencies that will typically dominate the way in which the text is understood. Although Gadamer went on to search for means by which the reader can suspend the horizon of understanding, I was much less impressed with this account than by the ambient resonances of this concept with other intellectual developments. In his work, *The structure of scientific revolutions*, Thomas Kuhn had demonstrated the ways in which the interpretation of scientific evidence is largely guided by a paradigm of understanding (or theoretical forestructure) central to the field at any given time. As he reasoned, the scientist carries out research and interprets the findings in terms of a theoretical (and metatheoretical) framework (or set of *a priori* assumptions) shared within a particular community. Much the same conclusion was reached, albeit on a different terrain, by the literary theorist, Stanley Fish. As Fish (1980) convincingly argued, when readers attempt to understand a text, they do so as members of an interpretive community. Their interpretations will inevitably bear the conventional understandings of the community.

As these various arguments converged, it became apparent that there is no reading of a "psychological interior" save through the presumptions one brings to bear. People's actions do not transparently reveal the character of their subjective worlds or mental processes; however, once psychologists bring a given theory to bear, they locate "internal events" in its terms. These theories have no basis in fact; any facts about the mind used in their support would have necessitated the use of such theories. In effect, the psychological world so dear to the heart of many social psychologists is a social construction, and the findings used to justify statements about this world are only valid insofar as one remains within the theoretical (and metatheoretical) paradigms of the field. Research findings don't have any meaning until they are interpreted, and these interpretations are not demanded by the findings themselves. They result from a process of negotiating meaning within the community.

One could, of course, see such conclusions as spelling the end of social psychology (and indeed, the end of science itself as a truth telling institution). However, such a dolorous conclusion is scarcely warranted. For, after all, the social constructionist critique is itself based on a set of premises, assumptions, and negotiations, and the pivotal concept within this domain is that of social process. Can we envision a social psychology, then, that views itself as inherently a social process and its contributions to the culture primarily in terms of social construction? The beginnings of this vision were developed in my 1982 book, *Toward transformation in social knowledge*. The exploration of its potential continues to the present.

Social Psychology in a Constructionist Key

As I presently see it, a social psychology informed by a constructionist view of knowledge vitally expands and enriches the scope of the field. Certain positive contributions of the past are salvaged, and the largely wasted efforts of the tradition abandoned. More importantly, a new range of significant endeavors is invited. I am not speaking here of a pie-in-the-sky vision, a dream on paper.

Rather, as I have tried to outline in a recent volume, *Realities and relationships*, movements toward a reconstructed psychology are in evidence throughout psychology [1] around the globe,[2] and resonate with similar movements across the human sciences and the humanities.[3] Michael Billig's contribution to the present volume is but one representative. Let me outline, then, what I see as the three major challenges of a social psychology in a constructionist mold, and describe representative offerings in each case:

The empirical challenge

There is nothing about a social constructionist psychology that rules out empirical research. However, the place of such research and its particular potentials are substantially refigured. From a constructionist perspective, the traditional attempt to test hypotheses about universal processes of the mind (cognition, motivation, perception, attitudes, prejudice, self-conception) seems at a minimum misguided, and more tragically, an enormous waste of resources (intellectual, monetary, temporal, material). Not only is the subject matter itself a social construction, thus not subject to empirical evaluation outside a particular tradition of interpretation, but such research represents the arrogation of a uniquely Western ontology of the mind to the status of the universal.

More positively from a constructionist perspective, traditional empirical research is most effectively deployed in (1) illustrating interesting or challenging ideas, and (2) tracing patterns of conduct of major significance to the society. In the case of bringing challenging ideas to life, the classic work of Asch (1952) on social conformity, and Milgram (1974) on obedience are illustrative. Neither of these inquiries proved anything about social life; they do not necessarily demonstrate anything about either conformity or obedience (which are themselves interpretations subject to challenge and negotiation). However, in the hands of these scholars, the data dramatically succeeded in bringing provocative ideas about human interaction to life, thus generating debate and dialogue. Both researchers raise fundamental questions about the power of social influence, and the needs and problems of both belonging to social groups and remaining independent of them. To be sure, there are many other resources for raising such issues, for example, in history, literature, and case studies. However, if the ethical and ideological burden is acceptable, the researcher's advantage is that he/she is able to craft the needed illustration in concrete terms and to demonstrate its potential generality in the population.

Many social psychologists, informed by constructionist concerns, are discontent with the political implications of human experimentation, and choose instead to explore the ways in which reality is constructed within the society. These studies, which focus on the discursive means by which we determine what is true and good, are emancipatory in their aims. Rather than trying to demonstrate universal principles, they use discourse analysis to foreground our particular habits of constructing the world and ourselves. The chief aim is to demonstrate the problems created by these discursive conventions and to open discussion on alternative intelligibilities. Thus, for example, investigators have used discourse analytic methods to unsettle the traditional gender distinction (Kitzinger, 1987), the concept of individual memory (Middleton & Edwards, 1990), the rationalities of social unrest (Potter & Reicher, 1987), accepted truths about alcohol (Taylor, 1990), and attributions of intention (Edwards & Potter, 1992), and the idea of factual or objective reports (Wooffitt, 1992). Others have been concerned with the ways in which forms of rhetoric or speech conventions inadvertently guide our presumptions of the real. In the case of the self, for example, Mary Gergen and I (Gergen & Gergen, 1988) have attempted to show how narrative conventions – or traditional ways of telling stories – provide the forestructure through which we make ourselves intelligible to others. In contrast to the traditional experimental work I described earlier, the self is viewed, then, as achieved through dialogic processes that are continuously in motion.

It should finally be added that traditional empirical methods have additional purchase in actuarial terms, that is, in providing information on recurring patterns of social conduct. The capacity of survey researchers to predict election outcomes, insurance companies to predict auto accidents, and population experts to forecast birth rates are illustrative of this potential. Laboratory research in social psychology is generally ill suited for this task, inasmuch as the research context is typically rarefied and the findings poor in ethological validity. However, attempts by social psychologists to predict health indicators (e.g. heart failure, cancer, length of life) have been especially promising. Largely removing the research from its laboratory confines, researchers trace the correlations between a range of social variables (e.g. social support, traumatic events, personal dispositions) and a range of health variables. The results of such research are often highly suggestive in terms of possible health policies and practices. To be sure, the phenomena in such research are socially constructed; labels such as heart failure and social support are culturally and historically contingent. However, because these constructs are widely shared in the culture, and are congenial to the prevailing ideology of health, the discipline contributes to the society by adopting its terms and furnishing information on patterns of action constructed in just this way.

The reflexive challenge

As we find, from a social constructionist perspective empirical research is not abandoned; its goals are simply revisioned in such a way that its outcomes are more directly keyed to societal concerns – provoking cultural dialogues, challenging traditional understandings, and furnishing information directly relevant to its investments. At the same time social constructionism invites a range of additional pursuits. Among the more prominent is that of reflexive deliberation. That people in relationships move toward collective agreements on what is real, rational, and right, and articulate these agreements in their forms of language, seems apparent enough. Whether a primitive society or a scientific subculture, we develop working languages for carrying out our collective lives. For the constructionist, however, there are significant dangers inhering in the solidification ("objectification") of any given way of constructing the world. Univocal agreements occlude possibilities for self-reflective appraisals. To reflect critically on one's pursuits, using the very rationalities that legitimate these pursuits, one can scarcely do other than rationalize the status quo. More importantly, those who do not share the premises are rendered "other," often dismissed, disparaged, or denigrated.

From this perspective, it is essential to set in motion processes of reflexive deliberation, processes which call attention to the historically and culturally situated character of the taken-for-granted world, which reflect on their potentials for suppression, and which open a space for other voices in the dialogues of the culture. These are indeed worthy goals, and specifically invited by a constructionist orientation to social psychology. Sensitive to the constructed character of our realities, to processes by which realities are generated and eroded, and the pragmatic implications of language formations, the constructionist social psychologist is optimally positioned to incite reflexive dialogue – both within the discipline of psychology, and within the culture more generally. Again, these are not idle speculations. Reflexive deliberation has been, and continues to be, a significant form of scholarship within the constructionist frame. Concerned with the potentially strangulating and oppressive potentials within the taken for granted assumptions of the discipline, psychologists have explored, for example, the limitations of traditional conceptions of individual psychological processes (Sampson, 1975, 1978), child development (Bradley, 1993), mental illness (Sarbin & Mancuso, 1980), and anger (Tavris, 1989). Concerned with the culture more generally, constructionist psychologists have probed, for example, the problems and potentials of the romanticist and modernist conceptions of the person (Gergen, 1991), the problematic assumptions underlying the way in which students are constructed in the educational sphere (Walkerdine, 1988), and the subtle sustenance of nationalist ideology (Billig, 1995)!

The creative challenge

Traditional social psychology largely contented itself with charting existing patterns of behavior. The task of the scientist, in this case, was to give accurate accounts of existing reality. Because existing reality is taken to be an instantiation of universal and transhistorical processes, the field took little interest in molding new futures for the society. Further, because contributions to new cultural forms would require a value commitment, and social psychology aimed to be value neutral, there was scant investment in professional pursuits directly concerned with social change. This attitude of cultural disengagement stands in stark contrast to a constructionist social psychology. Already we have seen the constructionist concern with ethical and political issues manifest itself in reflexive scholarship. To engage in critique is to presume a criterion of "the good," toward which effective critical analysis inherently strives. However, the constructionist mandate for social transformation is far more profound. For the constructionist, the discourses of the profession are themselves constitutive of cultural life. When they serve to mold the intelligibilities of the culture – making distinctions, furnishing rationales for action, and implicitly evaluating forms of conduct – they also prepare our future. This may be a future which simply recapitulates the past, which sustains the taken-for-granted assumptions of the culture. Such are typically the effects of a social psychology based on a realist (or objectifying) account of science. However, for the constructionist, social-psychological inquiry can enter into the creation of new forms of cultural life. With the development of new theoretical languages, research practices, forms of expression, and practices of intervention, so does the field invite cultural transformation.

Constructionism places no particular constraints or demands on the scholar in terms of preferred visions of the future. However, there has been perhaps an inevitable tendency among constructionist scholars to develop theories and practices that favor communalism over individualism, interdependence over independence, participatory over hierarchical decision making, and societal integration as opposed to traditionalist segmentation. Such leanings are virtually derivative of the constructionist view of knowledge as socially constructed. To illustrate the way in which theoretical work is used to effect such ends, let us return to the continuing theme of the self. As we found, within the experimentalist tradition self-conception is usually treated as more or less self-contained within the individual, a feature of universal and biologically based processes of mental functioning. Such a view perpetuates the long-standing individualist practices within the culture, stressing as it does the independent functioning of the individual. Social institutions, on this account, are byproducts of individual interaction. Or to play out the implications, friendship, marriage, family, and community are artificial contrivances, possibly resulting from our individual insufficiencies. The sufficient person is an independent being.

Eschewing the individualist tradition, and giving value to relationship over isolation, ultimately requires an alternative to the traditional conception of the self – in effect, creative theoretical work. In this vein, theorists such as John Shotter (1993a, 1993b), Edward Sampson (1993), and Hermans and Kempen (1993) have begun to develop a deeply socialized conception of self. Drawing importantly from earlier writings of Vygotsky (1978) and Bakhtin (1981), individual functioning is held to be inseparable from relationship. The vast share of human action grows out of interchange, and is directed into further interchange. As I write these lines I am reflecting myriad dialogues with professionals and students, for example, and am speaking into a relationship with readers. The words are not "my own," the authorship is misleading. Rather, I am a carrier of relationships, forging them into yet new relationships. This work is further complemented by a series of creative theoretical formulations attempting to reconstitute traditional psychological terms. For example, for Potter and Wetherell (1987), attitudes are not lodged within the heads of private individuals; to possess an attitude is to take a position in a conversation. For Billig (1987), there is little reason to examine the rational processes lying behind language, somewhere in the brain; rather, to speak rationally is to engage in accepted forms of rhetoric.

It will prove illustrative to contrast my work on the self-concept within the old paradigm (mechanistic, individualistic, experimental), with recent, relationally oriented explorations of emotion (Gergen, 1994). Let us first deconstruct the traditional emotional terms – concepts such as anger, love, fear, joy, and the like. That is, let us view such terms as social constructions, and not as indexing differentiated properties of the mind or the cortex. With the aid of such deconstruction we are relieved of the endlessly burdensome search for the signified – that is, the elusive essence of anger, love, and so on. Further, the individualist conception of such terms may be bracketed. This critique also enables us to view the language of emotion, not as a set of terms referring to off-stage properties of the mind, but as performatives. That is, when we say, "I am angry," "I love you," and the like, we are not trying to describe a far off land of the mind, or a state of the neurons. Rather, we are performing in a relationship, and the phrases themselves are only a constituent of more fully embodied actions, including movements of the limbs, vocal intonations, patterns of gaze, and so on.

At the same time, let us not view these performances as purely individual. Rather, they are more adequately viewed as integers in more complex patterns of relationship. They cannot be performed at random, but require the actions of others as invitations; and once performed, they invite only a circumscribed array of actions on the part of others. Let us view these extended patterns of interchange as *emotional scenarios*. In documenting emotional scenarios for anger, for example, we find that there are only certain actions that warrant anger as an intelligible response (e.g. insult, expressions of hostility). And, once anger has been performed, the other is not free to act in any way; convention requires that one react, for example, with an apology, with an exonerating explanation, or with anger. Or to put it more broadly, we find emotional expressions to be constituents of extended forms of interchange, somewhat like cultural dances, and they gain their intelligibility and importance only by virtue of their placement within such dances. Emotional performances are no more possessions of the single individual than are the words we speak.

Although innovative theoretical formulations such as these are one means of contributing to a process of societal transformation, we find additional professional means of pursuing such ends. For example, constructionist psychologists have also pursued alternative forms of methodology, reasoning as they do that research methods also convey values and ideologies. Feeling that experimental technologies place a divide between the scientist and subject, privilege the scientist's voice over the subject's, and invite manipulation, they seek means of broadening the range of research methods. Qualitative methodologies (Denzin & Lincoln, 1994) are one significant step toward an enriched social psychology, as are discourse analytic procedures. Further, we are invited to experiment with our very forms of scientific expression. Professional writings in social psychology inherit stale traditions of rhetoric; they are intelligible to but a minute community of scholars, and even within this community they are overly formal, monologic, defensive, and dry. The nature of the social world scarcely demands such an archaic form of expression. Constructionism invites the scholar to expand the repertoire of expression, to explore ways of speaking and writing to a broader audience, perhaps with multiple voices, and a richer range of rhetoric. Recent examples would include the feminist writings of Mary Gergen (1988, 1992), and the first undergraduate text in constructionist social psychology by Rogers et al (1995).[4]

In conclusion, I find a constructionist social psychology one that is unbounded in potential: it neither specifies the margins of the discipline nor fixes the parameters of inquiry in advance. It is psychology closely tied to cultural life; inviting passionate engagement; linking intellectual work with change-oriented practices; favoring provocative dialogue both within and external to the discipline; firing the imagination of futures; and yet, retaining considerable humility toward to its own assumptions and respect for the assumptions of others. The message of a social psychology in a constructionist frame is, then, profoundly optimistic.

Notes

1. See, for example, Kessen (1990) in developmental psychology, Hermans and Kempen (1993) in personality studies, Spence (1982) and Penn and Frankfurt (in press) in individual and family therapy, Hare-Mustin and Marecek (1988) and M. Gergen (1988) in feminist psychology, and Danziger (1990) in the historical analysis of psychology.
2. Among many others, we may include Ibanez (1991) in Spain; Bradley (1993) in Australia; White and Epston (1990) in New Zealand, Misra (1994) in India, Schnitman and Fuks (1993) in Argentina, Hermans and Kempen (1993) in the Netherlands, Engstrom (1990) in Finland, Middleton and Edwards (1990) in the UK, and Wilutzki in Germany, Stam (1990) in Canada, and Petrillo (1995) in Italy.
3. See, for example Coulter's (1989) work in sociology, Lutz (1988) work in anthropology, White (1978) in history, McNamee (1989) in communication, Fiske (1989) in cultural studies, and

Rorty (1991) in philosophy, and Gregory (1994) in geographic studies.

4. An additional work on social construction by Vivien Burr (1995) is also a significant new entry at the university text level, but the writing in this case is more traditional.

Further Reading

Burr, V. (1995). *An introduction to social constructionism.* London: Routledge. An introductory discussion of basic issues and challenges of social constructionist social psychology.

Gergen, K. J. (1994). *Realities and relationships: Soundings in social construction.* Cambridge, MA: Harvard University Press. A professional level treatment of the development and logic of social psychology in a social constructionist frame, along with an extended discussion of relational theory.

Middleton, D., & Edwards, D. (Eds.) (1990). *Collective remembering*. London: Sage. Contributions to understanding human memory as a social – as opposed to individual – phenomenon.

Shotter, J. (1993). *Conversational realities.* London: Sage. An advanced view of various intricacies of social construction in everyday life.

Shotter, J., & Gergen, K. J. (Eds.) (1989). *Texts of identity*. London: Sage. Contributions to understanding individual identity in terms of cultural texts.

References

Asch, S. (1952). *Social psychology*. Englewood Cliffs, NJ: Prentice-Hall.

Bakhtin, M. (1981). *The dialogic imagination.* Austin, TX: University of Texas Press.

Billig, M. (1987). *Arguing and thinking*. London: Cambridge University Press.

Billig, M. (1995). *Banal nationalism*. London: Sage.

Bradley, B. (1993). A serpent's guide to children's "theories of mind." *Theory and Psychology*, *3*, 497–521.

Burr, V. (1995). *An introduction to social constructionism.* London: Routledge.

Coulter, J. (1989). *Mind in action*. Oxford: Blackwell.

Danziger, K. (1990). *Constructing the subject: Historical origins of psychological research*. Cambridge: Cambridge University Press.

Denzin, N. K., & Lincoln, Y. S. (Eds.) (1994). *Handbook of qualitative research*. Thousand Oaks, CA: Sage.

Edwards, D., & Potter, J. (1992). *Discursive psychology*. London: Sage.

Engestrom, Y., & Middleton, D. (1990). Communal cognition in the workplace. In D. Middleton and D. Edwards (Eds.), *Collective remembering*. London: Sage.

Fish, S. (1980). *Is there a text in this class? The authority of interpretive communities.* Cambridge, MA: Harvard University Press.

Fiske, S. (1987). *Television culture*. London: Routledge.

Fiske, S. (1989). *Television culture*. London: Routledge.

Gadamer, H. (1975). *Truth and method.* New York: Seabury.

Gergen, K. J. (1965). Interactions goals and personalistic feedback as factors affecting the presentations of self. *Journal of Personality and Social Psychology*, *1*, 413–424.

Gergen, K. J. (1973). Social psychology as history. *Journal of Personality and Social Psychology*, *26*, 309–320.

Gergen, K. J. (1982/1991). *Toward transfor-*

mation in social knowledge. New York: Springer Verlag. 2nd ed. London: Sage.

Gergen, K. J. (1991). *The saturated self*. New York: Basic Books.

Gergen, K. J. (1994). *Reality and relationships, soundings in social construction*. Cambridge, MA: Harvard University Press.

Gergen, K. J., & Gergen, M. M. (1988). Narrative and the self as relationship. In L. Berkowitz (Ed.), *Advances in experimental social psychology* (Vol. 21, pp. 17–56). New York: Academic Press.

Gergen, M. M. (1988). Toward a feminist metatheory and methodology in the social sciences. In M. Gergen (Ed.), *Feminist thought and the structure of knowledge*. New York: New York University Press.

Gergen, M. M. (1992). From mod masculinity to post-mod macho: A feminist replay. In S. Kvale (Ed.), *Psychology and postmodernism*. London: Sage.

Gregory, D. (1994). *Geographical imaginations*. Cambridge: Blackwell.

Harré, R., & Secord, P. (1972). *The explanation of social behaviour*. Oxford: Blackwell.

Hare-Mustin, R., & Marecek, J. (1988). The meaning of difference: Gender theory, postmodernism and psychology. *American Psychologist*, *43*, 455–464.

Hermans, J., & Kempen, H. (1993). *The dialogical self*. New York: Academic Press.

Ibanez, T. (1991). Social psychology and the rhetoric of truth. *Theory and Psychology*, 1, 187–201.

Kessen, W. (1990). *The rise and fall of development*. Worcester, MA: Clark University Press.

Kitzinger, C. (1987). *The social construction of lesbianism*. London: Sage.

Kuhn, T. (1970). *The structure of scientific revolutions*. Chicago, IL: University of Chicago Press.

Lutz, C. (1988). *Unnatural emotions*. Chicago, IL: University of Chicago Press.

McGuire, W. (1973). The yin and yang of progress in social psychology: Seven koans. *Journal of Personality and Social Psychology*, *26*, 446–456.

McNamee, S. (1989). Creating new narratives in family therapy: An application of social constructionism. *Journal of Applied Communication Research*, *17*, 92–112.

Mead, G. H. (1934). *Mind, self and society from the standpoint of a social behaviorist*. Chicago, IL: University of Chicago Press.

Middleton, D., & Edwards, D. (1990). *Collective remembering*. London: Sage.

Milgram, S. (1974). *Obedience to authority*. New York: Harper & Row.

Misra, G. (1994). Psychology of control: Cross-cultural considerations. *Journal of Indian Psychology*, *12*, 8–45.

Penn, P., & Frankfurt, M. (in press). Creating a participant text: Writing, multiple voices, narrative multiplicity. *Family Process*.

Petrillo, G. (1995). Pragmatics of communication and psychosocial theories from a constructionist interactionist view. In I. Lubek, R van Hezewijk, G. Pheterson, & C. Tolman (Eds.), *Trends and issues in theoretical psychology*. New York: Springer Verlag.

Potter, J., & Reicher, S. D. (1987). Discourses of community and conflict: The organization of social categories in accounts of a riot. *British Journal of Social Psychology*, *26*, 25–40.

Potter, J., & Wetherell, M. (1987). *Discourse and social psychology: Beyond attitudes and behavior*. London: Sage.

Ring, K. (1967). Some sober questions about frivolous values. *Journal of Experimental Social Psychology*, *3*, 113–123.

Rogers, R. S., Stenner, P., Gleeson, K., & Rogers, W. S. (1995). *Social psychology: A critical agenda*. London: Polity Press.

Rorty, R. (1991). *Objectivity, relativism and truth*. New York: Cambridge University Press.

Sampson, E. (1975). Psychology and the American ideal. *Journal of Personality and Social Psychology*, *35*, 767–782.

Sampson, E. (1978). Scientific paradigms and social values: Wanted – a scientific revolution. *Journal of Personality and Social Psychology*, *36*, 1332–1343.

Sampson, E. (1993). *Celebrating the other: A dialogic account of human nature*. New York: Harvester.

Sarbin, T., & Mancuso, J. (1980). *Schizophrenia: Medical diagnosis or verdict?* Elmsford, NY: Pergamon.

Schnitman, D., & Fuks, S. (1993). Paradima y crisis. Entre el riesgo y law posibilidad. *Psyckhe*, *2*, 33–42.

Shotter, J. (1993a). *Cultural politics of everyday life*. Toronto: University of Toronto Press.

Shotter, J. (1993b). *Conversational realities.* London: Sage.

Spence, D. (1982). *Narrative truth and historical truth*. New York: Norton.

Stam, H. (1990). Rebuilding the ship at sea: The historical and theoretical problems of constructionist epistemologies in psychology. *Canadian Psychology*, *31*, 239–253.

Strickland, L. (1976). Priorities and paradigms. In L. Strickland, F. Aboud, & K. Gergen (Eds.), *Social psychology in transition*. New York: Plenum Press.

Tavris, C. (1989). *Anger: The misunderstood emotion*. New York: Simon and Schuster.

Taylor, C. (1990). *The ethics of authenticity*. Cambridge, MA: Harvard University Press.

Vygotsky, L. (1978). *Mind in society: The development of higher psychological processes.* Cambridge, MA: Harvard University Press.

Walkerdine, V. (1988). *The mastery of reason*. London: Routledge, Kegan & Paul.

White, H. (1978). *Tropics of discourse*. Baltimore, MD: Johns Hopkins University Press.

White, M., & Epston, D. (1990). *Narrative means to therapeutic ends*. New York: Norton.

Wilutzki, U. and Wiesner, M. (in press). Segregation or cooperation? A social constructionist perspective on drug use and drug work. *Journal of Systemic Therapies.*

Wooffitt, R. (1992). *Telling tales of the unexpected: The organization of factual accounts*. London: Harvester Wheatsheaf.

9

Social Life as Rule-governed Patterns of Joint Action

Rom Harré

Rom Harré began his academic career as a mathematician, lecturing in the University of the Punjab, Lahore. He did graduate work in philosophy under J. L. Austin. He has lectured in philosophy of science at Birmingham, Leicester and Oxford University. He is Emeritus Fellow of Linacre College, Oxford. Since 1978 he has been Adjunct Professor in the Computer Science and Philosophy program at Binghamton University, and since 1989 Professor of Psychology at Georgetown University, Washington DC. His publications include *Varieties of realism*, *Social being*, *Personal being*, *The explanation of social behaviour* with P. F. Secord, *Pronouns and people* with P. Muhlhausler and *The discursive mind* with Grant Gillett. He co-edited the *Blackwell Encyclopedic Dictionary of Psychology* with Roger Lamb.

Introduction: Choosing a Paradigm

Every science is built on the basis of some metaphysical scheme. In the course of its growth and development it may shift from its original foundation, even working with two incompatible metaphysics at one and the same time. This seems to be the state of affairs in contemporary social psychology. Many social psychologists set up their work within a framework of causal concepts targeted on different kinds of human behavior. They conceive of their empirical studies as experiments, and use statistical "packages" in the analysis of their "data." Research results are then presented as either as descriptions of patterns of behavior, or as hypotheses about the working of causal mechanisms. These alternatives are frequently elided under the auspices of a metaphysical theory about causality that derives ultimately from the eighteenth-century Scottish philosopher David Hume. For Hume, and many who have followed his lead, causality is no more than a pattern of regular concomitances among types of events. There may be contexts in which the Humean concept of causality is the appropriate metaphysical scheme, but there are also many in which it turns out to be seriously misleading. One of the main drawbacks of such an austere concept is that it tends to suggest that explanation and prediction are essentially the same, and this in turn leads to a neglect of theory. Some who have become critical of the Humean way with science have turned to cognitive science to delve deeper into the sources of behavior, but I believe that social psychology has made its most significant contributions to our knowledge of ourselves in a research frame drawn from a very different theoretical basis, one which is less beholden to any abstract metaphysical scheme. This is the paradigm based on the idea expressed in the title of this paper; the idea that social life consists mostly of patterns of joint action controlled by rules and conventions, some immanent in habitual action, some serving as explicit templates for proper behavior. The media by which these patterns are produced are mainly discursive, that is they consist in the joint use of symbolic tools to accomplish projects, both large and small.

The theoretical foundation for which explanations employ the concepts of "rule" and "meaning" been variously called "ethogenics," "social constructionism," and, more recently, "discursive psychology." The conceptual basis of the approach is the principle that we should take people to be active agents, whose conduct is to be seen as attempts to realize, together with others, plans, projects, and intentions according to the rules and norms of the local society. The means for realizing such projects, are, it is assumed, predominantly discursive. For example they would be realized in such social interactions as the setting up of organized groups under a leader, the cultivation of friendship and enmity, and so on, achieved by the use of various symbolic systems, prominent among which is language. Empirical studies framed in this theoretical scheme involve recording and analyzing real human conduct in real settings. The results of such studies would be presented, not as putative causal laws, but as systems of rules and conventions. Generalities, describing repeated *patterns* of joint action, are to be interpreted either as culturally modified ethological responses, or, more frequently, as recording the implementation of cultural conventions, effectively reporting hypotheses about the "grammars" of different kinds of joint action. The word "grammar" has come to be used in this context as a result of the realization that there is a strong analogy between the conventional patterning of language with respect to the significant arrangement of word classes and the way sequences of actions are organized with respect to act classes. For example an action serving as an excuse would normally follow a protest, though there are cases in which a subtle social point is made by performing the excuse bearing action prior to the infringement. Such moves exploit the existence of the standard convention, of course.

I shall call these two schemes the "causal" framework and the "action-rule" framework respectively. The complexity and multi-faceted character of human life is such that both schemes will be needed, each having its appropriate field of application. Some research territories, such as romantic love, are unlikely to be successfully explored without the complementary use of both.

Psychology: The Hybrid Science

The patterns of human life are of many kinds, falling into three broad families. There are cognitive activities, involving the skillful manipulation of symbols, both publicly and privately. Then there are patterns of behavior brought into being through the triggering of fixed action patterns, the propensities for which are inherited, but subject to much cultural refinement. There is a third family of patterns of behavior, those that are the result of the inculcation of habits and of training. Underlying all three families are the neural states and processes through which those manipulations, responses, and habits are implemented. To the planning of the study of the discursive activities through which cognitive tasks are accomplished concepts like "meaning," "intentionality" (that is directedness of an action to something other than itself), and "grammar" (the normative organization of action patterns) are germane; to the planning of the study of fixed action patterns concepts like "causality" and "mechanism" are appropriate. It would be too obvious a mistake to import biological concepts into the planning of studies of discursive interactions. But there are many activities one is trained to perform which, though discursive in origin, soon take the form of habits of mind, the performance of which may look very like the patterns of events produced by causal mechanisms. One must be on one's guard not to be tempted into transferring the metaphysics and methodology proper to genuinely causal processes to phenomena which only look like them. Sociality, in all its many facets, involves both the genetically maintained givens of human ethology, the study of which belongs to biology, and the locally ingrained habits and customs of human culture, the study of which belongs to an extended version of discourse analysis. Some of social psychology's peculiar difficulties and the seeming implausibility of many of its theories and the unsuitability of its experimental methods to its research material, stem from the fact that habit-driven forms of symbolic interaction may appear, at first sight very similar to causally driven forms of ethological interaction.

What does it matter whether social habits and customs are assimilated to causality or to "grammar?" There are two dimensions on which genuinely and pseudo-causal patterns differ significantly. One is how they can be changed, rules and genes coming under quite different technologies of transformation. The other is how they are acquired. Ethological responses are inherited, habits are learned. The research program of developmental social psychology will look very different depending on whether it is the sources of fixed action patterns that we seek or the origins of well-trained social habits.

In the action-rule framework social *psychology* is to be distinguished from micro-sociology by the insertion of individuals into the analytical scheme. This is done by the use of concepts such as "habit," "training," and "skill" to link individuals to the patterns of joint action in which they participate. This reflects the distinction between a cause-based explanatory scheme, in which the investigator aiming at more than merely reporting a Humean concomitance is under an obligation to develop hypotheses about mechanisms, and a rule-based scheme in which an investigator is under an obligation to account for how the individual actor comes to be able to follow the rules. As Wittgenstein (1953) emphasized, it makes sense to train someone to follow a rule by habit, almost as if the conditions for activating the habit functioned like a cause. It is by training that we learn to calculate in accordance with the rules of arithmetic, without, as adults ever consciously consulting them. It is by training that we learn to be polite to our elders, and to offer reasons for refusing invitations, and so on.

In moving from a mental process metaphysics to a discursive action framework we abandon more than just the causality principle. We also leave behind both the subjective/objective and the inner/outer distinctions, the merger of which has been a prominent organizing principle in traditional psychology of all fields, not just social! The metaphor of "internalization" has long served to refer to what an individual learns from collective resources and by participating in joint activities. This terminology tends subtly to reinforce the idea that there is a hidden realm of "inner processes" to which only the actor has access. Instead, new paradigm social psychologists make use of a distinction between discursive actions performed publicly and those performed privately. Sometimes the latter are done as part of a rehearsal for the former. In general we reject the methodological principle that public actions are the outward and visible product of a sequence of private actions. There are both public and private actions, falling largely under the same conventions of correctness and meaningfulness. Nor do we subscribe to the AI–cognitive science thesis that by analogy there must be a superprivate performance behind both public and private performances, "information processing" that is neither conscious manipulation of symbols nor chemical and physical goings on in the brain and nervous system. Of course this is not behaviorism because we do not suppose that either public or private actions are caused by environmental contingencies either mediately or immediately.

In what follows I shall be presenting not only some of the achievements of those who have based their work on the second foundation but also an important example of a research field in which both schemes are required. I should like to emphasize once again that the research domain of social psychology seems to require, in different topic areas, either one or, in some cases such as the social psychology of the emotions, a subtle interweaving of both the causal and the discursive metaphysics and methodologies.

Discursive Methodology

At this point an important caveat must be entered. The word "rule" is readily misunderstood, though less so if it is combined with the metaphor of a "grammar" of action. It is rare indeed that a group of people will knowingly control their everyday social conduct by reference to explicit rules, that is that they will *follow* rules. Where this does happen we usually recognize, even in exotic cultures, that we are witnessing (or taking part in) some formal or ceremonial occasion, such as a judicial trial set in a courtroom or a ceremony unfamiliar to most of the participants such as a bar mitzvah. In discursive psychology "rule" serves as a technical term for labeling what a social psychologist would write down to express the local norms of proper and improper behavior. Here we should speak of people acting "in accordance with" rules. Of course, people do have conscious recourse to rules in situations of disorder or uncertainty in which they tend to behave as social psychologists reminding themselves and others what the correct procedures are.

Within the discursive framework the upshot of a piece of social scientific research would consist of four items:

1. a specification of the intentions, aims and projects of the participants who engage in some social activity and their mutual "positions" in local moral orders;
2. a catalogue of the kinds of actions they performed, the structures or sequences into which these actions enter, and what the performance of this or that sequence achieves;
3. a set or sets of rules expressing the non-native constraints on action in the assumed settings;
4. a specification of the settings appropriate to this or that social activity and with criteria by which those settings are created/recognized as such.

What role is envisaged for the "experiment," the empirical technique that was supposed to guarantee that the reports of social psychologists had some authenticity as "science?" We need to be reminded that there are two ways in which complex, structured entities can be decomposed for scientific purposes. In an experiment a structured phenomenon is decomposed empirically, by separating its properties into two classes, those referred to by parameters, which will be held constant in the experiment, and those referred to by variables one or more of which will be changed and subsequent changes looked for in the others. It is essential for such a procedure to be of any scientific value that the properties to which empirically separated variables and parameters refer are the same properties as they referred to in the undecomposed state of the phenomenon (Vygotsky, 1962). This condition is rarely satisfied in social psychology (Harré & Secord, 1972). However, this does not mean that analytical decomposition must be given up as a project. In many sciences, complex structures are decomposed analytically, in thought experiments. In most cases this should be the route taken by social psychologists. By using techniques of discourse analysis and other ways of decomposing complex wholes into their significant parts the properties of complex wholes and those of their constituents are necessarily preserved during the analysis. A video record can be analyzed without destroying the phenomenon which has been recorded, whereas an intervention or a simplified experimental analog of some social interaction is almost sure to transform the phenomena into something else. To ask people what are their reactions to written descriptions of social phenomena, a technique which is sometimes presented as an experiment, is of course nothing of the sort. It is an exploration of the discursive skills of the participants. None the worse for that! But the results are about a text not about the phenomenon the text purports to describe.

One final methodological innovation must be highlighted. Analytical decomposition of recorded material from real episodes is carried on according to the promptings of a model or models. Taking yet another leaf from the book of the physical sciences, the work I shall be describing makes essential use of models in the sense of the physical sciences: namely, analogs. Models are used for the systematic development of a conceptual system, realized in a terminology, and used for analyzing the activities of participants in some class of social events. The models of most methodological significance have been the analogy of some social episodes to games and of others to conversations. Both are species of a more general model, the analogy between life episodes and stage plays, the dramaturgical model, but for the purposes of this exposition that generic model remains in the background. Games are at once a fertile source of insights into activities of everyday life, and themselves interesting social interactions capable of being researched with the same methodological framework as they themselves enliven. The same is true of the conversation model. Using speech-act theory (Austin, 1962; Searle, 1979) as the main analytical tool, according to which utterances are classified and their orderly production studied as if they were the performances of social acts, conversations can be seen as complex social interactions in which participants attempt to bring off their plans and intentions within a normative framework that is often local and particular to the social group engaged in mutual discourse. For example, in the reworking of traditional "attribution theory" we try to identify the discursive conventions by which persons who are differently positioned in a conversation use causal and moral concepts to accomplish a favorable interpretation of their actions or to achieve the more subtle upshot of having their actions taken as "things that befell them" (Hewstone, 1989) and so avoid taking responsibility for them.

Some Applications of Discursive Methodology

There have been four main groups of studies from which I would like to draw in this exposition. There have been those which have broken new ground, for example studies of the social psychology of public disorder (Marsh, Rosser, & Harré, 1977). Then there have been reworkings of some existing fields of study, for example of social aspects of the emotions (Lutz, 1988). There have also been studies in which the social psychology of social psychology has been the focus, for instance some recent work on attribution theory (Edwards & Potter, 1992). Finally there has been work on the social psychology of social change which seems to necessitate the use of an action-rule format for the analysis of the processes involved in the genesis of new social forms. In all these studies human conduct in real settings has been the research object. The explanatory framework has been non-causal, that is it has been assumed that what was being observed was purposeful action carried out in accordance with local rules and conventions by active agents.

The social psychology of hooliganism

This research was mainly the work of Peter Marsh and conducted primarily by participant observation with the Oxford United Football Club, although it has been replicated by several other in depth investigations. The focus of the work was on the seeming violent behavior of the supporters of rival teams culminating in skirmishes between groups of fans, sometimes during the game but for the most part before and after a match. How was this behavior to be described and how was it to be accounted for? It was obvious from the start that there was no place for causal concepts in this work. It was just not true that hooliganism was caused by any specific conditions that came to obtain at or near football grounds. It was something that people did, not something that happened to them. Nor, given the scale of the phenomenon, was there any prospect of a laboratory simulation, Zimbardo style, even had the ethical grounds for experiments in such conditions of potential violence been met. Marsh's work took two main directions. The first was a detailed study of the behavior in question, the apparently violent confrontations, seeming at first sight to be random acts of aggression, which was the way these events were portrayed by the national press. The most common phrase describing a football riot was "mindless violence". Yet as Marsh's work developed it soon became clear that clashes between fans were highly ordered, tightly structured, and bounded by strict limits as to the kinds of acts properly to be performed on such occasions. The second phase of the work was an investigation of the social structure of supporters' groups. This led to a study of how this structure was created, maintained, and transformed in relation to the "military" activities that took place on or near a football ground.

"Fights," on close inspection turned out to be ritual combats, in the sense that physical contact between protagonists of combative groups was rare. A standard repertoire of gestures, both threatening and insulting, were employed, seemingly to intimidate the rivals. At the same time a sequence of small steps of advance and retreat gradually led to one party occupying the bulk of the combat ground. Retrospectively these events were redescribed by the fans in the bloodiest and most violent terms, but nevertheless with a strictly maintained repertoire of possible redescriptions. Marsh recorded several incidents in which redescriptions that violated the implicit rhetorical norms were resisted and their perpetrators punished. The ritual character of the confrontations also emerged from a parallel research into the form and function of the chanting that has also been a notable feature of British football supporters' activities. Nigel Tattersfield (1981) collected a large number of chants, analyzed their content, and identified their occasions of use. Rival groups of supporters would arrive at the ground perhaps an hour before play was due to begin and, occupying opposite ends of the field, would begin antiphonal chanting, one replying to the other. Again this activity seemed to be highly ritualized and to be aimed at achieving a kind of dominance by one group over the other. Wit, somewhat simple and coarse grained, determination to outsing the opposition and the previous history of such encounters all played a role in the outcome of a bout of chanting.

This, then, was the complex social process by which something of value to the participants was accomplished. The "fights" and chanting could be looked at as games, contests played with standardized moves, and strictly controlled by rules, informally enforced by the older members of the supporter groups. The sequencing of acts had something of the character of a conversation analyzed in terms of speech-act theory. Both models were used with good effect.

Once the descriptive analysis had been completed two questions needed to be answered:

1. How did individuals come to be skilled in performances of these sorts, and what skills did they need to accomplish the repertoire of acts competently?
2. What was the point for the actors, of this elaborate "form of life"?

Marsh's investigations of the social structure of the "soccer tribe" revealed a formal hierarchy of roles and statuses, marked by costume, and consisting of differential rights and duties in the micro-society. The first of the above questions was answered by a careful study of how new members were gradually inducted into the group, and what skills they needed to be able to display at each stage of the induction of sufficient merit to rise in the status hierarchy. The elaborate "uniforms" of the fans, each club having its distinctive colors, were made up of items whose gradual acquisition and subsequent abandonment marked a "moral career," to use Goffman's vivid phrase for the patterns of status change in a micro-society. The second question was answered by the discovery that status was achieved, maintained, and transformed by performances in the ritual battles that I have described above. As a lad took part in more and more clashes, and played an honorable role in them, so he was permitted to acquire more of the uniform that marked a growing status. But as he became better known to the other members of his "tribe" and even to the members of other "tribes" so he could shed formal marks of belonging and of status. Marsh found a working terminology in use by the fans for describing status rankings among themselves.

The work of Elizabeth Rosser on violent outbreaks in schools revealed a very similar psychological background. Attacks on teachers were neither random nor spontaneous. They were highly ritualized and followed a tightly defined pattern in relation to the way the children interpreted what had been happening to them. Weak teachers were taken to be a sign that the authorities had written off a class, while strong teachers were admired and respected, their presence in the classroom an indication that this group of children were being taken seriously by the school management. The fact that these theories had little correspondence with the way that teachers saw the situation is, of course, irrelevant to the social psychology of violent attacks on teachers. But the disparity is of importance in large-scale studies of the entire institutional framework in which these dramatic performances take place.

Discursive psychology must subject its methods and results to itself. "To do the social psychology of discursive acts" is to engage in the production of a sequence of discursive acts oneself to the performers of which the same questions should be put as they put to the football fans. These questions were not addressed by Marsh and his co-workers, but they have been forcibly put by Potter and Wetherell (1987). Marsh et al. were, of course, engaged in a discursive enterprise, at least one of the points of which was to make available to the general public and to others in the profession of social psychologist a certain reading of the events in question. The version offered by Marsh et al. is a preferred reading, not because it reflects more accurately "what really happened" at the football grounds, but because it coheres with the fans' own accounts of "what really happened." In the light of those *accounts* the version created by Marsh el al. makes the events intelligible, and perhaps manageable.

But what about the great aim of science – to find the *truth*? Since social events are discursive events the discursive construction of events does indeed reveal a reality, one of many that may simultaneously exist in some social milieu. There is no second, deeper reality to which those constructions must conform. In physics there are the models created by physicists and there is the world of which they are models. But social reality just *is* an open set of models with which social actors, including social psychologists, manage their relations with one another, and strive to make their interactions mutually intelligible.

The social psychology of the emotions

In accordance with the action-rule oriented approach to psychology the most recent development in the treatment of the emotions, instanced by the work of such investigators as Wierzbicka (1992), is based on a functional thesis. Emotional displays and bodily feelings are for something. They happen to people but they are not just things that happen to people. This prompts the question: What is the role of displays of emotion in a strip of social life? The discursive account is based on the principle that emotion displays are expressions of trained, habitual, or inbuilt judgments. For example, a display of anger is an expression of the judgment that the angry person has been denigrated, abused, or injured in some way. Displays also frequently have illocutionary force as social acts; for example, the person to whom the anger is directed is thereby rebuked (Averill, 1982). Reapplying speech-act theory to displays of emotion as meaningful acts we are able to identify the illocutionary force of such display, that is to interpret it in terms of the local repertoire of social acts. Not only emotion displays, but that modern psychological phenomenon (Stearns & Stearns, 1988), emotion feelings, are to be treated the same way. So that a feeling interpreted, let us say, as anxiety, is an expression of a judgment that the situation that confronts one (or might confront one) is threatening, dangerous, worrisome, and so on and may have the illocutionary force of a warning.

The discursive turn in emotion studies moves the focus of research from the physiological states of individuals to the social acts that the public expression of these states serves to perform. Another consequence of this development is that attention needs to be paid to the local rules for expressing emotion. If emotions are primarily interpersonal acts and only secondarily expressed in intrapersonal subjective feelings, then the question of how a recipient of an emotional display is able to recognize the display as the performance of a particular act needs to be addressed. The recipient must be able to manage an open set of interpretative rules for the display and interpretation of emotions.

Care must be taken in how we interpret the general thesis that emotion displays are intentional acts, that is directed towards the social task of expressing public judgment of one's own behavior (embarrassment) or that of another (indignation) or of some state of affairs (grief). There is or should be no implication that an intentional act is a consciously directed act. Emotions, whether expressed in public displays or in private feelings, are generally not under the immediate second order control of the person who experiences or displays them. We can choose, once we have grown up a bit, whether to display or suppress the expression of an emotion (from whence perhaps has arisen the modern conception of an emotion as a private feeling). Intentionality refers to the semantic properties of an act rather than to the conscious state of an actor.

Yet another consequence of this approach to emotions is the expectation that there will be widely different systems of emotions in play in different cultures. It also follows that we shall have to consider the question as to how far and through what means local emotion systems are learned. A pioneering work (though not the first to adopt the intentional stance to the emotion displays of a distant culture) is Lutz's (1988) detailed study of the emotions of the Ifaluk people, a culture of the Pacific Ocean. Among the Ifaluk emotion displays seem to express a somewhat different range of social acts and interpersonal judgments than are highlighted among Americans. For example, the Ifaluk words for the cluster of emotions which would need some reference to fear or anxiety in the phrases needed to express their meaning in English, are focused on social rather than on physical dangers and threats. Physical danger is salient to a different emotion cluster in which our concept of fear plays either no role at all or a subordinate one. Emotion displays among the Ifaluk taken as patterns of social acts, just as in any other culture, have their place at specific sites in complex patterns of conversational structures of interpersonal interactions. For instance the main "anger" emotion, *sort*, expresses something like righteous indignation at being treated carelessly or without insufficient respect by a social inferior. That inferior, aware of the display of *sort*, displays *metagu* expressing a complex judgment roughly that he or she recognizes that the behavior was improper in that the person displaying *sort* is entitled to do so. In displaying *metagu* the delinquent expresses contrition.

At this point the importance of adopting the action-rule scheme rather than the cause–effect scheme becomes salient. Only with a scheme that enables one to make explicit the normative framework in which social life is lived can one take account of the important distinctions between correct and incorrect, proper and improper conduct. The use of the action-rule scheme allows very naturally for the question of norms of emotional displays to be addressed. Not only do we have to see emotion displays in the context of correct or incorrect conduct to which the emotion display is directed, as for example a display of embarrassment is directed to one's own improprieties, but that the display itself may be proper or improper in this or that context. Improper displays of joy, for instance in the context of someone else's failure or pain, are singled out in some cultures as distinct emotions, as for example, in emotionology they come under the generic heading of *Schadenfreude*. Psychiatrists are frequently required to cope with incorrect or unsuitable emotion displays or emotion feelings. For instance, fear of the outdoors is an emotion that can be readily construed as inappropriate to the situation that the person feeling or displaying the emotion finds themselves in. But how? As the bodily expression of a judgment, the judgment that the outdoors is dangerous, we have a mistaken or incorrect assessment of how things are. As a bodily expressed judgment it is hard to insert the necessary cognitive corrective, just as it is in more overtly cognitive acts such as the temptation many people feel to affirm the consequent, or to infer individual propensities from statistical distributions.

Moving to the action-rule frame also allows for the fact, not always sufficiently highlighted by students of the emotions, that the physiological aspect of emotion displays may not be specific to the emotion, or even be felt as a definite feeling at all. For instance the well-known phenomena that are central to "reversal theory" (Apter, 1992), that someone who is highly aroused may switch immediately from anxiety to elation, is an even more telling demonstration of the non-specific character of the emotion feeling than the classic studies by Schachter (1971). My own studies of "pride" show the same thing. People display pride in a great variety of ways, including widely differing postures, from the "cock-of-the-walk" strut to a display very similar to embarrassment. They may also display pride wholly by their manner of speaking, without any gestural or postural display at all. There is no common physiological state or process that could be said to be the natural groundwork of pride as there is for fear, be it primarily physical danger among Europeans and Americans, or primarily social threats as among the Ifaluk; in each case there is a flush of adrenalin.

Conceiving of emotion displays and emotion feelings as cognitive acts, expressions of judgments in the medium of bodily states or movements, allows one to introduce a further dimension to our studies that is missing from the cause–effect conceptual system. Emotion displays and emotion feelings have their place in a sequence of events, some of which are verbal, others happenings in the environment that have to be interpreted according to some conceptual scheme. The conversational model is invaluable at this point. We must look at the structure of an episode in which an emotional display occurs as if it were a conversation. If the acts that are performed in an episode conform to local dramaturgical or narrative conventions as to how such episodes should unfold the episode is taken as unproblematically intelligible. We expect displays of chagrin from some of our colleagues when merit raises or performance bonuses are announced. Without this attention to the context in which a display or a feeling is embedded the studies of emotion that fall in the mainstream are unrealistic. We need to know what came before and what came after a display or a feeling, not only in the sense of what caused it, but also in the sense of what justified it or did not justify it. We want to know just how the display or the feeling fell into just *that* place in the orderly flow of action engaged in by *these* people in *these* circumstances.

It is easy to see that both the causal framework and the action-rule framework are needed to complete an adequate study of the emotions, their genesis and their place in human life. There are cause–effect patterns, for which complex causal mechanisms will one day be found. These patterns are to be observed in the natural (ethological) reactions that humans have inherited as part of their repertoire of "fixed action patterns," the utility of which will surely have an evolutionary explanation. It may be that some patterns of response are so deeply trained into the members of a culture that they can be treated within the causal framework as if they were part of human ethology. But the effects of such processes, the feelings and displays that are felt heard and seen, are not just physiological states or muscular twitches. They are functionally the expressions of judgments, embodied not in words, but in feelings and displays. To their study the action-rule framework must be applied.

The reinterpretation in discursive terms of some traditional social psychological research

I believe that the most profound and important development in the whole of psychology, including social psychology, of the last two decades has been the advent of the discursive approach. It was widely assumed prior to the introduction of the discursive viewpoint that the "verbal responses" of the people taking part in experiments (significantly called "subjects"; Danziger, 1990) were to be interpreted as the outward signs of inner processes and states. This was the move adumbrated by the exponents of the first cognitive revolution initiated by Bruner and Miller at Harvard in the 1960s (Bruner, 1983). Questionnaires, rating scales, and so on were treated as if they served the same function in empirical studies in social psychology as thermometers and electroscopes served in physics, that is provided a more or less transparent window on to "inner processes," the real stuff of psychological research. If they did not exactly open a window then at least they offered the wherewithal for an application of hypothetico-deductive methodology for postulating "hidden mechanisms." Even now some social psychologists still assume this principle. For example, Argyle and Martin (1991), in their study of happiness, analyze what respondents say about how they feel when they have been Scottish dancing or watching television as if they were referring to some clearly differentiated and mutually intelligible inner state, perhaps to a bodily feeling. But of course, all Argyle could legitimately draw from his "data" is a rule or two about the uses of the word "happy," and its various congeners and synonyms in the discursive conventions for responding to questionnaires. The idea that there are mental processes and states that are revealed by answers to questions (cunningly posed to bypass "demand characteristics") was once very widespread. It led to some startling misinterpretations of early versions of discursive psychology. For instance, Nisbett thought that the fact that people said things that were not true descriptions of the thought had caused them to behave in this or that way, demonstrated that the anthropomorphic model of human functioning, proposed by Harré and Secord (1972), was invalid.

The rapid rise of discursive psychology, including the application of its main ideas and techniques to the investigation of problems of social conduct, has not only illuminated earlier topics of research, such as "attribution theory," but also allowed social psychologists to turn their attention to the social psychology of social psychology itself. The latter is a discursive practice, resulting in the production of documents of various sorts, framed within two major sets of discursive conventions.

The discursive turn in social psychology has been well summed up by Potter and Wetherell (1987, p. 160) where they say:

> Participants' discourse or social texts are approached in their own right and not as a secondary route to things "beyond the text" like attitudes, events or cognitive processes. [Participants' discourse is the cognitive process!] Discourse is treated as a potent, action-oriented medium, not a [semi] transparent information channel . . . research questions give priority to discourse, in any form and ask about its construction in relation to function.

The question that must be asked in any social psychological research will be "what are the functions of some sequence of discursive acts, and how are they accomplished?" Taking this point of view we can now reapproach much of traditional social psychology, delete the naive cognitivist assumption of the "semitransparent" instrument, and reinterpret the results discursively. For instance, Edwards and Potter (1992) have done this reinterpretative work with attribution theory. Now the various patterns of explanation of events, of the assigning of responsibility between oneself and the other, or the physical environment, are taken, not as the results of the working of some cognitive mechanisms, their "outward and visible sign" so to say, but as an indication of the grammar of explanatory discourses, the narrative conventions of this or that subculture.

The social psychology of social change

The complex phenomena of social change present a particularly paradoxical and intractable problem for a research program based on the cause–effect schema. If social behavior is the effect of causes then either change is impossible (the causal powers of electrons do not change) or we must contemplate a hierarchy of causal processes. It is difficult to image what such a hierarchy might be. Even Marxist social change theory did not envisage a *causal* account of superstructural behavior. Recently a number of attempts have been made to develop a mutation-selection theory of social change, premised on the principle that the patterning of social action is to be explained by reference to rules (van Parijs, 1981; Toulmin, 1972; Harré, 1992). Rules can change in a way that causal mechanisms, for instance in the neurobiology of ethology, cannot. Indeed, we are quite familiar with a variety of ways in which changes of rules can occur. For instance they can change by legislative action, as the rules of rugby football have recently changed. More often innovations gradually become apparent in the practices of daily life.

The mutation-selection hypothesis works by a comparison between gene-selection theory in biology and "meme-selection" theory in social life (Dawkins, 1981). A meme is an elementary bearer of a cultural practice, for example a rule, which can be transmitted from generation to generation by cultural means. In cases of the more conscious invention of a mutant social practice, an innovatory rule-set is proposed, and some people try to carry it out. For example new forms of address for men and women are proposed as well as new third person pronouns. The former mutation has survived in the current socio-economic climate which serves as a selection environment, so we all use the expressions "Mr" and "Ms." But the innovations in personal pronouns have not spread. No one uses "hesh," "hersh" or "shim." The rules for new forms of address and for new personal pronouns are like the genes for a new biological structure or fixed action pattern, and like genes, some have spread to new generations of speakers and actors, and others have not. Whether a gene (rule-set) is to be found in the social resources of subsequent generations is determined by the fate of the fixed action pattern (social practice) it causes (legitimates) in the relevant selection environment.

This action-rule based research program is still in its infancy. There are intriguing research questions to be answered, both with respect to how novel rule-sets come to be invented, and how they are favored or disfavored by this or that socio-economic environment, perhaps even including the local ecology (Harris, 1978).

Discursive analyses of programs of research in discursive psychology

There has been a great deal of research into the construction of "science," work that has unfortunately been situated outside the traditional academic frontiers of social psychology. Among the classic papers in this field is that by Gilbert and Mulkay (1982). In the study reported therein it emerged that the way of presenting the views of the group that one agreed with on some scientific issue, say the cross-membrane transport of protons, conformed to one set of discourse conventions, and the way the views of rivals, with whom one disagreed, was presented accorded with a different set. The fascinating thing about these two "interpretative repertoires" was that while the one drew on "official" (highly unrealistic and abstract philosophy of science) the other drew on common sense social psychological explanatory concepts, such as the deleterious effect on judgment of overenthusiastic commitment to a point of view, the effect of personal jealousy on the evaluation of the work of others, and so on. The point is not whether either of these discursive patterns captured the "truth of the matter," but that the discourses within which such issues as "the truth of the matter" arise, were patterned this way. The social psychology of a group of scientific workers in a specified field was not indicated by or revealed by the patterns of discourse, it *was* those patterns of discourse. The discursive skills of scientists are engaged in making available to readers and co-workers their versions of phenomena as reality.

Generalization of the Discursive Approach

The discursive point of view has begun to colonize fields of psychology rarely touched on by social psychologists. For example, many of the recent studies of the psychology of the self and of "personhood," summed up in Harré and Gillett (1994), have been based on the principles of discursive psychology, and so subsumed within a "social" point of view. As Potter and Wetherell pointed out (1987) discursive psychologists

> are not suggesting that the phenomena traditionally thought of as mental should be excluded from analysis because they are in some way private, mysterious, unknowable. . . . The language of the self and mental life is a public one which is available for analysis . . . In practice, much of the phenomenon of the mind is intersubjectively constituted as the person speaks, writes, reminisces, talks to others and so on.

From this point of view the disjunctions upon which traditional social psychology has been based, between "inner" and "outer" or "subjective" and "objective" states, are themselves discursive categories. Our grasp of this makes it clear that the question as to how well someone's behavior or declaration or answer matches or does not match their (inner) cognitive state is irrelevant. There are no "inner" cognitive states. Of course, this is not to deny that there is lots of private mental activity, but that too is discourse. As I remarked earlier in this paper the category of "discursive action" and the related categories such as the general category of a "grammar" or that of a rule-set that goes with it are equally applicable to the analysis and explanation of private patterns of thought. But as Vygotsky (1962) reminded us there is nothing in the sphere of private cognition that was not first in the sphere of public conversation.

References

(Those marked * are recommended for further reading.)

Apter, M. (1992). *The dangerous edge*. New York: Maxwell Macmillan.

Argyle, M., & Martin, P. (1991). The psychological causes of happiness. In F. Strack, M. Argyle, & N. Schuz (Eds.), *Subjective wellbeing*. Oxford: Pergamon Press.

Austin, J. L. (1962). *How to do things with words*. Oxford: Clarendon Press.

Averill, J. (1982). *Anger and aggression*. New York: Springer Verlag.

Bruner, J. S. (1983). *In search of mind*. New York: Harper and Row.

Danziger, K. (1990). *Constructing the subject*. Cambridge: Cambridge University Press.

Dawkins, R. (1976). *The selfish gene* (Chapter 1). Oxford: Oxford University Press.

*Edwards, D., & Potter, J. (1992). *Discursive psychology*. London: Sage.

Gilbert, G. N., & Mulkay, N. (1982). Warranting scientific beliefs. *Social Studies of Science*, *12*, 3–408.

Harré, R. (1992). *Social being* (2nd ed.). Oxford: Blackwell.

*Harré, R., & Gillett G. (1994). *The discursive mind*. London and Los Angeles: Sage.

Harré, R., & Secord, P. F. (1972). *The explanation of social behaviour*. Oxford: Blackwell.

Harris, M. (1978). *Cows, pigs, wars and witches*. London: Hutchinson.

Hewstone, M. (1989). *Causal attributions: From cognitive process to collective beliefs*. Oxford: Blackwell.

Lutz, C. (1988). *Unnatural emotions*. Chicago: Chicago University Press.

Marsh, P., Rosser, E., & Harré, R. (1977). *The rules of disorder*. London: Routledge and Kegan Paul.

Potter, J., & Wetherell, M. (1987). *Discourse and social psychology*. London: Sage.

Schachter, S. (1971). *Emotion, obesity and crime*. New York: Academic Press (Chapters 2–4).

Searle, J. R. (1979). *Meaning and expression*. Cambridge: Cambridge University Press.

*Stearns, C. Z., & Stearns, P. (1988). *Emotion and social change*. New York: Holmcs and Meier.

Tattersfield, N. (1981). Personal communication.

Toulmin, S. (1972). *Human understanding*. Princeton, NJ: Princeton University Press.

van Parijs, P. (1981). *Evolutionary explanations in the social sciences*. Totowa, NJ: Rowman and Littlefield.

Vygotsky, L. S. (1962). *Thought and language*. Cambridge, MA: MIT Press.

*Wierzbicka, A. (1992). *Semiotics, culture and cognition*. New York: Oxford University Press.

Wittgenstein, L. (1953). *Philosophical investigations*. Oxford: Blackwell.

10

Beliefs, Knowledge, and Meaning from the Perspective of the Perceiver: Need for Structure-Order

O. J. Harvey

Professor Harvey was born August 27, 1927. He received his doctorate from the University of Oklahoma in 1954 under the supervision of Professor Muzafer Sherif, with whom he co-authored his first paper in psychology in 1951. He was a post-doctoral research fellow at Yale University's Attitude Change Project, 1954–55; Assistant Professor of Psychology at Vanderbilt University, 1955–58; an Assistant, Associate, and Full Professor at the University of Colorado, 1958 until retirement. He was a Fellow, Center for Advanced Study, 1964–65, and NIMH Career Development Awardee, 1967–71. His theoretical and research interests have been mainly in group relations; and the formation, functioning, and change of attitudes and beliefs.

Introduction

Aristotle seems clearly to have been correct in his observation that all people seek knowledge. That an individual will strive to structure or pattern any unstructured situation of sensed importance to him or her and will ascribe meaning to that pattern is one of psychology's most basic and well-established principles. Within psychology, the *Gestalt* psychologists were the first to recognize this principle, systematically treat it as a basic human motive or need, and apply its implications to a wide array of psychological processes still of current interest, including perception (e.g. Koffka, 1922; Kohler, 1929), thinking and memory (e.g. Wertheimer, 1959), human growth and development, and other human organizational tendencies and outcomes as well (e.g. Kohler, 1929). Though *Gestalt* psychology never became widely popular under that name, its basic tenets were incorporated as central conceptions into such major veins of psychology as Bartlett's work on memory (1932) and thinking (1958); Sherif's work on norm formation, social judgment, and social influence (e.g. Sherif, 1935, 1936); Lewin's work on personality and group dynamics (1935, 1951); Asch's work on person perception and social influence (Asch, 1946, 1952); and Werner's work on human development (Werner, 1957).

The need for structure and meaning seems to influence most, if not all, cognitive processes and products, including one's beliefs about the world (Pepper, 1942) and what the believer considers as knowledge. While such a need presumably exists in all people capable of thought, individuals differ vastly in the ways in which they structure impinging stimuli or events; hence in their resulting beliefs and knowledge about those impingements and in the meaning they ascribe to them.

The focus of this chapter will be on *personal* beliefs, knowledge, and meaning as a product of the human need to structure, explain, control, and find meaning in the world, including one's relationship to and place in it. As Merleau-Ponty (1981) has maintained, knowledge assumed to exist independently of human experience – even if, in fact, it does – is inaccessible by psychology or any other existing human method. Accordingly, beliefs will be defined later in this chapter as *personal hypotheses*, or assumptions of what an outcome or state of affairs will be proven to be when tested by whatever test the *particular believer* accepts as valid. Knowledge will be defined as a validated or *confirmed* personal belief, without regard to whether the belief or its proof is valid or "true" according to the criteria of any other person or source. Meaning is the *import*, the implications of a belief or personal knowledge for feeling and/or action.

Following descriptions of some of the psychological processes supporting the tendency toward structure and patterning that result in beliefs, personal knowledge, and meaning – processes of particular concern to *Gestalt* and neo-*Gestalt* psychologists – beliefs, belief systems and personal knowledge will be characterized in greater detail. Individual differences in belief systems will then be described and the effect of these differences on such psychological products as open- and closed-mindedness, speed of closure, use of information, conservatism, authoritarianism, dogmatism, punitiveness, perspective taking, creativity, locus of control, and self-esteem will be presented.

Although belief, knowledge, and meaning will be treated in individual or *phenomenological* terms, their characterizations are consistent with the strong tendency for groups of people to share the same beliefs, personal knowledge and meaning about referents (objects or events) that are significant to their *reference group*, the group with which they identify and aspire to be like (e.g. H. Kelley, 1952; Sherif & Cantril, 1947). Consensus among reference group members is, in fact, among the more, if not the most, widely utilized source of a person's beliefs, personal knowledge, and meaning.

Tendency Toward Structure and Meaning

Few, if any, human tendencies appear stronger and more pervasive than to differentiate and pattern specie and/or personally relevant stimuli and to make personal sense of them. Probably no concern has so dominated human thought and effort as the unceasing search for access – by discovery, revelation, or personal construction, and attribution – to valid and reliable beliefs and knowledge through which, as *a system of personal effectance or causation* (de Charms, 1968; Harvey, 1963; Langer, 1983; MacMurray, 1956), the apparent vagaries of life can be predicted or managed in ways that support survival and attainment of other personal goals. This "cognitive drive," averred Pepper, "is for the most completely invariant evidence possible" (Pepper, 1942, p. 57), exemplified by magic, witchcraft, religion, science, and other systems of presumed control and causality which have arisen as part of this universal and interminable quest and endeavor (e.g. Cantril & Bumstead, 1960; Durkheim, 1912; Frazier, 1922; Polanyi, 1964; Werner, 1957). As Allport has noted, "Cantril and such existentialists as Frankl regard man's search for meaning, for the 'why' of his experience, as an ultimate – perhaps the ultimate – motive in life" (Allport, 1961, p. 217).

A person's patterning and interpretation of a stimulus situation need not be veridical to be treated as such. They need only to be *believed to be* accurate to evoke from the effectance system of the believer a mode of response and coping that the believer anticipates, consciously or habitually, will enable him or her to effect desired outcomes from the world or otherwise to deal effectively with it. This "effort after meaning," as Bartlett termed it (Bartlett, 1932), often extends to making sense out of nonsense, mistaking appearance for essence, and interpreting illusions as real. This is well illustrated in Sherif's classic demonstration that individuals and groups will erroneously judge a fixed pinpoint of light in a dark room as moving (the autokinetic effect), and with repeated exposures of the light will evolve a standardized judgment or group norm of the magnitude of the movement (Sherif, 1935, 1936; Sherif & Harvey, 1952). Equally illustrative is the practice of the Ojibwa Indians who, according to Hallowell (1949), take drastic steps to prevent the untrained child from eating or even touching *kinnebikonin*, snakeberries that are erroneously labeled as deadly poisonous by the adults.

Dean Kelley, a clergyman and theologian, has characterized the person "as an inveterate meaning-monger" who "tries to make sense out of his experience, even if he has to resort to non-sense to do it. His eye involuntarily finds patterns in any random visual stimuli presented to it, and thus the night sky becomes peopled with constellations where none exist" (Kelley, 1972, p. 38).

Veridical or not, the "real world" to the receiving individual is the world filtered through his or her beliefs. "It is this world, as distorted and unreal, as undifferentiated . . . as it may be, that the individual conforms to in his [or her] own behavior and demands similar conformity from others" (Harvey, Hunt, & Schroder, 1961, p. 47).

The tendency to pattern, form beliefs, and convert the beliefs into knowledge through proof from the perspective of the believer exists for corporeal or sensory referents and for incorporeal referents as well. The urgency and intensity of the motivation to pattern and ascribe meaning to wholly conceptual or incorporeal referents, such as "honor," "duty," "fairness," and "immorality," seems, in fact, to generally exceed that of highly structured corporeal referents, such as "sticks" and "stones," which are more accessible to direct sensory test and verification by the believer.

The greater concern of society with incorporeal referents disposes it toward greater social pressure for common beliefs and meanings about them than about sensory referents. The greater ambiguity of the incorporeal referents, in turn, renders the individual more susceptible to social definitions and pressures, a reflection of the principle that people are more socially influenceable under conditions of greater than lesser ambiguity and uncertainty (e.g. Asch, 1952; Sherif, 1936; Sherif & Harvey, 1952; Thrasher, 1954).

The greater centrality of incorporeal referents results additionally in beliefs about them becoming superordinate cognitive structures with which beliefs about the subordinate corporeal referents are rendered in agreement and supportive from the cognitive strain toward consistency between the subordinate and superordinate. For example, beliefs about "God," a superordinate referent for the majority of people, heavily influences, often determining completely, subordinate beliefs about referents related to creation or evolution of the universe.

As Kelley has noted, whether dealing with corporeal or incorporeal referents, the individual "finds patterns in his experience, and accordingly the universe has become peopled with shapes and rhythms, powers and beings, fates and forces which enable him to make sense of it" (Kelley, 1972, p. 38). "Some of these patterns are useful for managing the mundane affairs of life. But by far the most important patterns for man's life are the very biggest ones," which "explain the purpose of his existence, the nature of reality, the fate of the world, the character of the beings or forces that determine his destiny, and how he can relate to them. These largest patterns of meaning are the subject matter of religion" (D. Kelley, 1972, p. 38), a position of Paul Tillich (1952), another eminent theologian, as well.

Failure to find acceptable answers to these more profound questions and least manageable problems has often spawned nihilism with its accompaniments of cynicism, anger, powerlessness, a sense of purposelessness, meaninglessness, a vacuous and worthless self, and suicide – among unsophisticated people and famous scientists alike (e.g. Barrett, 1962; Tillich, 1952). Thus Pascal, renowned mathematician and father of the theory of probability, voiced his famous outcry for exchange of his own belief in scientific skepticism and sense of personal emptiness for the certitude of religious faith. "Not the God of philosophers," he entreated, "but the God of Abraham, Isaac, and Jacob," famous exemplars of faith according to religious history (Barrett, 1962, p. 116).

As painful as it is to the individual and as damaging as it is to his or her self not to develop trusted and effective systems of beliefs and personal knowledge, it appears to be even more devastating to have long-standing systems of effectance so negated that they are rendered inoperative and place their holders in a psychological void, exemplified by the "brainwashing" of American prisoners of war by their Chinese captors during the Korean war (Harvey et al., 1961) and, conceivably, by the more recently recognized effects of post-traumatic stress disorder as well.

The cynicism, nihilism, and despair evoked by the absence of trusted systems of beliefs, by failure to form them or by their utter negation especially, constitute the core of the belief system I have termed cynicism, one of the four to be discussed later in this chapter.

Meaning, Closure and Pragnanz

Both Sherif's demonstration of the formation of norms of the autokinetic phenomenon and Kelley's observation of people's tendency to form structure out of randomness represent instances of the well-known *Gestalt* principles of closure and pragnanz. "That we experience certain groups of stars does not mean that these stars themselves constitute groups," averred Kohler. "More generally: most groups (i.e. wholes with discrete members) are wholes only in our vision, whereas among themselves the members have no physical connections" (Kohler, 1928, p. 393).

The grouping of the stars represents an instance of closure, the tendency toward completing and stabilizing a tentative pattern or form by having successfully proceeded "towards the intrinsically appropriate end of a behavior sequence" (Kohler, 1929, p. 392), referred to by Bartlett (1958) as "closing the gap." Failure to close the gap and attain closure leaves the individual in a state of tension and unease that may be expressed in a variety of outcomes (Lewin, 1951). One of the better known of these effects is the tendency for individuals to remember uncompleted tasks and goals more than completed ones, referred to in the *Gestalt* lexicon as the "Zeigarnik effect," so named for the student of

Lewin who first experimentally demonstrated the phenomenon. As would be expected, this effect has been found to be stronger for uncompleted tasks or unattained goals of higher than of lower involvement to the individual (Larimer, 1962).

Closure, marked by a sense of completion and rest, tends to be experienced as a successful solution to a personal question and to be accepted as validation or invalidation of a percept, judgment, or belief. Augustine, for example, appealed successfully in the fourth century for reliance on the sense of completion and rest evoked by closure as validation of his beliefs about the essence of God, a factor in his becoming one of the more influential figures in Christendom even before his sainthood in the Catholic Church (Barrett, 1962; Markus, 1967).

Closure is subordinate to the law of *pragnanz* or *good form*, the dynamic process of change according to which every *Gestalt* becomes as "good as possible" within the constraints or boundaries of the pattern, percept, or meaning (Petermann, 1932, p. 247). The tendency toward organization and principle of good form "may be applied far beyond the limits of sensory fields," to "the processes of learning, of reproduction, of striving, of emotional attitude, of thinking, acting, and so forth" (Kohler, 1929, p. 193). "Quite apart from psychology the same will be true of ontogentic development, and other biological events, wherever they show the definite marks of self-distribution and self-regulation" (Kohler, 1929, pp. 193–194).

A *Gestalt*, defined by Kohler as "any segregated whole" (Kohler, 1929, p. 192) is rendered maximally distinctive through the processes of "making precise" and "leveling," terms used originally by Wulf to describe transitions of memory toward the attainment of good form, a better and more harmonious fit with the whole (Petermann, 1932, p. 247). Making precise, usually referred to as "sharpening," exaggerates "some particular distinction," emphasizes some specific aspect of the parts to increase their consonance with the whole while not changing the structure of the constraining whole. Leveling is the process of "minimizing asymmetries" to gain a better fit with the "whole" (Petermann, 1932, p. 247).

The work of Wulf on pragnanz, leveling, and sharpening elicited a number of important studies by psychologists not wholly or directly in the *Gestalt* school (e.g. Allport, 1930; Bartlett, 1932; Carmichael, Hogan, & Walter, 1932; Gibson, 1929), the best known of these being Bartlett's classic work on remembering (Bartlett, 1932). A more recent influence of Wulf's work may be seen, for example, in the work of Labov (1973) on the selective effects of language on addition and omission of cognitive elements necessary for consistency of the memory with the more dominant theme of structure and order. Though to the knowledge of this writer it has not been so noted, Wulf's work could also be meaningfully linked to several well known theories of "defense mechanisms" and possibly of dissonance and attribution as well.

The Meaning of "Meaning"

The concept "meaning" itself has many meanings, a cardinal feature, implicit or explicit, being that it is inevitably comparative and synthetic: the relating of an object or referent, corporeal or incorporeal, to a framework of internal standards that include existing beliefs and presumed knowledge, differentiating and placing the referent on a dimension or set of dimensions, and synthesizing these "readings" into a pattern of import, *a set of recognized implications for action and feeling*. As Bateson has written, "It is impossible to explain any pattern by invoking a single quantity. But note that a ratio between two quantities is already the beginning of a pattern" (Bateson, 1979, p. 53), an idea akin to one of the earlier expositions of the comparative nature of meaning, that of Bishop Berkeley in his landmark treatise *Three Dialogues Between Hylas and Philonous*, first published in 1713 (McCormack, 1925).

The mere presence of things, however, does not automatically evoke effort at patterning and meaning. As Kohler quoted Madam Curie, "before [such] natural processes can take place, 'it is necessary that certain elements of symmetry be absent. *Asymmetry* produces the course of nature. The absence of symmetrical elements is necessary for the occurrence of every natural event' " (quoted by Petermann, 1932, p. 49). Asymmetry at the psychological level, as I conceive it, is a psychological state of tension and unease created by the observer's sensing that his or her existing beliefs and/or presumed knowledge are at odds with the reading of the present situation. Without the motivation and cognitive selectivity engendered by asymmetry, the search for symmetry and meaning would not be evoked, and the world would remain an undifferentiated mass – unnoticed, meaningless, and devoid of information to the normless and neutral individual (James, 1890, Vol. 1).

As an incorporeal referent open to countless definitions, "meaning" has no standardized term in psychology. "Perception" is the term used most often to refer to it, even though individuals of similar sensory experiences (or perceptions) of the same stimuli may differ in their assignment of meaning. Thus a native of London and a chieftain from Swaziland who both perceived a London traffic officer raising his arm while directing city traffic were found to differ in the meaning they ascribed to the raised arm. To the London native, it meant a signal for traffic to stop. To the chieftain, it signified friendliness, as in his homeland (Allport, 1961; Bartlett, 1932).

Kohler has provided another example of similar sensory experiences resulting in different meanings:

> "Objects" cannot exist for us before sensory experience has become imbued with meaning. Who can deny that meaning fundamentally determines almost all experience? . . . The German noun "Igel" sounds to Germans as though no animal but a hedgehog could have this name. "Eagle", however, which in English is acoustically the same as

"Igel" is in German, sounds to an American as though only an "Adler" [the German word for "eagle"] could be called by this name. Here it is obvious that we have to discriminate between a genuine sensory experience, which is the same in both languages, and two different meanings connected with it in different countries. (Kohler, 1929, pp. 72–73)

To distinguish "meaning" from "perception," Allport (1961) proposed that "proception," a term coined by the philosopher Buchler (1955), replace "perception" to signify meaning. The suggestion has gone unheeded.

Some Precursors to Meaning

Meaning neither inheres in an object, as Locke argued in 1690 (Clapp, 1967), nor emanates isomorphically from direct sensory experience of it. Even common referents do not ensure common meaning, evidenced by the widely unrecognized fact, for example, that the "morning star" and the "evening star" both refer to the same entity, the planet Venus.

Like other cognitive products, meaning is *personally constructed* from a synthesis of experiences bipolarly determined by properties of both the external situation and internal factors of the organism. "This is so well known through recent studies on hunger, sexual behavior, and so forth that I scarcely need mention the fact," opined Kohler (1929, pp. 324–325), an opinion, however, that was premature and overly optimistic. Not until an amassing of research findings by the New Look Psychology (from 1935 until around 1960) was the level of information about the determinants implied by Kohler attained, with the idea of bipolarity being continued but more typically under the label of "frame of reference."

This concept was applied most prominently and widely by Sherif, who had attended Kohler's lectures at the University of Berlin in the early 1930s (Harvey, 1988). Assumptions embodied in his conception of frame of reference served as the starting point for all of Sherif's major works: his earlier seminal work on social perception and group norms (1935, 1936), and later his widely ranging works on self and ego-involvement (e.g. Sherif & Cantril, 1947), attitude change (e.g. Hovland, Harvey, & Sherif, 1957), social judgment (e.g. Sherif & Hovland, 1961), and group relations (e.g. Sherif, Harvey, White, Hood, & Sherif, 1961, 1988).

As in Kohler's idea of bipolarity, in Sherif's conception of "frame of reference" – the totality of external and internal factors operative at the time – either an external or internal factor from within the frame of reference, or the interaction of two or more such factors may dominate the meaning. "These weighty factors, or anchors, may be located in the stimulus field. At other times, the individual's desires or ingrained attitudes may anchor his perception, judgment, and action so securely that they affect what he selects for attention and how he interprets it" (Sherif & Sherif, 1969, p. 31); in Koffka's words, they may stand out as "figure," and "the kernel of the whole experience" (Koffka, 1922, p. 566).

Whether an internal or external factor is more influential on interpretation and meaning depends on the *ambiguity* of the stimulus field and the *intensity* of the internal factor(s), according to Sherif. High stimulus ambiguity and intense arousal of an internal state maximizes the influence of a dispositional factor and the tendency toward attribution, leveling and sharpening as a means of completing structure, exemplified by an individual seeking desperately to understand and relate to incorporeal referents of such personal and social significance as "truth," "fairness," and "immorality." The effect of stimulus or situational variables, conversely, is greatest under high stimulus structure and low intensity of internal arousal (e.g. Sherif & Sherif, 1969; Sherif & Harvey, 1952; Thrasher, 1954).

Factors in the frame of reference other than the main anchorages, however, generally are not without some influence. Most if not all of them serve in some degree as ground, or in the words of Koffka again, "the general level (niveau) upon which the figure appears" (Koffka, 1922, p. 566). Kindred notions, it may be noted, appeared in essential details early in the history of psychology in the writings of Locke (Clapp, 1967) and Berkeley (McCormack, 1925), and later in such concepts as "just noticeable difference" of early psychophysicists (Boring, 1942), the "stream of consciousness" of James (1890), and "adaptation level" proposed by Helson (1948) as a quantifiable conception of Sherif's conception of frame of reference.

For the *Gestalt* psychologists and Sherif alike, meaning is an *emergent* product that is different from the *sum* of external and internal factors or parts operative at any given time, a point well illustrated in experiments on impression formation spearheaded by Asch (1946). For example, two people described by lists of adjectives differing in only one central characteristic, such as warm–cold (Kelley, 1950), were perceived very differently, justifying the conclusion in Asch's view, "that a change of one quality produces a fundamental change in the entire impression" (Asch, 1952, p. 210).

The idea of emergence, illustratable by the effect of a list of adjectives or by the frame of reference being sharply altered by change in a single factor in ways not wholly predictable by an *additive* or *linear model* of reasoning and analysis, runs counter to the more dominant views of current psychology. It may prove to be the case, however, that while the weight of a factor in a closed system may be determined by a linear model of reasoning, the influence of a factor in a more unbounded, open, and fluctuating system, such as meaning, could best be determined and explained by a nonlinear model of thought and explanation in which a single or formerly neutral condition or stimulus may unpredictably dominate the outcome. This idea, which in its more essential details was advanced by Kohler more than sixty-five years ago (Kohler, 1929, pp. 103–147), has become so widely accepted among scientists concerned with such organizational issues as order, disorder, and chaos that a paradigm shift has already occurred among them (e.g. Gleick, 1987; Prigogine, 1976). This development, now beginning to be recognized by psychologists, is likely to strongly impact psychology in the future toward conceiving and analyzing at least certain psychological causes and outcomes in terms of nonlinear rather than, or in addition to, linear models.

Belief, Belief System, and Knowledge

Once evolved from the process of structuring and patterning of relevant impingements, belief systems and personal knowledge become internal factors where, as parts of or membership within the frame of reference, they heavily influence interpretation of and response to the world, especially under conditions of high personal involvement and ambiguous stimulus conditions. In the remainder of this chapter, beliefs and knowledge will be more fully defined, ways in which belief systems differ in their more central content and structure will be described, and effects of these differences on such outcomes as those noted earlier will be presented.

Definitions

As used in this chapter, belief is defined as an anticipated reality from the third person perspective: one's assumption of the transpersonal characteristics or essence of an object or situation *per se* without regard to the believer's own attitude toward it or any one else's belief or attitude toward it as well.

A belief system, in turn, is a constellation of beliefs with a root or core belief (Pepper, 1942) and a number of subordinate denotatively and connotatively consistent beliefs that relate to each other directly and/or through their relationship to the core belief (Harvey, 1986). A belief system is thus an interrelated set of well-anchored *expectancies* or *hypotheses* of what the reality regarding a related set of referents will be proven to be whenever tested according to whatever criteria *that believer* accepts as valid for the assumption being tested, be the criteria articles of folklore, faith, current social norms, logic, experimental science, or some other framework of reasoning and decision making. Belief as thus characterized makes no assumptions about the nature of what some might call "true reality," a reality presumed to exist independently of any person's conception or belief about it.

Confirmation of the belief according to the criteria of the tester converts the belief into knowledge for that believer, irrespective of the validity of that knowledge according to the standards of any other source.

A belief may contain the proof of its own validity in the view of many believers. In more undifferentiated and concretely functioning belief systems, high certitude alone tends to be mistakenly taken for validity, in sharp contrast to believers of more differentiated, open, and abstract systems who distinguish between certainty and validity and recognize that a person, including oneself, may be "completely certain" while at the same time being "completely wrong."

Beliefs distinguished from attitudes

Attitudes are being distinguished from beliefs because they are so often confused with and used interchangeably with each other. Much of the research on "attitudes" has actually been on beliefs, and vice versa.

Whereas a belief represents the third person perspective, an attitude represents the first person view, the "I" perspective. An attitude refers to a positive or negative valence or inclination of its holder toward an object, and neither contains nor conveys any direct information about the object *per se*. A belief, in contrast, is assumed by the believer to refer to attributes of the object without reference to any personal inclination toward it, to characteristics of an object or a referent as "it actually exists whether we think about it or not" and "no matter how we think about it" (Adler, 1985, p. 89). Owing to their indispensable role in defining reality for the believer and prescribing ways of responding to that perceived reality, most beliefs evoke higher negative affect, involve both a larger number and more central cognitive elements, and are more impactful on the self than most attitudes when threatened or negated.

Reciprocal effects of belief and experience

Beliefs and personal knowledge serve as a psychological bridge that mediates between the individual and the impinging world in much the way as do schemata as originally described by Kant in 1787 in the second edition of his *Critique of pure reason* (Walsh, 1967). Among their effects, they bias or render their holder selective in what aspects of the world are relevant, salient, discriminated, and, in the language of *Gestalt* psychology, what stands out as figure to him or her. They affect not only perception, short-term and long-term memory (e.g. Bartlett, 1932), especially under conditions of high involvement and stimulus ambiguity, they also influence a vast array of traditional social psychological phenomena, as noted in the introduction, some of which are to be detailed later.

Beliefs and personal knowledge operate as both "cause" and "effect," influencing experience and being influenced by it, either toward change or toward strengthening. As with the evolution of thought according to Piaget (1951), a belief system is the product of the reciprocal effects of "assimilation" and "accommodation," respectively, the incorporation of external influences into thought or belief through "molding" the impingement to fit the thought or belief, and changing the thought or belief toward the external impingement (Harvey et al., 1961). "These two aspects of thought are inseparable: thought organizes itself in adapting to objects and thought structures objects in organizing itself" (Piaget, 1951, p. 186).

This mutual dependence of belief and experience implies that the interpretation and meaning of each impingement modifies the underlying belief, perceptibly or imperceptibly, so "that no state once gone can recur and be identical with what it was before" (James, 1890, Vol. 1, p. 230). "Even though the objective characteristics of the impinging object or event may remain constant, each subsequent experience of the object must be different because its preceding exposure modified the conceptual standard [belief] in terms of which it was being gauged" (Harvey et al., 1961, p. 17).

This shift of the adaptation level toward properties of the impinging stimulus, manifested in such outcomes as habituation and boredom, are described particularly clearly by James (1890, Vol. 1, pp. 233–234) and by Koffka (1922, p. 566). Quite the opposite effects, however, may occur instead. Highly prejudiced and concretely functioning individuals, for example, may psychologically so mold even a highly disconfirming event that it confirms and strengthens existing beliefs instead of weakening or changing them toward the event (Harvey et al., 1961). Or, relatedly, a "boomerang effect" may occur, demonstrable, for example, by the recipient of a communication changing his or her position oppositely to that recommended by the source of the communication.

Individual Differences in Belief Systems, Knowledge and Meaning

Concreteness–abstractness of belief systems

Though seemingly universal, the human tendency to structure and find meaning is expressed among individuals in vastly dissimilar ways, including development of sharply differing systems of beliefs and consequent personal knowledge and meaning which, despite their differences, embody for their holders "the most completely invariant evidence possible" (Pepper, 1941, p. 57).

Of the many ways in which belief systems may differ, *content* and *structure* are among the more important. Content is what the beliefs are about (any object or referent of direct experience or imagination) and structure has to do with the extent to which and ways in which the content is differentiated and integrated. Especially important is the ability of the believer to differentiate and integrate beliefs of high ego-involvement and centrality to him or her. While individuals may differ somewhat even in the number of distinctions they can make within their beliefs of low centrality and in the ability to organize these differentiations into different patterns or gestalts, these differences are much greater for beliefs of high involvement and centrality (Harvey et al., 1968; White & Harvey, 1965).

The capacity to differentiate and integrate beliefs of high involvement and centrality into multiple patterns of different meanings is the cardinal definer of *concreteness–abstractness*, a superordinate property of cognitive functioning that affects a seemingly endless range of psychological processes. The greater this capacity, the more abstract the cognitive functioning. The less this ability, the fewer the differentiations and greater the fixity of the pattern(s) into which the distinctions can be organized or integrated, the greater the concreteness (e.g. Goldstein & Scheerer, 1941; Harvey et al., 1961; Piaget, 1951; Werner, 1957).

The concept of concreteness–abstractness occupied a central position in the classic work of Goldstein and Scheerer (1941) on the effects of damage to the human cortex on thoughts, beliefs and actions. Through their work, this concept also became a key idea in our own work on conceptual systems initially (Harvey et al., 1961), and especially in my own later work on belief systems (e.g. Harvey, 1986).

Some of the more significant social psychological effects, or at least correlates, of greater concreteness of beliefs demonstrated or reaffirmed since 1961 include: (1) greater traditionalism, conservatism, dogmatism, authoritarianism, and prejudice (Brigham & Severy, 1976; Harvey, 1966; Harvey, White, Prather, Alter, & Hoffmeister, 1966); (2) a greater need for cognitive consistency and greater negative affect from inconsistency (Harvey & Ware, 1967); (3) a greater tendency toward polarized ("black–white," "good–bad") judgments (White & Harvey, 1965); (4) lower flexibility, manifested in a lesser ability to break set, play a role, take the perspective of another or advocate a position counter to one's own stand (Harvey, 1966; Miller & Harvey, 1973; White & Harvey, 1965); (5) lower creativity (Harvey, 1966); (6) attainment of certitude from minimal information and overgeneralization of the resulting impressions, to the point of stereotypic functioning (Brigham & Severy, 1976; Harvey, 1966; Ware & Harvey, 1967); and (7) greater dictatorialness and punitiveness, together with a stronger belief that persons should be judged and punished on the basis of the act and not on the intent nor the circumstances of the action (Gore, 1985; Harvey, 1986; Harvey et al., 1968).

The relationship of greater abstractness to these outcomes is opposite from the relationship of concreteness to them.

Four Systems or Patterns of Beliefs

From a combination of levels of concreteness–abstractness and content of highest centrality and involvement to the believer, Harvey et al. (1961) deduced four prototypic systems of beliefs, which they at that time termed "conceptual systems."

It should be noted, in line with our earlier discussion of emergence and non-linearity, that while different thoughts or beliefs may share many or most of the same characteristics, difference on only two or three critical criteria may produce patterns that are qualitatively different from all the other systems or patterns, as may be seen in the work of Asch (1946) on impression formation, and in medical diagnoses of illness and disease. Conversely, while two patterns may differ on most characteristics, through sharing only two or three characteristics they may be perceived as qualitatively similar, as in the transposition of melody or in a chihuahua and a St Bernard both being recognizable as dogs. In either the pattern of dissimilarity or similarity, one or two critical characteristics may serve as "figure," "the kernel of the whole experience" (Koffka, 1922), and so dominate the definition of the pattern that other characteristics serve only as "ground."

As did Goldstein and Scheerer (1941), I view the four systems of beliefs described below as representing *qualitative* and not just *quantitative* differences in cognitive functioning.

Because of their strong influence on the definition of knowledge, methods of its attainment, and tests of its validity in the view of the believer, I have come to refer to the four systems of belief as the epistemologies of extrapersonalism, cynicism, egoism, and contextualism (e.g. 1986), single words intended to summarize the most distinctive features of each system. The more central assumptions and distinguishing characteristics of each system are summarized below in what is considered to be its prototypic form.

Extrapersonalism

This system of beliefs epitomizes the characteristics of more concrete functioning noted earlier. Central to this system is the assumption by its holder that his or her beliefs are an isomorphic or perfect copy of an unchangeable and universal truth decreed or otherwise created by an extrapersonal source of ultimate wisdom and power (Gore, 1985; Harvey, 1986), and hence for another's belief or knowledge to be correct it must correspond to that of the believer. Such a source of truth is usually conceived as some form of a godhead, although the believer may not so label the source. A charismatic leader, such as Hitler, Manson, Jones, or Koresh, a social movement (Kaufmann, 1973), an ascribed historical inevitability (Berlin, 1954), or even a social convention (Munro, 1969) may be attributed ultimate validity and causality and serve the function of a godhead, with or without full recognition or admission by the believer. Ascription of the origin of a belief to an extrapersonal source endows it with unshakable validity and unimpeachable truth in the view of the extrapersonalist. Certitude of and compliance with this belief earn the source's grace and, in the view of the extrapersonalist, empower him or her with personal causation and effectance. Strength of belief in God, importance of the relationship with God, and frequency of church attendance are much higher for extrapersonalists than for representatives of the other three systems (Batres, 1984; Gore, 1985; Harvey & Felknor, 1970).

Extrapersonalists agree more strongly than persons of the other systems with such statements from the belief systems test, an objective measure of belief systems developed by Gore (1985), as "God is the ultimate cause of the universe and its principles of functioning," "God reveals the truth to those who believe in him," "I can influence my own life only by working through God's Master Plan," "My worth as a person depends solely on my knowledge of and obedience to God's will," "Truth is the same for all people, for all actions and for all times," "There is no such thing as partial truth: something is either true or false," and "All people may be classified as good or evil."

Cynicism

This system of beliefs, little if any more abstract than extrapersonalism, is opposite to extrapersonalism in its valence toward most of the more socially significant referents of belief. As part of a deep and pervasive distrust, cynics tend to perceive their fate controllers as inconsistent, unpredictable, unfair, and untrustworthy. To safeguard against potential control and hurt from others, they are generally highly wary of interpersonal dependencies on representatives of institutions and even of the interdependencies in intimate relationships. Suspicion, defensiveness, intransigence, dogmatism, and interpersonal distancing are accompanied by low self-disclosure, hostility, a sense of alienation, and social exclusion, and generally by feelings of social powerlessness and low self-esteem, often to the point of nihilism, despair, and depression (Batres, 1984; Gore, 1985; Harvey, 1966). Cynics tend to attribute causation of negative events to powerful other persons, and positive outcomes to luck, chance, or freedom from the adverse effects of control by others. They attend church only rarely, if ever, although they may claim belief in a god of some form.

Cynics agree more strongly than representatives of the other systems to such items from the belief systems test as "Most people in authority are frauds," "Success in life is simply a matter of knowing the right people," "I feel helpless when it comes to changing anything," "My spirits are low most of the time," and "It's stupid to trust anyone but yourself."

Though hostile toward authority sources and their espoused norms and behavior, cynics may display toward persons they perceive as of lower status than themselves behavior that is similar to that of authority figures whom they denounce, and use previously rejected norms of authority sources when they perceive doing so as instrumental to their own objectives (Ware & Harvey, 1968).

Egoism

This system of beliefs is more abstract and humanistic than either extra-personalism or cynicism. While maintaining more strongly than persons of the other systems that people are by nature unique, good, and deserving (Gore, 1985), egoists at the same time view the world narcissistically, tending to view self as a specially deserving person (Raimy, 1975), and to rely on personal feelings more than on God or information in making major decisions. They rate themselves higher on characteristics generally considered socially desirable, such as sociability, self-disclosure, nurturance, and sympathy, and also higher on self-esteem and self-causation of positive outcomes than do representatives of the other three systems (Gore, 1985; Harvey, 1966).

Though they *publicly* present themselves as believing strongly in equality, a principle of distributing positive outcomes equally among those participating in achieving them, they *privately* advocate distribution of outcomes in terms of equity, the distribution of proceeds in terms of *deservedness*, which may include not only amount of contribution to the outcome, but claimed status, goodness and other personal characteristics aimed at rendering the claimant more deserving than others. Like cynics, egoists score high on hedonism (Gore, 1985). But unlike cynics, who feel that only a fool would not take advantage of a rare opportunity, egoists tend to justify their hedonism as an inherent entitlement or as a dividend earned through self-ascribed humanism, especially care for and nurturance of others.

Egoists agree more strongly than persons of the other systems with such statements from the belief systems test as "There is no such thing as fate other than a person's control of his/her own life," "I can do anything I want to if I really make up my mind to do so," "Every person has the right to maximize his/her own pleasure as long as no one is harmed by it," "Generally one's feelings should be trusted more than one's intellect," "My relationship to other people is more important to me than my relationship to God," and "There is no such thing as a bad person; only bad experiences."

Contextualism

This, the most abstractly functioning of the four systems, is organized around the belief that beliefs themselves are personally constructed and are not the product of some extrapersonal source, and that interpretations of the world depend upon the changing context comprised of these beliefs, other personological, and situational factors operative at the moment, the opposite particularly of extrapersonalism. Contextualists score highest of the four systems in reflexivity (conception and evaluation of self from the third-person perspective), ability and tendency to take the role of the other (Harvey, 1966; Miller & Harvey, 1973), creativity (Harvey, 1966), intrinsic motivation, in valuing competence and basing decisions on information (Gore, 1985). They score lowest in dogmatism and authoritarianism (Harvey, 1966) and, unlike extrapersonalists and cynics particularly, believe more in remediation than in severe punishment for crimes, including most capital offenses (Harvey, 1986).

Contextualists agree more strongly than representatives of the other systems with such items from the belief systems test as "There is no such thing as complete truth," What is truth depends upon the context or situation," "The one thing of which we can be 100 percent certain is that everything changes with time," and "There is nothing in the universe that is not in the process of constant change."

The relationship of belief systems to numerous psychological outcomes in addition to those noted have been examined, including parent–child relations, college major, career choice, use of formal authority and power, teaching style, preferred leadership style, art preference, stand on social and political issues, interpersonal interaction, personal values, and several aspects of religion. Report of these relationships here, however, are precluded by space limitation.

Recapitulation and Conclusion

The four belief systems may be viewed as human forms of patterning aimed at rendering the more central and ego-involving aspects of the world intelligible, controllable, and meaningful, each system in its own qualitatively different way: extrapersonalists through reliance on and conformity to what they believe to be the principles or edicts of an omnipotent and omniscient force with whom they have an assumed personal relationship; cynics through negative independence and avoidance of dependence on and control by powerful others; egoists through a self presentation as unusually deserving and entitled; and contextualists through competence, information, and self reliance based on flexibility born from openness and the assumption that "facts" and "truth" are tentative.

As noted earlier, the greatest effect or strongest engagement of a particular belief system occurs under conditions of high ego-involvement and from moderate to fairly high levels of stress (Harvey et al., 1968; Miller & Harvey, 1973). Under familiar and low stress conditions, the difference between systems is at its lowest – though not necessarily zero – with shared social norms becoming more influential in the interaction between the individual and the environment, particularly the social environment. In recognition of this, the test we have used most extensively to assess belief systems, the "this I believe" test (e.g. Greaves, 1971; Harvey, 1966, 1986), requires the respondent to indicate his or her beliefs by writing at least two sentences about a referent of high personal significance under timed conditions that require quick responses with little or no time for reflection and deliberation.

High involvement and stress are associated with conceptual closedness, lessened ability to differentiate and integrate, and generally decreased ability to process information for concretely functioning systems while the reverse is true for more abstractly functioning systems, at least up to fairly high levels of stress (Harvey, 1966; Harvey et al., 1968; Miller & Harvey, 1973). The functioning of concrete and abstract belief systems under stress appear to be governed by different organizational principles that result in the interpretation and response to the world in qualitatively different ways. Concrete systems seem to follow the principles of "equilibrium structures" as described by Prigogine (1976), that is, structures of closed and stationary states, such as an ice crystal, that participate in minimal interchange of energy with their surrounding environment. Abstract systems, contrastingly, appear to be organized and to operate in accordance with the principle of "order through fluctuation" a "dissipative structure" which "requires a non-linear mechanism" for its open and more unpredictable interchange with its world (Prigogine, 1976, p. 95).

References

(Those marked * are recommended for further reading.)

Adler, M. J. (1985). *Ten philosophical mistakes*. New York: Macmillan.

Allport, G. W. (1930). Change and decay in the visual memory image. *British Journal of Psychology*, *21*, 133–148.

Allport, G. W. (1961). *Pattern and growth in personality*. New York: Holt, Rinehart & Winston.

Asch, S. E. (1946). Forming impressions of personality. *Journal of Abnormal and Social Psychology*, *41*, 258–290.

*Asch, S. E. (1952). *Social psychology*. New York: Prentice-Hall.

Barrett, W. (1962). *Irrational man: A study in existential philosophy*. New York: Doubleday-Anchor.

Bartlett, F. C. (1932). *Remembering: A study in experimental and social psychology*. Cambridge: Cambridge University.

Bateson, G. (1979). *Mind and nature a necessary unity*. New York: Dutton.

Batres, A. R. (1984). *Parental methods of control/influence as antecedents to belief systems*. Unpublished doctoral dissertation, University of Colorado.

Berlin, I. (1954). *Historical inevitability*. Oxford: Oxford University Press.

Boring, E. G. (1942). *Sensation and perception in the history of experimental psychology*. New York: Appleton-Century-Crofts.

Brigham, J. C., & Severy, L. J. (1976). Personality and attitude determinants of voting behavior. *Social Behavior and Personality*, *4*, 127–139.

Buchler, J. (1955). *Nature and judgment*. New York: Columbia University.

Cantril, H., & Bumstead, H. C. (1960). *Reflections on the human venture*. New York: New York University.

Carmichael, L., Hogan, H. P., & Walter, A. A. (1932). An experimental study of the effect of language on the reproduction of visually perceived forms. *Journal of Experimental Psychology*, *15*, 73–86.

Clapp, J. G. (1967). John Locke. In *The encyclopedia of philosophy* (Vol. 4). New York: Macmillan.

de Charms, R. (1968). *Personal causation*. New York: Academic Press.

Durkheim, E. (1912). *The elementary forms of the religious life*. Trans. J. W. Swain. Glencoe: Free Press.

Frazier, J. G. (1922). *The golden bough* (abr. ed.) New York: Macmillan.

Gibson, J. J. (1929). The reproduction of visually presented forms. *Journal of Experimental Psychology, 12*, 1–30.

Gleick, J. (1987). *Chaos: Making a new science.* New York: Penguin Books.

*Goldstein, K., & Scheerer, M. (1941). Abstract and concrete behavior: An experimental study with special tests. *Psychological Monograph*, *53*, Whole No. 239.

Gore, E. J. (1985). *Development of an objective measure of belief systems.* Unpublished doctoral dissertation, University of Colorado.

Greaves, G. (1971). Harvey's "This I Believe" test: Studies of reliability. *Psychological Reports, 28*, 387–390.

Harvey, O. J. (1963). Overview. In O. J. Harvey (Ed.), *Motivation and social interaction*. New York: Ronald.

Harvey, O. J. (1966). System structure, flexibility and creativity. In O. J. Harvey (Ed.), *Experience, structure and adaptability* (pp. 39–66). New York: Springer Verlag.

*Harvey, O. J. (1986). Belief systems and attitudes toward the death penalty and other punishments. *Journal of Personality*, *54*, 143–159.

*Harvey, O. J. (1989). Obituary: Muzafer Sherif (1906–1988). *American Psychologist*, 1325–1326.

Harvey, O. J., & Felknor, C. M. (1970). Parent–child relations as an antecedent to conceptual functioning. In R. A. Hoppe, G. A. Milton, & E. C. Simmel (Eds.), *Early experiences and the processes of socialization.* New York: Academic Press.

Harvey, O. J., & Ware, R. (1967). Personality factors in dissonance resolution. *Journal of Personality and Social Psychology*, *7*, 227–230.

*Harvey, O. J., Hunt, D. E., & Schroder, H. M. (1961). *Conceptual systems and personality organization.* New York: Wiley.

Harvey, O. J., Prather, M., White, B. J., & Hoffmeister, J. K. (1968). Teacher beliefs, classroom atmosphere and student performance. *American Educational Research Journal*, *5*, 151–166.

Harvey, O. J., Reich, J. W., & Wyer, R. S. (1968). The effect of attitudinal intensity and structure of beliefs upon differentiation. *Journal of Personality and Social Psychology*, *10*, 472–478.

Harvey, O. J., White, B. J., Prather, M., Alter, R. D., & Hoffmeister, J. K. (1966). Teacher beliefs and preschool atmospheres. *Journal of Educational Psychology*, *57*, 373–381.

Helson, H. (1948). Adaptation level as a basis for a quantitative theory of frames of reference. *Psychological Review*, *55*, 297–313.

Hovland, C. I., Harvey, O. J., & Sherif, M. (1957). Assimilation and contrast effects in reactions to communication and attitude change. *Journal of Abnormal and Social Psychology*, *55*, 244–252.

James, W. (1890). *Principles of psychology* (Vol. 1). New York: Henry Holt.

Kaufmann, W. (1973). *Without guilt and justice*. New York: Peter H. Wyden.

Kelley, D. M. (1972). *Why conservative churches are growing*. New York: Harper & Row.

Kelley, H. H. (1950). The warm–cold variable in first impressions of persons. *Journal of Personality*, *18*, 431–439.

Koffka, K. (1922). Perception: An introduction to gestalt-theory. *Psychological Bulletin*, *19*, 531–558.

*Kohler, W. (1929). *Gestalt psychology*. New York: Liveright.

Labov, W. (1973). *Sociolinguistic patterns.* Philadelphia, PA: University of Pennsylvania Press.

Langer, E. J. (1983). *The psychology of personal control*. Berkeley, CA: Sage.

Larimer, G. S. (1962). *Some effects of values on social judgment*. Unpublished master's thesis, University of Utah.

Lewin, K. (1935). *A dynamic theory of personality*. New York: McGraw Hill.

Lewin, K. (1951). *Field theory in social science* (Ed. D. Cartwright). New York: Harper.

McCormack, T. J. (Ed.) (1925). *George Berkeley: Three dialogues between Hylas and Philonous.* Chicago, IL: Open Court Publishing.

MacMurray, J. (1956). *The self as agent.* London: Faber.

Markus, R, A. (1967). St. Augustine. In *Encyclopedia of philosophy* (Vol. 1, pp. 198–297). New York: Macmillan.

Merleau-Ponty, M. (1981). *Phenomenology of perception* (Rev. ed., Trans. C. Smith). New York: Routledge and K. Paul.

Miller, A. G., & Harvey, O. J. (1973). Effects of concreteness–abstractness and anxiety on intellectual and motor performance. *Journal of Consulting and Clinical Psychology*, *3*, 444–451.

Munro, D. J. (1969). *The concept of man in early China.* Stanford: Stanford University.

*Pepper, S. C. (1942). *World hypotheses.* Berkeley: University of California Press.

*Petermann, B. (1932). *The gestalt theory and the problem of configuration.* New York: Harcourt Brace.

Piaget, J. (1951). Principal factors determining intellectual evolution from childhood to adult life. In D. Rappaport (Ed.), *Organization and pathology of thought.* New York: Columbia University.

Piaget, J. (1954). *The construction of reality in the child.* New York: Basic Books.

Polanyi, M. (1964). *Science, faith and society.* Chicago: University of Chicago.

Prigogine, I. (1976). Order through fluctuation: Self-organization an social system. In E. Jantsch & C. H. Waddington (Eds.), *Evolution and consciousness.* Reading, MA: Addison Wesley.

Raimy, V. C. (1975). *Misunderstandings of the self.* San Francisco: Jossey-Bass.

Sherif, M. (1935). A study of some social factors in perception. *Archives of Psychology*, No. 187.

*Sherif, M. (1936). *The psychology of social norms.* New York: Harper & Row.

Sherif, M., & Cantril, H. (1947). *The psychology of ego-involvements.* New York: Wiley.

Sherif, M., & Harvey, O. J. (1952). Elimination of stable anchorages in individual and group situations. *Sociometry*, *15*, 272–305.

Sherif, M., Harvey, O. J., White, B. J., Hood, W. R., & Sherif, C. W. (1961/1988). *Intergroup conflict and cooperation: The robbers cave study.* Norman, Institute of Group Relations, University of Oklahoma, Middletown, CT: Wesleyan University.

Sherif, M., & Hovland, C. I. (1961). *Social judgment: And contrast effects in communication and attitude change.* New Haven: Yale University.

*Sherif, M., & Sherif, C. W. (1969). *Social psychology.* New York: Harper & Row.

Thrasher, J. D. (1954). Interpersonal relations and gradations of stimulus structure in judgment variation. *Sociometry*, *17*, 228–241.

Tillich, P. (1952). *The courage to be.* New Haven: Yale University.

Walsh, W. H. (1967). Kant, Immanuel. In *Encyclopedia of philosophy* (Vol. 4), pp. 305–324.

Ware, R., & Harvey, O. J. (1967). A cognitive determinant of impression formation. *Journal of Personality and Social Psychology*, *5*, 38–44.

Ware, R., & Harvey, O. J. (1968). *Effects of source characteristics and belief systems on social judgment.* Unpublished manuscript, University of Colorado.

Werner, H. (1957). *Comparative psychology of mental development.* New York: International Universities Press.

Wertheimer, M. (Ed.) (1959). *Productive thinking.* New York: Harper.

White, B. J., & Harvey, O. J. (1965). Effects of personality and own stand on judgment and production of statements about a central issue. *Journal of Experimental Social Psychology*, *1*, 334–347.

11

Three Lessons from Social Psychology: Multiple Levels of Analysis, Methodological Pluralism, and Statistical Sophistication

Miles Hewstone

Miles Hewstone (born 1956) studied psychology at the University of Bristol, published his first paper in 1979, and obtained his doctorate from Oxford University in 1981 (supervised by Jos Jaspars). He has held chairs in social psychology at the universities of Bristol and Mannheim, and is now Professor of Psychology at the University of Wales, Cardiff. He has published widely on the topics of attribution theory, social cognition, stereotyping, and intergroup relations. He is co-founding editor of the *European Review of Social Psychology*, and a former editor of the *British Journal of Social Psychology*, a past recipient of the British Psychological Society's Spearman Medal, and a former Fellow at the Center for Advanced Study in the Behavioral Sciences, Stanford.

Introduction

Before proceeding to the idiosyncratic, and for me intellectually rewarding, exercise of considering what lessons I have learned from social psychology, I

I am grateful to the editors for their constructive comments on an earlier version of this chapter. I would also like to take the opportunity to thank the following persons who have been my "teachers" explicitly or implicitly, and contributed in a major way to my developing the view of social psychology contained herein: Howard Giles, the late Jos Jaspars, Charles M. Judd, Serge Moscovici, Wolfgang Stroebe, the late Henri Tajfel, and John Turner.

have to begin by adding to the editors' useful prologue in which they define *social psychology*. While I agree with most of what they write, for some years now I have applied a rather more specific definition to myself – or subscribed to a more specific (sub-) discipline – that of contextual social psychology.

The term *contextual social psychology* was coined by Pettigrew (1981) and contrasted with two other "wings" of social psychology – *experimental social psychology* and *symbolic interactionism*. In fact, my self-definition overlaps with Pettigrew's experimental and contextual variants. I subscribe to experimental social psychology's focus on controlled experimentation, emphasis on individual psychological processes as mediators of social and situational effects rather than personality factors, and detailed analysis of cognitive processes. I also follow the journals he associates with this sub-field: e.g. *Journal of Personality and Social Psychology*, *Journal of Experimental Social Psychology* and the *European Journal of Social Psychology*. But I disagree with the unrelieved reliance on laboratory experimentation – indeed I make this one of my main lessons from social psychology!

I strongly identify with contextual social psychology because of its "consistent attention to individual factors in the context of macrostructural factors" and its "consistent simultaneous use of individual and social variables in both its theory and research" (Pettigrew, 1981, p. 308), but I think its output is represented widely in the journals mentioned above, and neither exclusively nor even predominantly in what Pettigrew calls its "chief journal outlets" – *Social Psychology Quarterly* (formerly *Sociometry*) and the *Journal of Social Issues*. Indeed, none of my own research, which I draw on below for illustrative purposes, has been published in these two outlets, and most of it has been published in the journals Pettigrew associates with experimental social psychology. These disagreements aside, I endorse the three emphases of contextual social psychology which, as Pettigrew points out, are shared in each case with one of the other forms of social psychology, but combine to provide a distinct approach: (1) an emphasis on cognitive factors at the individual level, i.e. the study of individually held knowledge structures and associated processes, such as attitudes, causal attributions, and stereotypes; (2) a commitment to quantitative methods, although these are as likely to involve quasi-experiments, field studies, and so on as they are to be laboratory experiments; (3) the willingness to strike a balance between maximizing both external and internal validity, which is seen in the attention paid to real-world data and the study of applied problems. According to Pettigrew, the pantheon of contextual social psychologists includes such figures as Sherif, Kelman, and D. Campbell, and Pettigrew applies the group name to himself, too. I would add the names of three prominent Europeans each of whom has had a major influence on my own work – Henri Tajfel, Jos Jaspars, and Serge Moscovici.

Thus my own definition of social psychology would be something like:

The scientific study of how personal, situational and societal factors influence the cognition, motivation and behavior of individuals and (members of) social groups. It ranges from intra-personal processes (e.g. how we perceive other people), to interpersonal relations (e.g. friendship, marriage), to intergroup relations (e.g. ethnic prejudice and stereotyping), and societal analyses (e.g. the beliefs shared by large numbers of people within a society).

More succinctly, what I think is unique about the perspective of social psychology is its analysis of individuals' subjective (cognitive) representations of social factors and how these guide perceptions and behavior in social contexts. It is in terms of this view of the discipline that I have enumerated the following lessons that I have learned.

Lesson One: Levels of Analysis

Levels of analysis in social-psychological research

As the editors of this volume acknowledge in their introduction, there are many ways to interpret the "social" in social psychology. Although this question has all the attractions of an intellectual black hole, it is important in establishing the boundaries and the scope of our discipline. One of the most important lessons I have learned, and have tried to bring to bear on my own research, is that there exist different levels of analysis at which social psychology can be, and should be, studied. Doise (1980, 1986) distinguished four levels of analysis in social-psychological studies:

1. The *intraindividual* level focuses on the mechanisms by which people organize their perception and evaluation of the social environment (level I).
2. The *interindividual* and *situational* level concerns interindividual processes as they occur in a given situation; the different positions that persons occupy outside the situation are not taken into account (level II).
3. The *social-positional* level is concerned with extra-situational differences in social position, such as the different group or categorical memberships of participants (level III).
4. The *ideological* level refers to systems of beliefs, representations, evaluations and norms that subjects carry with them into an experimental situation (level IV).

Doise used this scheme to analyze published work and he identified a dominant tendency in social-psychological research, both American and European, to limit the analysis to levels I and II. He noted, however, that European social psychology did attempt, more than its American counterpart, to introduce level-III and -IV analyses into both theory and research.

Both the prosecution of research at different levels and the integration of that body of research will surely yield a more complete understanding of phenomena than any one level can achieve alone. I try to illustrate this in the following section for the field of attribution theory. Just as Doise noted, it is a field in which American researchers have tended to work at levels I and II, whereas Europeans became more associated with levels III and IV. Later, however, researchers (including myself) began to "cross the divide," often back and forth, resulting in a broader notion of attribution and a more ambitious attempt to integrate studies across the levels of analysis.

Illustration from my own research: levels of attribution

Attribution theory, the study of common sense causal explanations, yields clear illustrations of Doise's four levels of analysis (see Hewstone, 1989). Level I, the intraindividual level, is limited to psychological or intrapersonal processes that deal with how individuals organize their perception, evaluation, and behavior in the social world. The emphasis is on how (i.e. the mechanisms by which) individuals process information. A prototypical example of attribution work at this level is Kelley's (1973) analysis of variance model of how individuals process information to arrive at a cause: they use three different types of information (consensus, consistency, and distinctiveness) to identify the conditions which covary with a particular event and thus "cause" it.

Level II, the interindividual or situational level, concentrates on the dynamics of interpersonal processes within a given situation. Individuals are seen as occupying essentially equal positions and are considered as interchangeable actors. The research on actor-observer differences in attribution, based on Jones and Nisbett's (1972) hypothesis, is a prototype of this level of analysis: actors tend to focus outwards on the situation as a cause of their behavior, whereas observers focus on the dispositional characteristics of the actor as the cause of observed behavior.

Level III, the socio-positional level, studies the effects of social categorization on attribution, and specifically whether identical behaviors or outcomes are explained differently as a function of targets' and perceivers' group memberships. This is illustrated by Taylor and Jaggi's (1974) study of Hindu perceivers' attributions for positive and negative acts by Hindu and Muslim targets. Hindus tended to give more internal (person) attributions for socially desirable than undesirable behavior performed by in-group members; they also tended to give somewhat more internal attributions for socially *un*desirable than desirable behavior enacted by out-group members. Remarkably, because of the traditional North American dominance of attribution research, there has long been a reluctance, at worst due to ignorance, to accept that there exists both an "intergroup" approach to attribution and an "attributional" approach to intergroup relations. The former emphasizes category-based and not just interpersonal attribution; the latter shows how attributional processes such as "explaining away" positive, disconfirming behavior by an out-group member can maintain intergroup conflict and block stereotype change (see Hewstone, 1989, Chapter 6, for a detailed analysis).

Level IV, the ideological level (which I prefer to call the "societal" level), studies the beliefs that are shared by large numbers of people within a society. A prototypical study is Miller's (1984) analysis of cross-cultural patterns of attribution, showing a developmental increase in dispositional attributions for an American sample, but an increase in contextual explanations for an Indian Hindu sample. At this level, attribution theory can be married to Moscovici' s (1976) analysis of social representations (see editors' introduction) to provide an analysis of the overlooked question, "where do attributions comes from?" (see Hewstone, 1989, Chapter 7).

The benefits of multiple-level research

One of the most often-heard criticisms of social psychology (from within the discipline!) is that we have a propensity to generate mini-theories which spawn mini-studies. As critics have argued, we should be engaged in more integrative, unifying work:

> An adequate understanding of either a phenomenon or a theory requires that it can be investigated through a program of research planned to reveal the wide range of circumstances that affect the phenomenon and the rich set of implicit assumptions that limit the theory, thus making explicit the contexts in which one or another relationship obtains. (McGuire, 1983, p. 22)

> Instead of adding to [the] proliferation of minitheories, researchers should focus on those fundamental principles of psychological functioning that have the potential to unify and organize the sprawling mass of research findings within one theoretical framework. (Tetlock and Manstead, 1985, p. 74)

Doise's analysis suggests that the integration (or "articulation," as he calls it) of different levels represents the next major challenge. As Doise wrote, "If there is a case for distinguishing four levels of analysis, it is in order to unite them better in future research" (1986, p. 28; see also Doise, 1984). I believe this is true not just for attribution or for any other theory in our field, but for the whole field itself. The advantages of a multi-level approach to attribution are several and obvious. First, the use of a levels model can be thought of in terms of Campbell's (1969) concept of "triangulation," the idea that multiple vantage points enable the researcher to "fix" on a common object in a way that would be impossible from a single point (Brewer & Collins, 1981). Thus the topic of attributional biases looks quite different when a purely information-processing perspective is supplanted with a societal level of analysis. For example, the "fundamental attribution error" (Ross, 1977) – broadly the tendency to make dispositional rather than situational attributions – might be explained cognitively in terms of differential rates of forgetting for situational and dispositional causes, but also societally in terms of social and cultural norms. Second, the pursuit of a social psychology in this mould encourages methodological diversity (e.g. the extremes of level I and level IV analyses will tend to capitalize on the respective strengths of laboratory and field research). I will argue in more detail for methodological pluralism in the following section.

Lesson Two: Methodological Pluralism

The case for programmatic research

As social psychologists we have at our disposal a broad range of research strategies which differ in terms of the representativeness of data that are collected, the realism of the setting in which data are collected, and the degree of control we as researchers have over the setting in which data are collected (see Manstead & Semin, 1996). These strategies include survey research, experiments, and quasi-experiments (in quasi-experiments subjects cannot be randomly assigned to conditions), field studies and archival research.

Although social psychologists could, and sometimes do, employ a wide range of methodological techniques, in practice many of them do not, and the range of techniques used seems to vary with the topic studied. Towering above all other methods is the laboratory experiment. It has become "the core research method in social psychology" (Aronson, Brewer, & Carlsmith, 1985, p. 443) because it is the method best suited to testing theory rather than merely describing the world as it is. It permits the experimenter a great degree of control over possible random variation and, even more advantageous, allows him or her to assign research subjects at random to experimental conditions. Thus laboratory experimentation, allied to probabilistic statistics, has paved the "royal road" to causal inference (Aronson et al., 1985). Notwithstanding the strengths of the laboratory experiment, I have learned that I can place greater faith in a theory that has been tested with multiple methods in different settings. Aronson et al., far from ignoring this point, champion what they call "programmatic research" (p. 476), based on the interplay of laboratory and field experimentation such that "*different* experimental procedures are used to explore the same conceptual relationship" (p. 480). I would like to go a stage further and remove the word "experimental" from the preceding quotation. Intersecting evidence from multiple methods (and not merely from different experimental procedures) increases convergent validity (Campbell & Fiske, 1959) and should be a goal to which more of us strive more of the time.

Illustrations from my own research: cognitive models of stereotype change

Over the last four years I have carried out a series of studies (with colleagues) investigating cognitive models of how stereotypes might change in response to different patterns of disconfirming information. We began in the laboratory, where we sought to replicate and extend the research of Weber and Crocker (1983). They compared stereotyping under two patterns of stereotype-disconfirming information: concentrated and dispersed. In the concentrated condition, disconfirming information is concentrated in a few group members, each of whom strongly disconfirms the group stereotype. In the dispersed condition, the same amount of disconfirming information is dispersed across several group members, each of whom only mildly disconfirms the stereotype. Like them we reported weaker stereotyping (by inference, more change) in response to the dispersed rather than the concentrated pattern of information (Johnston & Hewstone, 1992; see Hewstone, 1994, for a review). This finding was consistent with a "subtyping" model of stereotype change: extreme disconfirmers in the concentrated condition are seen as unrepresentative group members and are set aside from other group members or subtyped; the stereotype is thereby insulated from change. We reasoned, further, that disconfirming attributes are most likely to become associated with the stereotype if they belong to an individual who is otherwise a very good "fit" to the category prototype, and showed that the "disconfirmers" (those group members described by any disconfirming information) were seen as more typical of the group in the dispersed than the concentrated condition. We also showed that, when subjects were asked to sort group members into piles based on perceived similarities and differences, extreme disconfirmers were cognitively represented in a separate subcategory, especially in the concentrated condition. We replicated and extended these effects in subsequent studies, using a variety of dependent measures.

Later we had the opportunity to carry out a large field study which applied this cognitive perspective on stereotype change to an evaluation of the "police–schools liaison" program run by one British police force. The idea behind this program was, simply, that one could effect change in young people's views of the police through direct contact between the police and young people. The particular program assigned full-time "school police officers" to some secondary schools ("target" schools) but not to others ("control" schools). Because only one police officer was assigned to each school, we argued that this intervention was based implicitly on – and provided a real-life application of – the conversion model of stereotype change.

We predicted that even if pupils formed a positive overall view of their target policeman, this image would be unlikely to generalize to their stereotype of the police in general unless the school police officer was seen as highly typical; and pupils would subtype the school police officer as distinct from the police in general. These hypotheses were tested in two field studies (a large-scale survey of stereotypes and a smaller, detailed analysis of subtyping as a cognitive process that impedes stereotype change). The longitudinal survey included a key comparison of stereotypes of the "police in general" and the "school police officer" held over the course of a year by target-school pupils (because only they had contact with and could therefore evaluate the stimulus, school police officer; see Hewstone, Hopkins, & Routh, 1992, Study 1). The school police officer was seen as quite different from (and more positive than) the police in general at both time 1 and 2. But there was no evidence that pupils had generalized from a positive view of their school police officer to a more positive view of the police in general at time.

To provide a more detailed analysis of whether these targets were subtyped in some cognitive sense, and thus excluded from the category of the police in general, we carried out an additional study. The second study (Hewstone et al., 1992, Study 2) investigated how pupils in a new target school categorized various sorts of policemen, authority figures, and significant others. The pupils were given twenty-five cards and asked to group the cards they felt were similar in some way. Pupils' card-sorts were analyzed using a computer-modeling program. The most striking feature of these data was the relatively tight clustering which included all the types of police officer ("foot patrol police officer," "woman police officer," "police officer in transit van" and "mounted police officer") *except* the "school police officer." It was clear that the psychological distance between the school police officer and the other police officers was much greater than that existing between the various other police officers. The results of this study suggested that these pupils viewed their school police officer as being quite distinct from the police in general and subtyped him accordingly. This evidence is, however, suggestive rather than definitive, given that the card-sorting measure of subtyping is a somewhat forced measure. We then went back to the laboratory to develop a more spontaneous measure of subtyping, based on clustering in free recall of information. We reasoned that if subjects do subtype disconfirmers more in the concentrated than dispersed condition, then they should organize their recall more in terms of the two separate subcategories, confirmers and disconfirmers. This is exactly what we found (Hewstone, Macrae, Griffiths, Milne, & Brown, 1994, Experiment 1).

The benefits of methodological pluralism

Of course, these field studies can provide only indirect evidence for or against certain cognitive models of stereotype change, because we did not *manipulate* different patterns of stereotype change. However, the research program as a whole derives validity from the plurality of methods, measures, and settings and makes me, at least, more confident that we are developing a model that is not restricted to, for example, artificial laboratory settings and specific measures. Thus I have learned the lesson taught by Festinger (1953) that the overall research program is best seen as a process of coming and going between the laboratory and the outside world.

Lesson Three: Statistical Sophistication

Statistical sophistication: all things in moderation . . . and mediation

One of the most crucial lessons I have learned about social-psychological research (I have had to learn it, since editors increasingly demand it, as in my view they should) is that the results of initial analyses (typically analysis of variance) are but the first step. There was a time when internal analysis of simple correlations would suffice as the second step. But more recent contributions by scholars who are both social psychologists and statisticians have indicated that something far more sophisticated is both available and necessary (Baron & Kenny, 1986; Judd & Kenny, 1981).

The moderator–mediator variable distinction in social-psychological research

Rarely has my reading of a paper reaped such rich personal rewards as my reading of Baron and Kenny (1986). These authors set out with exemplary clarity the key distinction between moderator and mediator variables, and demonstrate its importance for the field of social psychology. As they explain, the distinction is best understood in terms of the kinds of questions one is asking in research: moderator variables address "when" questions (e.g. *when* does contact between members of different groups lead to an improvement in out-group attitudes?), whereas mediator variables address "how" or "why" questions (e.g. *how* or *why* does exposure to different patterns of stereotype-disconfirming information have differential impact on stereotype change?). Both moderation and mediation effects involve more than two variables; that is, they both deal with what happens when a third variable comes into play. But they do so in very different ways. Moderation implies that the *level* of the third variable can change the relationship between the other two variables, whereas mediation implies that the relationship between the two variables can actually be created by the third variable. For example, schoolgirls may perform better in school than boys, but only *when* they are educated in single-sex schools (i.e. type of school *moderates* performance); further research might show *how* this comes about, for example through greater attention and effort, fewer class interruptions and so on (i.e. psychological processes and classroom variables *mediate* performance).

This volume is not the place to detail the statistical nature of the argument, which has in any case already been done by Baron and Kenny (nor, as my friends will attest, is this author the person to do it!). It is more important to state why the distinction matters and to refer, briefly, to the appropriate statistical solutions. The distinction matters, first, because the terms moderation and mediation should not be used interchangeably. However, Baron and Kenny include in their article examples of authors who have done just this; I relate this fact not with *Schadenfreude* but more with relief (there but for the grace of God went I). The distinction matters, second, as Baron and Kenny explain, because it has implications for our choice of experimental designs, research options, and planned statistical analyses. I would go even further and argue that it should affect the theories we develop. Kenny (1985) commented that the analysis of variance had become no longer merely an analytical tool but the framework in which we think about theoretical and research issues. I will try to illustrate from my own research program why I think that this new framework is necessary.

Illustrations from my own research: intergroup contact

Since Allport (1954/1979) first explored the "contact hypothesis" in social-psychological research, research has studied what situational factors (such as intimacy, cooperation, and equal status) maximize the positive benefits of bringing members of two hostile groups into contact with each other (see Amir, 1976). Together with Rupert Brown, I have argued that it is also crucial to ensure that group affiliations, social categorizations, are still evident in contact situations – we call this "intergroup" contact. If this is not the case there will be merely a change in interpersonal perceptions of isolated out-group members and not generalized change in attitudes towards the out-group as a whole (Hewstone, 1996; Hewstone & Brown, 1986). Thus we are talking about *when* contact leads to decreased prejudice, and that "when" implies a moderational approach.

We recently tested this idea with survey data, including European students' self-reported contact with Germans and attitudes towards living in Germany (Vivian, Brown, & Hewstone, 1996). Our measures included three types of contact – the amount of contact, its intimacy, and whether it was cooperative or competitive. In each case we argued that the effect of contact on attitude would be *moderated* by whether the contact could be considered to be "intergroup" (of course the cross-sectional survey data do not allow us to determine the direction of causality implied by figure 11.1, and the original article acknowledges this qualification). We assessed this in three ways, by asking respondents in the survey: (1) how often they and a German contact partner reported making references to one another's country or nationality in their encounters; (2) to rate how typical the other person was of his or her national group; and (3) to rate the perceived homogeneity–heterogeneity of the other national group as a whole.

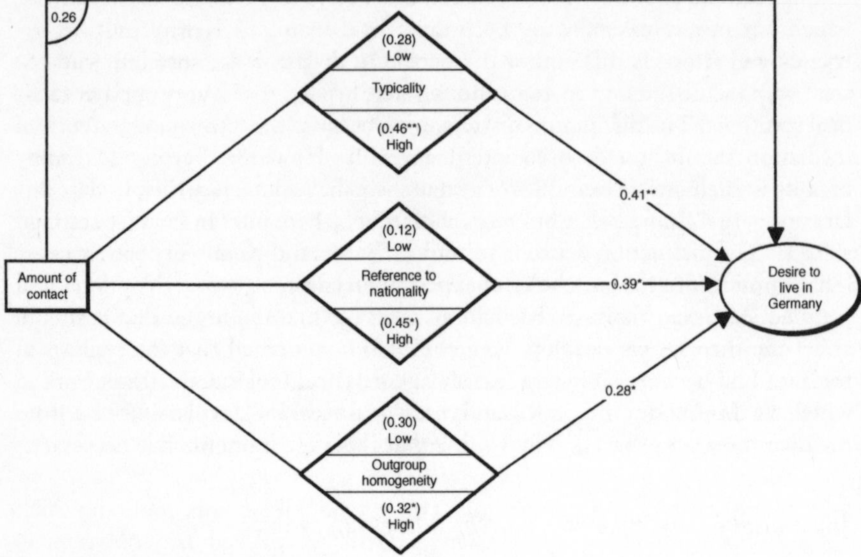

Figure 11.1 "Intergroup" contact moderates the effect of contact on attitude

We reasoned that "intergroup" contact would involve more references to nationality, contact with someone seen as typical of the out-group, and an out-group seen as relatively homogeneous.

The results of our moderational analysis for "amount of contact" are shown in figure 11.1. Statistically this analysis involves adding a moderator variable (each of typicality, references, and homogeneity in turn) and its product (or interaction) with the independent variable (amount of contact) to a regression equation containing the independent variable alone. We do this to see whether each interaction term (e.g. amount qualified by typicality) has a significant effect on its own. Independent effects for the interaction terms indicate moderation. As figure 11.1 shows, although amount of contact affects "desire to live in Germany" on its own, all three interaction terms are significant (0.41, 0.39, 0.28), indicating moderation effects. We then assessed the effects of each potential moderator separately by dichotomizing the moderator into "low" and "high" categories; and reassessed the effects associated with the independent variable at different levels of the (dichotomized) moderator variable. As figure 11.1 shows, the amount of contact was more strongly associated with desire to live in Germany in respondents who reported contact with highly typical Germans (0.46), reported relatively frequent references to nationality during contact (0.45), and perceived relatively high out-group homogeneity (0.32). These data are strongly supportive of our intergroup model of contact and test its moderational assumption correctly: out-group contact has a stronger effect on out-group attitude *when* contact is intergroup in nature.

Our intergroup model of contact also makes a *mediational* assumption about how stereotype-disconfirming information can change stereotypes. It implies that disconfirming attributes are most likely to become associated with the stereotype if they belong to an individual who is otherwise a very good fit to the category (Rothbart & John, 1985). Somewhat counter-intuitively, stereotype-disconfirming information should therefore be linked to typical out-group members (see also Wilder, 1984), a view that is consistent with Hewstone and Brown's (1986) idea that categories should be maintained in contact settings. Unless this is the case, people tend to react to stereotype-disconfirming information not with generalization, but with "subtyping."

In a recent study we used mediational analysis to test whether the impact of different patterns of stereotype-disconfirming information on stereotyping was mediated by perceived typicality and/or subtyping (Hewstone, Hassebrauck, Wirth, & Waenke, 1995). As Baron and Kenny (1986) explain, to ascribe a mediator function to a third variable implies that it represents the "generative mechanism" through which the independent variable is able to influence the dependent variable. We reasoned that two potential mediators could in principle fulfill this function. First, change could be blocked by subtyping of disconfirming members (measured by the extent to which disconfirming and confirming groups members are clustered separately in memory) which we knew to be greater in the concentrated condition could block change. Second, the perceived typicality of "disconfirmers" (those members of the out-group who show any disconfirming behavior), which we knew to be greater in the dispersed condition, could play the crucial role in generalizing change.

Statistically, testing mediation requires the researcher to test a series of regression models in order to explore the relationship between variables (Judd & Kenny, 1981). These regression equations ask simple questions such as "what is the relationship between patterns of stereotypical information and psychological processes?" and "what is the relationship between stereotyping and the pattern of information respondents are exposed to?" In the first equation, the potential mediators (subtyping, typicality) are regressed on the independent variable (concentrated vs dispersed patterns, contrast coded +1 and −1, respectively). The independent variable *must* affect a mediator if the latter is to be considered a possible mediator of the independent variable's effect on the dependent variable. As figure 11.2 shows, this is only the case for typicality (−0.554, i.e. the dispersed condition is associated with greater perceived typicality). In the second equation, the dependent variable (stereotyping index) is regressed on the independent variable (pattern). To establish mediation the independent variable must affect the dependent variable (and does so with a significant coefficient of 0.274). In the third equation, the dependent variable is regressed on both the independent variable and the mediators. To establish mediation, the mediator(s) must still affect the dependent variable (only typicality is significantly associated with decreased stereotyping, −0.560). Thus

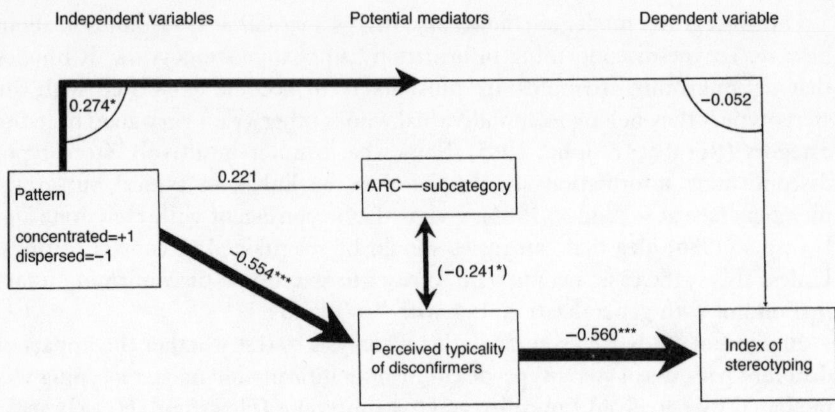

Figure 11.2 Perceived typicality of disconfirmers mediates the impact of different patterns of disconfirming information on stereotyping

perceived typicality is the only credible mediator. The final test of mediation involves comparing the effect of the independent variable on the dependent variable in equations two and three; the effect must be less in three than two and this is the case (−0.052 vs 0.274). Perfect mediation holds if the independent variable has no effect when the mediator is controlled.

This kind of analysis seems crucial to testing our theories properly. In this case, it led me to re-evaluate the nature of subtyping, and to see perceived typicality of disconfirmers as the key process, one consequence of which is that disconfirmers will be subtyped, thus ruling out their impact in the long term. This is, of course, quite different from asserting that subtyping (measured by the ARC measure of clustering in recall) mediates stereotype change, which is clearly not the case.

The role of statistics in our discipline

I fear that some readers (and especially those who, like me, find statistics a challenging topic) may feel that a volume like this one should be about theoretical, and not statistical, issues. I agree, but when we are using statistics to test our theories inappropriately, then the issue *is* theoretical. I hope to have demonstrated, in relatively non-technical language, the importance of the moderation–mediation distinction. There is now a growing number of papers that illustrate the application of these analyses to a wide variety of areas, and some of which are particularly clear in the way they test, rather than assume, central relationships in fields such as social influence (Baker & Petty, 1994), or intergroup relations (Gaertner, Mann, Dovidio, Murrell, & Pomare, 1990). To test sophisticated theory in a sophisticated manner we need to keep moving forward statistically.

Conclusion

In this chapter I have tried to share three of the lessons that I personally have learned from social psychology. I am not arguing that they are more important than some of the others I might have listed, nor do I wish to imply that there will be no further lessons to learn in the future. Indeed, had it not been used already in an engaging account of lessons learned about the application of statistics to psychology, I might have entitled this chapter: "Things I have learned (so far)" (Cohen, 1990).

Nonetheless, these three lessons (multiple levels of analysis, methodological pluralism, and statistical sophistication) do seem to me to constitute something of the essence of social psychology – the quantitative analysis of the individual in social settings – the characteristics that set it apart from related, complementary disciplines. Finally, I do not wish to appear Panglossian, uncritically contented with the state of our discipline. Had the editors' emphasis been somewhat different, I might, for example, have written about my concern that we as social psychologists pay relatively little attention to the nature of theory (with honorable exceptions such as Pettigrew, 1991) – but that is a lesson still to be learned. I do though take seriously the charge of irrelevance that has been leveled at social psychology, especially when the accusers have been senior scholars who have made major contributions to the field:

> [M]any contemporary studies seem to shed light on nothing more than a narrow phenomenon studied under specific conditions . . . some current investigations seem to end up in elegantly polished triviality – snippets of empiricism, but nothing more. (Allport, 1968, p. 68)

> [I]mpressive gains in technical competence have been . . . something of a mixed blessing, for the fascination with technique seems all too often to have replaced a concern for substantive significance. (Cartwright, 1979, p. 87)

But I believe that holding true to these three lessons makes the phenomena identified broader, the conditions studied more general, and the significance of our contributions substantial as well as statistical.

References

(Those marked * are recommended for further reading.)

Allport, G. W. (1954/1979). *The nature of prejudice*. Cambridge/Reading, MA: Addison Wesley.

Allport, G. W. (1968). The historical background of modern social psychology. In G. Lindzey & E. Aronson (Eds.), *Handbook of social psychology* (2nd ed., Vol. 1, pp. 1–80). Reading, MA: Addison Wesley.

Amir, Y. (1976). The role of intergroup contact in change of prejudice and ethnic relations. In P. A. Katz (Ed.), *Towards the elimination of racism* (pp. 245–308). Elmsford, NY: Pergamon Press.

Aronson, E., Brewer, M. B., & Carlsmith, J. M. (1985). Experimentation in social psychology. In G. Lindzey & E. Aronson (Eds.) *Handbook of social psychology* (3rd ed., Vol. 1, pp. 441–486). New York: Random House.

Baker, S. M., & Petty, R. E. (1994). Majority and minority influence: Source-position imbalance as a determinant of message scrutiny. *Journal of Personality and Social Psychology*, *67*, 5–19.

* Baron, R. M., & Kenny, D. A. (1986). The moderator–mediator variable distinction in social psychological research: Conceptual, strategic, and statistical considerations. *Journal of Personality and Social Psychology*, *51*, 1173–1182.

* Brewer, M. B., & Collins, B. E. (Eds.) (1981). Perspectives on knowing: Six themes from Donald T. Campbell. In M. B. Brewer & B. E. Collins (Eds.), *Scientific inquiry and the social sciences: A volume in honor of Donald T. Campbell*. San Francisco, CA: Jossey-Bass.

Campbell, D. T. (1969). Reforms as experiments. *American Psychologist*, *24*, 409–429.

Campbell, D. T., & Fiske, D. W. (1959). Convergent and discriminant validation by the multitrait-multimatrix method. *Psychological Bulletin*, *56*, 81–105.

Cohen, J. (1990). Things I have learned (so far). *American Psychologist*, *45*, 1304–1312.

Cartwright, D. (1979). Contemporary social psychology in historical perspective. *Social Psychology Quarterly*, *42*, 82–93.

* Doise, W. (1980). Levels of explanation in the *European Journal of Social Psychology*. *European Journal of Social Psychology*, *10*, 213–231.

Doise, W. (1986). *Levels of explanation in social psychology*. Cambridge/Paris: Cambridge University Press/Maison des Sciences de l' Homme. (Originally published as *L'explication en psychologie sociale*. Paris: Presses Universitaires France, 1982.)

Festinger, L. (1953). Laboratory experiments. In L. Festinger & D. Katz (Eds.), *Research methods in the behavioral sciences*. New York: Dryden. [Reprinted in S. Schachter & M. S. Gazzaniga (Eds.), *Extending psychological frontiers: Selected works of Leon Festinger* (pp. 510–541). New York: Russell Sage Foundation.]

Gaertner, S. L., Mann, J. A., Dovidio, J. F., Murrell, A. J., & Pomare, M. (1990). How does cooperation reduce intergroup bias? *Journal of Personality and Social Psychology*, *59*, 692–704.

Hewstone, M. (1994). Revision and change of stereotypic beliefs: In search of the elusive subtyping model. In W. Stroebe & M. Hewstone (Eds.), *European Review of Social Psychology* (Vol. 5, pp. 69–109). Chichester: J. Wiley.

Hewstone, M. (1989). *Causal attribution: From cognitive processes to collective beliefs*. Oxford, UK/Cambridge, MA: Blackwell.

* Hewstone, M. (1996). Contact and categorization: Social-psychological interventions to change intergroup relations. In C. N. Macrae, C. Stangor, & M. Hewstone (Eds.), *Foundations of stereotypes and stereotyping* (pp. 323–368). New York: Guilford.

Hewstone, M., & Brown, R. J. (1986). Contact is not enough: An intergroup perspective on the "contact hypothesis." In M. Hewstone & R. J. Brown (Eds.), *Contact and conflict in intergroup encounters* (pp. 1–44). Oxford: Blackwell.

Hewstone, M., Hassebrauck, M., Wirth, A., & Waenke, M. (1995). *Mediation of stereotype change via perceived typicality of disconfirmers*. Unpublished manuscript, Universities of Cardiff, Wales and Mannheim.

Hewstone, M., Hopkins, N., & Routh, D. A. (1992). Cognitive models of stereotype change: (1) Generalization and subtyping in young people's views of the police. *European Journal of Social Psychology*, *22*, 219–234.

Hewstone, M., Macrae, C. N., Griffiths, R., Milne, A., & Brown, R. (1994). Cognitive models of stereotype change: (5) Measurement, development, and consequences of subtyping. *Journal of Experimental Social Psychology*, *30*, 505–526.

Johnston, L., & Hewstone, M. (1992). Cognitive models of stereotype change: (3) Subtyping and the perceived typicality of disconfirming group members. *Journal of Experimental Social Psychology*, *28*, 360–386.

Jones, E. E., & Nisbett, R. E. (1972). The actor and the observer: Divergent perceptions of the causes of behavior. In E. E. Jones, D. E. Kanouse, H. H. Kelley, R. E. Nisbett, S. Valins, & B. Weiner (Eds.), *Attribution: Perceiving the causes of behavior* (pp. 79–94). Morristown, NJ: General Learning Press.

Judd, C. M., & Kenny, D. A. (1981). Process analysis: Estimating mediation in evaluation research. *Evaluation Research*, *5*, 602–619.

Kelley, H. H. (1973). The processes of causal attribution. *American Psychologist*, *28*, 107–128.

Kenny, D. A. (1985). Quantitative methods for social psychology. In G. Lindzey & E. Aronson (Eds.), *The handbook of social psychology* (3rd ed., Vol. 1, pp. 487–508). New York: Random House.

Manstead, A. S. R., & Semin, G. R. (1996). Methodology in social psychology: Putting ideas to the test. In M. Hewstone, W. Stroebe, & G. M. Stephenson (Eds.), *Introduction to social psychology: A European perspective* (2nd ed., pp. 74–106). Oxford: Blackwell.

McGuire, W. J. (1983). A contextualist theory of knowledge: Its implications for innovation and reform in psychological research. In L. Berkowitz (Ed.), *Advances in experimental social psychology* (Vol. 16, pp. 1–47). Orlando, FL: Academic Press.

Miller, J. G. (1984). Culture and the development of everyday social explanation. *Journal of Personality and Social Psychology*, *46*, 961–978.

Moscovici, S. (1961/1976). *La psychoanalyse, son image et son public* (2nd ed.). Paris: Presses Universitaires de France.

Pettigrew, T. F. (1981). Extending the stereotype concept. In D. L. Hamilton (Ed.), *Cognitive processes in stereotyping and intergroup behavior* (pp. 303–331). Hillsdale, NJ: Lawrence Erlbaum.

Pettigrew, T. F. (1991). Toward unity and bold theory: Popperian suggestions for two persistent problems of social psychology. In C. W. Stephan, W. Stephan, & T. F. Pettigrew (Eds.), *The future of social psychology* (pp. 13–27). New York: Springer-Verlag.

Ross, L. (1977). The intuitive psychologist and his shortcomings: Distortions in the attribution process. In L. Berkowitz (Ed.), *Advances in experimental social psychology* (Vol. 10, pp. 173–220). New York: Academic Press.

Rothbart, M., & John, O. P. (1985). Social categorization and behavioral episodes: A cognitive analysis of the effects of intergroup contact. *Journal of Social Issues*, *41*, 81–104.

Taylor, D. M., & Jaggi, V. (1974). Ethnocentrism and causal attribution in a South Indian context. *Journal of Cross-Cultural Psychology*, *5*, 162–171.

Tetlock, P. E., & Manstead, A. S. R. (1985). Impression management versus intrapsychic explanations in social psychology: A useful dichotomy? *Psychological Review*, *92*, 59–77.

Vivian, J., Brown, R., & Hewstone, M. (1996). *Changing attitudes through intergroup contact: The effects of group membership salience*. Manuscript under review.

Weber, R., & Crocker, J. (1983). Cognitive processes in the revision of stereotypic beliefs. *Journal of Personality and Social Psychology*, *45*, 961–977.

Wilder, D. A. (1984). Intergroup contact: The typical member and the exception to the rule. *Journal of Experimental Social Psychology*, *20*, 177–194.

12 Biases in Social Cognition: "Aboutness" as a General Principle

E. Tory Higgins

Tory Higgins, Professor of Psychology, Columbia University, was born in Montreal, Canada in 1946. He honored in anthropology and sociology as an undergraduate at McGill University, and then received his M.A. in social psychology at London School of Economics and Political Science. During these early years he became interested in the interrelation among language, thought, and society. He received his doctorate in psychology from Columbia University (1973) where he worked with Janellen Huttenlocher in psycholinguistics, Robert Krauss in interpersonal communication, and Stanley Schachter in health psychology. He was a co-founder of the Ontario Symposium of Personality and Social Psychology, a Fellow at the Center for Advanced Study in the Behavioral Sciences, and a recipient of a MERIT award from the National Institute of Health. He is associate editor of *Social Cognition* and has co-edited several volumes on social cognition and on motivation and cognition.

You watch a debate and observe a debater's strong advocacy of a position. Even though you know that the debating coach assigned each position to be advocated, you decide that the position advocated was the debater's true personal opinion. Shortly after exercising you meet a guy who bothered you earlier in the day and you feel more angry at him than you did when the incident happened. A friend of yours who clearly dislikes a woman you just met at a party asks your impression of her. Although the conversation has little immediate effect on your memory of what happened at the party, weeks later you misremember the woman as having behaved badly at the party. These examples illustrate well-established cases of social-cognitive shortcomings – correspondence bias, misattribution, and saying is believing, respectively. This paper describes how these and other biases in social cognition, such as false consensus, perseverance, overjustification, priming effects, and change-of-standard effects, can all be understood in terms of a single basic principle of social cognition – the "aboutness principle" (for some related ideas, see also Higgins & Bargh, 1987).

The "aboutness" principle refers to the following tendency. When people perceive a response (their own or another person's), they represent what the response is about, and whatever is represented as what the response is *about* is inferred to be the *source* of the response. Before describing various ways in which social cognition is led astray by the aboutness principle, two initial questions must be briefly considered. First, why do people represent what perceived responses are about? Second, why is the operation of the aboutness principle problematic?

When a person responds to some input, such as an emotional response to some object or event, the response, if not itself an action, provides information to take action. But in order to take action, it is necessary for the person to represent what the response is about. A fear response to an input, for example, provides information to avoid something, but avoid what? It is necessary to represent that the fear response is about "X" in order to take action to avoid "X." When observing the response of another person it is also important to represent what the response is about. For example, just categorizing another person's facial expression as "frowning" provides little information that is useful for taking action. To take action it is important to represent whether this person's expression is about the circumstances surrounding its production or is about the emotional tendencies of the person who produced it. Thus, perceiving the responses of self or others in the world will not serve its self-regulatory function unless there is some representation of what the response is about. The answer to the first question, then, is that people represent what perceived responses are about to facilitate taking action.

Given the adaptive benefits, or even necessity, of representing what responses are about, why is the operation of the aboutness principle problematic? When people represent what a response is about they naturally represent it as about some*thing*, a response associated with some particular object or event. And whatever is represented as what a response is about becomes emphasized as the source of the response. But what a response is about is *not* the same as the source of the response. Moreover, a response typically has multiple sources rather than a single source. For example, one's performance on a course exam might be represented as being about one's knowledge of the course material; but knowledge of the course material is only one source of exam performance. Motivation while taking the exam and exam difficulty are additional sources of exam performance. Thus, the tendency to infer that what a response is about is the source of the response often fails to take into account sufficiently other sources of the response. This is why the operation of the aboutness principle is problematic. Let us now review specific cases where the operation of the aboutness principle produces biases in social cognition. The review of these biases is organized in terms of three basic conditions of person perception: the nature of the input, the state of the perceiver, and the context of perception.

The Nature of the Input

Even something as apparently simple as observing another person's behavior typically involves rather complex input. There is the behavior, the person who produced the behavior, some entity to which the behavior was directed, and the surrounding circumstances of the behavior. For example, consider the input in a classic study by Jones and Harris (1967). Each participant in the study was shown an essay that either supported or opposed Fidel Castro, the communist Cuban president, and was told either that the author had freely chosen to advocate the position taken in the essay or that the author was a member of a debating team and had been assigned the position by the debating coach. In one key condition of the study, then, the input involved an essayist who produced a supportive behavior directed toward Castro after being told to do so by the debating coach. This is a rather complex input. What did the participants in the study make of this input?

The surprising finding was that the participants in this condition tended to judge the essayist as personally having a favorable attitude toward Castro despite the fact that the essayist was told to take a favorable position toward Castro by the debating coach. This tendency for people to infer that the source of an observed behavior is a disposition in the actor that corresponds to the behavior he or she produced rather than the situation in which the behavior took place (i.e. either the entity toward which the behavior was directed or the surrounding circumstances) has been called the "observer bias" (Jones & Nisbett, 1972), the "fundamental attribution error" (Ross, 1977) or the "correspondence bias" (Gilbert & Jones, 1986; see also Jones, 1979). This specific tendency may appear to be pervasive because in many studies the participants believe that the study is *about* an individual who has performed a certain behavior, and the procedures of the studies typically promote this perception (see Quattrone, 1982). Thus, the participants are likely to represent the behavior as being about the actor. According to the aboutness principle, then, the participants will emphasize the actor as being the source of the behavior rather than the situation in which the behavior occurred.

The aboutness principle, however, does not assume that there is some general or fundamental tendency to infer a particular kind of source for perceived responses, such as a fundamental tendency to infer that the source of another person's behavior is a disposition corresponding to that behavior. Depending on additional qualities of the input (e.g. Quattrone, 1982; Taylor &

Fiske, 1975), or even the explanatory predispositions of the perceiver (e.g. Miller, 1984; Newman, 1993), perceivers will represent an actor's behavior as being about either the actor or the situation and infer that the source of the behavior was either the actor's disposition or situational forces, respectively (see Higgins & Bargh, 1987). Trope and Liberman's hypothesis-testing perspective on inferential processes also assumes that either dispositional or situational biases can occur depending on what the inference is represented as being about; that is, is the hypothesis, and the evidence used to test it, about the person's disposition or about the person's situation (see Trope & Liberman, in press)?

The same essay communication, for example, is more or less likely to be represented as being about the communicator depending on whether the perceivers are told the communicator composed the essay or copied the essay, respectively, and perceivers are less likely to infer that the communicator's disposition is the source of the essay when they do not represent the essay as being about the communicator (e.g. Snyder & Jones, 1974). Perceivers are also less likely to infer that a communicator's disposition is the source of a message when the communication circumstances suggest that the message might have been about characteristics of the audience to which it was addressed (Newtson & Czerlinsky, 1974). Imagine, for example, an adult trying to teach a 3-year-old how to play some game. Because the childlike quality of the message is clearly about the child audience, a perceiver is likely to infer that the source of the message's childlike quality is the child to whom the message was addressed rather than the communicator's childlike disposition.

A study by Pryor and Kriss (1977) provides especially compelling evidence for the importance of aboutness in attributions to personal dispositions versus situational forces. They manipulated the salience of either the person or the entity in a person–entity sentiment relation by varying which appeared first as the topic of the sentence (e.g. "Joe likes the film" versus "The film was liked by Joe"). In one study they found that subjects' recognition responses for the entity relative to the person were quicker when the entity versus the person had been made linguistically salient. In another study they found that subjects were more likely to make entity attributions when the entity rather than the person was made linguistically salient. These results suggest that language rules can communicate what a target person's response is about, which then affects perceivers' inference concerning the source of the response.

There is also social-cognitive research suggesting that even when behaviors are not represented in terms of situational forces, the likelihood of inferring that the source of a behavior is the actor's personal disposition can still vary depending on the aboutness representation. An actor's behavior, for instance, can be represented as being about the actor as an individual or as being about the actor as a member of some social category. Studies have found that perceivers are more likely to consider social category membership as the source of a response when an actor is less individualized by the input information (e.g. Yzerbyt & Dardenne, 1995). Conversely, research on the "dilution effect" demonstrates that even information pretested to be nondiagnostic, such as information about the actor's home town for predicting the actor's tolerance for shock, can reduce the use of social category information when making inferences (e.g. Nisbett, Zukier, & Lemley, 1981). This effect could occur because the nondiagnostic information individualizes the actor, which makes potential responses more about the actor's personal dispositions than about the actor's social category membership.

The classic case of the "representativeness" error (Kahneman & Tversky, 1973) can also be understood in these general terms. In Kahneman and Tversky's (1973) study, participants were told that a panel of psychologists had administered personality tests to thirty engineers and seventy lawyers, which provided the base rate probability that any randomly selected target would be an engineer. The participants were asked to estimate the likelihood that a specific target was one of the engineers. When no individualizing information about the target was provided, perceivers used the base rate information when making their inference. But perceivers were less likely to use the base rate information appropriately when individualizing information was provided, including only nondiagnostic information, such as information that the target person was 30 years old, was married with no children, and was a man of high ability and high motivation who was well liked by his colleagues. Instead, the perceivers based their inference on the target person information as if that was what the input information was about.

Interestingly, when Zukier and Pepitone (1984) placed participants in the role of "scientist," rather than the more "clinical" role of "trying to understand another person" that previous studies have typically emphasized, perceivers were more likely to use the base rate information appropriately. This is presumably because scientific input is more about base rates whereas clinical input is more about personal characteristics. Similarly, when Ginossar and Trope (1987) told participants that the problem was a game of chance in which both the base rate and the target person information they received would be a matter of chance, the base rate information was used more appropriately.

There is considerable evidence, then, that perceivers' inferences from input information vary in the extent to which the personal characteristics of the target actor are emphasized. Even in the classic case of perceivers receiving information about a target person's response to some entity in some situation, it is not always the case that perceivers will infer that the source of the response is the person's disposition. Thus, the fundamental source of bias in making inferences from input information is not the general overutilization (or underutilization) of any specific type of input information. Instead, as suggested by the aboutness principle, the problem is that people represent the input information, and especially perceived responses, as being about some *thing* when in fact it is typically about multiple things. When subsequent inferences emphasize just the part of the input information represented as being what the input was about, then the inferences will necessarily be biased because other parts of the input will not be taken into account sufficiently. Let us turn now to other cases of this bias that derive from another condition of person perception – the state of the perceiver.

The State of the Perceiver

What perceivers represent an actor's response to be about can vary depending on the kinds of input information they are given, as we have seen. The state of the perceiver at the time of exposure to the input information can also influence the representation of what an actor's response is about. This state can be relatively temporary or relatively chronic (when it is often referred to as a perceiver trait). Although the previous section was concerned with variations in input information, two variables mentioned as influencing aboutness involve the state of the perceiver. One was the explanatory predispositions of the perceiver, such as different individuals or members of different cultures holding different theories concerning what people's behaviors are about (e.g. Miller, 1984; Newman, 1993). Another was the momentary role of the perceiver that influences the perceived relevance of different kinds of information, such as exposure to input information when in the "clinical" role versus the "scientist" role (e.g. Zukier & Pepitone, 1984).

The applications of the aboutness principle considered thus far have involved inferences about another person. The aboutness principle also applies to inferences about oneself, and some of the best known cases of biased self-perception involve variations in the state of the perceiver. Consider, for example, the state of the perceiver in a classic study by Schachter and Singer (1962). As part of a supposed study on the effects of vitamin supplements on vision, the participants were injected with epinephrine or a placebo and were or were not told that the drug had specific side effects. In one condition the participants were injected with epinephrine, which increases arousal, and were misinformed about the side effects of the drug (e.g. "you will have an itching sensation over parts of your body"). While waiting for the supposed vision drug to take full effect, these participants were more likely than those in control conditions to express either anger or euphoria, depending on whether a stooge in the waiting room with them acted in an angry or euphoric manner, respectively. One interpretation of this study is that the participants in this condition experienced high arousal from the epinephrine but could not attribute their experience to the drug because they had been told that it had different side effects. Thus, they attributed their experience to the emotional state suggested by the behavior of their waiting room partner.

The phenomenon implied in this interpretation has been called "misattribution" because perceivers' attribution for their response to the drug is attributed to an emotional state rather than to the drug that actually produced it. A related phenomenon in the literature is the "excitation transfer" effect (see Zillmann, 1982). In one study by Zillmann, Johnson, and Day (1974), the participants were first provoked by another person, next engaged in strenuous physical exercise, and then were given the opportunity to retaliate against the person who had provoked them earlier. The study found that the participants were more likely to retaliate when given the opportunity several minutes after their exercise than immediately after. One interpretation of this finding is that immediately after exercise there are many clear cues that one's arousal is due to the exercise, but as time goes by it becomes less clear that one's remaining arousal is due to the exercise. It becomes more likely, then, that whatever arousal (or excitation) remains from the exercise will be misattributed (or transferred) to one's anger when meeting the provoker again, thus increasing the likelihood of retaliation.

The above phenomena can be understood as compelling cases of people applying the aboutness principle to their own responses. The participants in the "epinephrine/misinformed" condition of the Schachter and Singer (1962) study could not represent their response to epinephrine as being about the drug and thus represented it as being about the emotional situation defined by their partner in the waiting room. They then inferred that the source of their response was the emotion corresponding to the emotional situation, without the drug being taken into account sufficiently as the source of their response.

In the Zillmann et al. (1974) study, those participants who had some time to recover from their exercise before remeeting their provoker did not represent their remaining arousal as being about their previous exercise, but quite naturally represented all of their arousal, including the arousal remaining from the exercise, as being about their anger at the provoker. They then inferred that the source of their response was their anger at the provoker's prior behavior to them, producing retaliation, without their previous exercise being taken into account sufficiently as the source of their response. It should be noted that such misattribution of phenomenal experiences, including not only feelings (e.g. Schwarz, 1990) but cognitive experiences as well (e.g. Jacoby, Kelley, Brown, & Jasechko, 1989; Schwarz, Bless, Strack, Klumpp, Rittenauer-Schatka, & Simons, 1991; Tversky & Kahneman, 1973), is a very general phenomenon that can be understood in terms of the aboutness principle.

The aboutness principle might also underlie other phenomenon involving perceptions of one's own responses. Ross, Greene, and House (1977), for example, conducted a study supposedly on communication techniques where they asked participants to walk around campus for half an hour wearing a large sign with the message "EAT AT JOE'S." Some agreed to wear the sign while others refused to do so. When the participants were asked to estimate whether other people would agree or refuse to wear the sign, there was a clear bias to predict that most other people would make whatever decision they themselves made. This bias was especially problematic for those who had refused to wear the sign because they were in the minority but believed that they were in the majority. This "false consensus" effect can be understood in terms of people representing their response, such as their refusal to wear the sign, as being about wearing the sign, such as how much time it would take or how unattractive it would be. According to the aboutness principle, perceivers would then infer that the source of their response was the inherent properties of wearing the sign. If this is so, then the same inherent properties should influence most other people's responses (cf. Ross et al., 1977).

In another area of self-perception, Ross, Lepper, and Hubbard (1975) gave participants false feedback while they performed a novel task. The false feedback communicated to participants that they had either succeeded or failed on the task. The participants were then given a standard "debriefing" session in which they were told that the feedback was completely unrelated to their actual performance on the task and was predetermined before they had even begun the task. After the feedback had been totally discredited, the participants were asked to estimate their true ability on the type of task they had been given. The participants' estimated that they had higher ability when they had received false success feedback than when they had received false failure feedback.

This "perseverance" effect can be understood in terms of people representing their original response when given success or failure feedback as being about how well they were doing on the novel task. According to the aboutness principle, the perceivers would then infer that the source of their response was their ability to do well on this type of task. This inference would activate other information consistent with this conclusion; that is, reasons why either success or failure on this type of task makes sense. These activated reasons would continue to influence participants' self-perceptions regardless of the performance feedback itself being discredited later (cf. Ross et al., 1975).

Biased self-perceptions not only influence judgments; they can influence subsequent motivation and behavior as well. An important motivational phenomenon is the "undermining of intrinsic interest" or "overjustification effect" that offering rewards for behavior can produce (e.g. Deci, 1971; Kruglanski, 1975; Lepper, Greene, & Nisbett, 1973; Ross, 1975). In an illustrative study by Lepper et al. (1973), children received multicolored felt-tipped pens and drawing paper, had the opportunity to draw freely, and were promised (and later received) an award for helping out an adult by drawing pictures. Compared to children who were not promised an award and did not receive one, these children spent much less time drawing in a subsequent free-play situation where they could draw or engage in other activities. According to the aboutness principle, the perceivers in the promised award condition represented their response to the drawing activity as being about the future award they would receive for drawing pictures. They then inferred that the source of their engagement in drawing was the promised award, rather than the inherently enjoyable properties of the activity. Given that there was no promised award for engaging in drawing in the subsequent free-play situation, there would be little reason to engage in drawing again (cf. Lepper et al., 1973).

From the perspective of the aboutness principle, it should not matter, in principle, whether inferences concerning some behavior are being made by the actor or by the observer. If the actor and observer represent what the behavior is about in the same way, then they should make the same source inference and have a tendency for the same bias. In their classic paper, Jones and Nisbett (1972) described how the causal inferences of actors and observers can diverge, with actors tending to make situational attributions for their behaviors, and observers of the same behaviors tending to make dispositional attributions.

As has already been noted, however, observers will make situational attributions under a variety of conditions and self-perceptions can involve dispositional attributions as well as situation attributions. What matters in these different cases is what the behavior is represented as being about. The different variables suggested by Jones and Nisbett (1972) as possibly accounting for the "actor/observer effect," as well as more motivational explanations (e.g. Bem, 1972), can be interpreted in terms of conditions that are likely to produce differences in how actors and observers represent what a behavior is about. Without discussing all these conditions in detail, one especially useful illustration of the importance of aboutness for more complex actor/observer differences might be instructive.

Ross, Amabile, and Steinmetz (1977) assigned some participants in their "quiz game" study to the role of contestant or "answerer" where they had to answer challenging general knowledge questions prepared by other subjects who had been assigned the role of "questioner." In addition to the "questioner" observers, additional participants in a separate study were assigned the role of audience "observer" and saw a live simulation of the quiz game. All participants later rated the general knowledge of the "answerer" and the "questioner." Both the "answerer" participants and the audience "observer" participants rated the questioners as being more knowledgeable than the answerer, despite the fact that they knew that the roles of questioner and answerer had been randomly assigned and that the questioner had been specifically asked to compose difficult questions from areas in which they happened to have expertise. This effect was not found for the "questioner" observers who on average did not rate their knowledge as being superior to that of their answerer.

These findings are quite challenging to the notion of an "actor/observer" effect. First, there was no difference between the "answerer" actors and the audience "observers." They both gave higher knowledge ratings to the questioner than to the answerer. Second, the "questioner" observers *did* differ from the audience "observers" in that they did not rate the answerer and questioner differently. Given that these findings do not reflect an "actor/observer" effect, what might be going on? A closer look at the Ross et al. (1977) findings indicates that the major effect was the high rating of the questioners' general knowledge by both the answerers and the audience observers but not by the questioners themselves. The questions asked by the questioners were clearly difficult and challenging. The contestants on average answered only about 40 percent of them. The audience observers and the answerers probably represented the questions as being about the questioners and then inferred that the source of the challenging questions was the high general knowledge of the questioners. The questioners themselves, however, were more likely to represent their questions as being about the situational demand to construct challenging questions, which they probably found difficult to do. For the questioners, the source of their responses, which they knew were highly selective, was not their high general knowledge but the experimental instructions to compose difficult questions, as well as the experimenter-provided hints of how to do so.

There is another very different phenomenon in social cognition that concerns how the state of the perceiver at the time of input exposure can produce biased judgments. Consider, for example, the state of the perceiver in a study by Higgins, Rholes, and Jones (1977). The participants in this study were initially exposed to one or another set of trait-related constructs as an incidental part of a supposed study on "perception." They later participated in an unrelated study on "reading comprehension" where they were asked to characterize the ambiguous behaviors of a target person, such as the following: "Once Donald made up his mind to do something it was as good as done no matter how long it might take or how difficult the going might be. Only rarely did he change his mind, even when it might well have been better if he had." Previous pilot testing revealed this behavior to be equally characterized as either "stubborn" or "persistent." Half of the participants in the prior "perception" task involving color-naming were exposed to the word "stubborn" as an incidental part of the task while the other half were exposed to the word "persistent." The study found a strong tendency for participants to use whichever trait construct had been primed in the "perception" task to categorize the target person's behavior in the subsequent "reading comprehension" task.

In the Higgins et al. (1977) study, the prior "perception" study primes or activates a particular construct stored in memory, which increases its subsequent accessibility or activation potential. This increased accessibility makes it more likely that the construct will be used later when categorizing input information, even when the construct has very little relation to the input or there are equally appropriate constructs that could have been used. This "accessibility bias" has proven to be a very robust phenomenon. The biasing effect of accessibility can also last a long time under certain exposure conditions (e.g. Smith, Stewart, & Buttram, 1992; Srull & Wyer, 1979) or when a construct is among a person's chronically accessible constructs (e.g. Bargh, Lombardi, & Higgins, 1988).

The aboutness principle provides a useful account of how the accessibility bias occurs. When perceivers categorize a target person's behavior it would be natural for them to represent their response to the behavior as being about the behavior. According to the aboutness principle, the perceivers would then infer that the source of their response to the behavior was simply the behavioral stimulus information itself. The problem with this inference is that the behavioral stimulus information is only one source of perceivers' categorizations. Indeed, if the stimulus information was the only source of categorization the perceivers would have categorized the behavior in an ambiguous manner. But only a small minority of perceivers in these studies categorize the behavior in an ambiguous, or even qualified, manner. The great majority of perceivers categorize the behavior in an unambiguous manner. The source of this disambiguation is the higher accessibility of one of the alternative constructs that is applicable to the behavior.

Thus, the relative accessibility of different stored constructs, whether from recent priming or from chronic accessibility, is another source of perceivers' categorizations. By not taking this additional source into account sufficiently, perceivers give too much credit to the stimulus information as the source of their categorization. And this overemphasis can create additional problems because the categorization is used in later processing as if it were based solely on the stimulus information. Perceivers' own personal attitudes toward the target person, for example, are influenced by their previous categorizations as if those categorizations were simply objective summaries of the target person's behavior. Thus, perceivers exposed to identical behaviors of a target person, but differing in the relative accessibility of their stored constructs, will later express different attitudes toward the person because the accessibility differences produce different categorizations that are treated as reflecting different target person behaviors (see Higgins et al., 1977).

The importance of aboutness for accessibility biases has become even clearer recently from studies where perceivers become aware that the recent priming events might influence their responses to the target person behaviors. Under conditions where perceivers are aware of the recent priming events, the increased accessibility of the primed constructs no longer produces judgments that are assimilated to the accessible constructs (e.g. Lombardi, Higgins, & Bargh, 1987; Martin, 1986; Newman & Uleman, 1990). Thus, when perceivers represent their accessible response to a target person behavior as being about the recent priming events, they no longer infer that the source of their response was the behavior and do not assimilate their subsequent judgment to the accessible construct.

This section has reviewed various ways in which the state of the perceiver can influence responses to input information without the contribution of the state to the response being taken into account sufficiently in subsequent inferences and processing. The next section reviews some ways in which the context of perception can also influence responses to input information with insufficient acknowledgment. Indeed, depending on how broadly one defines the context of perception, one might consider recent priming as a case of the context of perception influencing responses with insufficient acknowledgment. In the cases to be considered next, however, the response and the unacknowledged variables influencing it occur in the same spatiotemporal context rather than in the "unrelated" contexts typical of most social cognition priming studies.

Context of Perception

There are many circumstances in everyday communication where people are under some social pressure to express ideas that are not their own. What is significant is that these communicators often end up believing whatever they said or planned to say (e.g. Festinger & Carlsmith, 1959; Higgins & Rholes, 1978; Janis & King, 1954; Zimmerman & Bauer, 1956). In one example of this phenomenon, the participants in a study by Higgins and Rholes (1978) read an essay describing the behaviors of a target person, Donald, and then communicated their impressions of him to an audience. The communicators were led to believe that their audience liked or disliked Donald already. The communicators tailored their message to suit their audience's attitude by disambiguating ambiguous behaviors in the direction of the attitude and by deleting unambiguous behaviors that were discrepant from the attitude. The study found that the communicators' own attitudes toward Donald and their memory of his behaviors became consistent with their message about him, and the effect on memory actually increased over a two-week period – the "saying is believing" effect.

When communicators produce (or prepare) a message on some topic, it would be natural for them to represent their message responses as being about the topic. In the Higgins and Rholes (1978) study, for example, it would be natural for communicators to represent their summaries of Donald's behaviors as being about Donald. According to the aboutness principle, these communicators would then infer that the source of their summaries was Donald's characteristics as reflected in his behaviors. As these perceivers become less able over time to remember the specific details of the stimulus information, they are likely to rely increasingly on their prior message summaries to decide what they saw and how they feel about it. This would not be a problem if the source of the summaries was only Donald's characteristics as reflected in his behaviors. But this is not the case. Another important source of the message summaries was the audience to which the message was directed. Indeed, because of the power of this source of their response, communicators who read exactly the same information about Donald but communicated to different audiences had very different recollections and evaluations of him two weeks later.

When perceivers are exposed to target person information the context of perception can also include additional non-target information that functions as a reference point or standard for judging the target. Such contextual standards can produce "contrast effects." In a study by Manis and Armstrong (1971), for example, the participants were asked to describe a target set of photographs of neutral emotional expressions in the context of an array of other photographs of emotional expressions. Compared to a control condition where the contextual array contained a full range of emotional expressions, the participants' descriptions of the same target expressions were more pleasant when the contextual array contained all unpleasant expressions and were less pleasant when the contextual array contained all pleasant expressions. Similarly, Higgins and Lurie (1983) found that perceivers judged the sentencing decisions of the same target trial judge to be "harsh" when they read about other relatively lenient trial judges and to be "lenient" when they read about other relatively harsh trial judges. Other recent studies of perceivers' attempts at "correction" of judgmental biases from context effects have revealed that subjects' theories concerning how context might influence their responses determine whether judgmental assimilation or contrast occurs, providing further evidence of the importance of aboutness in social-cognitive biases (see Wegener & Petty, 1995).

Higgins and Lurie (1983) also found that the judgmental contrast effect obtained in their study produced substantial memory errors later if the category norm for sentencing decisions at the time of recall was different from the earlier context standard. The category norm for sentencing decisions was varied by having participants return for a second session and read about the sentencing decisions of an additional set of trial judges. Apparently, the perceivers at the time of recall used the category norm as the standard to reconstruct the referential meaning of their earlier judgment of the target person without taking into account sufficiently that their earlier judgment had been made in relation to the context standard – the "change-of-standard" effect. When perceivers make their original judgment of the target trial judge it is natural for them to represent their judgmental response as being about the target person. According to the aboutness principle, the perceivers then infer that the source of their judgment is the target person's lenient or harsh nature as a trial judge as displayed in his behaviors. When later reconstructing the target's sentencing decisions, the perceivers use the category norm to interpret the meaning of being a lenient or harsh trial judge, following the natural rules of language. But the source of the original judgment was not just the target's sentencing decisions. The context of sentencing decisions by other trial judges also strongly influenced their judgment. Because this additional source of their original judgment was not taken into account sufficiently, the perceivers' recall of the target's sentencing decisions was distorted.

It might also be noted that there are other kinds of "contrast effects" in which "aboutness" plays an important role. Schwarz, Strack, and Mai (1991), for example, asked participants in their "survey" study to report first on their "happiness with marriage" and second on their "happiness with life-as-a-whole," after telling them that the survey wanted to learn about two areas of life that may be important for people's overall well-being. They found that the respondents reported higher life satisfaction when they were unhappily married and lower life satisfaction when they were happily married. Schwarz et al. (1991) suggest that when the participants respond to the second "happiness with life-as-a-whole" question they exclude the amount of happiness associated with their response to the first "happiness with marriage" question – a contrast effect from "exclusion." As they further suggest, this exclusion occurs because the "given-new" rule of everyday conversation (Grice, 1975) requires that their response to the second question be about something new; that is, something not already given in their response to the first question. A question for future research, then, is how do perceivers represent their second answer – as being about the "given-new" rule or as being only about their life satisfaction? And if it is the latter, which is likely, how might this distort their subsequent processing?

Context not only produces contrast effects. It can produce "assimilation effects" as well. An emotional expression, for example, will be assimilated to its surrounding context, such as a perceiver identifying an actor's ambiguous expression as "fearful" when the actor is in a dangerous situation. Trope (1986) reports that perceivers treat such identifications as if they reflected solely the properties of the actor; that is, they represent the input as being about just the actor and not the situation. They then use these identifications as independent evidence when making subsequent inferences about the actor's disposition. This produces errors in dispositional inference. "Placebo effects" can also be understood in these terms because the placebo induction can bias self-perception, such as perceiving oneself as "aroused," which is then used as independent evidence to infer that one is an "anxious" person (see Trope, 1986).

Concluding Remarks

This chapter has reviewed many different types of biases in social cognition. I have proposed that one basic principle might underlie these various biases – the aboutness principle. This refers to the tendency for people, when they perceive a response made by themselves or another person, to represent what the response is about and then infer that whatever the response is *about* is also the *source* of the response. The operation of the aboutness principle is problematic because people naturally represent a response as being about some*thing* and then infer that the source of the response was that thing, whereas a response typically has multiple sources rather than a single source. Therefore, the operation of the aboutness principle fails to take into account sufficiently additional sources of a person's response.

This chapter has been concerned with biases in social cognition. It must be emphasized that the existence of such biases does not justify a negative evaluation of people's abilities. It is simply the case that people have limitations, as all living things have limitations, along with their equally obvious strengths. Given that people have information-processing limitations, the important question becomes, "How do people function within their limitations?" As discussed earlier, the aboutness principle describes a process that begins with people representing what a perceived response is about. This representation is adaptive; it is necessary in order to take action. The problem arises when this representation is used to infer the source of the response. But there is no easy solution to this problem. After all, there are some sources that perceivers are unlikely to ever take into account, such as their own chronically accessible constructs, and there are other sources that perceivers might try to take into account but are not able to calibrate accurately, such as audience effects. Thus, people do the best they can, and their best often produces biases in social cognition. Still, it would be helpful if people recognized that their processing is often biased to some extent because this could increase tolerance, open-mindedness, and prudence (Higgins & Bargh, 1987).

The discussion of the aboutness principle in this chapter is obviously incomplete. There is a need to identify when the aboutness principle is most likely to operate. Given its role in taking action mentioned earlier, one might speculate that the aboutness principle is most likely to operate when there are strong pressures to take immediate action. For example, it might be that the aboutness principle is more likely to operate when people are under time pressure (cf. Kruglanski, 1990). There is also a need for systematic consideration of what determines the aboutness representation itself. The present chapter has simply mentioned various possibilities, such as perceivers' culture-based theories of what behavior is about, communication rules concerning what verbal responses should be about, instructional sets or role assignments concerning what perceivers' responses to input should be about, and so on. There are also suggestions in the literature, such as the proposal that *Gestalt* principles, including spatio-temporal proximity and similarity, might determine perceptions of what responses are about (e.g. Heider, 1944; Quattrone, 1982; Ross, 1977). It should be noted, however, that the *Gestalt* notion that "behavior engulfs the field" is not helpful in this regard because one still has to know which variables determine the representation of what the behavior is about. A model that identifies these variables in a systematic way holds the promise of accounting for a wide variety of social-cognitive biases in terms of a single principle – the aboutness principle. Moreover, it might help to explain why politicians, and couples for that matter, invest considerable energy debating what the problem they confront really is about.

Bibliography

(Those marked * are recommended for further reading.)

Bargh, J. A., Lombardi, W. J., & Higgins, E. T. (1988). Automaticity of chronically accessible constructs in person × situation effects on person perception: It's just a matter of time. *Journal of Personality and Social Psychology*, *55*, 599–605.

Bem, D. J. (1972). Self-perception theory. In L. Berkowitz (Ed.), *Advances in experimental social psychology* (Vol. 6, pp. 1–62). New York: Academic Press.

Deci, E. L. (1971). Effects of externally mediated rewards on intrinsic motivation. *Journal of Personality and Social Psychology*, *18*, 105–115.

Festinger, L., & Carlsmith, J. M. (1959). Cognitive consequences of forced compliance. *Journal of Abnormal and Social Psychology*, *58*, 203–211.

*Fiske, S. T., & Taylor, S. E. (1991). *Social cognition* (2nd ed.). New York: McGraw Hill.

Gilbert, D. T., & Jones, E. E. (1986). Perceiver-induced constraint: Interpretations of self-generated reality. *Journal of Personality and Social Psychology*, *50*, 269–280.

Ginossar, Z., & Trope, Y. (1987). Problem solving in judgment under uncertainty. *Journal of Personality and Social Psychology*, *52*, 464–474.

Grice, H. P. (1975). Logic and conversation. In P. Cole and J. L. Morgan (Eds.), *Syntax and semantics* (Vol. 3): *Speech acts* (pp. 365–372). New York: Seminar Press.

Heider, F. (1944). Social perception and phenomenal causality. *Psychological Review*, *51*, 358–374.

*Higgins, E. T., & Bargh, J. A. (1987). Social cognition and social perception. *Annual Review of Psychology*, *38*, 369–425.

Higgins, E. T., & Lurie, L. (1983). Context, categorization, and memory: The "change-of-standard" effect. *Cognitive Psychology*, *15*, 525–547.

Higgins, E. T., & Rholes, W. S. (1978). "Saying is believing": Effects of message modification on memory and liking for the person described. *Journal of Experimental Social Psychology*, *14*, 363–378.

Higgins, E. T., Rholes, W. S., & Jones, C. R. (1977). Category accessibility and impression formation. *Journal of Experimental Social Psychology*, *13*, 141–154.

Jacoby, L. L., Kelley, C., Brown, J., & Jasechko, J. (1989). Becoming famous overnight: Limits on the ability to avoid unconscious influences of the past. *Journal of Personality and Social Psychology*, *56*, 326–338.

Janis, I. L., & King, B. T. (1954). The influence of role-playing on opinion change. *Journal of Abnormal and Social Psychology*, *49*, 211–218.

Jones, E. E. (1979). The rocky road from acts to dispositions. *American Psychologist*, *34*, 107–117.

Jones, E. E., & Harris, V. A. (1967). The attribution of attitudes. *Journal of Experimental Social Psychology*, *3*, 1–24.

Jones, E. E., & Nisbett, R. E. (1972). The actor and the observer: Divergent perceptions of the causes of behavior. In E. E. Jones, D. Kanouse, H. H. Kelley, R. E. Nisbett, S. Valins, & B. Weiner (Eds.), *Attribution: Perceiving the causes of behavior* (pp. 79–94). New York: General Learning Press.

Kahneman, D., & Tversky, A. (1973). On the psychology of prediction. *Psychological Review*, *80*, 237–251.

Kruglanski, A. W. (1975). The endogenous-exogeneous partition in attribution theory. *Psychological Review*, *82*, 387–406.

Kruglanski, A. W. (1990). Motivations for judging and knowing: Implications for causal attribution. In E. T. Higgins & R. M. Sorrentino (Eds.), *Handbook of motivation and cognition: Foundations of social behavior* (Vol. 2). New York: Guilford.

Lepper, M. R., Greene, D., & Nisbett, R. E. (1973). Undermining children's intrinsic interest with extrinsic reward: A test of the overjustification hypothesis. *Journal of Personality and Social Psychology*, *28*, 129–137.

Lombardi, W. J., Higgins, E. T., & Bargh, J. A. (1987). The role of consciousness in priming effects on categorization. *Personality and Social Psychology Bulletin*, *13*, 411–429.

Manis, M., & Armstrong, G. W. (1971). Contrast effects in verbal output. *Journal of Experimental Social Psychology*, *7*, 381–388.

Martin, L. L. (1986). Set/reset: Use and disuse of concepts in impression formation. *Journal of Personality and Social Psychology*, *51*, 493–504.

Miller, J. G. (1984). Culture and the development of everyday social explanation. *Personality and Social Psychology*, *46*, 961–978.

Newman, L. S. (1993). How individualists interpret behavior: Idiocentrism and spontaneous trait inference. *Social Cognition*, *11*, 243–269.

Newman, L. S., & Uleman, J. S. (1990). Assimilation and contrast effects in spontaneous trait inference. *Personality and Social Psychology Bulletin*, *16*, 224–240.

Newtson, D., & Czerlinsky, T. (1974). Adjustment of attitude communications for contrasts by extreme audiences. *Journal of Personality and Social Psychology*, *30*, 829–837.

Nisbett, R. E., Zukier, H., & Lemley, R. (1981). The dilution effect: Nondiagnostic information weakens the effect of diagnostic information. *Cognitive Psychology*, *13*, 248–277.

Pryor, J. B., & Kriss, M. (1977). The cognitive dynamics of salience in the attribution process. *Journal of Personality and Social Psychology*, *35*, 49–55.

*Quattrone, G. A. (1982). Overattribution and unit formation: When behavior engulfs the person. *Journal of Personality and Social Psychology*, *42*, 593–607.

*Ross, L. (1977). The intuitive psychologist and his shortcomings: Distortions in the attribution process. In L. Berkowitz (Ed.), *Advances in Experimental Social Psychology* (Vol. 10, pp. 173–220). New York: Academic Press.

Ross, L., Amabile, T. M., & Steinmetz, J. L. (1977). Social roles, social control, and biases in social-perception processes. *Journal of Personality and Social Psychology*, *35*, 485–494.

Ross, L., Greene, D., & House, P. (1977). The "false consensus effect": An egocentric bias in social perception and attribution processes. *Journal of Experimental Social Psychology*, *13*, 279–301.

Ross, L., Lepper, M. R., & Hubbard, M. (1975). Perseverance in self-perception and social perception: Biased attribution processes in the debriefing paradigm. *Journal of Personality and Social Psychology*, *32*, 880–892.

Ross, M. (1975). Salience of reward and intrinsic motivation. *Journal of Personality and Social Psychology*, *32*, 245–254.

Schachter, S., & Singer, J. E. (1962). Cognitive, social and physiological determinants of emotional state. *Psychological Review*, *69*, 379–399.

Schwarz, N. (1990). Feelings as information: Informational and motivational functions of affective states. In E. T. Higgins & R. M. Sorrentino (Eds.), *Handbook of motivation and cognition: Foundations of social behavior* (Vol. 2, pp. 527–561). New York: Guilford.

Schwarz, N., Bless, H., Strack, F., Klumpp, G., Rittenauer-Schatka, H., & Simons, A. (1991). Ease of retrieval as information:

Another look at the availability heuristic. *Journal of Personality and Social Psychology*, *61*, 195–202.

Schwarz, N., Strack, F., & Mai, H. P. (1991). Assimilation and contrast effects in part-whole question sequences: A conversational-logic analysis. *Public Opinion Quarterly*, *55*, 3–23.

Smith, E. R., Stewart, T. L., & Buttram, R. T. (1992). Inferring a trait from a behavior has long-term, highly specific effects. *Journal of Personality and Social Psychology*, *62*, 753–759.

Snyder, M. L., & Jones, E. E. (1974). Attitude attribution when behavior is constrained. *Journal of Experimental Social Psychology*, *10*, 585–600.

Srull, T. K., & Wyer, R. S. (1979). The role of category accessibility in the interpretation of information about persons: Some determinants and implications. *Journal of Personality and Social Psychology*, *37*, 1660–1672.

Taylor, S. E., & Fiske, S. T. (1975). Point of view and perceptions of causality. *Journal of Personality and Social Psychology*, *32*, 439–445.

Trope, Y. (1986). Identification and inferential processes in dispositional attribution. *Psychological Review*, *93*, 239–257.

*Trope, Y., & Liberman, A. (in press). Social hypothesis testing: Cognitive and motivational mechanisms. In E. T. Higgins and A. W. Kruglanski (Eds.), *Social psychology: Handbook of basic principles*. New York: Guilford.

Tversky, A., & Kahneman, D. (1973). Availability: A heuristic for judging frequency and probability. *Cognitive Psychology*, *5*, 207–32.

Wegener, D. T., & Petty, R. E. (1995). Flexible correction processes in social judgment: The role of naive theories in corrections for perceived bias. *Journal of Personality and Social Psychology*, *68*, 36–51.

Yzerbyt, V. Y., & Dardenne, B. (1995). *Judgeability concerns in social perception*. Paper presented at the Society of Experimental Social Psychology, Washington, DC.

Zillmann, D. (1978). Attribution and misattribution of excitatory reactions. In J. H. Harvey, W. J. Ickes & R. F. Kidd (Eds.), *New directions in attribution research* (Vol. 2, pp. 335–368). Hillsdale, NJ: Lawrence Erlbaum.

Zillmann, D., Johnson, R. C., & Day, K. D. (1974). Attribution of apparent arousal and proficiency of recovery from sympathetic activation affecting excitation transfer to aggressive behavior. *Journal of Experimental Social Psychology*, *10*, 503–515.

Zimmerman, C., & Bauer, R. A. (1956). The effect of an audience on what is remembered. *Public Opinion Quarterly*, *20*, 238–248.

Zukier, H., & Pepitone, A. (1984). Social roles and strategies in prediction: Some determinants of the use of base rate information. *Journal of Personality and Social Psychology*, *47*, 349–360.

13

Dynamic Social Impact: The Societal Consequences of Human Interaction

Bibb Latané

Now Professor of Psychology at Florida Atlantic University, Bibb Latané taught at Columbia, Ohio State, and North Carolina after receiving a Minnesota doctorate and a Yale B.A. Viewing social psychology as the interdisciplinary mother of the social sciences rather than as a sub-specialty of psychology, Latané is a two-time winner of the AAAS Behavioral Science Prize, a recipient of the Donald T. Campbell Career Research Award and Cattell and Guggenheim Fellowships, and past President of the Midwestern Psychological Association and the Society for Personality and Social Psychology. He helped start the *Personality and Social Psychology Bulletin* and the *Review of Personality and Social Psychology* and founded the Nags Head Conference Center, which hosted its 133rd scientific conference in 1996. Married to social psychologist Deborah Richardson, he lives by the seashore and rides a bike to work.

For me, as I suspect for most of my colleagues, the message of social psychology is both personal and public. In what follows, *italics* express my personal views, and roman type presents a more objective position.

When I was eight, headlines screamed the success of the Hiroshima bomb in ending the world war. Subsequent news about the bomb's potential for also ending the world led to a view of science as scourge as well as salvation and the need to redress the balance by making advances in social science comparable to the stunning advances in physical science. These headlines made me greatly aware of my identity as an American, a representative of the most advanced nation on earth, the birthplace of democracy and its underpinnings – education, freedom of speech, and the marketplace of ideas (only subsequently did I learn that this chauvinistic view was not entirely correct). I shared this identity with everyone else in Chappaqua, New York, a small town then inhabited largely by housewives, children, and men who came home at night from jobs on Wall Street or Madison Avenue.

Other identities differentiated me from my classmates. As a transplanted southerner, I was a representative of a defeated nation with different customs, values, and beliefs, some admirable and some otherwise, a region characterized by a sense of tradition and continuity. As the only person in my school with a French name, I was a representative of a ruthlessly persecuted religious minority, the Huguenots, dimly remembered for the Massacre of St Bartholomew's Eve, the Revocation of the Edict of Nantes, and my ancestors' exodus from France (the origin of the word refugee). Finally, as the descendant of a long line of professionals – ministers, doctors, lawyers, and educators – I was a representative of a tradition of using one's knowledge and intelligence to solve other people's problems. All of these identities led me later to set a goal – to study social science in order to solve the problems of conflict and war – to see if science could help humans convert sword-carrying into helping hands and create a world of harmony rather than strife. Although it is not obvious in every study, this goal has driven much of my research and has resulted in a theory of dynamic social impact – a theory of the emergence and maintenance of culture from and by the interaction of individuals – a theory which exemplifies my conception of what should be the message of social psychology.

Broadly speaking, my research can be divided into four major lines – on bystander intervention, social attraction, social loafing, and social impact, which culminate in a fifth – a new theory of the emergent dynamics of social interaction.

Research on Bystander Intervention, Social Attraction, Social Loafing, and Social Impact

Bystander intervention

My best-known research is probably my work with John Darley, Judith Rodin, and others on bystander intervention in emergencies. This line of research was stimulated by the idea that what made the failure of bystanders to inform the police of the fatal New York assault in 1966 on Catherine Genovese so newsworthy – namely that there were thirty-eight rather than one or two witnesses – may have also contributed to their inaction. This line of research created realistic but controllable emergencies in both laboratory and field settings, testing the generality of the phenomena by creating a wide variety of different emergencies. For example, students at New York University hearing a conversation partner apparently undergo an epileptic seizure and Columbia students finding themselves in a room filling up with smoke or overhearing a young lady in the next room fall from a chair were all less likely to intervene if other people were involved than if they were alone. John Darley and I produced a prize-winning book (Latané & Darley, 1970) that introduced the cost–reward, decision-tree analysis of the intervention process that has guided most later research in the area of prosocial behavior and documented the existence of three independent forms of social inhibition of bystander intervention: (1) audience inhibition, in which being in public makes people less likely to act; (2) social influence, in which seeing that no one else has yet responded makes each witness conclude that nonresponse is the appropriate action; and (3) diffusion of responsibility, in which the onus on each person to act is reduced. These findings have been widely replicated by other investigators and represent one of the most consistent phenomena in social psychology. Latané and Nida (1981) summarized dozens of studies employing several thousand participants all providing supportive evidence.

This research has been indirectly influential because two Columbia graduate students involved in running the studies, Dick Nisbett (who played the role of the seizure victim) and Lee Ross (who ran the smoke-filled room study) came to realize the importance of the situation rather than personality or character in determining individual action. This idea seems to have become accepted as one of the defining characteristics of social psychology. Perhaps their further idea of the fundamental attribution error (Nisbett & Ross, 1980) helps explain the media's continued tendency to blame citizen "apathy" rather than situational circumstance for failures of intervention.

Further research has shown that social inhibition applies to nonemergency settings as well. For example, two studies conducted in elevators showed that people are less likely to pick up dropped coins (Latané & Dabbs, 1975) or take a coupon for a free hamburger (Petty, Williams, Harkins, & Latané, 1977) if there are other people present. Even the size of tip in restaurants seems to be reduced as the number of people eating together increases (Freeman, Walker, Borden, & Latané, 1975). A recent large-scale replication (Latané, Harton, Rockloff, Bourgeois, & Wheeler, in preparation) of the original Latané and Rodin (1969) lady in distress study shows that the social inhibition of bystander response is still powerful almost thirty years and a major cultural shift later.

Social attraction

A second major line of research explored the sources of social attraction in animals, using as subjects laboratory rodents such as rats, mice, gerbils, and hamsters. With an ever-changing group of graduate students I developed new techniques for assessing attraction (using the pair as the unit of analysis) and set out to systematically explore the stimulus determinants of affiliation. The major finding of more than two dozen published studies was the central importance of *interaction* as the key source of attraction – animals were not very much attracted to unresponsive partners, no matter how similar, but were very much attracted to appropriately responsive partners, no matter how different (Latané & Hothersall, 1972). The most striking example of this phenomenon is that, with familiarity, rats can learn to spend almost as much time approaching a responsive human hand as another rat (Werner & Latané, 1974). A second major theme of this research was the idea of social interaction as a motivated system – rats are responsive to social deprivation and social satiation – regulated with respect to the amount of time they spend in social contact rather than the distance between them (Latané & Werner, 1978). I discontinued this line of research twenty years ago, as social psychology's turn to the cognitive reduced the enthusiasm of research assistants and editors alike for animal models, and these themes of interaction and self-regulated systems lay dormant until recently.

Social loafing

Steve Harkins, Kip Williams, and I were able to put together another prize-winning series of laboratory experiments in the mid-1970s on people's tendency to exert less energy if their efforts were unidentifiable than if they worked alone (Latané, Williams, & Harkins, 1979). Some of the tasks involved noise production (clapping and shouting), some idea generation (brainstorming), but all seemed to lead to less than optimal effort when people participated in-groups (indeed, the major problem with the research was that we all had a tendency to wait around for the others to do the work). Such phenomena undoubtedly impair not only productivity but the quality of life in all the myriad organizations and institutions that constitute modern existence.

Social impact

My initial research on social impact theory (Latané, 1981) grew as an extension of the idea that other forms of social pressure could, like responsibility, be multiplied and divided. After reviewing the literature on such topics as imitation, argumentation, and intimidation, I concluded that three broad categories of variables seemed to have consistent effects on many forms of social influence. Specifically, a metaphor of social forces operating in a social force field suggested that social influence should generally be proportional to a multiplicative function of the strength (representing individual differences in wealth, power, or intelligence), immediacy (representing closeness in space or absence of filters or barriers) and number (representing how many) of sources of social influence that impinge on an individual. Empirical data on aggression, conformity, contagion, crowding, minority influence, obedience, and stage fright, as well, of course, as helping, all support the basic metaphor.

Some people find the predictions of social impact theory banal, others find them incredible, many prefer narrative accounts of specific psychological processes to general mathematical models designed to explain many phenomena. Unlike physics, where a theory is considered simply to be the pasting of a bit of mathematics to a bit of reality, social psychologists often seem to feel a verbal description is necessary to make for satisfactory explanation. Thus, a number of social psychologists have dismissed social impact theory as being descriptive rather than explanatory. Whatever the virtue of social impact theory in explaining as well as describing the reactions of individuals to the presence and actions of others, it is a well-tested, general metatheory of social influence, and since it is stated with sufficient specificity to provide the basis for computer simulation, it becomes a uniquely powerful tool for predicting the self-organizing behavior of groups, both small and large.

A Dynamic Theory of Social Impact

Cultures can be seen as regionally clustered, historically evolving bundles or correlated sets of beliefs, values and practices. In 1908 William McDougall wrote that the fundamental problem for social psychology was "to show how, given the native propensities and capacities of the individual human mind, all the complex mental life of societies is shaped by and in turn reacts upon the individual" (p. 18). I agree and take this still to be our major task. I believe culture can be seen as an inductive combination of partially correlated behavioral or stylistic elements.

Traditional views, which have the great advantage of being solvable with conventional mathematics, assume linear change and predict convergence. To the extent that people are influenced by each other in a linear, incremental fashion, they should gradually move closer to each other and become more moderate, eventually converging on a middle of the road position that represents the average of the initial opinions. Instead, I believe we should think of individual change as being often nonlinear or nonincremental and that societal psychology can be approached as the nonlinear dynamics of a complex system (Waldrop, 1992). Unlike traditional linear dynamics, where people react to discrepancies by making small adjustments, nonlinear change is nonincremental or catastrophic, like the camel's response to the last piece of straw.

Nonlinear dynamics are not easily amenable to traditional analytic techniques, and computer simulation is, even for mathematicians and physicists, often the best way to understand them. Computer simulation can be used as a "derivation machine," a way of finding out what your theories predict. In order to use computer simulation, we need a very concrete, well-specified theory, but in order for the results to be meaningful, the theory must be quite general.

Dynamic social impact theory (Latané, 1996a; Nowak, Szamrej, & Latané, 1990) has four main elements. First, I assume that individual human beings, varying in strength and other attributes, are distributed in social space. Strength has to do with how much power people have to influence others, how wise and articulate they are, how much they are listened to and imitated.

Second, I assume that with respect to any given attribute, each person is influenced by their own individual experience (here called *b* for bias) and by others in proportion to a multiplicative function of their strength, immediacy, and number.

Third, I suggest that unless total persuasive impact ($\hat{\imath}_p$), that is the pressure to change to a different position outweighs supportive impact ($\hat{\imath}_s$) plus bias (*b*) or the pressure to stay where you are, an individual will not change. Otherwise, he or she will. So a given person will change if and only if persuasive impact is greater than supportive impact plus bias (this feature is what makes this model nonlinear).

Fourth, the computer calculates dynamic social impact as the cumulative effect of the iterative, recursive influence of interacting people on each other (i.e. interactions at time 1 affect interactions at time 2 and so on).

This theory is quite general, referring to any socially influenceable attribute of a person, including not only beliefs and attitudes but habits, moods, and lifestyles – anything, that is, that is affected by the presence or actions of other people.

SITSIM: A Derivation Machine

What does the theory predict? To find out, I use SITSIM, a computer program conceived with the help of Andrzej Nowak (Nowak & Latané, 1994). SITSIM's control panel allows you to vary twenty attributes of the simulation, each with two to five choices of specific theoretical assumptions, system characteristics, parameter values, and initial conditions – more than 200 billion possible combinations in all! Having made your choices, the computer calculates person-by-person, step-by-step what's going to happen.

For each of two issues, each open face in figure 13.1 represents a person adopting the majority position, and each dark face a member of the minority. The initial positions are randomly distributed in social space with no correlation between the two issues – the results would be even stronger if some initial clustering and/or correlation were allowed. The computer looks at each person in turn, calculating whether they will change based on the relative strength, immediacy, and number of nearby people with similar or different attributes, but then a minute later calculating whether these other people are themselves going to change. And it does this over and over again until it finds what will happen to the group as a whole. These outcomes are typical of hundreds of

Before influence, values of two attributes of each of 400 people varying in strength are spatially random and uncorrelated

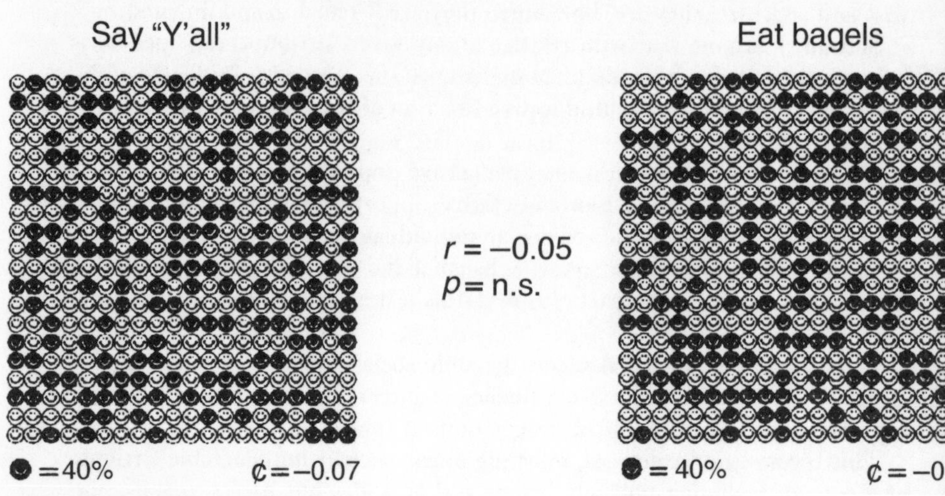

After 30 rounds of influence, attributes have become spatially clustered and correlated, while the minority although reduced in size, persists

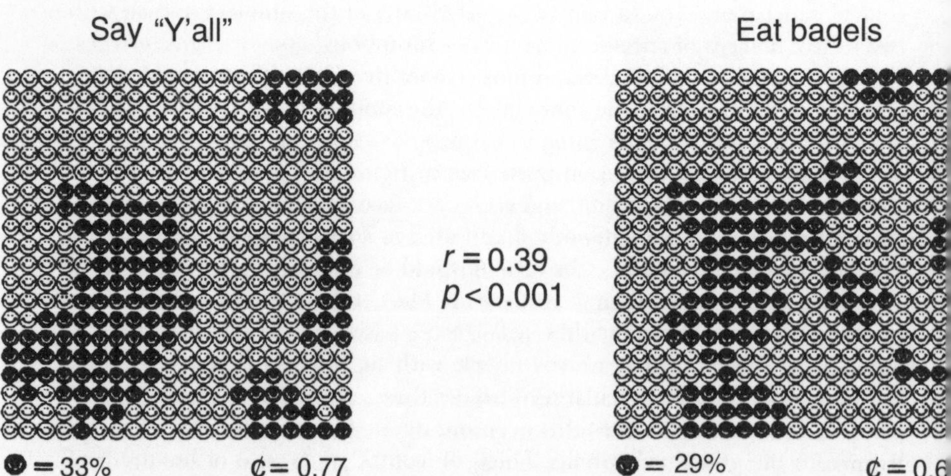

Figure 13.1 Example of a SITSIM outcome

thousands of simulations we have run. They exemplify four ways in which these systems self-organize.

First, please notice the decrease in the number of people adopting each minority position. In these cases, the original 40 percent minority has been reduced to 33 percent and 29 percent respectively. Such a *consolidation* results when minorities are more exposed than majorities to adverse social influence, although minorities occasionally can increase in size, especially if they have the better arguments. Consolidation represents a loss of diversity and is also the predicted outcome of traditional linear models, but not of those who advocate a special role for minority influence (see Latané, 1996b; Latané & Wolf, 1981).

Second, notice the emergence of obvious spatial clustering. *Clustering* results from people being more influenced by neighbors than strangers. In some regions of the USA, now, everybody says "Y'all," while in others nobody does. The emergence of clustering obviously depends not only on having a spatially distributed population but on the fact that people are more influenced by neighbors than strangers. Clustering is a novel prediction of dynamic social impact theory, but I suspect it is surprising only if you are dubious about the immediacy principle of social impact.

Third, notice the new degree of *correlation* between the originally independent attributes (saying "y'all" and eating bagels). In part, correlation emerges as a result of a perpetuation of the strength structure, with highly influential people able to impose their views on several different issues. Primarily, however, correlation is caused by the reduction in degrees of freedom resulting from clustering (Latané, 1996c). Instead of being a population of 400 independent actors, the system now acts as if there were a greatly reduced number of independent agents. The prediction of correlation is not only novel but highly surprising – a fair candidate for the coveted category of "counter-intuitive" (although Bob Abelson suggested a similar phenomenon back in 1979).

The final remarkable finding is the maintenance of continuing diversity. Continuing diversity is maintained by clusters that preserve minorities from extinction. People who live inside minority clusters are shielded from majority influence and have no reason to change, so that even with continued rounds of influence, the minority won't disappear. Continued diversity is possible only if two theoretical conditions are met: there must be some degree of nonlinearity in the change process to prevent populations from compromising themselves into uniformity, and there must be some form of individual difference to prevent minority clusters from eroding at their edges (Latané & Nowak, 1996). To the extent that human social systems are characterized by the first of these conditions, they will be similar to complex systems in the physical world. To the extent the second condition is true, they will be different.

In summary, social systems of people influencing each other self-organize in four different respects. Consolidation comes about because minorities are usually more exposed to opposition than majorities and therefore more vulnerable to social influence. Clustering results from people being more influenced by their neighbors than they are by strangers. Correlation between originally independent attributes emerges as a result of both the perpetuation of the strength structure and the reduction of degrees of freedom that results from clustering. And, finally, continuing diversity is maintained by clusters that have the effect of making everybody think they're in the majority.

These features seem to be the inevitable result of dynamical systems. In fact, a systematic series of hundreds of thousands of SITSIM simulations shows these consequences to be extremely robust with respect to theoretical assumptions, parameter values, system characteristics, and initial conditions (Latané & Nowak, 1996). They are not just some idiosyncratic quirk of a fine-tuned simulation, but would result from any program with the general characteristics I have described. This nontrivial discovery is reported in a major physics journal (Lewenstein, Nowak, & Latané, 1992) and illustrates that complex systems are not necessarily chaotic with small initial differences leading to big changes in the outcome. On the contrary, in self-organizing social systems such as those I describe, very different starting points lead to identical outcomes, at least at the group level.

Dynamic social impact theory is an ambitious attempt to explain the emergence of group-level phenomena at very large scales – up to the level of culture itself. As such, it is not easily amenable to the methods of laboratory studies typically employed by researchers interested in-group behavior. Most laboratory studies of group process are constrained by logistical necessity to a few people spending at most an afternoon in the laboratory. A reasonable experimental test of dynamic social impact would require the ability to repeatedly poll a large group of spatially distributed people as they influence each other over time under controlled conditions on a variety of specified issues. Getting large groups together, controlling who communicates with whom and about what, and recording their changing opinions is logistically very difficult – it is hard to see how such an experiment could be accomplished with face-to-face groups.

Empirical Results Supporting Dynamic Social Impact Theory

Self-organization in electronic juries

As a first step in testing the predictions of dynamic social impact theory under controlled conditions, my research group turned to computer-mediated communication for three reasons. First, the fact that computer discussion can be asynchronous alleviates the practical problems associated with assembling large groups of people at the same time. Second, electronic mail networks make it easy to test the effects of different configurations of social space independently of physical space by controlling who may send messages to whom. Finally, the fact that participants enter their messages at a keyboard ensures a record of all episodes of communication. I present here the methods and results of two novel tests of DSIT in some detail because they represent a new research paradigm. Each of these studies, in which participants were allowed to discuss issues over electronic mail was conducted on CAPS, a computer administrated panel study I conduct each semester at Florida Atlantic University. CAPS typically employs 120 undergraduates per semester to work at computer terminals for five hour-long sessions spread over two and one-half weeks as part of "a large-scale study of new information technology." After an initial orientation session, students are able to log in by themselves at their appointed time and work their way through a series of research modules, reading messages on the computer screen and entering responses on their keyboards. Different experiments were conducted in different semesters with messages involving a variety of topics.

Figure 13.2 shows the life history of a real 12-person mock jury, the members of which were CAPS participants playing the roles of jurors on a student honor court trying to come up with lenient or punitive verdicts for cases

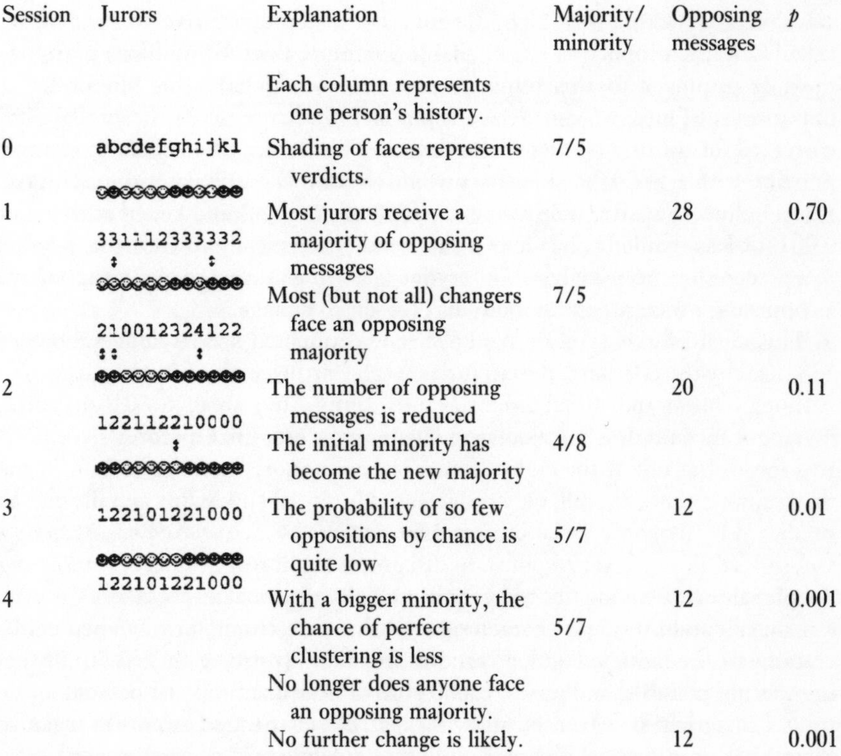

Session	Jurors	Explanation	Majority/minority	Opposing messages	*p*
		Each column represents one person's history.			
0	abcdefghijkl	Shading of faces represents verdicts.	7/5		
1	331112333332	Most jurors receive a majority of opposing messages		28	0.70
	210012324122	Most (but not all) changers face an opposing majority	7/5		
2	122112210000	The number of opposing messages is reduced		20	0.11
		The initial minority has become the new majority	4/8		
3	122101221000	The probability of so few oppositions by chance is quite low	5/7	12	0.01
4	122101221000	With a bigger minority, the chance of perfect clustering is less	5/7	12	0.001
		No longer does anyone face an opposing majority.			
		No further change is likely.		12	0.001

Figure 13.2 Spatial clustering of jury verdicts

involving a dormitory assault, a ruined dress, a cheating accusation, and too much noise (Jackson & Latané, 1995). Each column represents the changing verdicts of a different person, with the color of the face representing whether they voted innocent or guilty. Like real courtrooms, juries deliberated by sending messages to each other – unlike real juries, however, they communicated only by email and only with their one or two nearest neighbors on either side. So, although they actually were communicating by reading and writing two-line messages at a computer terminal, the jurors functionally were spatially distributed, much as if they were sitting around a table talking only to their neighbors on either side. Messages written during one session were delivered and read the following session two or five days later. Communication was therefore asynchronous, like airmail, voice mail, or email.

The first row for each session shows the number of opposing messages each person got. Those people who got the most opposing messages were most likely to change, as shown by the double arrows. As the temporal evolution of this jury proceeds, jurors become more similar to their neighbors, as those who found themselves in disagreement were most likely to change. This resulted in a decrease in the number of opposing messages. We can use this number to calculate the degree to which the jury is clustered, relative to chance, by calculating the proportion (p) of all 12! (i.e. more than 479 million) permutations of groups with this minority size that would have this few or fewer oppositions. Thus, we can derive a number that represents the probability, corrected for continuity, that such a degree of clustering could occur by chance. Starting with a p of 0.70, slightly anti-clustered, this particular group achieved perfect clustering after only two exchanges of messages and ended with a p of 0.001, or less than one chance in a thousand (we typically convert this p-value to a z-score for meta-analysis). Everyone is getting at least as many supportive as opposing messages and nobody has reason to change.

This clustering is typical. We have now conducted spatial deliberations of 138 cases by thirty-nine different juries, each starting with no initial clustering. Although often the initial minority was simply too small to self-organize, making it meaningless to calculate a clustering score, final z-scores were positive for all but ten of the eighty-four cases with more than one person in the final minority and, overall, clustering was substantial and highly significant. As predicted by dynamic social impact theory, therefore, clustering seems to be a widespread group-level response to disagreement in real groups of interacting people, allowing minorities to become spatially organized.

Consolidation was also characteristic of these electronic juries. When deliberations were conducted under a random geometry (thirty-eight cases), clustering was not possible, and juries reached full or near unanimity 61 percent of the time. Clustering, however, by allowing spatially distributed groups to organize themselves into distinct, spatially coherent subcultures, allowed minorities to survive, being eliminated or reduced to a single holdout only 39 percent of the time, thus contributing to the maintenance of continuing diversity. In the context of a jury trial, of course, these subcultures prevent groups from reaching verdicts. In the larger society, we may think them more desirable.

This study provides a new method for observing social influence processes, the electronic student honor court, and introduces a new procedure for calculating clustering statistics, using probability values. The present findings suggest that spatially coherent sub-groups or clusters can and do emerge from initially random distributions of opinions as a result of discussion. Even in-groups as small as twelve-person juries passing messages on involving issues to and from as few as two neighbors, dynamic social impact leads to the emergence of small-scale minority subgroups that become resistant to majority influence. DSIT conceptualizes communication in social space as a continuous process, with influence assumed to decrease with increased distance in social space. The email paradigm, in contrast, assigns social space a discrete, all-or-none character, as people are permitted to communicate only with their immediate neighbors. Computer simulations by Latané and Nowak (1996) suggest that consolidation and clustering should be even more pronounced if social space were allowed to vary continuously. Consolidation and clustering emerged in-groups as small as twelve persons with as few as two messages – but would they characterize larger groups? They occurred in a one-dimensional spatial geometry resembling a group seated around a table – but would they show up with higher dimension or "clumpier" geometries, which may be more generally characteristic of the outside world? Continuing diversity in the form of hung juries was common despite peoples desire to reach consensus – but what would happen if the motive to conform were made even more powerful?

Self-organization in email discussion groups

Dynamic social impact theory predicts that four forms of self-organization at the group level should result from social influence at the individual level: consolidation from the fact that minorities are more exposed, clustering as neighbors become more similar, correlation because even clusters formed independently on different issues will overlap, leading to a loss of independence, and continuing diversity from the protection afforded minorities by clusters. Furthermore, it follows from DSIT that consolidation and clustering should be enhanced in proportion to the tendency to conform to others, while correlation should be proportional to clustering. Finally, even when individuals are motivated to conform to the majority, groups should be able to maintain continuing diversity. In 1995 Martin Bourgeois and I succeeded in testing each of these predictions in a single (large) study (Bourgeois & Latané, 1995). We recruited 240 people and organized them into ten 24-person groups. Participants communicated with their four nearest neighbors in a social space constructed like a ribbon of families – six four-person groups, each with two connections each to the neighboring families on either side. Participants exchanged messages with four other people – each other person in their own family and also with one person from another subgroup during five communication rounds over two-and-a-half weeks. Again, messages written during one session were delivered and read the following session two or five days later. The results were striking, perhaps the most satisfying set of data I have ever collected.

Varying influenceability

We chose three activities designed to vary the degree to which people were likely to be subject to social influence. (1) In the conformity game, participants were promised a $1 reward for predicting the majority position on each of six uninvolving issues such as "Which mathematician (Euler or Hilbert) will the majority of your 24-person group prefer?" We expected people to be very responsive to the opinions of their neighbors on these issues and they were, changing almost 70 percent of the time when the majority opposed their prediction, less than 3 percent otherwise. (2) For the political/social forum, participants were asked to rate their agreement with a series of statements on six-point scales including a two-line statement of reasons. Topics included judgments of human rights violations (H), political policies (P), social issues (S), and four items from the authoritarian personality inventory (F). People were somewhat less responsive, but still paid attention to their neighbors' arguments with respect to the political and social issues – over one-third changing when faced with unanimous disagreement compared to the 10 percent who changed after being exposed to disagreement from one or two neighbors. (3) Finally, the deviation game was similar to the conformity game except that group members were rewarded for being in the minority, giving them no incentive to become similar to their neighbors. As one might expect, change in the deviation game was inversely related to the amount of opposition – with over 50 percent switching to differentiate themselves from a unanimous set of agreeing neighbors compared to less than 15 percent changing when faced with unanimous disagreement.

These differences in the degree of social influence according to the type of topic should be reflected in corresponding differences in the resulting emergence of consolidation, clustering, and correlation. Specifically, these forms of self-organization should be greater for conformity game than for political and social issues, and should completely disappear for the deviation game. Statistical analyses were conducted by computing the average degree of consolidation and clustering across all issues of a given type for each of the ten independent groups and then calculating *t*-tests on planned comparisons.

Consolidation This was commonplace, especially among the conformity game issues for which there was a net reduction of 37 percent in the size of the initial minority ($p < 0.001$) and a complete unification at the majority position for 17 percent of the issues. Although people were much less responsive to social influence for the political-social issues, there was still a significant ($p < 0.001$) degree of consolidation with an average of 14 percent of the initial minority converting to the majority. However, again as expected, there was significantly ($p < 0.01$) less consolidation for these attitudes than for conformity game issues. Finally, there was no sign of consolidation for the deviation game items, with a net change of less than 2 percent in the size of the minority.

Clustering This was again consistent, statistically significant with positive final z-scores on every one of the fifty-five conformity game items that did not unify (z was significant for fifty-two of these cases), and the average increase in z-score was 3.19. I believe there can be no remaining doubt that clustering is an extremely powerful phenomenon if social influence is sufficiently strong. But is it restricted to trivial conformity game topics?

The answer is no! Clustering was still quite robust for the political-social issues, with the final z being positive on 79 percent of the 110 cases, averaging 1.08 and significant ($p < 0.001$). It was significant even for a set of four F-scale items measuring authoritarian personality orientations. As expected from the lower degree of individual change, clustering was significantly lower than for the conformity game. Furthermore, rather than clustering, the deviation game items actually showed a tendency towards anticlustering, with an average final z of -0.94 ($p = 0.07$). Thus, clustering is a powerful emergent force, and it is exhibited when and to the degree predicted by dynamic social impact theory. It characterizes both important and trivial issues, over a wide range of susceptibility to social influence.

Correlation Perhaps the most surprising prediction of DSIT is that correlations should emerge among previously unrelated issues, not because people discover hidden relationships between them, but simply from the loss of independence due to clustering. To test the significance of this effect, we counted, separately for each of the ten independent groups, the number of statistically significant ($r > 0.40$) correlation coefficients among all possible combinations of issues of each type before and after discussion. Before discussion, there was only a chance level of correlation among the six conformity game items (5 percent of the 150 possible coefficients) or between the six conformity game and the ten or twelve political-social issues (5 percent of the 660 possible correlations). There was a somewhat higher degree of correlation among the political-social issues, with 8 percent of 555 being significant at the 0.05 level before discussion.

As a result of the clustering induced by discussion, the number of significant correlations among the conformity game responses rose dramatically from 5 to 35 percent and their average absolute value from 0.16 to 0.31, both increases being significant ($p < 0.001$). These correlations, which ranged up to 0.83, are simply a result of dynamic social influence separately applied to each of the issues, and presumably do not yet represent the emergence of anything like an ideology. The number of significant correlations involving political-social items rose to 14 percent, with their average final degree of correlation rising to 0.21 (both p's < 0.01). Since there was less social influence and less clustering with respect to the social-political items, we should expect a lower degree of correlation to result from communication, and indeed the results bear this out, demonstrating that correlation is determined by the degree of clustering, and not by ideological connections among the issues. Finally, the emergence of correlation entirely depended on clustering. In the deviation game, in which people strove to be dissimilar from their neighbors, there was no clustering and only 2 percent of the 165 possible correlations were significant after discussion, down from 6 percent before.

Social identity emerging from discussion The emergence of clusters of correlated attitudes from dynamic social impact should lead to the development of subgroups of people with similar attributes. Figure 13.3 represents the post-discussion opinions on the six conformity game issues of a typical group of twenty-four CAPS participants. Each feature (left and right eyebrow, eye, and side of mouth) corresponds to a different issue, about which the person can hold one of two positions (smile vs. frown). Clustering and correlation have produced strong "family resemblances" within most sub-groups. Although not possible for participants to detect in the present paradigm, such patterns in the outside world may become identifiable and form the basis for friendship choices, stereotypes, in- versus out-group feelings, and all the other features of social life.

Social impact and social representations The patterns of beliefs and behaviors formed by dynamic social influence can be considered rudimentary social representations as conceived by Moscovici (1984) – they apply to ideas, values, practices, and any other socially influenceable attribute of an individual, they are collectively realized, in the sense that different people possess different aspects of the whole, and they form complete descriptions of pieces of social reality, which can acquire iconic form, allowing them to become the means as

Figure 13.3 Family resemblances in a typical group after discussing six issues (facial features represent opinions)

well as the objects of influence. Thus, dynamic social impact theory has the potential to account for how social representations, clustered bundles of culture elements self-organized through social interaction, emerge from everyday communication (Huguet & Latané, 1996). By being the means as well as the result of communication, these social representations can help enhance the degree of self-organization in-groups.

Conclusion

Conceiving society as a complex nonlinear system of interacting individuals, dynamic social impact theory explores how individual experience and social influence processes lead to the regional differentiation and temporal evolution of culture. Changes in the attributes (e.g. moods, attitudes, habits) of spatially distributed individuals resulting from the interactive, reciprocal, and recursive operation of social influence processes can be modeled through computer simulation, using dynamic social impact theory, a simple but very general model of social influence. Surprisingly, several macro-level phenomena can be predicted to emerge from the operation of these micro-level processes, including a consolidation with reduced diversity of attributes, a clustering of minorities into spatially coherent sub-groups of people protecting each other from exposure to outside influence, a correlation of peoples positions on different issues, and an ultimate maintenance of continuing diversity, as minority positions are enabled to survive.

I am currently conducting empirical research on college students and other people interacting not only in electronic mail networks but in lecture halls and dormitories to test the predictions of dynamic social impact theory. The results to date are highly encouraging – not only do actual groups exhibit the phenomena predicted by dynamic social impact theory (Harton, Green, Jackson, & Latané, under review; Latané & L'Herrou, 1996), but simulations succeed in predicting the postdiscussion responses of individuals (Bourgeois & Latané, in press; Rockloff & Latané, in press). In addition, I am extending the theory to deal with the development of stereotypes, social identities, political ideologies, and social representations from individuals' perceptions of correlated attributes in their local environment. I hope this research will contribute to understanding the complex interaction between individual psychological processes and social outcomes in-groups ranging in size from families and other small groups to organizations, communities, and even nations. Concepts and procedures developed in this research should be applicable to understanding the historical development of regional differences in customs, values, and beliefs, social determinants of moods, norms, lifestyles, and behaviors, both constructive and maladaptive, and such elusive phenomena as social movements, consumer confidence, national character, social representations, and public opinion. This approach aligns social psychology with the interdisciplinary study of complex self-organizing systems, and contributes to and draws upon related work in physics, economics, and biology. It leads to a conception of social psychology as an interdisciplinary amalgamation unifying the social and mathematical sciences and enabling a rational approach to understanding social problems.

Dynamic social impact theory has many implications for practice, varying in plausibility and ease of implementation. The modern world is embarking on a massive experiment in new forms of communication – the Internet. What will this do to regional and temporal differences in such elements of culture as public opinion and the mood of the public? Perhaps dynamic social impact theory will be helpful in finding out. If a goal in a democratic society is to preserve opinion diversity while encouraging a full discussion of issues, dynamic social impact theory may also help show how electronic discussion could best be organized. Rather than allowing a large number of participants to jam the channel as everyone tries to talk to everyone else, perhaps online chats should be organized in a ribbon or family geometry, allowing everyone to talk with their desired number of correspondents in a way likely to allow the full development of minority as well as majority perspectives. Seating assignments in classrooms may facilitate not only learning but (as schoolteachers already know) the control of disruptive behavior. Perhaps new systems of assigning seats in national assemblies such as the US Congress or work groups in organizations could even lead to new combinations of ideological elements and a burst of creative policy.

Dynamic social impact theory views culture as a continuing human creation to which everyone contributes. Based on the psychology of the individual human being, living in a social world, dynamic social impact theory assumes that culture is generated from the bottom up in the form of inductive combinations of culture elements that become spatially distributed social representations. The theory sees human society as a collection of subcultures, an organic changing entity responsive to, and possibly controllable through, the technology that determines the shape, the geometry of social space, the technology of social interaction. Although I hope this theory may lead to understanding sociological, political, and economic phenomena, it will probably be best suited to explaining the form rather than the content of historical, cultural, and regional differences, as nothing in the theory tells us what the nature of a particular culture will be. According to this theory, there will be two kinds of cultural universals, those originating in the nature and experience of individuals (the *b* or bias term in the theory) and the macro-level emergent consequences of their interaction (dynamic self-organization).

Finally, many of you should be happy that this theory assures a central role for social psychology in solving the master problem of social science,

McDougall's task of showing how individuals create and are shaped by society. I hope this chapter will contribute to the integration of differing perspectives in helping us address this challenge.

Fears of atomic holocaust seem to have faded in the fifty years since the bomb was first unleashed; today's headlines tell instead of tribal warfare, ethnic conflict, religious intolerance, teenage violence, and political stalemate. The problems may have changed, but the imbalance between the physical and social sciences seems as pronounced as ever. Perhaps this is because we have such a hard time getting our stories told.

Along with other social scientists, I often receive calls from such media powerhouses as the Associated Press, the Oprah Winfrey show, NBC Dateline, or the BBC, wanting me to explain why a marketplaceful of English people watched as Jamie Bulger was dragged to his death in 1993 by two pre-teenaged bullies, or why a bridgeful of Detroiters failed to save Deletha Word from drowning in 1995 after an altercation with a crazed assailant. Although the media often carry a short graf citing me or some other social scientist, they seem instinctively to want to revert to the "apathy" label initiated by Abe Rosenthal, managing editor of the New York Times, *who broke the original Genovese story (Rosenthal, 1964). Although millions of students in introductory psychology and social psychology courses have now learned about the pre-eminence over apathy of such situational factors as the number of bystanders, the* Times, *despite its excellent stable of science writers, doesn't seem to have yet caught on. This may reflect either a mindless desire to preserve its original slant on the story, or a more general tendency to blame character rather than circumstance for the foibles of others.*

Nevertheless, along with most of the other contributors to this volume, I believe social psychology still has much to offer – if we can make the public aware of the enormous power of situational influences. Perhaps we can be most useful, not in giving answers to specific policy questions, but in suggesting how groups and organizations can best find the answers themselves. The old view of social engineering, in which a central elite made informed decisions for the widespread masses, has been discredited. Democracy, with its underpinnings of education, freedom of speech, and the marketplace of ideas, seems to do a good job of enabling society to organize itself through dynamic social impact. Perhaps social psychology will have a role in helping specify conditions which will allow groups of all sizes, from neighborhoods to nations, to organize themselves most effectively, eliminating bad ideas and practices while maintaining healthy diversity. Thus, I believe the science and profession of social psychology is still the one best hope for those of us who wish to apply human knowledge and intelligence to creating a world of harmony rather than strife.

Further Reading

Latané, B. (1989). Social psychology and how to revitalize it. In M. R. Leary (Ed.), *The state of social psychology: Issues, themes, and controversies*. Newbury Park, CA: Sage Publications. I present results of a survey of social psychologists and discuss problems and prospects facing social psychology.

Latané, B. (1996a). Dynamic social impact: The creation of culture by communication. *Journal of Communication 46*(3). This invited symposium, with papers co-authored with Jim Liu, Marty Bourgeois, Howard Lavine, Pascal Huguet, and Mark Schaller, includes a formal statement of dynamic social impact theory, a discussion of the nature of social space, some empirical results, and suggestions for new directions in explaining ideology, social representations, and stereotypes.

Latané, B. (1996b). Strength from weakness: The fate of opinion minorities in spatially distributed groups. In E. Witte & J. Davis (Eds.), *Understanding group behavior: Consensual action by small groups* (pp. 193–219). Hillsdale, NJ: Lawrence Erlbaum. I argue that the language of social impact theory may be especially useful in describing minority influence effects, and suggest six ways in which minorities may gain disproportionate influence.

Latané, B. (1996c). Dynamic social impact: Robust predictions from simple theory. In R. Hegselmann, U. Mueller, & K. Troitzsch (Eds.), *Modelling and simulation in the social sciences from the philosophy of science point of view*. Dordrecht: Reidel. I discuss the role of multi-agent simulation in social psychology and contrast dynamic social impact theory with three other approaches to social simulation.

Latané, B., & Nowak, A. (1994). Attitudes as catastrophes: From dimensions to categories with increasing involvement. In R. Vallacher & A. Nowak (Eds.), *Dynamical systems in social psychology* (pp. 219–249). New York: Academic Press. The chapter presents a nonlinear model of individual attitude change designed to explain why discussion can intensify disagreement; other chapters introduce dynamical systems to social psychology.

Latané, B., & Nowak, A. (1996). Self-organizing social systems: Necessary and sufficient conditions for the emergence of consolidation and clustering. In G. Barnett & F. Boster (Eds.), *Progress in communication sciences: Persuasion*. Norwood, NJ: Ablex. A thorough simulation-based analysis of the central and boundary conditions leading to continuing diversity.

References

Bourgeois, M. J., & Latané, B. (1995, July). *Dynamic social impact causes spatially clustered and correlated opinions*. Poster presented at the annual meetings of the American Psychological Society, New York.

Bourgeois, M. J., & Latané, B. (in press). Simulating dynamic social impact: Four levels of prediction. In E. Chattoe & R. Conte (Eds.), *Evolving societies: The computer simulation of social systems*. London: UCL Press.

Freeman, S., Walker, M., Borden, R., & Latané, B. (1975). Diffusion of responsibility and restaurant tipping: Cheaper by the bunch. *Personality and Social Psychology Bulletin*, *1*, 584–587.

Harton, H. C., Green, L. R., Jackson, C., & Latané, B. (under review). *Discussion leads to consolidation, clustering, and correlation*

– *and (sometimes) the correct answer: A classroom demonstration of dynamic social impact.*

Huguet, P., & Latané, B. (1996). Social representations as dynamic social impact. *Journal of Communication, 46*(3).

Jackson, C., & Latané, B. (1995). *Dynamic social impact on trial: The emergence of subgroups in electronic juries.* Poster presented at the annual meetings of the American Psychological Society, New York.

Latané, B. (1981). The psychology of social impact. *American Psychologist*, *36*, 343–365.

Latané, B. (1996a). Dynamic social impact: The creation of culture by communication. *Journal of Communication, 46*(3).

Latané, B. (1996b). Strength from weakness: The fate of opinion minorities in spatially distributed groups. In E. Witte & J. Davis (Eds.), *Understanding group behavior: Consensual action by small groups* (pp. 193–219). Hillsdale, NJ: Lawrence Erlbaum.

Latané, B. (1996c). The emergence of clustering and correlation from social interaction. In R. Hegselmann & H. O. Peitgen (Eds.), *Order and chaos in nature and society*. Vienna: Hîlder-Pichler.

Latané, B., & Dabbs, J. (1975). Sex, group size and helping in three cities. *Sociometry*, *38*, 180–194.

Latané, B. & Darley, J. M. (1970). *The unresponsive bystander: Why doesn't he help*? Englewood Cliffs, NJ: Prentice Hall.

Latané, B., Harton, H. C., Rockloff, M. J., Bourgeois, M. J., & Wheeler, L. (in preparation). *Answering the call: Distinguishing three sources of social inhibition in emergencies and nonemergencies.*

Latané, B., & Hothersall, D. (1972). Social attraction in animals. In P. C. Dodwell (Ed.), *New horizons in psychology II*, Penguin Books.

Latané, B., & L'Herrou, T. (1996). Social clustering in the conformity game: Dynamic social impact in electronic groups. *Journal of Personality and Social Psychology, 71*, 1218–1230.

Latané, B., & Nida, S. (1981). Ten years of research on group size and helping. *Psychological Bulletin*, *89*, 308–324

Latané, B., & Nowak, A. (1996). Self-organizing social systems: Necessary and sufficient conditions for the emergence of consolidation and clustering. In G. Barnett & F. Boster (Eds.), *Progress in communication sciences: Persuasion*. Norwood, NJ: Ablex.

Latané, B., & Rodin, J. (1969). A lady in distress: Inhibiting effects of friends and strangers on bystander intervention. *Journal of Experimental Social Psychology*, *5*, 189–202.

Latané, B., Williams, K., & Harkins, S. (1979). Many hands make light the work: Causes and consequences of social loafing. *Journal of Personality and Social Psychology*, *37*, 822–832.

Latané, B., & Werner, C. (1978). The regulation of social contact in laboratory rats: Time, not distance. *Journal of Personality and Social Psychology*, *36*, 1128–1137.

Latané, B., & Wolf, S. (1981). The social impact of majorities and minorities. *Psychological Review*, *88*, 438–453.

Lewenstein, M., Nowak, A., & Latané, B. (1992). The statistical mechanics of social impact. *Physical Review A*, *45*, 703–716.

McDougall, W. (1908). *Introduction to Social psychology*. London: Methuen.

Moscovici, S. (1984). The phenomenon of social representations. In R. M. Farr & S. Moscovici (Eds.) *Social representations*. Cambridge/Paris CUP/Maison des Sciences de L'Homme.

Nisbett, R. E., & Ross, L. (1980). *Human inference: Strategies and shortcomings of social judgment*. Englewood Cliffs, NJ: Prentice Hall.

Nowak, A., & Latané, B. (1994). Simulating the emergence of social order from individual behavior. In N. Gilbert & J. Doran (Eds.), *Simulating societies: The computer simulation of social phenomena* (pp. 63–84). London: University College London Press.

Nowak, A., Szamrej, J., & Latané, B. (1990). From private attitude to public opinion: A dynamic theory of social impact. *Psychological Review*, *97*, 362–376.

Petty, R. E., Williams, K. D., Harkins, S. G., & Latané, B. (1977). Social inhibition of helping yourself: Bystander response to a cheeseburger. *Personality and Social Psychology Bulletin*, *3*, 579–582.

Rockloff, M. J., & Latané, B. (in press). Human choice in social context. In U. Mueller & K. Troitzsch (Eds.), *Social science microsimulation: A challenge for computer science*. Springer Lecture Notes in Economics and Mathematical Systems, Berlin: Springer Verlag.

Rosenthal, A. M. (1964). *Thirty-eight witnesses*. New York: McGraw Hill.

Waldrop, M. M. (1992). *Complexity: The emerging science at the edge of order and chaos*. New York: Simon & Schuster.

Werner, C., & Latané, B. (1974). Interaction motivates attraction: Rats are fond of fondling. *Journal of Personality and Social Psychology*, *29*, 328–334.

14

Going Beyond the Banalities of Bubbapsychology: A Perspectivist Social Psychology

William J. McGuire

William J. McGuire, born in New York City in 1925, obtained a B.A. (1949) and M.A. (1950) from Fordham University, a doctorate (1954) from Yale University, and an honorary doctorate (1990) from Eötvös Loránd University (Budapest). At the University of Illinois, Columbia University, University of California, and Yale University, he taught and did research on attitude change, immunization against persuasion, the self-concept, and thought systems. He has received fellowships from the Social Science Research Council, the National Institute of Health, the Guggenheim Foundation, and the Center for Advanced Study in the Behavioral Sciences. Among his awards are the 1988 Distinguished Scientific Contribution Award from the American Psychological Association and the 1992 Distinguished Scientist Award from the Society of Experimental Social Psychology.

The editors in their introduction to this volume point out that one of the distinctive features of social psychology is that it deals with processes that are frequently experienced in daily life. Such familiarity has the attraction that our discipline grapples with universally relevant questions but presents the danger that our answers tend to be trite. This chapter proposes ways of pursuing social psychology that provide extraordinary answers to ordinary questions.

To illustrate the problem, consider the student coming home from her seminar in social psychology and being greeted by her grandmother with the question, "So, what's new in social psychology?" The student might reply,

"We went over a couple of interesting experiments that confirmed the hypothesis that the more physically attractive people are, the more desirable they are judged to be as marriage mates." The grandmother may have to exercise heroic restraint to keep from asking, "Is it to learn this that you have gone to school for 20 years?" At least her bubba is spared the further paradox that such obvious hypotheses often prove difficult to confirm empirically. The malaise of social psychology is that in our empirical work we tend to labor mountainously to bring forth mousy conceptualizations. The entering student is often aware of the field's banalities but as he or she acculturates tends to settle for its trivialities. It need not be so. This chapter describes techniques that can provoke and empower social psychologists to go beyond the trite to more striking formulations. First, though, I shall describe the aberrant "perspectivist" epistemology that guides and motivates these procedures for going beyond the bubba-psychological banalities.

The Nature of Knowledge: A Perspectivist Epistemology

The nature of knowledge is a topic of central personal and professional relevance to social psychological students, teachers, and researchers, but my perspectivist approach will be described here only as regards three issues: What is it "to know," what are the criteria by which alternative knowledge formulations are to be evaluated, and how can enlightening knowledge formulations be generated? These are the three issues most relevant to the purposes of this volume. A fuller discussion of perspectivism can be found elsewhere (McGuire, 1973, 1983, 1984, 1986, 1989, 1994).

What is it, to know? The origins of knowledge

It is easier to grasp what knowledge is if one first considers why knowing developed. Knowledge probably had its origins in the dependence of the organism (whose needs and capacities vary over time) on an environment whose gratifications vary over time and place. One mode of coping with such a situation is for the species to evolve so that the organism has the capacity to monitor its own momentary needs and capacities and the environment's varying satisfactions and threats. Such monitoring would allow the organism to coordinate its own behavior efficiently with the environment's possibilities. This mode of coping would be cost-effective to the extent that the onerousness of the monitoring and coordination functions is kept to a minimum by selectively monitoring only the most crucial and manageable aspects of the situation. The knowing process probably involves the person's putting some aspect of the knowledge apparatus (e.g. cerebral circuits, sensory-organ orientation, postural adjustments, etc.) into one-to-one correspondence with a few crucial environmental aspects, constituting a metaphorical representation of the environment that covaries with its crucial aspects.

The tragedy of knowledge

Knowledge representations are triply flawed misrepresentations marred by underrepresentations, overrepresentations, and malrepresentations. (1) Underrepresentation is necessitated by the fact that knowing is very expensive histologically and metabolically (e.g. the brain has vastly more cells than the rest of the body combined and is an energy glutton, consuming a quarter of the total oxygen and glucose used by the resting body). This limits the person to monitoring only the most essential aspects of the known (e.g. over the vast spectrum of electromagnetic waves that are impinging on humans, we can monitor directly only the tiny range of visible light). (2) Overrepresentation arises because, if knowledge is to provide information for coordinated reaction, the knower must supplement the incoming information with inferences based on past experiences and current needs (e.g. we must infer three-dimensional space from a flat retinal image; and from observing others' behavior in like past situations we must extrapolate their likely behavior in the present new situation). (3) Besides over- and underrepresentation, knowledge necessarily involves malrepresentation because it is informed by the nature of the knower as well as the known (e.g. the visual representation in the occipital lobe is vastly different from the seen object itself). Consider, for example, two representations a writer might have of his desk, the phenomenal representation as a solid hardwood surface versus the atomic physics representation as mostly space with a scattering of infinitesimal particles. As different as these two representations are from one another, they are probably more similar to each other than they are to the table.

That such underrepresentation, overrepresentation, and malrepresentation distort our knowledge gives rise to my perspectivist epistemology to cope with the tragedy that our necessary representations are necessarily misrepresentations. The evolutionary process has probably honed to a fine edge of adequacy human's representation of pervasive actualities like local space, so that we can locomote through it and manipulate objects in it with high accuracy. As knowledge proceeds to more abstract levels and more novel tasks, as in social-psychological theories, the inherent misrepresentations involved in knowledge become gigantic. We have the cold comfort that even worse than knowing is not knowing; and that while all knowledge representations are inadequate, some may be identifiable as less inadequate than others.

Perspectivist epistemology, by recognizing the flaws in the scientific process (both in its *a priori* conceptual confrontational aspects and in its *a posteriori* empirical confrontational aspects – both aspects of social psychology that are discussed below) helps the researcher cope with this tragic situation. Great expectations as regards broad and generally valid laws must be replaced by modest hopes to identify restricted conditions in which some knowledge representation provides a limping but useful metaphor of the situation known. It is not only the social scientist who must recognize (and exploit) the limitations of knowledge. The classical physicist may propose that the distance traversed by a falling body is $d = 1/2gt^2$ and is independent of the body's mass. However all empirical tests would disprove these hypotheses which would be valid, if ever, only in a hypothetical vacuum. A skilled center fielder chasing a fly ball has an implicit theory much more predictive than the more austerely lovely formal physics model, $d = 1/2gt^2$. Perspectivism guides our proper use of conceptual and empirical confrontations that constitute research for their true purpose, discovering the circumstances in which any knowledge representation is and is not useful.

Pursuit of the dismal perspectivist bottom line that every knowledge representation is triply a misrepresentation leads to perspectivism's most upbeat implication, perspectivism's radical position that every knowledge representation (including every social psychological hypothesis) is true, as adumbrated in William Blake's aphorism, "Everything possible to be believed is an image of truth." The derivation and exploitation of this perspectivist insight that all hypotheses (even mutually contradictory ones) are true can be accomplished by several approaches including the quasi-logical argument that if every proposition is false (due to over-, under-, and malrepresentation) then the contradictory of every proposition is true, which implies that every proposition is true as well as false.

The perspectivist resolution of this paradox is that every hypothesis is usually inadequate but occasionally adequate from some limited perspective, in some specific context. The purpose of conceptual and empirical research in social psychology and other fields is not the critical one of testing whether a set hypothesis (and its theoretical housing) is true or false, but the creative one of discovering the perspectives from which it is true or false. As regards criteria for judging which knowledge representation is more adequate from a given perspective (or from which perspective a given hypothesis is more adequate), perspectivism ecumenically recognizes a plethora of criteria and proposes use of a mix of them, as a corrective to the current narrow overemphasis in social psychology and other sciences of the one criterion of survival of disconfirmation when put to the jeopardy of empirical test.

Criteria for Judging the Adequacy of a Knowledge Representation

The knowledge representations whose adequacy concerns us in social psychology are our hypotheses (i.e. statements of relations between variables, such as the prediction that persons perceive their ingroups as more heterogeneous than their outgroups) and the broader theoretical formulations from which these specific hypotheses can be derived (e.g. self-categorization theory; see Turner, Hogg, Oakes, Reicher, & Wetherell, 1987). The traditional criterion for judging the adequacy of such a hypothesis is whether, when put in empirical jeopardy, it survives the test. A perspectivist analysis calls this orthodoxy into question. Perspectivism proposes over a dozen additional criteria (including independent and even mutually contradictory criteria) and asserts that the orthodox empirical-confirmation criterion is not and should not be dominant.

Intrinsic criteria

Criteria that judge the adequacy of a knowledge representation by characteristics intrinsic to the representation itself will be considered first, and then extrinsic criteria which judge the representation's adequacy against some external standard. One quite familiar intrinsic desideratum is internal consistency: a theoretical formulation is judged inadequate to the extent that it yields mutually contradictory implications. A second desideratum is, paradoxically, internal inconsistency. A Hegelian-Marxist dialectician might argue that, because the society itself has internal contradictions, so should a theory describing it; and that in any case internal inconsistencies are creatively provocative in instigating search for a higher synthesis that will account for the thesis and antithesis. Novelty and banality are a second pair of contradictory intrinsic criteria. Scientists prize knowledge representations more highly if they yield a dramatically new insight rather than simply being a minor variation on a familiar theme. On the other hand, banality is also prized in that explanations are acceptable only to the extent that they use concepts currently acceptable to high-table science (e.g. social psychologists may accept a physiologizing explanation but reject parapsychologizing explanations as too radically outside current orthodoxy). Other intrinsic criteria for judging the adequacy of knowledge representations (such as social-psychological hypotheses and theories) include other curiously opposite pairs, such as completeness and open-endedness, parsimony and rococo extravagance, elegance and heuristic provocativeness, as discussed by McGuire (1989).

Extrinsic criteria

The adequacy of knowledge representations may be judged also by extrinsic criteria, a half dozen of which will be mentioned here. (1) One such external standard is derivability from an accepted set of premises such as Whitehead and Russell's axioms (1910–13), the Bible, the Marxist-Leninist corpus, or a legal compilation. Other external criteria include (2) the status of the author; (3) acceptance by valued constituencies; (4) a subjective sense of acceptability;

(5) pragmatic value; and (6) survival of disconfirmation when put in empirical jeopardy. It is this last criterion which receives most explicit recognition in empirical sciences such as social psychology.

This long but still incomplete list of criteria for judging the adequacy of knowledge representations includes many that are independent of or even contrary to one another, which should caution social psychologists against epistemological oversimplifications, however orthodox. The optimal weighting to give a set of criteria depends on the perspective from which a problem is viewed. The banality of most social-psychological formulations is due in part to overemphasis on a few traditional criteria (e.g. internal consistency, derivability from a set of accepted postulates, survival of empirical jeopardy) to the neglect of others (e.g. novelty, heuristic provocativeness, pragmatic value). Perspectivism redresses the conventional imbalance by reducing the conventional overemphasis of critical, hypothesis-evaluating criteria relative to creative, hypothesis-generating criteria.

From logical empiricism to perspectivism

Since the fall of the Roman empire, European epistemology has been dominated by five successive knowledge criteria, from dogmatism to rationalism to positivism to logical empiricism to an incipient perspectivist ascendancy (McGuire, 1989). The hegemonic succession has passed from one to the other with increasing speed, perspectivism now waiting in the wings about to enter center stage. The five successive periods represent an accelerating evolution toward increasing sophistication. Here I shall describe the transition only from the current to the impending favored positions, from logical empiricism to perspectivism.

Precedence of theory over data collection The Vienna circle and their followers ingeniously combined contrasting insights of the two preceding hegemonies, rationalism and positivism, into a provocative epistemology that can be encapsulated in four tenets, two having to do with the *a priori* conceptual confrontation aspects of scientific inquiry and two having to do with the *a posteriori* empirical confrontation aspects. In keeping with rationalism's reaction to radical positivism, a first tenet of logical empiricism is that empirical observation should be preceded and guided by explicit knowledge representations, including a hypothesis and a theory from which it can be derived. It recognizes that researchers typically have preconceptions likely to distort their observations and interpretations, which are best made explicit so that their prejudicing effects can be taken into account and so that they can guide data collection and interpretation economically and equitably.

Perspectivism accepts this first tenet of logical empiricism and extends it by asserting that the researcher should focus, not only on an initial hypothesis but also on its contrary, following Simone Weil's prescription that whenever one formulates an attractive proposition one should immediately generate circumstances in which its contrary would be the case. As regards *a priori* theory, perspectivism agrees with the logical empiricist prescription that one should have an explicit theory from which one's hypothesis can be derived, but goes further by asserting that one is not enough, that our research programs should be designed to test at least two alternative theoretical explanations for the initial hypothesis and at least two for its contrary.

The reconcilability of contrary hypotheses A second logical empiricist tenet pertinent to *a priori* aspects of research is its assumption that between contrary hypotheses at least one must be erroneous. Perspectivism takes issue with this contention, arguing that all propositions are true, including even a proposition and its contrary, each being true even if only rarely and in limited contexts (such as the hypothetical vacuum where the physics law $d = 1/2gt^2$ may obtain). Perspectivism regards the conceptual and empirical riches of scientific research as residing, not in the critical determination of whether one's set hypothesis as formulated is right or wrong, but in discovering the circumstances in which it does or does not obtain. As regards the theories from which the hypothesis is derived, current orthodoxy encourages researchers to espouse one theory and (at least implicitly) to regard other theories as antagonistic. Perspectivism asserts rather that any hypothesis obtains for multiple reasons and prescribes generating at least two theories to account for any hypothesis. Social psychologists pursuing the current orthodoxy are likely to start with an obvious hypothesis embedded in one theory and then carry out an experiment purportedly to test whether the hypothesis and theory are true. The perspectivist starts rather with the hypothesis and its contrary, investigating the extent to which each is accounted for by multiple, mutually supplementary theories in various contexts. The perspectivist approach better exploits the social psychologist's initial inspiration and lessens the banality stemming from the orthodox approach.

The desirability of a posteriori empirical confrontation A third basic tenet of logical empiricism is that the hypothesis, after *a priori* conceptual clarification, should be subjected to *a posteriori* empirical confrontation. Perspectivism is in accord with this useful corrective to the tendency in everyday thinking (and even in some more formal humanistic thinking) for the knower to act as if having thought of a hypothesis is evidence of its adequacy, but departs from logical empiricism's assumption of a discontinuity (and even reversal) between the *a priori* conceptual confrontation as creative and the *a posteriori* empirical confrontation as critical. Perspectivists use both aspects as primarily creative and secondarily critical, with the empirical confrontation continuing the *a priori* discovery process by exploring the evolving meaning of the hypothesis by other criteria, both confrontations clarifying the contexts in which the hypothesis does versus does not obtain.

Empirical confrontation as test versus discovery A fourth logical empiricist tenet, which like the third has to do with the *a posteriori* empirical confrontation, is that the purpose of this empirical confrontation is to test whether the initial hypothesis and the theory in which it has been housed are correct or at least confirmed sufficiently to increase one's confidence in them. Perspectivism differs radically on this tenet, maintaining that the purpose of the empirical confrontation is not to test the validity of a fixed knowledge representation, but to continue the process of discovering what this representation means, that is, the perspectives from which and contexts in which it does and does not adequately represent the known.

Perspectivist revisionism has both prescriptive and descriptive implications. Perspectivism's basic position that all propositions are true (if only from a few perspectives in very limited contexts) prescribes that the purpose of empirical confrontation should not be to indicate whether the hypothesis is true in any general sense but rather the more exciting purpose of discovering what it means, that is, identifying the limited circumstances in which the hypothesis does versus does not serve. However, I go beyond prescription to description in asserting that even adherents to orthodox logical empiricism do not themselves use empirical confrontation to test their hypothesis but rather, after carrying out an experiment whose results do not agree with the hypothesis, are likely to say that the experiment "did not come out right," thus rejecting the experiment and not the hypothesis. The researcher is likely to tinker with the experiment, changing this and that aspect until it "works." Indeed, even before carrying out the first formal experiment that failed to confirm, the researcher has ordinarily carried out numerous thought experiments and empirical pre-studies and explorations of materials, subjects, procedures, modifying them until the experiment shows good promise of "working." Analogous to these laboratory actualities, the field researcher explores around the natural-world environment until he or she finds a situation in which the hypothesis is most likely to obtain.

When researchers claim to themselves and others that they are using the empirical aspect of research in one manner when actually they are using it in so different a manner it may have a corrupting effect. The perspectivist here is not criticizing what is done (e.g. pre-studies searching for an experimental situation in which the hypothesis will come out right) but condemning rather the failure to recognize and admit that this is what one is and should be doing. The perspectivist's use of the empirical confrontation to discover the fullness of one's initial inspiration allows the researcher to use empirical confrontation efficiently, organizing the "pre-studies" and follow-up studies programmatically, doing justice to a complex initial insight by elaborating it systematically as regards the contexts in which (and the reasons for which) it is adequate or not.

Correcting the Neglect of the Creative Aspects of Methodology

Failure to appreciate that the empirical confrontation best serves a discovery, rather than testing, function contributes to the frequent banality of social psychological hypotheses and theories because it results in our methodology courses overemphasizing the critical hypothesis-testing aspects of the scientific process, to the neglect of its creative hypothesis-generating aspects. Most social psychologists will readily grant that good research depends on creative hypothesis-generating at least as much as on critical hypothesis-testing. Yet our psychology methodology courses deal almost exclusively with the critical, hypothesis-testing topics (e.g. how to measure or manipulate variables, how to control for extraneous variables, experimental design, and inferential statistics). Our methodology courses spend little if any time on how to create provocative hypotheses or how to construct novel theories that account for them, however much we recognize that one first has to catch one's hypothesis before one can test it. The colossal imbalance between the creative and the critical in our methodology courses sends our students the wrong message and leaves them ill equipped for making the contributions of which they might be capable with better balanced training.

That our teachers neglect the creative aspect of methodology even while recognizing its importance may be due to their feeling that creativity is such an elusive process that it cannot be described, much less taught, and perhaps their suspicion that creatives, if not born, are made much earlier than entry into graduate school. At best, mentors may encourage protégés to read studies by creative researchers or to enter into an apprentice relationship with them in hope that some creativity will rub off on the protégé. Perspectivism serves as a corrective to this neglect of the creative in a number of ways. It encourages pursuing the validity, not only of trite hypotheses, but also of their counter-intuitive contraries and, by recognizing the contextual limitations of any social psychological hypothesis, encourages search for higher order interaction effects in addition to the more obvious main effects. Perspectivism also promotes creative explorations by emphasizing that any relation obtains for multiple theoretical explanations. Social psychologists of all epistemological orientations should work harder at introducing explicit training in creativity into methodology courses and tutoring research students to encourage and equip them to create a social psychology that goes beyond banality.

Sociological studies show that creativity can be promoted by institutional arrangements that encourage innovations; some such studies use nomothetic multivariate data collection and analysis techniques (Andrews, 1979) while others use idiographic case studies (Latour & Woolgar, 1979; Goodfield, 1981). As a psychologist I shall discuss the possibilities on the individual level of training students in creativity-promoting techniques, both in the strategic planning of programs of research and in the tactical use of a variety of creative heuristics to enhance the novelty and adequacy of specific hypotheses. The next two sections deal successively with creativity-teaching possibilities on the strategic level (McGuire, 1989) and then on the tactical level (McGuire, 1997).

Strategic-level creativity training in planning programs of research

In social-psychology methodology courses I use a series of cumulative worksheets to guide students through a perspectivist approach to programmatic research planning, launched by each student's own initial hypothesis, which is often banal; but by the time the program has been designed the student is usually surprised by the creativity of his or her end product. The series of worksheets (McGuire, 1989) begins by asking the student to suggest three or four interesting social psychology hypotheses and to indicate why each sounds interesting (e.g. what difference it would make in theory or in practice whether the hypothesis were true or not). I react to the students' proposed hypotheses and give them further exercises to help each choose one hypothesis as the point of departure for developing a research program. An attraction of a perspectivist approach is that it is not a problem that most of these initial hypotheses are fairly obvious (e.g. "People tend to like better other people who are similar to themselves," or "People tend to be more persuaded by sources whom they like than they dislike"). Worksheets then guide the student through playing word games with the two variables in their hypothesis, better to exploit their meaning. The students are encouraged to partition the initial variables into subscales, each separately measured, when their initial conceptual confrontation does not allow them to decide which of several related meanings underlying their label best catches their insights.

The student is then guided through generating at least two explanatory theories from which the hypothesis can be derived. Then the student is given a more specifically perspectivist task: he or she is asked to stand the hypothesis on its head, as Marx did Hegel, and assert the contrary of their initial hypothesis (e.g. "People like best those who are least like themselves," and "People are most persuaded by those whom they like least"). Again, for this contrary hypothesis the student is asked to give at least two explanatory theories from which it can be derived.

The students are then asked to formalize their four-plus theories, each of which usually takes the form of a mediational explanation that can be formally expressed as a syllogism. For example, when asked to generate an explanatory theory by completing the sentence, "People tend to like others who are least like themselves because . . ." They complete it with explanations such as ". . . because dissimilar others are more interesting" or ". . . because people who are unlike themselves better complement their own needs." Formalizing such theories involves putting the explanation into syllogistic form. The minor premise that, "The more dissimilar to oneself a person is, the more interesting he or she tends to be" combined with the major premise that, "The more interesting a person tends to be, the more one tends to like him or her" yields as a valid conclusion the contrary hypothesis being explained, that "The more dissimilar to oneself that a person is, the more one tends to like him or her." Researchers sometimes feel that such syllogistic formalization stifles creative thinking, but actually it gives one a half-dozen advantages over an informal statement of the theory. It provides a check on the theory's validity, detects tautology, provides a diagnostic plausibility check, identifies mediational variables, tests the distinctness of alternative explanations, and allows each premise to serve as a launching pad for creatively generating implied interaction hypotheses. These six dividends of formalization are described more fully elsewhere (McGuire, 1994).

The sixth dividend is a particularly powerful tool for the creative generation of additional interactional hypotheses for inclusion in one's research program. Each premise energizes and diversifies the generation of situational and dispositional variables that will multiply the relation in the initial hypothesis insofar as that theoretical explanation accounts for the hypothesis, leaving the student with a plethora of additional hypotheses. An efficiently organized program of research can then be constructed by setting priorities among the main and interaction predictions yielded, beginning with variables that are easily measured, interesting in themselves, and constitute predictions implied distinctively by only one of the multiple theories.

This cryptic account of programmatic planning procedures illustrates how a student who might start with a pedestrian initial hypothesis can be trained to generate a plethora of predictions, many interesting in their own right and gaining additional interest by the role they play in an organized program of research.

Tactical-level creativity training

Turning from the strategic creation of programs of research to the tactics of generating individual hypotheses, there are two types of tactical aids that can enhance the social psychology student's prowess in generating more interesting hypotheses and theories. One type involves content-free heuristic stances that one can take that sensitize one to interesting questions for research. The other type is more content-specific, being ways of transforming a given trite hypothesis into something more interesting. Tactics of each type will be described in the two sections that follow.

Generating new insights by content-free creative heuristics McGuire (1997) lists dozens of creative heuristics for generating new hypotheses, grouped into subtypes, each described with instances of its use in social psychology and suggestions about how it might be taught. A first class of creative heuristics for generating new hypotheses involves recognizing and analyzing provocative naturally occurring events. Examples are exploiting the relevance and shortcomings of practitioners' rules of thumb, extrapolating from similar problems already solved, and recognizing and accounting for paradoxical occurrences. An example of the latter is Festinger's (1957) deriving his dissonance theory in part from his studies of rumors revealing the paradoxical tendency for communities that had just experienced a traumatic event to predict disturbingly the immanence of further traumatic events.

A second class of provocative heuristics involves simple direct conceptual analyses. Examples are partitioning a variable into distinctive sub-variables, dividing a process into sequential sub-components, or pushing a reasonable hypothesis until its implications become implausible. For example, when one pushes the reasonable hypothesis that perceived liking increases with eye contact to the extremity where one person stares at another 100 percent of the time, it reminds the researcher that eye contact can be perceived as threatening as well as a sign of affection.

A third set of creative heuristics involves more complex mediated inference. For example, one can posit multiple mediators to account for a known relation, or can use the hypothetico-deductive method to derive novel hypotheses from banal axioms, or use an available check list to generate variables (e.g. using the Murray needs list to generate possible drug gratifications that can be countered in an anti-drug campaign, as in McGuire, 1991).

A fourth set of creative heuristics goes beyond the observational and the conceptual techniques used in the first three sets by calling for reinterpretations of previous research outcomes, such as reconciling conflicting outcomes or failures to replicate in multiple past experiments, or doing deviant-case analysis, or interpreting serendipitous interaction affects. For example, Petty and Cacioppo (1986) in analyzing why source credibility sometimes does and sometimes does not increase persuasive impact developed their notion of multiple paths to persuasion and their elaboration-likelihood model. Meta-analysis can serve as a formal tool in such reinterpretations.

A fifth set of provocative heuristics pushes one still further in the empirical direction in that they involve collection of new or reanalysis of old data. This can range from exploratory procedures such as multivariate-analysis fishing expeditions and doing content analyses of open-ended responses, to more directive explorations such as mathematical modeling and structural-equation modeling. For example, Brock (1965) pitted source similarity and source expertise against each other in exploring how the source's perceived experience on the issue can modify surprisingly his or her persuasive impact on a naive audience.

Generating new insights by transforming a given hypothesis Training social psychology students in the five sets of topic-free creative techniques just mentioned involves giving them general stances that promote their noticing anomalies and facilely formulating creative hypotheses in any topic area. Social psychologists can also be trained to master content-specific techniques that involve creatively transforming their initial, often pedestrian hypotheses. The examples of such creative transformations described below all start with the familiar hypothesis about what makes people likeable and how people's likeability affects their persuasive impact.

One such transformation is to partition the independent variable of an obvious relation into sub-variables that may relate differently to the dependent variable. The familiar hypothesis that the more similar two people are, the more they tend to like each other was made more interesting when Rokeach (1960) and Triandis (1961) distinguished between and argued about the relative importance of demographic versus ideological similarity. Alternatively, the researcher can partition the dependent variable of an obvious relation into sub-variables, as when the hypothesis that the perceived power of a source enhances attitude change is qualified by taking into account public versus private attitude change.

Another interest-enhancing transformation of an obvious hypothesis is to add striking partial definitions of the obvious independent variable. For example, the hypothesis that the persuasiveness of a source increases with his or her physical attractiveness becomes more interesting when one adds provocative concepts about what constitutes physical attractiveness. The neoteny research shows that male faces are judged more attractive and expert as they depart from the neonatal configurations, whereas women's faces are judged more attractive and trustworthy as they stay close to the neonatal configuration. This leads to the prediction that large-eyed women will be more persuasive on topics where trustworthiness is crucial while heavy-eyebrowed men will be more persuasive on topics that involve expertise (Brownlow & Zebrowitz, 1990).

Another transformation involves recognition that researchers have used some independent variable label ambiguously, and so untangling the two meanings will clarify a confusing body of findings. For example, the audience's "involvement" in the persuasive topic has been conjectured by Sherif & Hovland (1961) to reduce, and by Festinger (1957) to increase, the persuasive impact of a given message. Zimbardo (1960) clarified past findings and suggested new studies by proposing that these opposed theorists were using "involvement" in different senses. If the audience thought that the issue was important then this would increase persuadability; however, if the audience felt committed to their initial positions this would decrease persuadability.

The student can be trained to go beyond generating a single plausible explanation for a hypothesized relation by generating multiple theoretical explanations. For example, when Hovland, Lumsdaine, and Sheffield (1949) conjectured why soldiers might have shown delayed-action effects after seeing army propaganda films, they proposed not only the subsequently studied "discounting cue" sleeper effect explanation (that as time passes the suspect source of the arguments is forgotten) but also a half-dozen other possible explanations.

Another provocative transformation is to explore the parameters of a familiar hypothesis, such as that liking and persuasive impact increase with perceived similarity between source and receivers. Such similarity could enhance liking by being either a cue or a reinforcement. Whether the importance of the similarity characteristic affects the slope or the height of the similarity-liking curve depends on whether similarity is operating as a cue or a reinforcer (Byrne, 1971). Unfortunately, psychological measurement is usually too crude to allow such parameter analysis. Advances in conjoint and functional measurement (Anderson, 1982) may partially solve this situation.

A more complex transformation of the initial hypothesis is to decompose nonmonotonic relations into underlying monotonic ones. A finding that audience age is nonmonotonically related to persuadability with maximum persuadability near age 12, with younger and older children harder to persuade, can be broken down into two mediating processes: (1) ability to comprehend the arguments and (2) tendency to yield to them, both increasing persuadability but with comprehension increasing and yielding declining with age (McGuire, 1968).

Exploring the limits of an obvious relation can also transform a banal hypothesis interestingly. Heider's (1958) rather obvious P-O-X hypothesis (that two people tend to like each other insofar as both like (or dislike) the same things) can be transformed by generating cases where two people actually like each other more if they disagree on their liking for a third topic. For example, a traditional couple may be happier if the macho husband loves football and his admiring wife hates it, leaving each spouse to love the other all the more for adhering to contrasting sex roles. In this case the obvious P-O-X model is transformed into something more interesting by taking role attributions into account.

One can also add interest to a frequently confirmed relation by recognizing that its study has been restricted to a circumscribed range of conditions. For example, past studies find women tend to be more persuadable than men (McGuire, 1969; Eagly, 1978) but one notices that persuasion studies typically involve "male" issues and male experimenters. One can then check (either informally or by a meta-analysis) whether such contextual uniformities call for reinterpretation of past findings of sex differences in persuadability.

Well-known relations are often ascribed to one conventional causal path and so a useful corrective transformation is to consider other possible causal links. For example, Newcomb's (1943, 1961) Bennington study on opinion formation in college groups found that familiarity affects liking, which affects ideological similarity; however, beyond this unidirectional causal chain each of these three variables affected the other two. Again, the theory of reasoned action (Fishbein & Ajzen, 1975; Fishbein, 1980) makes the obvious prediction that attitude affects behavioral intention which in turn affects overt behavior; but new insights are evoked by hypothesizing that attitude also affects overt behavior directly, without going through behavioral intention (Bentler & Speckart, 1979).

Some more elaborate transformations make use of analytical procedures such as multiple regression analysis, factor analysis, meta-analysis, or structural equation modeling. For example, a common working assumption in social psychology is that source credibility, attractiveness, and power are the three major independent determinants of the source's persuasive impact; but it would be useful to get multiple indices of each of the three and subject them to factor analyses to determine if source characteristics do group into these three conventional variables and *if* the three are mutually orthogonal.

A particularly fertile transformation of a trite hypothesis is the perverse one of asserting its contrary and then conjecturing special conditions under which this nonobvious contrary relation obtains. For example, while it is tritely obvious to predict that source expertise, trustworthiness, likeability, similarity, power, and so on, all enhance persuasive impact, one can transform each prediction by asserting that the contrary is the case, that each reduces persuasive impact. For example, perceived expertise might reduce persuasive impact by making the source seem distant or prejudiced (Brock, 1965). Again a source's likeability may decrease his or her persuasive impact in contexts where there is insufficient justification, traumatic initiation, praise from a stranger, identification with the aggressor, or safety in deviating. This contrary transformation is in keeping with the basic tenet of perspectivist epistemology that every hypothesis and its contrary are true, each in its appropriate context.

Conclusions

The editors introduce this volume by identifying a distinctive feature of social psychology that contributes greatly to its relevance, namely, its accounting for processes that everyone experiences in daily life. This chapter has made the further point that accounting for these ordinary processes often requires extraordinary explanations. A perspectivist epistemology exposes the limitations of even trite explanations and the need for and power of nonobvious explanations. Taking William Blake's aphorism, "Everything possible to be believed is an image of truth" as a working hypothesis, this chapter has described how *a priori* conceptual confrontations and *a posteriori* empirical confrontations can be used to identify perspectives from which even the most extraordinary explanations are pertinent and provocative.

The perspectivist approach highlights how peculiar it is that social psychology methodology courses deal almost exclusively with the hypothesis-testing aspects of research to the neglect of the hypothesis-creation aspects. As a corrective, this chapter has suggested innovations in the training of social psychologists that can enhance their motivation and ability to generate novel hypotheses. Some of these innovations release the researcher's creativity on the strategic level of designing whole programs of research. Other of these innovations augment the researcher's creativity on the tactical level of producing more innovative hypotheses, either by generating them at the outset or by creatively transforming more banal initial hypotheses.

References

(Those marked * are recommended for further reading.)

Anderson, N. H. (1982). Methods of information integration theory. New York: Academic Press.

Andrews, F. M. (Ed.) (1979). *Scientific productivity: The effectiveness of research groups in six countries*. New York: Cambridge University Press.

Bentler, P. M., & Speckart, G. (1979). Models of attitude–behavior relations. *Psychological Review*, *86*, 452–464.

Brock, T. C. (1965). Communicator–recipient similarity and decision change. *Journal of Personality and Social Psychology*, *1*, 650–654.

Brownlow, S., & Zebrowitz, L. A. (1990). Facial appearance, gender, and credibility in television commercials. *Journal of Nonverbal Behavior*, *14*, 51–60.

Byrne, D. (1971). *The attraction paradigm*. New York: Academic Press.

Eagly, A. H. (1978). Sex differences in influenceability. *Psychological Bulletin*, *85*, 86–116.

Festinger, L. (1957). *A theory of cognitive dissonance*. Stanford: Stanford University Press.

Fishbein, M. (1980). A theory of reasoned action: Some applications and implications. In H. Howe & M. Page (Eds.), *Nebraska Symposium on motivation, 1979*, (Vol. 27). Lincoln, NB: University of Nebraska Press, pp. 65–116.

Fishbein, M., & Ajzen, I. (1975). *Belief, attitude, intention and behavior: An introduction to theory and research*. Boston, MA: Addison-Wesley

Goodfield, J. (1981). *An imagined world: A story of scientific discovery*. New York: Harper & Row.

Heider, F. (1958). *The psychology of interpersonal relations*. New York: Wiley.

Hovland, C. I., Lumsdaine, A. A., & Sheffield, F. D. (1949). *Studies in social psychology in World War II*. Vol. 3: *Experiments on mass communication*. Princeton, NJ: Princeton University Press.

Latour, B., & Woolgar, S. (1979). *Laboratory life: The social construction of scientific facts*. Beverly Hills, CA: Sage.

McGuire, W. J. (1968). Personality and susceptibility to social influence. In E. F. Borgatta & W. W. Lambert (Eds.), *Handbook of personality theory and research* (pp. 1130–1187). Chicago: Rand McNally.

McGuire, W. J. (1969). Attitude and attitude change. In G. Lindzey & E. Aronson (Eds.), *Handbook of social psychology* (Vol. 3, pp. 136–314). Reading, MA: Addison-Wesley.

*McGuire, W. J. (1973). The yin and yang of progress in social psychology: Seven koan. *Journal of Personality and Social Psychology*, *26*, 446–456.

*McGuire, W. J. (1983). A contextualist theory of knowledge: Its implications for innovation and reform in psychological research. In L. Berkowitz (Ed.), *Advances in experimental social psychology* (Vol. 16, pp. 1–47). New York: Academic Press.

McGuire, W. J. (1984). Perspectivism: A look back at the future. *Contemporary Social Psychology*, *10*(5 & 6), 19–39.

McGuire, W. J. (1986). A perspectivist looks at contextualism and the future of behavioral science. In R. Rosnow & M. Georgoudi (Eds.), *Contextualism and understanding in behavioral science: Implications for research and theory* (pp. 271–301). New York: Praeger.

*McGuire, W. J. (1989). A perspectivist approach to the strategic planning of programmatic scientific research. In B. Gholson, W. R. Shadish, Jr., R. A. Neimeyer & A. C. Houts (Eds.), *The psychology of science: Contributions to metascience* (pp. 214–245). New York: Cambridge University Press.

*McGuire, W. J. (1991). Using guiding-idea theories of the person to develop educational campaigns against drug abuse and other health-threatening behavior. *Health Education Research: Theory and Practice*, *6*, 173–184.

McGuire, W. J. (1994). The psychology of behavior and the behavior of psychologists. *Revista Mexicana de Análisis de la conducta* [*Mexican Journal of Behavior Analysis*], *20, Monographic issue*, 75–100.

*McGuire, W. J. (1997). Creative hypothesis generating in psychology: some useful heuristics. *Annual Review of Psychology*, 48.

Newcomb, T. M. (1943). *Personality and social change*. New York: Dryden.

Newcomb, T. M. (1961). *The acquaintance process*. New York: Holt, Rinehart, & Winston.

Petty, R., & Cacioppo, J. T. (1986). *Attitude change: Central and peripheral routes to persuasion*. New York: Springer Verlag.

Rokeach, M. (1960). *The open and closed mind* (pp. 132–168). New York: Basic Books.

Sherif, M., & Hovland, C. I. (1961). *Social judgment: Assimilation and contrast effects in communication and attitude change*. New Haven, CT: Yale University Press.

Triandis, H. C. (1961). A note on Rokeach's theory of prejudice. *Journal of Abnormal and Social Psychology*, *62*, 184–186.

Turner, J. C., Hogg, M. A., Oakes, P. J., Reicher, S. D., & Wetherell, M. S. (1987). *Rediscovering the social group: a self-categorization theory*. Oxford: Blackwell.

Whitehead, A. N., & Russell, B. (1910–1913). *Principia mathematica* (3 vols). Cambridge: Cambridge University Press.

Zimbardo, P. G. (1960). Involvement and communication discrepancy as determinants of opinion conformity. *Journal of Abnormal and Social Psychology*, *60*, 86–94.

15

Situations, Belongingness, Attitudes, and Culture: Four Lessons Learned from Social Psychology

Antony S. R. Manstead

Tony Manstead (born May 16, 1950) did his doctoral research at the University of Sussex, under the supervision of Peter B. Smith, and was awarded his doctorate in 1978. His first academic publication was in 1979. Prior to his current position as Professor of Social Psychology at the University of Amsterdam, he held academic positions at the University of Sussex and the University of Manchester. He is an Associate Editor of *Personality and Social Psychology Bulletin* and of *Cognition and Emotion* and currently the President of the European Association of Experimental Social Psychology. His publications focus on the psychology of emotion and the psychology of attitudes and attitude change.

Introduction

The editors' invitation to identify the principal lessons to be learned from social psychology initially struck me as intriguing. Later, when I began writing this piece, it struck me as frustrating. To begin with the latter reaction, since it is the fresher of the two in my mind, the notion that all (or even most of) the key lessons I have learned from studying social psychology can be captured within a 5,000 word essay is simply unrealistic. There is much more than can be accommodated within the space available. On the other hand, the editors are

I would like to thank Agneta Fischer, Stephanie van Goozen, Gün Semin, Russell Spears, and the editors for their helpful comments on an earlier draft.

surely correct in thinking that if someone has spent more than twenty years studying a discipline, it should be possible for him or her to provide a succinct summary of at least the principal lessons that have been learned in the process. What follows is necessarily highly selective: the list could easily be extended. What I have tried to do in the first half of this essay is identify what I see as the key lessons I have learned from social psychology, and to provide some rationale for my selection. I do not claim that these lessons could not also have been learned from other disciplines, but I would be surprised if they would all emerge so clearly from another single discipline in social or behavioral science. In the second half of the essay I try to illustrate three of these lessons by drawing on some of my own research.

Lessons Learned from the Study of Social Psychology

Social situations are powerful

The editors of this volume suggest, in the opening chapter, that the discipline of social psychology can be divided conceptually into three components: social perception and judgment, social influence, and social interaction. This is a perspective on social psychology that places social influence processes at the heart of the discipline, since they constitute a two-way link between individual cognition and interpersonal behavior. This view of the discipline nicely reflects the fact that many of the studies now regarded as "classic" experiments in social psychology are studies of social influence: Sherif's (1935) studies of norm formation, Asch's (1951) studies of group pressure, Milgram's (1963) studies of obedience, and Latané and Darley's (1968) studies of bystander intervention are obvious examples. This tradition represents what is in many ways the backbone of the discipline. The most obvious lesson to be drawn from this line of work is that *social situations are powerful*. In each of the studies referred to above, a substantial proportion of individuals were shown to be influenced by the behaviors – or in some cases simply the mere presence of – other people. Anyone familiar with social psychological research cannot fail to be impressed by the fact that when individuals are placed in situations in which there is some conflict between individual preferences or perceptions and the preferences or perceptions of others, the latter prevail more frequently than most laypersons would predict. Understanding *why* situations have this power to influence an individual's thoughts, perceptions, and actions is of course the most interesting issue. The classic account of why social situations are powerful is the one provided by Deutsch and Gerard (1955). They explain social influence in terms of a distinction between informational influence and normative influence. Informational influence arises from the assumption that other people are often good sources of information about the world; if several other people agree with each other it is irrational to ignore such consensus. Normative influence arises from the perception that the opinions and actions of the majority in a social group constitute a group norm; by conforming to this norm one avoids rejection and/or increases acceptance. Whatever the advantages and disadvantages of this "dual-process" explanation of social influence (cf. Turner, 1991), it is clear that what is often referred to as normative influence plays a key role in conformity and social influence.

In the explanations offered by Sherif, Asch, Milgram, and Latané and Darley, and others who have investigated social influence phenomena, one theme tends to recur, namely the difficulty people have in ignoring the opinions and behaviors of others. Sherif described the "frame of reference" provided by others' judgments when an individual is asked to judge ambiguous stimuli; Asch discussed the need to be accepted by others in a group as a motive for conforming to their judgments; Milgram described the difficulty of disengaging from a situation in which an authority figure instructs one to act against one's better judgment; and Latané and Darley discuss the fear of appearing to overreact as a reason for not responding to an apparent emergency when other bystanders are present. A common element of each explanation is that the individual is regarded as attaching great importance to the way in which he or she is or would be evaluated by others, even where these others are complete strangers.

Human beings need social bonds

Why are we so preoccupied with the way in which others evaluate us? The answer to this question constitutes a second lesson to be drawn from social psychology, namely that *human beings desire social bonds*. Although the strength of this need may vary across individuals, it applies to enough people to warrant singling out as a "lesson of social psychology." We care about how others evaluate us, not because we are egotistical or insatiably curious about any information concerning us, but because how we are evaluated by others indicates how likely it is that we would be accepted by them as acquaintances or friends. We are attuned to the opinions of others because knowing what they think (about things in general, and us in particular) helps us to accomplish one of the key goals of human existence, namely the forming and maintaining of social bonds.

The general thesis that humans have a basic "need to belong" has recently been articulated by Baumeister and Leary (1995). They propose a "belongingness hypothesis," which states that

> human beings have a pervasive drive to form and maintain at least a minimum quantity of lasting, positive, and impactful interpersonal relationships. Satisfying this drive involves two criteria: First, there is a need for frequent, affectively pleasant interactions

with a few other people, and second, these must take place in the context of a temporally stable and enduring framework of affective concern for each other's welfare. (p. 497)

In support of this hypothesis, Baumeister and Leary review a broad range of studies which demonstrate, among other things, that social bonds are formed very readily, that they are broken only with great reluctance, that the existence of or potential for social relationships shapes cognition and emotion, and that relationship deprivation has negative consequences. This pattern of evidence suggests that the need to belong is indeed fundamental and pervasive.

If the belongingness hypothesis is correct, then the need to form and maintain social bonds is likely to be a motivational force at the heart of many social-psychological phenomena, ranging from the formation of interpersonal relationships and group formation to variations in self-presentation and conformity to group norms. The hypothesis also suggests that those who for one reason or another find it difficult to form or maintain relationships will suffer as a result of the non-fulfillment of the fundamental need to belong. Indeed, there is plenty of evidence that children who are socially isolated or rejected do suffer as a result of their lack of social bonds, in the sense that they are more likely to experience mental health problems in later life (see Kupersmidt, Coie, & Dodge, 1990). Given this well-established link between childhood social rejection and later psychiatric problems, it is of considerable importance to understand why children are isolated or rejected.

Attitudes are important

If the "lessons of social psychology" were to end here, the task of those charged with changing the practices of people in order, say, to protect the environment, or improve health, should be a simple one. If changing situations brings about changes of behavior, and if individuals accommodate their behavior to the perceived wishes and expectations of others in order to fulfill a need to belong, a logical conclusion would be that bringing about behavior change must be a relatively straightforward business. Even a cursory examination of the history of research on the impact of persuasive communications, both inside and outside the laboratory, shows us that this conclusion is incorrect. Bringing about changes in attitudes and intentions, let alone changes in behavior, is generally an uphill struggle, and the closer one gets to real-life behaviors the more difficult it is to bring about the sought-for change.

How can this observation be squared with the first two "lessons?" Of course, human beings are not infinitely malleable; one of the psychological factors involved in setting limits on this malleability is the individual's need for a consistent sense of self. That need for a consistent sense of self, or identity, is served by intraindividual consistency in beliefs, attitudes, and behaviors. This consistency is seemingly at odds with the plasticity of human behavior suggested by the first two "lessons," and this need for some temporal consistency in beliefs, attitudes, and behaviors helps to account for the difficulties encountered by health educators, for example, in promoting behavior change. While there are undoubtedly many facets of an individual (e.g. physical characteristics, gender, religion, occupation, nationality) that combine to establish his or her sense of identity, from a social-psychological perspective there are good reasons for focusing on a person's *attitudes*. Attitudes have long been a central focus of theoretical and empirical interest in social psychology, with the result that we know more about them than about other possible contributors to a stable sense of identity. Attitudes help to establish what Greenwald (1980) called the "totalitarian ego." Greenwald used this term to refer to the way in which the human mind resists cognitive change: we select and interpret information in ways that make it consistent with our established attitudes, even to the extent that we may "rewrite" our memories of past thoughts and deeds to make them more coherent with current attitudes and actions.

A simple extension of this argument is that established attitudes have an impact on current and future behaviors, and there is indeed ample evidence that attitudes have an impact on perceptions and behaviors, ranging from Hastorf and Cantril's (1954) classic study of the way in which supporters of rival football teams arrived at divergent perceptions of a game involving the two teams, to research showing that attitudes measured at one point in time are substantially predictive of later behavior (for a review, see Kraus, 1995). A third lesson of social psychology, then, is that *attitudes play a key role in human social cognition and behavior*, helping individuals to achieve a sense of personal coherence and identity, shaping the way in which they perceive, interpret, and remember social information, and guiding the way in which they behave, but at the same time rendering them more resistant to social influence. If attitudes do play a key role in shaping human social behavior, it follows that identifying precisely *how* they exercise this influence would be helpful in any attempt to modify that behavior.

Culture has consequences

A further lesson of social psychology arises from the combined impact of two factors identified in previously described "lessons." The human preoccupation with social context, resulting in the need to accommodate ourselves to the mores of the social milieu in which we find ourselves, implies that *socialization* – involving extended exposure to a specific social milieu subscribing to a particular configuration of social mores – will have a strong influence on the individual. The lasting quality of this influence is attributable to the need for a sense of identity, with a semi-permanent set of beliefs, attitudes, and behaviors. This implies that the cultural context in which we develop psychologically should have a powerful impact on the way in which we construe the world around us. This, indeed, is the fourth lesson I would want to draw from social psychology: *culture has consequences* (cf. Hofstede, 1980), in the sense that those who are socialized into a particular culture adopt certain values that have a lasting effect on the way in which they construe the social environment, and thereby on their social behavior. The impact of culture on thoughts, feelings, and behaviors is a subtle yet important one. Landman (1996) expresses it in terms of the "worldview" that is provided by a particular culture. A worldview is

> a set of fundamental values, beliefs, and sentiments about reality which are often tacit and taken for granted. It works like a giant lens through which we characteristically and implicitly perceive, organize, remember, interpret, and emotionally experience the raw material of life. A worldview is difficult to put your finger on, and therefore difficult to analyze. Yet it is every bit as real and as powerful as your parents. It is not acquired through magic; undoubtedly worldviews develop and are sustained through many of the same methods entailed in other forms of socialization. A common worldview is one thing that makes a culture a culture rather than a set of unconnected individuals. Individuals in the same culture share a worldview; they can't help it – it comes with the culture. Yet worldviews are not monolithic; individuals in the same culture differ in the extent to which they have internalized every detail of a prevailing worldview. (p. 90)

As Landman points out, it is hard to put your finger on a worldview, which in turn makes it difficult to research. Later I will summarize a study in which my colleagues and I tried to demonstrate how worldviews subtly influence our conceptions of emotion.

Illustrative Research

The first of the four lessons described above is in my view so well documented in social psychological research that it requires no further illustration here. The other three may be regarded as more contentious. I now draw on some of my own research to illustrate those three lessons.

Rejection, relationships, and emotional competence

"Emotional competence" (Gordon, 1989; Saarni, 1990) and "emotional intelligence" (Salovey & Mayer, 1990) are terms used by theorists who are interested in the adaptive significance of emotion. Despite some differences of emphasis, it is apparent that there is considerable overlap in what theorists mean by the terms emotional competence or emotional intelligence. One aspect of this construct that is prominent in all three definitions concerns the communication of emotion. In our own research (Manstead & Edwards, 1992), we were concerned with communicative aspects of emotional competence in children. Our particular concern was with the relationship between a child's ability to read others' emotions from facial cues, on the one hand, and the quality of his or her relations with peers, on the other. There are grounds for predicting that those who are high in emotional competence should enjoy better relations with their peers than those who are low in emotional competence. As Salovey and Mayer (1990) put it, emotionally intelligent people "are aware of their feelings and those of others . . . Such awareness will often lead to the effective regulation of affect within themselves and others, and so contribute to well being. Thus, the emotionally intelligent person is often a pleasure to be around and leaves others feeling better" (p. 201). Drawing on these ideas, we predicted that a child who finds it difficult to understand what others feel on the basis of their facial behavior would be less popular than a child who finds it easy to infer another's emotions from his or her facial behavior.

We conducted a four-wave panel study in which we measured emotion recognition ability and peer popularity in 153 children over a two-year period. The children were approximately 5 years old at wave 1. The other waves were conducted approximately one year, eighteen months, and two years later. Emotion recognition ability was assessed by asking the child to make judgments about photographs of facial expressions. Peer popularity was assessed by asking the children to make positive and negative nominations of classmates (e.g. those whom they would [or would not] invite to a birthday party). Subtracting the negative nominations received by each child from his or her positive nominations provided an index of *social preference*. Summing the positive and negative nominations provided an index of *social impact*. Combining these two indices results in four sociometric "quadrants": *popular*, i.e. children above the median in social preference and social impact; *amiable*, i.e. children above the median in preference but below the median in impact; *neglected*, i.e. children below the median in preference and in impact; and *rejected*, i.e., children below the median in preference but above the median in impact.

When we compared the number of correct recognitions of facial expressions made by children in the different sociometric groups, we found substantial differences. Children in the popular and amiable sociometric groups scored significantly higher on the facial expression measure than did children in the rejected group. There was a less consistent tendency for the popular and amiable children to score significantly higher than children in the neglected group. We then examined the issue of how peer popularity and facial expression recognition are causally related by conducting a series of multiple regression analyses in which we exploited the longitudinal nature of the research design. The pattern of results we found argues against the idea that causality flows *unidirectionally* between emotion recognition and preference. How able a child was to recognize emotions from facial expressions at age 5 helped to predict how popular he or she would be with peers two years later, even when differences in popularity at age 5 were partialed out. This suggests that emotion recognition does play a role in determining peer popularity. However, how popular a child was with his or her peers at age 5 helped to account for how well he or she performed on an emotion recognition task two years later, even when differences in emotion recognition at age 5 were partialed out. This suggests that popularity plays a role in shaping emotion recognition ability. Clearly, the only causal model with which these data are consistent is one in which there is reciprocal influence between the two variables.

As argued earlier, one lesson from social psychology is that humans have a basic need to belong, and that if this need remains unsatisfied negative consequences will ensue. There is ample evidence that isolated or rejected children are more likely to experience mental health problems in later life. It is therefore important to understand the antecedents of social isolation or rejection. What our research suggests is that *one* cause of early isolation or unpopularity in children is a deficit in ability to recognize emotion from facial expression cues. The research also suggests that there is a reciprocal causal relationship between popularity and emotion recognition; thus children can begin by being isolated or unpopular because of their relative inability to recognize facial expression information, but the resulting lack of close relationships with peers then denies these children the opportunity to learn about the meanings of facial expressions, thereby exacerbating their isolation or rejection.

Changing attitudes changes behavior

As proposed above, another lesson to be learned from studying social psychology is that attitudes are important. They influence how we perceive, interpret, evaluate, remember, and act. Especially important in the history of attitude theory and research has been the relationship between attitudes and behavior. Although this relationship was widely regarded as a "troubled" one in the 1960s and 1970s, the efforts of a number of theorists, notably Fishbein and Ajzen (1975; Ajzen & Fishbein, 1977, 1980) led to a general re-evaluation of the relationship. It is now generally accepted that – assuming that certain conditions are satisfied – attitudes do exercise a causal impact on behavior (cf. Kraus, 1995). However, convincing evidence of this causal role requires experimental research in which attitudes are changed in an experimental group, left unmanipulated in a control group, and the behavioral consequences are measured. If it could be shown that participants in the experimental group change their intentions and/or behavior in a direction consistent with the manipulated attitude change, whereas the intentions and behaviors of control group participants remain stable, this would support the proposition that attitudes do indeed determine behavior.

Just such a study was conducted by Beale and Manstead (1991). We examined the ability of Ajzen's (1988) theory of planned behavior (TPB) to account for mothers' intentions to manage their infants' sugar consumption. Before describing the research, it may be helpful to summarize the essential features of the TPB. The immediate determinant of behavior in this model is *behavioral intention*, in other words how the individual intends to act. Intention, in turn, is determined by the individual's *attitude to the behavior* in question, by his or her *subjective norm*, and by his or her *perceived control over the behavior* concerned. Attitude to behavior refers to the extent to which the person sees performing the behavior as a good or a bad thing to do. Subjective norm reflects the degree of perceived social pressure on the individual to perform or not to perform the behavior. Perceived behavioral control represents the individual's perception of how easy or difficult it is to perform the behavior in question. A basic assumption of the TPB is that individuals form intentions to engage in a behavior to the extent that they have positive attitudes to the behavior, see important others as expecting them to engage in the behavior, and believe that the behavior is one that is possible for them to perform.

Returning to the Beale and Manstead (1991) study, the focus of this research was on restricting the frequency of infants' sugar consumption. This is a behavior that was advocated in a program of dental health education designed to encourage the mothers of six-month-old children to care for their children's teeth. At this age most babies have just grown their first tooth, or will shortly do so; the program was intended to capitalize on the interest in teeth that this event generates in parents. The link between sugar intake and dental decay is well established, but it is the reduction in *frequency* of sugar intake rather than in total amount of sugar consumption that is important in the control of dental decay. Thus the dental health education program used in the present research advocated that mothers should restrict their babies' sugar intake to mealtimes only.

The study provided an opportunity to measure the components of the TPB in one group before and after an experimental manipulation – the dental health education program – and in a second, control group, allowing comparisons to be made between the two groups and before and after the manipulation. This should enable any change in mothers' intentions attributable to the intervention to be traced back through the predictors of intentions as specified by the TPB and ultimately to the content of the educational program. This would provide support for the theory of planned behavior and also have clear implications for the planning and evaluation of health education programs. Because the program emphasized only the benefits of performing the advocated behavior, it was expected that change in the experimental group would be reflected in attitude to behavior and its antecedents, leaving subjective norm and perceived behavioral control unchanged.

As expected, intentions to perform the advocated behavior became stronger and attitudes to the behavior became more positive between the two interviews in the experimental group but did not do so in the control group. Further comparisons of the two groups at the level of behavioral beliefs and outcome evaluations (regarded in the TPB as the precursors of attitudes to behavior), and normative beliefs and motivations to comply (the theoretical precursors of subjective norm) revealed only one significant difference. This was with respect to the behavioral belief that reducing an infant's sugar intake would mean that he or she would get less tooth decay. Mothers in the experimental group regarded this as more likely than did mothers in the control group. Since this was the only one of the five behavioral beliefs we measured that was directly addressed by the intervention, this difference combines with the remaining data in providing consistent support for the proposition that attitudes act as determinants of future behavioral intentions. Given the substantial body of evidence that intentions are in turn predictive of actual behavior (see Ajzen, 1988), it is reasonable to conclude that attitudes determine behavior.

Returning to the corresponding lesson of social psychology, we can see that the present research provides experimental support for a proposition that typically rests on correlational evidence. How people behave depends on their attitudes to that behavior; if through an intervention you can change these attitudes, corresponding behavioral change should follow.

Worldviews influence emotion prototypes

The extent to which emotions are universal across cultures has been the subject of much speculation, controversy, and research. On the one hand there are theorists who regard emotions as shaped to an important degree by biological factors and evolutionary processes (e.g. Ekman, 1992). According to this view, "basic" emotions should be characterized by a large degree of cross-cultural consistency in the way they are experienced subjectively, in the patterns of physiological activity associated with them, and (in the absence of "display rules"; Ekman & Friesen, 1969) in the way in which they are expressed facially. On the other hand there are theorists who regard emotions as shaped to an important degree by social and cultural processes (e.g. Lutz & Abu-Lughod, 1990). According to this view, there is considerable scope for cultural variation in the experience and expression of emotions. Not only might a given emotion play a more central role in some cultures than in others; there might even be emotions that exist in some cultures but not in others.

In our own research on this issue (Fischer, Manstead, & Rodriguez Mosquera, 1995), we assumed that if a culture is to influence the way in which people experience and express emotions, this influence is most likely to be observed in the way in which emotions are conceptualized within the culture. More specifically, we assumed (1) that differences at the level of conceptualization will have an impact at the level of emotional experience and expression; and (2) that the way in which individuals experience and express emotions come to be reflected in the way in which the emotions concerned are conceptualized, such that differences at the level of experience and expression are apparent at the level of conceptualization.

The two countries we studied were Spain and the Netherlands. There is evidence that these countries represent distinct cultures, and that they differ in the importance they attach to specific values. One such difference is the more central role played by "honor" in Spanish culture. Whereas honor in itself probably does not constitute what Landman (in press) calls a worldview, we would argue that it is a central element in a network of values that could in combination be regarded as constituting a worldview. In "honor" cultures self-respect is not independent of the respect one receives from others: honor refers to a person's respect and esteem, which is dependent on his or her value in the eyes of others. The more central role of honor in Spanish culture suggests that differences between Spanish and Dutch cultural prototypes of emotion should be especially apparent for those emotions that are experienced when honor is gained or lost, such as pride, shame, and anger. Specifically, we anticipated that, as compared with Dutch respondents, Spanish respondents would provide a greater range of examples of the prototypical components of these emotions; would be more likely to mention prototypical components referring either to honor being at stake or to the interpersonal consequences of the emotions; and would mention more social consequences with respect to these emotions, because honor is a culturally significant concern.

Our findings were generally consistent with these predictions, especially with respect to pride and shame. These emotions were more salient and more disruptive for Spanish respondents, in that they were expected to have more far-reaching consequences for oneself and for one's relations with others. This pattern of differences is consistent with the notion that honor plays a more important role in Spanish culture. The enhancement of one's honor was a more typical antecedent of pride and the loss of one's honor was a more typical antecedent of shame in Spanish culture; as a consequence, thinking about the enhancement or loss of honor was a more typical ingredient of pride and shame, respectively.

Our conclusion is that culture-specific values such as honor can serve three different functions with respect to emotions. First, they may act as "concerns" (cf. Frijda, 1986), in the sense that they elicit particular emotions when they are advanced or threatened. This was demonstrated in the present study: Spanish respondents were more likely to mention antecedents of pride and shame in which their honor was enhanced, lost, or threatened. Second, they may constitute part of the emotional experience itself, in the sense that the contents of these values are reflected in the thoughts, wishes, or tendencies that characterize the emotion. There was also evidence to support this in the present study, for example in the Spanish descriptions of the thoughts they typically have during pride or shame experiences (e.g. "they will disrespect me"). Third, values may influence the consequences of emotion for oneself in relation to others. In the present study this appeared to be the case for pride and shame: Spanish respondents were especially aware of the negative social consequences of these emotions.

These findings are consistent with the proposition that "worldviews" influence cultural prototypes of some emotions. Although we have not established that such worldviews influence the experience and expression of these emotions, it seems reasonable to assume that differences at the level of conceptualization would be accompanied by differences at the level of experience and expression.

Conclusion

I have argued that studying social psychology teaches us four "lessons" (among many others): that social situations can and often do have a powerful impact on behavior; that humans have a fundamental need to belong; that attitudes help to shape perceptions, judgments, and actions; and that cultural variations have significant consequences for social cognition, emotion, and behavior. These are the most important – but by no means the only – lessons I have learned from studying social psychology. While they no doubt reflect my personal preferences and experiences (i.e. my worldview), I hope that they have value beyond providing an insight into one person's perspective on the discipline. If there is a "meta-message" to be derived from these four lessons, and from the research examples I have summarized, it concerns the theoretical and practical utility of the research methods that are typically used by social psychologists. By applying empirical methods in general, and experimental or quasi-experimental methods in particular, social psychologists have been able to provide insights into issues and problems that are of practical significance beyond the immediate concerns of their own discipline. A keenness to study real-world problems empirically, preferably experimentally, and guided by a theory, was of course a hallmark of the work of Kurt Lewin, who can legitimately be regarded as the father of modern social psychology. As the editors of the *Journal of Social Issues* put it in an issue devoted to the heritage of Kurt Lewin, "There is still nothing so practical as a good theory – one with sophisticated concepts and replicable operational definitions of well-defined interventions, whose effects are systematically assessed; one that attempts to conceptualize all the important and relevant variables active in the situation, not just one or two" (Bargal, Gold, & Lewin, 1992, p. 5). If we take "interventions" to include "experimental manipulations," this statement strikes me as an excellent prescription for social psychological research in general. Following such a prescription should help us to contribute to the understanding of social issues and the solution of social problems.

Further Reading

Ajzen, I. (1988). *Attitudes, personality, and behavior*. Milton Keynes: Open University Press and Chicago, IL: Dorsey. An excellent introduction to the methodological and theoretical issues involved in studying the attitude–behavior relationship.

Baumeister, R. F., & Leary, M. R. (1995). The need to belong: Desire for interpersonal attachments as a fundamental human motivation. *Psychological Bulletin*, *117*, 497–529. An interesting review of psychological research relevant to the authors' thesis that the "need to belong" is a key motivation.

Harris, P. L. (1989). *Children and emotion: The development of psychological understanding*. Oxford: Blackwell Publishers. A compelling account of the way in which children's understanding of emotion develops, and how this influences and is influenced by their experience.

Markus, H., & Kitayama, S. (1991). Culture and self: Implications for cognition, emotion, and motivation. *Psychological Review*, *98*, 224–253. An influential analysis of how culture influences psychological processes, stressing the role played by different conceptions of self.

Turner, J. C. (1991). *Social influence*. Milton Keynes: Open University Press and Pacific Grove, CA: Brooks/Cole. A sophisticated introduction to the topic, including a critique of the classic "dual-process" explanation.

References

Ajzen, I. (1988). *Attitudes, personality, and behavior*. Milton Keynes: Open University Press and Chicago, IL: Dorsey.

Ajzen, I., & Fishbein, M. (1977). Attitude–behavior relations: A theoretical analysis and review of empirical research. *Psychological Bulletin*, *84*, 888–918.

Ajzen, I., & Fishbein, M. (1980). *Understanding attitudes and predicting social behavior*. Englewood Cliffs, NJ: Prentice-Hall.

Asch, S. E. (1951). Effects of group pressure upon the modification and distortion of judgments. In H. Guetzkow (Ed.), *Groups, leadership, and men* (pp. 177–190). Pittsburgh, PA: Carnegie Press.

Bargal, D., Gold, M., & Lewin, M. (1992). Introduction: The heritage of Kurt Lewin. *Journal of Social Issues*, *48*, 3–13.

Baumeister, R. F., & Leary, M. R. (1995). The need to belong: Desire for interpersonal attachments as a fundamental human motivation. *Psychological Bulletin*, *117*, 497–529.

Beale, D. A., & Manstead, A. S. R. (1991). Predicting mothers' intentions to limit frequency of infants' sugar intake: Testing the theory of planned behavior. *Journal of Applied Social Psychology*, *21*, 409–431.

Deutsch, M., & Gerard, H. B. (1955). A study of normative and informational social influences upon individual judgment. *Journal of Abnormal and Social Psychology*, *51*, 629–636.

Ekman, P. (1992). An argument for basic emotions. *Cognition and Emotion*, *6*, 169-201.

Ekman, P., & Friesen, W. V. (1969). The repertoire of nonverbal behavior: Categories, origins, usage, and coding. *Semiotica*, *1*, 49–98.

Fischer, A. H., Manstead, A. S. R., & Rodriguez Mosquera, P. (1995). Cultural differences in prototypes of anger, pride and shame: A comparison between Spain and the Netherlands. Unpublished manuscript, University of Amsterdam.

Fishbein, M. and Ajzen, I. (1975). *Belief attitude, intention and behavior: An introduction to theory and research*. Reading, MA: Addison-Wesley.

Frijda, N. H. (1986). *The emotions*. Cambridge: Cambridge University Press.

Gordon, S. L. (1989). The socialization of children's emotions: Emotional culture, competence, and exposure. In C. Saarni & P. L. Harris (Eds.), *Children's understanding of emotion* (pp. 319–349). New York: Cambridge University Press.

Greenwald, A. G. (1980). The totalitarian ego: Fabrication and revision of personal history. *American Psychologist*, *35*, 603–618.

Hastorf, A. H., & Cantril, H. (1954). They saw a game: A case study. *Journal of Abnormal and Social Psychology*, *49*, 129–134.

Hofstede, G. (1980). *Culture's consequences*. Beverly Hills, CA: Sage.

Kraus, S. J. (1995). Attitudes and the prediction of behavior: A meta-analysis of the empirical literature. *Personality and Social Psychology Bulletin*, *21*, 58–75.

Kupersmidt, J. B., Coie, J. D., & Dodge, K. A. (1990). The role of poor peer relationships in the development of disorder. In S. R. Asher & J. D. Coie (Eds.), *Peer rejection in childhood* (pp. 274–305). New York: Cambridge University Press.

Landman, J. (1996). Social control of "negative" emotions. In W. G. Parrott & R. Harré (Eds.), *Emotions: The embodiment of social control* (pp. 89–116). London: Sage.

Latané, B., & Darley, J. M. (1968). Group inhibition of bystander intervention in emergencies. *Journal of Personality and Social Psychology*, *10*, 215–221.

Lutz, C., & Abu-Lughod, L. (1990). *Language and the politics of emotion*. New York: Cambridge University Press.

Manstead, A. S. R., & Edwards, R. (1992). Communicative aspects of children's emotional competence. In K. T. Strongman (Ed.), *International Review of Studies on Emotion* (Vol. 2, pp. 167–195). Chichester: Wiley.

Milgram, S. (1963). Behavioral study of obedience. *Journal of Abnormal and Social Psychology*, *67*, 371–378.

Saarni, C. (1990). Emotional competence: How emotions and relationships become integrated. In R. A. Thompson (Ed.), *Socioemotional development: Nebraska Symposium on motivation, 1988* (pp. 115–182). Lincoln, NE: University of Nebraska Press.

Salovey, P., & Mayer, J. D. (1990). Emotional intelligence. *Imagination, Cognition and Personality*, *9*, 185–211.

Sherif, M. (1935). A study of some social factors in perception. *Archives of Psychology*, *27*, 1–60.

Turner, J. C. (1991). *Social influence*. Milton Keynes: Open University Press and Pacific Grove, CA: Brooks/Cole.

16

Nonmaterial beliefs: Theory and Research in Cultural Social Psychology

Albert Pepitone

Albert Pepitone was born in Brooklyn, New York City where he attended public schools and Seth Low Jr. High School. He graduated from New York University with a B.A. in music (orchestration and composition) and psychology, and went on to Yale to receive an M.A. in experimental psychology. During World War II, he worked in the US Air Force psychological research units on the selection of pilots, navigators, and bombardiers. Following the war, while working in a human relations research group with Stuart Cook on techniques to reduce prejudice, he was invited by Kurt Lewin to join the graduate program of the Research Center for Group Dynamics at MIT. After Lewin's death he moved with the Center to the University of Michigan where he completed this doctorate under the direction of Leon Festinger. He accepted an assistant professorship at the University of Pennsylvania, where, except for Fulbright Fellowships and visiting professorships at Groningen, Rome, and Bologna, he has remained as undergraduate and graduate teacher until his retirement in 1993. His publications over four decades cover a range of social psychological issues from social perception, to group dynamics, history and theory. In recent years, his research has dealt with cultural belief systems.

Prologue

If there is one shortcoming of social psychology that has stuck for at least a quarter century, and still applies even through fundamental paradigm shifts, it is that the field has neglected macro-social structure and culture in its theories and research (Pepitone, 1976). The failure to conceive individuals as imbedded in socioeconomic environments, as role players in organizational structures, as positioned in multiple communication channels and networks, and as members of cultural groups, has discouraged theoretical accounts and representations of human social behavior that accurately map what is observed in the real world as people know it. To the discerning lay person and the novelist nothing is more real and powerful in affecting the way people think, act, and feel than their socio-economic status, occupational role, commitment to style, their generational age, and their ethno-religious identity.

Yet any unbiased overview of the history of social psychology must conclude that the field has been steered by meta-theoretical perspectives that focus theory and research on the individual and to a lesser extent on the small group. Clearly, the mainstream theories and models that dominate the enterprise have been, in essence, statements about intrapsychic processes and structures (Pepitone, 1986). Thus, in the now defunct behavioristic paradigm which guided conceptualization and research on social learning, frustration-aggression, nonverbal behavior, and attitude change, theories were based on reinforcement mechanisms that govern the formation and change of S–R associations. In the now regnant cognitive paradigm, theories refer to the processing, storage, and retrieval of information. Both paradigms center on what theoretically goes on in the head of the individual under a given stimulus or informational input.

Further about culture, the major subject of this essay, its neglect by social psychology reflects – with no small irony – the convergent influence of cultural norms. In the United States, where social psychology has flourished more than anywhere else, the individuocentrism is wholly consistent with the economic values of entrepreneurial capitalism, the achievements of the self-made "captains" of industry, the imagery of rugged cowboys taming the wild West, as well as the celebrated values of political freedom and legal justice. This ethos, instantly recognized by visitors from abroad, nourishes the conception of the independent individual as the proper and productive unit of analysis in psychology.

But it is the "science culture," and particularly the values that prescribe theory-building and empirical research, that have fostered individualism. Thus, it is a foundational principle in scientific psychology – as in all empirical sciences – that theories should not only be empirically validated but be *generally* valid (Pepitone & Triandis, 1987). A good theory should be valid across the domains represented by the dependent and independent variables. If, for example, the theory is $K = F(M)$, the function should be the same for all empirical instances of K and M. Adherence to this principle has encouraged *process* theories and an indifference if not an aversion to distinctions based on content. Unless explicitly delimited, process theories convey the impression of exhaustive generality.

A more direct promoter of individuocentrism is the principle that a theory be general across socio-cultural samples, that it apply to all individuals everywhere. "Theories seek universals," is the operative slogan. When comparisons across cultural groups reveal differences, the universality of the theory may be compromised. Thus, strategically, there is a disincentive to theorize about cultural dynamics and to carry out comparative research.

There are, of course, some aspects of cognition, emotion, and action that exclusively reflect individual, self-contained intrapsychic processes. But the full comprehension of the social human being in the real world will require analysis, observation, and theoretical integration of the effects of the "prime movers": social structure, culture, and biology. According to this view, the ultimate theories of social psychology will consist of conceptual statements that generally represent these influences converging at a given time and in given situations, to produce individual and group behavior. Rather than regard culture, social structure, and the individual as different "levels of analysis," assigning the structural to sociology, the cultural to anthropology, and to psychology the individual, cultural social psychology aims to comprehend and conceptually synthesize data from all levels, *as the observed phenomena require*. In this vision, new areas of research and theoretical insights will emerge from examining all interactions among the prime-mover variables. Thus, the cultural social psychologist will be stimulated to address the effects of both individual needs and group dynamics on the evolution of cultural norms, the cultural determinants of social structures, how social structures constrain cultural norms, and so on.

With respect to culture, unlike the inventory descriptions of whole societies, social psychologists are likely to investigate specific cultural systems that are known to affect lives in significant ways. Our entry point into culture focuses on systems of normative beliefs evolved in and maintained by societies and other groups, that have been internalized by individuals who are identified with the cultural group or exemplar.

Nonmaterial Beliefs

The profound influence of culture on individual cognition and collective behavior is nowhere more evident than when we observe the effects of beliefs, especially the large class that includes spiritual agents and their powers, impersonal transcendental laws, paranormal abilities, metaphysical concepts, mystical energies, magic, or generically, *nonmaterial beliefs*. Such beliefs refer to agents, powers, processes, things, laws, places, events, etc. that do not exist in any objective, physical sense and cannot be confirmed empirically by known scientific methods.

Ethnographic observations of historically and geographically separated samples, indicate that spiritual (e.g. deities), mystical (e.g. astrological), and magical (e.g. witchcraft) beliefs, are found *in some form* in all societies in the world sample (Murdock, 1945, 1980). There is also physical evidence that nonmaterial beliefs were held and expressed by human groups early in the evolution of culture. The wall paintings in the remote recesses of the Lascaux caves testify to beliefs in sympathetic magic among our Cro-Magnon ancestors at least 15,000 years ago. Further, widely separated ancient peoples buried their dead along with objects that would be useful, or symbolize their status, in an afterlife. And, in the first urban societies of 5,000 years ago, we find elaborated systems of beliefs that include cosmologies, Gods, witchcraft, and justice.

One has to ask – how is it that since neolithic times nonmaterial beliefs were maintained and evolved into vibrant systems in societies throughout the world? The "success" of religion compellingly suggests that nonmaterial beliefs perform psychologically adaptive functions for individuals and groups in dealing with life conditions and events. Three categories of functions may be proposed. (1) Such beliefs satisfy basic needs, wishes, and emotions. Thus, belief in Gods and their powers allows one to hope for miracles when facing life threats and losses; life after death relieves anxiety over the prospect of one's own death and the death of loved ones. The belief in luck helps one handle risks, losses and gains. (2) Such beliefs and their ritualized communal expressions serve to increase the cohesion of groups at deep levels. Thus, belief in God or totem binds the believers in a mystical unity and common identity – "We are all God's children." (3) Such beliefs enhance the individual's comprehension of inexplicable and problematic life experiences by providing explanations, evaluative frameworks, and attributions of causality.

Although, when stated explicitly, the functionality of nonmaterial beliefs is almost self-evident, it is necessary to specify *a priori* and confirm empirically the life events and conditions in which one or more of the functions of nonmaterial beliefs is being served. In addition, we want to know how general are such hypotheses relating to belief-functions, and especially if they are valid cross-culturally. In this essay, we examine some theoretical issues and programmatic research that move the inquiry toward these objectives. But first, we must raise a fundamental question about a theory built on functions.

How can nonmaterial beliefs be *adaptive* when they are contradicted by objective, material reality, and worse, when holding them *per se* invites aggression and death? Thus, there are occasions when God is not on the side of a warring party though believed to be so, when holding certain despised religious beliefs is a target for annihilation, and when reliance on Lady Luck costs the gambler a bundle of real money.

There is no single or simple answer to the question but a number of theoretical reasons for the tenacity of nonmaterial beliefs in human groups may be considered.

First, the persistence of such beliefs is inherent in their ontological status. Although powers, laws, spirits, and the like, are not real by physical standards, they are experientially and psychologically no less real for the believers. While conceding that the referents of their beliefs may not be material, believers would insist that materiality is not the sole criterion of reality. Thus, as part of a separate and autonomous order of reality, nonmaterial beliefs are protected from disconfirmation by real objective events, difficult to falsify and delete from the cognitive structure. Secondly, nonmaterial or psychological realities can be actively defended by denial of physical reality through the intervention of counter-beliefs. Illness, for example, even when caused by a diagnosed organic disease, can be considered by believers to be a spiritual malaise, and physical death can be denied by beliefs in resurrection and reincarnation. Thirdly, when denial does not work and objectively real events call psychological reality into question, we would expect disturbing dissonance to be generated by the contradiction between two systems of reality. Strong motivation would then be directed toward restructuring the systems to preserve the threatened nonmaterial beliefs. In this restructuring process, the latter are likely to be more labile and supple than material beliefs because they are not constrained by any empirical validation pressure (Pepitone, 1964). Thus, when God fails to perform a miracle cure, the believer can make various adjustments or reweightings without changing the belief in Him and His powers: "We will all meet in Heaven; remember, life on Earth is a transitory phase on the way toward salvation and acceptance into the Kingdom of God," "We are being punished for our Sins," "God moves in mysterious ways," "It is the work of the Devil," and, of course, "God is testing our faith." Finally, as noted earlier, beliefs are not single and isolated structures but part of systems that are organized. Thus, change in any one nonmaterial belief may be resisted because of the potential effect on other beliefs with which it is interdependent.

The present essay will focus on three common systems of nonmaterial beliefs and their interrelationships. Arguably, *Fate*, *justice*, and *God* are among the most common and influential beliefs in all world cultures. The discussion centers on the distinctive properties of these beliefs, hypotheses about their functions in life events, and experimental tests of such hypotheses, including cross-cultural comparisons.

The Force of Fate

Not only grandmother from the "old country" or the backwoods believes that significant events are "meant to be." Even in modern societies, one often encounters the belief that deaths, accidents, illnesses, births, natural cataclysms, the course of romantic relationships, discoveries and encounters, are the workings of a mysterious force, generated and directed by an impersonal transcendental power or law, such as that which governs the movement of the stars. As we elaborate below, the belief in fate tends to be invoked when life events are associated with a person's past experience, giving the impression that they are predestined, and when the life event outcome is completely under the control of a mysterious external agency, giving the impression that it is inevitable. In some fatalistic systems, the ultimate destiny of the individual is specified, though the time, place, and circumstances are not certain. More generally, individuals believe in the power of fate but do not know what fate has in store; indeed, from the earliest times, "satellite" belief systems have evolved – horoscopes, palmistry, cards, numerology, etc. – to function as diviners of destiny.

Fated outcomes are not contingent on the prior conduct of the individuals affected, which distinguishes fate from the beliefs in justice and God. In this sense, fate is "blind," and in being uncontrollable and more or less unpredictable, shares some characteristics with the belief in luck and chance. It should be noted, however, that neither of the latter influences are believed to be pre-ordained and inevitable.

The belief in fate may serve one or more of the functions proposed earlier: To enhance comprehension, at a primitive level, fate provides order and simplicity to life. At a higher cognitive level, fate identifies a causal agency and provides explanations of life events. Functioning to satisfy needs and emotions, the belief that life and death are pre-ordained provides relief from chronic anxiety associated with seeing oneself as responsible for unhappy and harmful life events.

The Selective Functioning of Fate

With respect to the cognitive function, it is intuitively plausible that when people are unable to understand the conditions and events of life on the basis of their beliefs about material things and processes, nonmaterial beliefs are brought into play for this purpose. However, the state of ignorance that "triggers" this intervention is not easy to define in general terms. For one thing, people don't usually know what they don't know. Further, not all individuals are automatically motivated to understand, even if they know that understanding would be good for them. Moreover, the degree and kind of comprehension considered to be adequate depend on culture – for example, on the value of science and proof. In what are loosely called Western societies, empirically tested physical definitions of reality have a higher value in the process of understanding life events than metaphysical, spiritual, or mystical conceptions. But even granting such individual and cultural variability, given (experimentally created) life events in which there is a paucity of cues for understanding in terms of material processes, relatively frequent use of nonmaterial beliefs would be expected. Simply stated, the hypothesis is that nonmaterial beliefs tend to fill the "vacuum" created by the inability to deploy material beliefs.

A more subtle hypothesis about the cognitive function of nonmaterial beliefs is that they are selective of the life events which they are employed to understand. Over a long period, my students and I have collected samples from newspapers, magazines, and personal anecdotes, of what people say in response to various life events they or others have experienced. What stands out consistently in this assorted material is not only that nonmaterial beliefs are used to explain, attribute causation to, and grasp the meaning of the life events, but that there is a selective correspondence between the beliefs used in this way and the features of the life events. The general thesis strongly suggested by the informal survey data, and later backed up by pilot studies, is that nonmaterial beliefs are more or less "specialized" in their cognitive function. Saffiotti (1990) tested the two hypotheses by constructing life event cases with features that played to the special, distinctive properties of six nonmaterial beliefs: fate, God, luck, just reward, just punishment, and chance. Subjects (a large sample of young male and female students from middle and lower middle class backgrounds, attending an urban university) were asked to write brief comments on twelve life event cases (two designed to be selected by each of the six nonmaterial beliefs).

The results, based on a reliable content analysis, supported the general hypothesis about the use of nonmaterial beliefs and the specific belief-selectivity hypothesis. Almost two-thirds of the subjects (65.9 percent) explicitly referred to one of the six nonmaterial beliefs in their spontaneous comments about the cases. And, among those subjects who did so, there was a clear relationship between the pair of life events and the particular nonmaterial beliefs predicted to be employed. Statistical analysis of the selectivity shown by subjects commenting on the life event cases (i.e. of the frequency with which the nonmaterial beliefs were used to explain the predicted life events) yielded a significant correlation (Saffiotti, 1990).

Of interest here, the two life events that were designed for the belief in fate included one or both of two main features – a *predestined* (pre-ordained) and/or an *inevitable* outcome. Operationally, a predestined outcome had a meaning that was directly associated with a singular, important event in the person's past. Outcomes were made to appear inevitable by placing them – the act that decided the outcome or earlier actions that decisively put the actor in position for the outcome – completely under someone else's control. To illustrate, the life event case that contained both features was that of the "long lost brother."

> A man on vacation in a place he did not prefer, a place decided by his wife, went into a shop to purchase an item that had been requested by his neighbor. There, he met his brother, a salesman, with whom he had lost contact since the end of World War II when they were involuntarily separated.

The analysis of the subjects' comments indicated a marked preference for the category of fate, which contained by far the modal frequency of subjects (41 percent), more than chance (24 percent), luck (17 percent), God (15 percent) just reward (2 percent), and just punishment (0 percent). The selectivity prediction was most impressively upheld, however, in response to the above life event containing both features. In the second life event case where only external control over outcome was manipulated to convey inevitability, without the preordination manipulation, the belief in fate was the second most frequent reference, second to the belief in luck. It would appear that for fate to be primarily selected, by North American samples, the connection between the outcome and an important past experience is a necessary feature of the life event.

An estimate of cultural generality of the cognitive function of the belief in fate may be provided by the results of the same experiment with a comparable sample from Northern India. For these subjects, the selectivity of the belief in fate (as well as of the five other nonmaterial beliefs) is seen unambiguously in *both* life event cases (Parsuram & Sharma, 1994). Confirmation of hypotheses by cultural samples that are so palpably different strengthens the claim of universality. We are not advancing that claim, however, simply because the prevalence and strength of the six nonmaterial beliefs may not be the same in cultures which, in overall description, are more similar to that of the North American region. Societies which are closer culturally may not show such belief selectivity. In other words, if it describes one cultural system, universality does not necessarily describe all the systems that make up a culture. As to the finding that the belief in fate was for the Indian sample selective in response to both life event cases, we do not see this as a challenge to the hypothesis that a principal eliciter of fate for the cognitive function is the feature of predestination, nor that, operationally, an association of outcome with an important past experience conveys the impression of predestination. What seems to be a simpler interpretation is that predestined life events are so commonly assumed in Indian culture, and mediated by so many diverse cues, that past association need not be explicit to elicit the belief for its cognitive function. To put the matter differently, North American culture is less fatalistic than Indian culture and hence requires tl e features of life events that invite the belief in fate to be more salient.

Really Fatal Fatalism

It is somewhat paradoxical that even if the nonmaterial beliefs in fate has no basis in objective physical reality, it can have real physical effects on individuals and groups. Consider the "placebo effect." Here, those in the control group who believe in the efficacy of the treatment for their illness show the same improvement as those in the experimental groups. The same kind of psychosomatic influence is observed in the context of post-hypnotic suggestion, and presumably plays a decisive role in psychotherapy. Of course, religious faith, and particularly faith in God, is widely claimed to effect dramatic and decisive cures that are called miracles. It is more paradoxical that the nonmaterial belief in fate, used for adaptive purposes like enhanced understanding, can also have physically harmful effects. Those who refuse to see doctors or to follow medical treatment programs, or to stop injurious lifestyles, because they believe that life and death are governed by preordained and inexorable laws, and that they will die when and only when "their number is up," are indeed likely to have shorter lives than nonbelievers.

Fatalistic beliefs are highly prevalent in China. According to one system, the power of fate originates in the transit of the stars through five phases. The individual's fate is determined by the birth year which is aligned with one of the five phases. The original feature of the Chinese system is that the preordained influence is on a particular organic destiny; each birth year is vulnerable to a specific organic disease – heart, lung, kidney, etc. Thus, a believer "knows" that death will be due to a given disease or organ failure.

Philips, Todd, and Wagner (1993) examined the death records of more than 28,000 Chinese-Americans who had died in California hospitals in the thirty-year period 1960–90. Focusing their study on the fifteen leading causes of death (mostly circulatory diseases and cancers), they divided the sample into those who died from a disease that was fated by their birth year and those who died from the same disease *not* predicted by their birth year. In thirteen of the fifteen diseases, the age at death was lower in the former sample, and the mean age of death over the fifteen comparisons was significantly lower for this sample (see the original article for statistical arguments).

Among several control checks carried out, one analysis showed that the difference between fated and nonfated death age was even greater in the subsample of Chinese born in China (and thus presumably more deeply committed to the fatalistic belief system) than in American-born Chinese. Of critical importance in interpreting these astonishing effects of the belief in fate, the investigators could find no differences in behavior or health habits that could be inferred from the death certificates. Unless there are, in fact, differences in health behavior common to those who know their fate, such as delayed medical treatment, we are left with the psychosomatic hypothesis that the belief *per se* works to undermine the vulnerable organ.

Fate and Responsibility

Not all systems of fate beliefs are astrological. In India, for example, fate is linked to the belief in karma which is part of a metaphysical worldview shared by Hindus, Buddhists, Jainists, Sikhs, and other religious communities comprising the vast majority of the population. Metaphysically, karma is a universal law that human actions have consequences. It is a belief in fate in that the conditions and events of life – miseries, joys, wealth, poverty, and caste – are pre-ordained and inevitable; it is a belief in justice since they are consequences of one's past deeds and in that sense deserved. Even though those deeds were committed in a previous existence, responsibility for them attaches to the conception of a continuous soul in endless cycles of birth and rebirth. Believers in karma should therefore be inclined to attribute responsibility for injustices to the victims; what they are reaping is what they have sowed.

In a carefully constructed interview study, Desai-Carroll (1989) asked samples of Indians living in the United States selected from Hindu temples, Muslim mosques, and Christian churches, to respond to several thumbnail descriptions of negative life conditions that were apparently the result of injustice, including disproportionate minority unemployment, criminal convictions, sex-discrimination, and increases in poverty. At a standard point in the interview, the respondents were given cards on which there were three categorical sources of responsibility for each of the conditions: society, the victim(s), and the culture (e.g. the way the victims were brought up). Subjects were told they had 100 percentage points to distribute over the three categories. Averaging the responses over all five cases, the Hindus were found to allocate the highest mean number of their points to the victims while the Muslims and Christians, in that order, showed the opposite pattern, assigning more of their points to society. The percentages allocated to the culture alternative were about the same for each of the three samples. Statistical analysis of these mean allocations of responsibility to the victim and to society among the three religious groups were significant.

The finding is, of course, suggestive rather than conclusive concerning the belief in karma and justice. Since there is no "true" distribution of responsibility in these cases, the obtained allocations could have been due to an overweening propensity of Christians to *avoid* attributing responsibility to the victims. Or, the results could have been due to both Hindu and Christian tendencies.

The Belief in Justice

The concept of justice is a central feature of religions, legal systems, and moral philosophy, and has been investigated by social psychologists in a variety of group settings where costs and benefits are allocated such as jury decisions and work, largely under the rubrics of distributive and procedural justice. Justice has also been studied in interpersonal relations more generally where favors, gifts, affection, help, and other rewards and punishments are exchanged.

It is not surprising that definitions of justice differ in this body of research. A minimalist definition is that rewards and costs should be allocated or exchanged in accordance with some criterion of deservingness. That is, it is unjust merely when a person's rewards are arbitrary. More specifically, justice demands that benefits and costs be in proportion to what is deserved. Just pay, for example, should be proportional to productivity or the amount of labor (and not based on kinship with the owner of the factory), just prison sentences are proportional to the severity of the crime (and not the race of the criminal). In interpersonal relations, justice is defined as "equity," which includes the element of social comparison. If benefits are given in a proportion to one person's effort, equity is experienced when the same proportion is used to assess everyone's benefits; all parties to the relationship should receive equal relative gains (Walster, Walster, & Berscheid, 1978).

Common observation makes it plain that what is considered just, right, and fair depends upon the kind of outcomes involved. Some believe execution of a convicted murderer is never just because it is too severe, while others, obeying *lex talionis*, find it unjust because it is not severe enough. What is justice also varies with the purposes of the groups in which distributions are made and with other contextual features. In criminal contexts, justice is often mixed with humanitarian values, as suggested by the phrase "justice tempered with mercy." And in political contexts, where an egalitarian ideology dominates all else, only absolute equality of all material things satisfies justice.

Another line of justice research in social psychology is concerned with a generalized belief in individuals that the world is just, a world in which people get what they deserve. In an early conceptualization, basic cognitive needs for order and predictability were assumed to be the dynamics underlying the belief. So strong is the need to believe that, under certain conditions, the believer may distort the responsibility attributed to victims of punishment. By blaming victims, believers can maintain their just world belief (Lerner, 1970, 1980). Recent thinking in the just world framework is somewhat more specific about deservingness in conceiving justice as a psychological entitlement. Justice is done when outcomes satisfy entitlements (Lerner, 1991). The sense of entitlement is assumed to come from social norms including reciprocity, the obligations of social roles and statuses, and legal rights.

Looking at the entire body of research on justice, except for the developmental approaches – and the Piaget, Kohlberg stage-theories in particular – justice as a *moral concept* plays no significant role. Of course, in the realm of distributive justice, the rules of resource allocation are not necessarily moral or wholly moral in nature. Although widely applied with firm conviction, and when violated, causing righteous indignation, they are, in essence, policy conventions or directives which can be modified to suit the interested parties; hence their variability. But from a cultural perspective, the belief in justice, especially about the conditions and events of life, has to be seen as a moral imperative that is laid down by God or an impersonal transcendental law. In its generic and prototypic form, the moral belief in justice refers to a simple state that ought to prevail in society and life events: "good things should happen to good people (as individuals and groups); bad things should happen to bad people."

Guided by this conceptualization, Pepitone and L'Armand (in press) proposed a model of moral justice in life events based on the relation between the valence of the outcome of the event, i.e. the psychological value of the cost or benefit it delivered, and the valence of the person(s) who experiences the outcome: that is, the goodness or badness of the person on moral dimensions. A state of justice is perceived when the outcome and person valences have the same signs or are similar in magnitude; injustice is perceived when they have opposite signs or differ widely in magnitude.

In the experiment, subjects were presented with a life event case in which the person and outcome valences were systematically designed and combined in all four ways; the person in the cases was made out to be good or bad, and the outcome experienced by the person was either positive or negative. After reading the cases, subjects were asked simply to write down their spontaneous comments about the case, and then to rate the degree of justice and injustice on a 100-point rating scale. The results strongly supported the hypothesis and were consistent in both nondirective, qualitative and the direct, quantitative measures. The statistical analysis showed that the effect on the spontaneous references to, and ratings of, justice, of goodness and badness of the person, depends on whether the outcome is similarly positive or negative. When person and outcome are good and positive, and when they are bad and negative, the mean ratings and mean presence/absence of mentions of justice in the free-response data, are higher than when they are opposite in sign.

Moreover, that the perception of just and unjust life events is a simple equality of the person and outcome valuations was also shown unambiguously by comparable Chinese samples (Lee & Pepitone, 1994), Korean samples (Hong, 1994), and Indian samples (Prachi, 1994).

There is one exclusive implication of the conception of justice as a moral belief. If justice is a law of the universe or the enforceable will of God, believers not only want life events to be just because that's the way things *should be*, but tend to *expect* that there are forces to bring about justice, at least ultimately. Thus, if people are perceived to be good or bad, the most likely outcomes to happen to them will have the same respective valences.

To test this hypothesis, Lee and Pepitone (1994) presented subjects with a list of personal characteristics of a Mr M. In one condition, they conveyed the impression of a good person (e.g. "honest," "loyal," etc.) while in a second condition, Mr. M was a bad person in terms of polar opposite adjectives ("dishonest," "disloyal," etc). The dependent variable was a set of scales that measured the valence of the most likely outcome for Mr M: "will lose job" . . . "will keep job," "will stay in good marriage" . . . "will get divorced," and so on.

The results are clear: good persons are expected to have significantly more positive outcomes than bad persons, while for the latter, the expectations are significantly more negative. The valences of expected outcomes thus reflect the transcendental law of justice or the will of God.

Religiosity and Justice

It is obvious that believers in God see a close connection between God and justice. God stands for justice and wants justice in the world; justice is voiced in God's laws, and in ancient religions, there is a goddess of justice. Yet, the relationship between the belief in God and the belief in justice implies opposite predictions. On the one hand, the believer in God who identifies with God and the supreme value of justice can be expected to be more sensitive to just and unjust life events. Such believers would be inclined to perceive just life events as more just and unjust life events as more unjust. On the other hand, as suggested by the discussion above, believers in God not only value justice but believe that God has the enforceable power to bring it about. These believers can be expected to overestimate the justice of those life events in which person and outcome valences are the same or equal and underestimate the dissimilar and unequal valences. Evidence from a questionnaire study supports this second prediction (Rubin & Peplau, 1975). Our evidence confirms such a "religiosity bias" (Pepitone & L'Armand, 1996). Subjects made self-estimates of their religiosity on the basis of their belief in God and their participation in religious services. The four-step scale ranged from: "extremely religious," "moderately," "slightly," or "not at all religious." The mean justice rating (on the 100-point scale) by the extremely religious subjects (65.7) was significantly higher than the mean rating by the nonreligious subjects (46.4), with the other means falling inbetween. The statistical analysis revealed that the effect of religiosity on the estimation of justice was independent of the person–outcome valence conditions. Thus, regardless of whether the person was good or bad and whether the outcome was positive or negative, the highly religious subjects tended to perceive life events as more just than their less religious counterparts.

Epilogue

Of central interest in this essay is the theoretical question of how it is that people believe in things that have no objective material existence, and the empirical question of how such nonmaterial beliefs affect the perception of life events. Though the boundary between the nonmaterial and the material is not always distinct, many of the former kind of beliefs are readily identified in everyday life – the belief that guardian angels are standing by, that HIV infection is God's punishment, that someone is bewitched or possessed of the devil, that upon death the soul rises to heaven, that what happens in life is written in the stars, and that Lady Luck can advise a player to draw on an inside straight. Indeed, some of the most influential beliefs in the nonmaterial repertoire like God, the power of fate, luck and justice are, in one version or another, as common as almost any other psychological characteristic found in humans throughout world cultures.

Rather than summarize the theoretical analysis and research data presented in the paper, it would be useful at this point to look at this field of inquiry from a more general perspective as articulated by the following propositions.

1. Nonmaterial beliefs are an integral part of a group's (society, tribe, community, etc.) culture, no less than its customs, mode of subsistence, and rules of inheritance. Such beliefs are conceived not as discrete structures, but organized as cultural systems in which they are more or less interrelated.
2. Nonmaterial beliefs can also be conceived to be part of the individual's cognitive structure. As such, they include references to the existence and reality of something, and, frequently, an evaluation of that something, which is to say that beliefs are often combined with values. For example, the belief in justice is not only a conviction that justice exists or will exist, but a reference to the goodness of justice. Indeed, it is the value component of beliefs that motivates actions and arouses emotions. The believer not only believes in the existence of God but effectively worships God, wants to be near God, wants ultimately to be in a spiritual union with God.
3. Beliefs are conceived as *joint* properties of group culture and individual cognitive structure by virtue of being shared with individuals who are identified with the culture. To be shared means not only that the beliefs are replicated among culture-members, but that they are normative, prescribing the reality and the valuation of nonmaterial forces, things, powers, laws, processes, beings, and places. These normative prescriptions, moreover, have been more or less internalized by individuals, so that their effects are self-induced, independently of influence pressure from the group.
4. Ethnographies provide strong evidence that in some generic and prototypic form, spiritual, mystical, and magical beliefs are widely distributed throughout world cultures. Presumably, to some extent, this reflects cultural diffusion; to some extent, universal dynamics of individuals and groups. Nevertheless, the cultural generality of particular hypotheses about nonmaterial beliefs has to be tested empirically.
5. The evolution and maintenance of nonmaterial belief norms depend generally on their serving psychologically adaptive functions for the individual and group.
6. Three broad classes of functions can be specified: (a) satisfaction of individual needs and emotions, (b) enhanced comprehension of life conditions and events, and (c) preservation of the integrity and identity of the group.

7. (a) We referred to experimental evidence that the common and influential nonmaterial beliefs including God, fate, and justice are invoked to enhance understanding of life events when the possibilities for understanding such events in material terms are limited, and evidence that this cognitive function is selective; that nonmaterial beliefs are more or less specialized in the life events for which they provide explanations.

   (b) The dependence of the cognitive function on the information available in life event cases with which to interpret life events, and the selectivity of the function shown by our North American sample were also reliably shown by a comparable sample from a manifestly different society – India. From this replication, however, there can be no inference that the cognitive function of the set of nonmaterial beliefs and their selectivity are universal. Although, plainly, there are societies whose cultures overall are more similar to the North American culture than Indian culture, the particular set of nonmaterial beliefs used in the research described may be less prevalent and weaker in these societies. Comparable samples (middle class university students) drawn from European cultures, for example, may be less spiritual, less inclined to believe in fate, and so on. Only further empirical research can determine more precisely the cross-cultural generality of belief hypotheses.

In conclusion, the perspective we have outlined in the study of nonmaterial beliefs is based on the conception that nonmaterial beliefs are joint properties of culture and individual cognitive structures – internalized norms that prescribe the reality-status and valuation of spiritual, supernatural, and transcendental phenomena which have historically remained outside the domain of scientific social psychology. But if social psychology is to be concerned with the experiences of real people and of all the realities in their world, the study of nonmaterial beliefs must be placed on the theory and research agenda.

Further Reading

Baroja, J. C. (1965). *The world of the witches* Chicago, IL: University of Chicago Press. A wide-ranging history of witchcraft in Europe and the ancient world, and its relationship with Christianity and the Devil.

Cohen, J. (1960). *Chance, skill and luck*. Baltimore and Mitcham (Victoria): Penguin. A program of simple and often incisive experiments on the effects of (the belief in) luck and chance.

Durkheim, E. (1915, 1965). *The elementary forms of religious life*. New York: Free Press. A highly original and now classic analysis of the essential characteristics of Totemic religion, which is seen as the prototype.

Malinowski, B. (1948). *Magic, science and religion*. New York: Free Press. A highly informative discourse on primitive religion and magic, and particularly how they relate to the evolution of scientific knowledge.

Pepitone, A., & L'Armand, K. (in press). The justice and injustice of life events. *European Journal of Social Psychology*.

References

Desai-Carroll, K. (1989). *A study of the interrelationships among belief systems: Religion, control, and justice*. Unpublished doctoral dissertation. University of Pennsylvania.

Lee, T., & Pepitone, A. (1994). *Symmetry on the perception of justice*. Paper presented at the meeting of the Society for Cross-Cultural Research, Santa Fe, NM.

Lerner, M. (1970). The desire for justice and the reaction to victims. In J. Macaulay & L. Berkowitz (Eds.), *Altruism and helping behavior*. New York: Academic Press.

Lerner, M. (1980). *The belief in a just world: A fundamental delusion*. New York: Plenum Press.

Lerner, M. (1991). Interpreting societal and psychological rules of entitlement. In R. Vermunt & H. Steensma (Eds.), *Social Justice in Human Relations* (Vol. 1). New York: Plenum Press.

Hong, G. (1994, February). Korean beliefs in the justice of life events. Paper presented at the meeting of the Society for Cross-Cultural Research, Santa Fe, NM.

Murdock, G. (1945). *The common denominator of culture*. New York: Columbia University Press.

Murdock, G. (1980). *Theories of illness: A world survey*. Pittsburgh, PA: University of Pittsburgh Press.

Pepitone, A. (1964/1968). *Attraction and hostility*. New York: Atherton Press; London: Tavistock Press.

Pepitone, A. (1976). Toward a normative and comparative biocultural social psychology. *Journal of Personality and Social Psychology*, *34*, 641–653.

Pepitone, A. (1986). Culture and the cognitive paradigm in social psychology. *Australian Journal of Psychology*, *3*, 245–256.

Pepitone, A., & Triandis, H. (1987). On the universality of social psychological theories. *Journal of Cross-Cultural Psychology*, *4*, 471–496.

Pepitone, A., & L'Armand, K. (in press). The justice and injustice of life events. *European Journal of Social Psychology*.

Philips, D., Todd, R., & Wagner, L. (1993). Psychology and survival. *The Lancet*, *342*, 1142–1145.

Parsuram, A., & Sharma, R. (1994). *Life events and belief selectivity*. Unpublished manuscript, Psychology Department, University of Delhi.

Prachi, S. (1994). *Reactions to cases of justice and injustice*. Unpublished doctoral dissertation, University of Delhi.

Rubin, Z., & Peplau, L. (1975). Who believes in a just world? *Journal of Social Issues*, *31*, 65–87.

Saffiotti, L. (1990). *The selective use of beliefs to interpret major life events*. Unpublished doctoral dissertation, University of Pennsylvania, Philadelphia.

Walster, E., Walster, G., & Berscheid, E. (1978). *Equity: Theory and research*. Boston, MA: Allyn & Bacon.

17

The Evolution of Theory and Research in Social Psychology: From Single to Multiple Effect and Process Models of Persuasion

Richard E. Petty

Richard E. Petty received his B.A. from the University of Virginia in 1973 and his doctorate in social psychology from Ohio State University in 1977. In 1987, he left his position as Middlebush Professor at the University of Missouri to return to Ohio State where he won the University Distinguished Scholar Award in 1994. He is the author of seven books and over 150 journal articles and chapters. Dr Petty is a fellow of the American Association for the Advancement of Science, the American Psychological Association, and the American Psychological Society. He is former editor of the *Personality and Social Psychology Bulletin* and currently serves on the editorial board of six journals.

Are similar people attracted to each other, or do opposites attract? Are men more effective leaders than women? Are attractive people more persuasive than unattractive ones? Furthermore, if people are more attracted to similar others, or if men are more effective leaders than women, or if attractive people are more persuasive, *why* is this the case? For example, if attractive people are more persuasive than unattractive people, is this because we pay more attention to what attractive people say, or is it because we agree with attractive people so that they will like us? Humans have a natural curiosity about such questions and social psychologists study these issues scientifically.

Notice that the way in which each of these questions is framed appears to assume that there is one correct answer or outcome for each of the variables involved. That is, the questions seem to imply that *either* men *or* women are more effective as leaders or that *either* attractive *or* unattractive people are more persuasive. I refer to this as the *single-effect assumption* – that variables such as source attractiveness have just one effect on any one outcome measure (such as how much persuasion they produce). Furthermore, the questions seem to imply that whichever effect is obtained, there is one explanation for or reason for why this outcome is produced. I refer to the latter as the *single-process assumption*.

Just as people who are not trained as social psychologists tend to think about questions this way, so too do social psychologists – especially when they are at the earliest stages of examining a new phenomenon. Inevitably, however, it seems to turn out that whatever some initial investigation shows (e.g. that attractive people are more persuasive than unattractive people), some subsequent study will eventually show the opposite (i.e. that attractive people are less persuasive than unattractive people). In fact, McGuire (1983) has suggested that the opposite of virtually every social-psychological finding is also true. The fact that opposite results are often obtained can be frustrating in that it can leave both scientists and laypersons baffled as to what to believe. Ironically, the production of opposite results sometimes leads not to confusion, but to a new and better understanding of the phenomena under study. In fact, theories developed to predict and explain opposite results can be quite powerful and can simplify our understanding of complex outcomes.

Another complicating factor in understanding human behavior is that it turns out that it is rarely the case that any one explanation for any one outcome is universally correct. This means, for example, that sometimes people might be attracted to similar others for one reason (e.g. we are attracted to similar others because they enjoy similar activities), but at other times, another reason provides a better explanation for the same outcome (e.g. we are attracted to similar others because they can read our emotions better and communicate with us more easily).

In this essay, I address and critique the single-effect and single-process assumptions that have guided early social-psychological work in general, and social-psychological research on attitude change and persuasion in particular. I focus on attitude change research because of its long and illustrious history in social psychology (cf. Allport, 1935), and also because (quite frankly) it is an area I know more about than others!

Single Versus Multiple Effects of Variables

First generation research

Scientific work on persuasion began in the twentieth century (e.g. Knower, 1935), although speculation about how people come to be influenced by various source and message factors can be traced to the ancient Greeks (e.g. see Aristotle's *Rhetoric*). The early or *first generation* researchers concerned with understanding attitude change wondered about such fundamental issues as: Are expert and attractive people more persuasive than non-experts and unattractive people? Is it better to present people with logical arguments or with appeals based on emotion? Is fear a good emotional tool or does it turn people off? In the initial tests of these notions, researchers would give people a persuasive message on some topic and would manipulate whether the message contained an expert source or not, or included fearful elements or not. In this way, the investigator could determine if the critical variable (e.g. fear or an expert source) was beneficial or harmful for persuasion. Most often, the study was guided by some underlying theory or notion of *why* the variable would be harmful or beneficial.

For example, one of the earliest general theories of persuasion was based on learning theory principles (Hovland, Janis, & Kelley, 1953). In its simplest form, this theory held that anything that facilitated attending to, comprehending, and learning the contents of the message would be good for persuasion, and anything that would disrupt attending, comprehending, and learning would be bad for persuasion. Thus, for example, distracting someone from the message should reduce persuasion because distraction is generally bad for attention, comprehension, and learning. Although some research has supported this notion, as I forewarned you, other research has found the opposite (see Petty & Brock, 1981, for a review). For example, Festinger and Maccoby (1964) presented college fraternity men with a message that advocated that fraternities should be abolished. They found that those who were distracted during the message ended up agreeing *more* with the message than those who were not distracted. To account for this, these researchers hypothesized that attitude change depended not so much on verbatim learning of a message, but on whether or not people *counter-argued* the arguments that were presented. They reasoned that people who disagreed with a message resisted by counter-arguing the message points during its presentation. Distraction could disrupt this counter-arguing and thereby increase the likelihood of persuasion by undermining this resistance mechanism.

Thus, learning theory predicts one outcome – that distraction is bad for persuasion, and counter-arguing theory predicts the opposite – that distraction is good for persuasion. It would be more parsimonious if one theory could explain both outcomes (i.e. how distraction can both increase and decrease persuasion). Petty, Wells, and Brock (1976) hypothesized that distraction could produce either outcome if distraction disrupted whatever people were thinking, rather than counter-arguments in particular. That is, if undistracted people would have been thinking favorable thoughts about the message, then distraction would disrupt these positive thoughts and would result in less persuasion than if no distraction were present, but if undistracted people would have been thinking unfavorable thoughts (counter-arguments), distraction would disrupt these negative thoughts and result in more persuasion. To test this thought disruption idea, Petty et al. (1976) developed two messages. One message was designed to elicit mostly favorable thoughts when people were paying careful attention to it (i.e. a *strong message* containing compelling arguments), and another message on the same topic was pre-tested to elicit mostly unfavorable thoughts when people were paying careful attention to it (i.e. a *weak message* containing specious arguments). These messages were then given to people who were exposed to either a minimal or a moderate amount of distraction during message exposure. The results of the study are presented in the top panel of figure 17.1. As expected by the thought disruption hypothesis, distraction was good for persuasion when the arguments were weak, but was bad for persuasion when the arguments were strong.

Following the report of this study in 1976, many other such studies were conducted that included both strong and weak arguments along with some variable of interest. These studies generally showed that many variables that were initially thought to have just one effect (i.e. either increasing or decreasing persuasion) could both increase and decrease persuasion depending on whether or not the variable was paired with a strong or a weak message (see Eagly & Chaiken, 1993; Petty & Cacioppo, 1986, for reviews). As another example of this dual outcome finding, consider the learning theory approach to message repetition. Learning theory suggested that repeating a message a few times would increase the likelihood of persuasion because with more exposures, people would have a greater chance to attend to, comprehend, and learn the message. However, research that varied the quality of the message that was presented along with message repetition found that going from one to three exposures of a strong message led to more persuasion, but going from one to three exposures of a weak message led to less persuasion (e.g. Cacioppo & Petty, 1989; see middle panel of figure 17.2). This suggested that learning *per se*, was not critical, but that increased repetition gave recipients a greater opportunity to think about and evaluate the arguments.

The persuasion work on distraction and message repetition supported a *cognitive* response (Greenwald, 1968; Petty, Ostrom, & Brock, 1981) or *elaboration likelihood model* of persuasion (Petty & Cacioppo, 1981, 1986). That is, variables could increase or decrease persuasion by influencing the likelihood that people would elaborate or think about the arguments presented (see also, Chaiken, Liberman, & Eagly, 1989). Some variables, like distraction, decreased

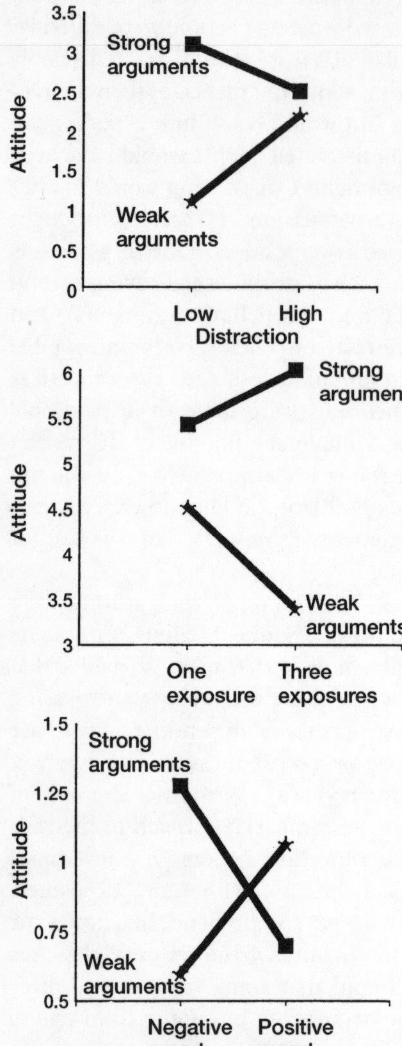

Figure 17.1 Examples of "second generation" research on message processing: Variables can increase and decrease persuasion by either increasing or decreasing message processing. Top panel: distraction reduces message processing (data from Petty, Wells, & Brock, 1976). Middle panel: message repetition increases message processing (data from Cacioppo & Petty, 1989). Bottom panel: positive mood reduces message processing (data from Worth & Mackie, 1987).

the likelihood that people would elaborate or generate cognitive responses to the message arguments, whereas other variables, like repeated exposure, increased the likelihood of the recipient cognitively responding to or elaborating the message arguments.

Second generation research

Because so many variables were shown to be associated with both increased and decreased persuasion since they influenced the likelihood of thinking about the

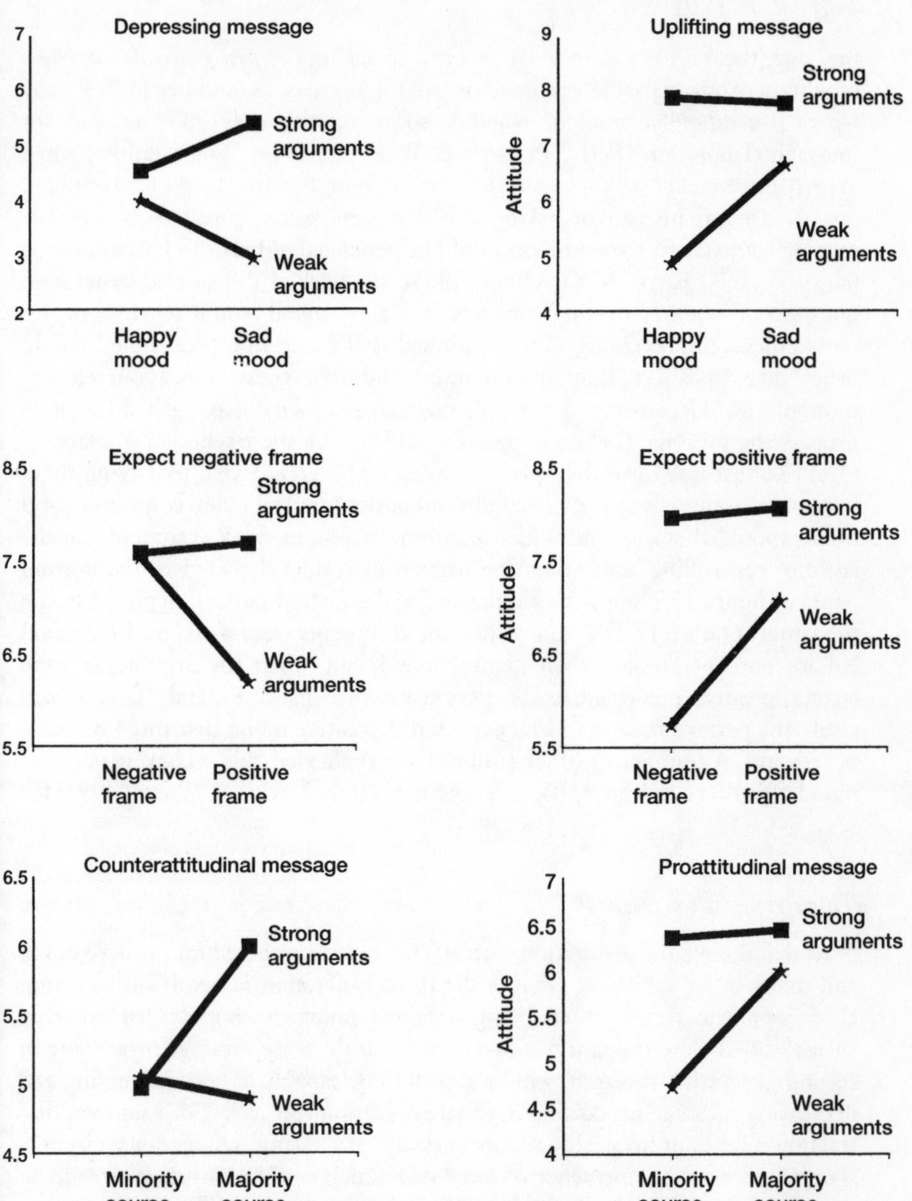

Figure 17.2 Examples of "third generation" research on message processing: Variables can both increase and decrease message processing. Top panel: positive mood can enhance or reduce message processing (data from Wegener, Petty, & Smith, 1995). Middle panel: positive message framing can enhance or reduce message processing (data from Smith & Petty, 1996). Bottom panel: minority sources can enhance or reduce message processing (data from Baker & Petty, 1994)

message, the field began to move away from asking the *first generation question* of whether some variable was good or bad for persuasion, and began to ask the *second generation question* of whether some variable was good or bad for message elaboration (Petty, Priester, & Wegener, 1994). For example, when Worth and Mackie (1987) began their research on the effects of positive mood on persuasion, instead of asking the first generation question of whether putting someone in a good mood would be beneficial or harmful for persuasion (e.g. see Janis, Kaye, & Kirschner, 1965), they asked the second generation question of whether putting someone in a good mood would increase or decrease message processing. They reasoned that being in a good mood would bring many positive thoughts to mind and that these message-irrelevant thoughts would consume a person's cognitive capacity making it difficult to process the message (i.e. good mood would reduce the likelihood of elaboration). To test this idea, they placed students in a good mood by having them win some money (happy mood condition) or not (neutral mood condition), and then exposed them to a message containing strong or weak arguments on the issue of controlling acid rain. The pattern of results depicted in the bottom panel of figure 17.1 was very similar to the distraction pattern depicted in the top panel of figure 17.1. That is, when the arguments were weak, positive mood led to more persuasion than neutral mood, but when the arguments were strong, positive mood led to less persuasion than neutral mood. This is precisely the pattern that would be expected if positive mood disrupted message processing. A number of other studies have replicated this second generation mood effect (see Schwarz, Bless, & Bohner, 1991; Mackie & Worth, 1991, for reviews).

Third generation research

Now that the second generation research has been conducted for positive mood and many other variables, what is the third generation issue? If our warning about opposite results often being obtained holds, it should turn out that variables that were thought to *either* increase *or* decrease message processing in second generation research, will be shown to be capable of both increasing *and* decreasing message processing in third generation research. For example, distraction might not invariably reduce message processing. Under some circumstances, perhaps, the presence of some distraction could motivate people to be especially diligent in thinking about the message.

This "third generation" opposite effect on processing has not (yet) been shown for distraction. However, third generation effects have been shown recently for other variables. Let's return to the effect of positive mood on persuasion. We now know that positive mood is not invariably good or bad for persuasion as reviewers of the first generation of research on positive mood concluded (e.g. see McGuire, 1985). Rather, second generation researchers and reviewers concluded that a pleasant mood could be good *or* bad for persuasion because a pleasant mood was invariably bad for message processing (Schwarz et al., 1991; Mackie & Worth, 1991; e.g. see bottom panel of figure 17.1). The third generation question would address the possibility that a pleasant mood could either be good or bad for message processing.

To account for both effects on message processing, a new explanation was needed for why mood affected thinking about a message. Wegener, Petty, and Smith (1995; see also Petty, Gleicher, & Baker, 1991) noted that second generation investigations of positive mood and persuasion used message topics that were rather unpleasant, counterattitudinal, and/or depressing (e.g. acid rain; tuition increases). Thus, happy people may not have thought about these messages because doing so would have destroyed their current good feelings. If the messages had been on topics that were pleasant and non-threatening, then perhaps people in a positive mood would be very interested in thinking about the messages because thinking about them would insure that their good feelings would be continued (Isen, 1993; Wegener & Petty, 1994).

To examine this idea, college students were first placed in a happy or sad mood by watching a video and reading an article that induced these states (Wegener et al., 1995, experiment 2). Then, the students were led to believe that the next article they would read (i.e. the persuasive message), would either make them feel happy (pleasant expectation condition) or sad (unpleasant expectation condition). The messages actually presented the same strong or weak arguments in favor of a new university service proposal. The top panel of figure 17.2 presents the results. Note that when the students expected the message to be unpleasant or depressing (first row, left panel), those in a positive mood were less attentive to message quality than those in a sad mood. When argument quality has a large effect on attitudes (as in the depressing message, sad mood condition), one can assume that people are attending to and thinking about the message, but when argument quality has a small (or no) effect on attitudes (as in the depressing message, happy mood condition), it appears that people are not forming their opinions based on an objective assessment of the merits of the proposal. This finding of reduced message processing for those in a positive mood replicates the second generation research suggesting that positive mood disrupts message processing (e.g. Worth & Mackie, 1987). Note however, that when the students expected the message to be uplifting and pleasant (first row, right panel), those in a positive mood actually engaged in *greater* message processing than those who were in a negative mood. This result, of course, suggests that positive mood does not invariably reduce message processing as the second generation research indicated, but can actually increase it. These results also provide support for a new explanation for why mood influences to message processing. Specifically, this research suggests that sometimes, the underlying motivation for message processing is to manage one's mood.

Other variables are beginning to receive the third generation treatment. For example, consider the long-standing question of whether it is better to present the arguments in a message in a positive frame (e.g. "if you stop smoking you will live a long, healthy life") or in a negative frame (e.g. "if you don't stop smoking, you will die sooner"). As with virtually all other persuasion variables, initial research and theory suggested that one framing was better for persuasion than the other. In this case, the evidence suggested that negative framing was more effective (e.g. Meyerowitz & Chaiken, 1987). Later, evidence was presented to support the second generation conclusion that negative framing tended to enhance information processing activity (e.g. Ditto & Lopez, 1992). Smith and Petty (1996) posed the third generation question of whether negative framing could both enhance and reduce message processing. They reasoned that people often expect persuaders to present the benefits of taking some action or agreeing with some position. Thus, when a message presents the costs of not taking some action, this is unexpected, and this surprise leads to greater information processing activity (see Olson, Roese, & Zanna, in press). This violation of expectancies notion suggests that if people were led to believe that a message would present the costs of not taking some action, but it instead presented the benefits of taking the action, this should lead to surprise and the (unexpected) positive framing would lead to greater information processing than the (expected) negative framing.

To test this idea, Smith and Petty (1996) led students to expect that an advertisement for a new vitamin would either present the benefits of taking the vitamin (positive expectancy condition) or the damages from not taking it (negative expectancy condition). The message then presented weak or strong arguments of the type expected or not. As the results in the middle panel of figure 17.2 demonstrate, people considered the arguments more in forming their attitudes when the arguments were of the type that were not expected (i.e. when the recipients were surprised). That is, when people expected a negatively framed message, greater message processing took place when the message used positively framed arguments (i.e. argument quality had a larger effect on attitudes when the arguments were framed positively than negatively; see left panel), but when people expected a positively framed message, greater message processing took place when the message used negatively framed arguments (i.e. argument quality had a larger effect on attitudes when the arguments were framed negatively than positively; see right panel).

As a final example, the bottom panel of figure 17.2 presents the results of a third generation study examining the variable of majority or minority sources. More specifically, this research addressed how learning that a message is endorsed by either a substantial majority or a small minority of other people affects information processing and persuasion. We can now bypass the first generation question (i.e. does majority or minority endorsement produce more persuasion? e.g. Asch, 1956), and the second generation question (does majority or minority endorsement produce more message processing? e.g. Harkins &

Petty, 1981; Moscovici, 1980), and turn directly to the third generation question. Baker and Petty (1994) hypothesized that since people generally expect other people to agree with them (the "false consenses effect", false consensus effect; Ross, Greene, & House, 1977), they would be more surprised when the message implied that a majority rather than a minority of other people took a position that disagreed with them. On the other hand, they would be more surprised when only a minority rather than a majority took a position that agreed with their own. Whichever position was the more surprising would produce the most message processing.

To test this notion, Baker and Petty (1994) presented students with opinion polls that indicated that either a majority or a minority of students and residents of their state favored a position that they also favored, or that either a majority or minority favored a position that they opposed. These pro- and counter-attitudinal positions were supported in a message with either strong or weak arguments. As the results in the bottom panel of figure 17.2 demonstrate, people engaged in greater processing of the message when the advocacy was not expected (i.e. the majority taking a counterattitudinal position [see left panel] and the minority taking a proattitudinal position [see right panel]), rather than expected (i.e. the majority taking a proattitudinal position and the minority taking a counterattitudinal position).

In sum, researchers investigating positive/negative message framing and majority/minority sources initially examined which framing and which type of source was best for persuasion (the first generation question). Then, researchers examined which framing and which source was best for message processing (the second generation question). Most recently, work on both variables has concluded that either framing (positive/negative) or source (majority/minority) can be better for message processing depending on which induces the most surprise. That is, the third generation conclusion is that *surprise leads to more message processing*, and suggests that sometimes the underlying motivation for message processing is to provide understanding of an unexpected occurrence.

Fourth Generation Research

Now that some third generation studies have clearly indicated that any one variable is capable of both increasing and decreasing message processing, what is the fourth generation issue? Fourth generation research involves taking the general information processing principles uncovered in the third generation research – such as surprise leading to more message processing – and considering the opposite – that surprise can lead to less message processing. Fourth generation research would address the conditions under which this opposite result would occur, and the overall mechanism(s) that could account for this. Note that at each generation of research, the overall conclusion is stated as a general prediction (e.g. negative framing leads to more persuasion, or negative framing leads to more message processing, or surprise leads to more message processing). The conclusions at each generation must account for the findings of the current and the previous generations. For example, the second generation principle that *negative framing leads to more processing* accounts for the first and second generation findings that negative framing can lead to more or less persuasion. Then, the third generation principle that *surprise leads to more processing* accounts for the second and third generation findings that negative framing can lead to more or less message processing and specifies the conditions under which each outcome occurs. The fourth generation general principle (not yet identified) would need to account for the finding (not yet obtained) that surprise can lead to more or less message processing. At this point, it is not clear how many generations of research will be needed before some *universal principles* of message processing are identified (i.e. principles for which the opposite does not occur or occurs under such unusual or near impossible circumstances that it need not be incorporated into a general theory of social behavior).

Summary of progress in each generation

In the domain of persuasion research (as in other social psychological areas of study), first generation research is important in documenting that some variable has *any* impact on persuasion (or some other socially relevant dependent measure). If some variable cannot be shown to either enhance or reduce persuasion (or increase or decrease aggression, altruism, prejudice, etc.), it is unlikely to be of much interest to social psychologists. As I noted, however, once a variable is shown to increase (or decrease) the measure of interest, the opposite result is often observed as well. When this occurs, second generation research is valuable when it uncovers a mechanism that can account for *both* effects. In the field of persuasion, the mechanism that was most successful in accounting for how any one variable could both increase and decrease persuasion had to do with the extent to which the variable influenced how much people processed or elaborated the message that was presented to them (e.g. Petty et al., 1976). The third and fourth generation research then builds on the second generation process identified. If the second generation mechanism had been different, then (as discussed further below) the third and fourth generation questions and conclusions would also be different.

In this regard it is important to note that our discussion of generational mechanisms has used the simplifying assumption that although the persuasion outcomes for any variable can be very different (i.e. the presence of a variable such as distraction sometimes leads to more and sometimes leads to less persuasion), the underlying mechanism by which a variable influences attitude change is the same (i.e. the mechanism by which variables influence persuasion is by affecting the extent of message processing). However, this assumption is flawed. Just as there is not only one outcome associated with most persuasion variables, there is not only one mechanism by which variables produce attitude change. It is to this issue that I turn next.

Single Versus Multiple Process Models

The examples of different generations of persuasion research in the previous section seem to imply that persuasion is a rather thoughtful process and that variables can have an impact on persuasion by influencing the amount of thought that takes place. Furthermore, our discussion seems to imply that the thinking people do about messages is rather objective in that it is guided by the quality of the arguments presented. If the arguments are compelling and people are motivated and able to think about them, they will generate favorable thoughts and will be persuaded. On the other hand, if the arguments are specious, and people are motivated and able to think about them, they will generate unfavorable thoughts and will resist influence or even move in the direction opposite to that advocated. Is this the only means by which attitudes are changed, or are there other mechanisms of persuasion? For example, are people ever *biased* in their consideration of messages rather than objective? Also, what happens when the likelihood of thinking is low and people are not thinking very carefully (if at all) about the merits of the arguments presented? Can persuasion still take place, and if so, what is responsible for persuasion then?

Biased thinking

The accumulated research clearly suggests that thinking about a message can sometimes be biased rather than objective. Biases can be produced by both individual and situational factors (see Petty & Cacioppo, 1986; Petty et al., 1994). In one early study, for example, Petty and Cacioppo (1979a), developed a message with strong arguments advocating that college seniors should be required to take a comprehensive exam in their major as a prerequisite to graduation. Two variables were manipulated. Some students were led to believe that the proposal would affect their graduating class (high relevance) whereas other students were led to believe that the proposal would not affect their class (low relevance). In addition, some students were told that the speaker was specifically trying to change their attitudes (forewarning condition), whereas the other subjects were not warned (no forewarning condition). Following exposure to the message, the students' attitudes toward the proposal were assessed.

In the unwarned conditions, the effect of increasing relevance was to increase persuasion. This is the effect that is expected if increasing relevance motivates people to consider the strong arguments in a relatively objective fashion. If the arguments had been weak, and relevance increased thinking, then the effect of increasing relevance would have been to decrease persuasion (Petty & Cacioppo, 1979b, 1990). However, an interesting result occurred when the students were warned that the speaker was trying to persuade them. When the warning was given, increasing relevance *decreased* the amount of persuasion even though the arguments were strong. What is going on? To account for these data, Petty and Cacioppo (1979a) hypothesized that ordinarily (i.e. without the warning), relevance increases thinking about the strong arguments in a relatively objective fashion. However, when people are forewarned that someone is trying to persuade them, they feel a threat to their freedom to think as they wish (i.e. they experience "reactance"; see Brehm, 1966). To restore their freedom, people are motivated to resist or counter-argue the message. So, when relevance is high and people are motivated to think about the issue, the reactance induced by the warning biases thoughts in a negative manner. Consistent with this explanation, when the warning was absent, increased relevance was associated with increased favorable thoughts, but when the warning was present, increased relevance was associated with increased counterargumentation (i.e. unfavorable thoughts). In sum, a warning on a high relevance topic did not lead to objective thinking about the strong arguments, but to biased thinking. Other studies have also demonstrated clear evidence of biased thinking on the part of message recipients (e.g. Liberman & Chaiken, 1992).

Low elaboration effects

We have seen that when people are motivated and able to think about a persuasive message, persuasion can result from either relatively objective thinking or from relatively biased thinking about the information presented. But what, if anything, is responsible for persuasion when thinking is low? The accumulated research has documented two types of effects that can occur when the extent of thinking about a message is low.

One type of low elaboration outcome occurs as a result of processes that are virtually identical to those that occur when thinking is high, but the processes are of a reduced magnitude (*a quantitative effect*). For example, consider a person who is exposed to a message containing eight strong arguments. The high elaboration objective processor might think of two or three favorable implications of each of the arguments whereas the low elaboration processor might think of only one or two favorable implications (since he or she is not thinking as much). The effect of this is that the high elaboration processor will have more favorable attitudes toward the issue than the low elaboration processor because he or she will have generated more favorable implications of the strong arguments presented. An alternative way to bring about this effect is if the low elaboration processor thinks diligently, but about fewer arguments (e.g. if the person generates two or three favorable thoughts to the first four arguments and does not think at all about the last four). This would also leave this person with a less favorable attitude than the person who thought carefully about all of the arguments.

This second (quantitative) low elaboration process – thinking about fewer arguments – can lead to some interesting effects. For example, what if the message contained four strong arguments followed by four weak ones? A high elaboration processor who thought about all of the information in a relatively objective manner would likely have a moderate opinion about the issue because the arguments are mixed (Friedreich, Fetherstonhaugh, Casey, & Gallagher, 1996; Petty & Cacioppo, 1984). However, an individual who considered only the early arguments would likely have a more favorable opinion because only the strong arguments were given careful consideration. If the message had four weak arguments followed by four strong ones, then the low elaboration processor would have a less favorable opinion than the high elaboration processor who considered all of the arguments objectively.

In addition to these quantitative effects, low elaboration attitude change can also be produced by processes that are substantively different from the argument consideration processes just described (*qualitative effect*). For example, consider another person who is exposed to the message with eight arguments. We have noted that the high elaboration processor would tend to think about all of the information. Also, we have noted that if the motivation to think was reduced, the recipient might think about each argument less carefully, or think about fewer arguments. However, other mechanisms of attitude change could occur when the elaboration likelihood is low that do not involve thought about the substantive merits of the arguments at all. For example, a low elaboration processor might simply count the arguments and reason that "if there are eight reasons to favor it, it must be worthwhile" (see Petty & Cacioppo, 1984). Note that this process is qualitatively different from the argument elaboration process in that this mechanism does not involve consideration of the merits of the arguments but instead involves reliance on a rule of thumb or heuristic that the person generates or retrieves from memory (see Chaiken, 1987, for more on heuristic processing). Other relatively low effort mechanisms that are capable of producing attitude change without processing the substantive merits of the arguments include: classical conditioning (Staats & Staats, 1958; Cacioppo et al., 1992), identification with the source of the message (Kelman, 1958), misattribution of affect to the message (Petty & Cacioppo, 1983; Schwarz & Clore, 1983), and mere exposure effects (Bornstein, 1989; Zajonc, 1968).

Multiple roles for variables

If the same persuasion outcome can be produced by different psychological processes, then theories of persuasion need to accommodate this. We have already noted that a single-process theory that can account for multiple and complex effects is generally better than one that can account for only one effect. Yet even the best single process theory accounting for the most complicated of effects (such as those depicted in figure 17.2) will be insufficient to account for human behavior because effects are often not produced by just one process.

Consider a very simple effect that could be observed in an experiment – that good mood leads to more persuasion than bad mood. In figure 17.1 (bottom panel) we saw that this could occur if good mood influenced information processing activity. For example, if a message was on an unpleasant topic and the arguments were specious, greater persuasion would result when in a positive rather than a neutral or negative mood because people in a good mood would be less likely to think about and generate unfavorable thoughts to the weak arguments (see also figure 17.2, top row). This outcome presumes that mood influences persuasion by affecting how much thinking a person is doing about a communication. However, can mood influence persuasion by other means? Just as we need to consider that any one process can bring about multiple effects, we must also consider that any one effect can be brought about by multiple processes.

Consider some of the persuasion processes that we mentioned above. Could mood bias processing of a message, or could mood influence attitudes by some qualitatively different means that did not involve affecting the amount or nature of information processing that took place? Petty, Schumann, Richman, and Strathman (1993) noted that previous research on positive mood and message processing did not attempt to render the likelihood of message elaboration as especially high or low. With the likelihood of elaboration not already preset by some other variable (such as distraction), mood was free to influence the extent of message processing. They hypothesized that if people were already highly motivated and able to think about a message for some reason other than their mood, then a positive mood would bias the thoughts that came to mind and could result in more persuasion than if the person was not feeling good. On the other hand, if the person was not at all motivated or able to think about a message, then positive mood would influence attitudes without affecting thinking. For example, people without scrutinizing the arguments at all might infer (falsely) that if they feel good, it's because they like or agree with the message (a misattribution of their positive feelings to the communication).

To examine this hypothesis, in two studies Petty et al. (1993) gave college students a task that either induced a good mood (e.g. watching a humorous video) or a relatively neutral mood (e.g. listening to classical music). Then, the students were exposed to a persuasive message either under conditions that would foster message thinking (e.g. the message was on a topic of high personal relevance) or not (e.g. the message was on a topic of low personal relevance; Petty & Cacioppo, 1979b). The results of this research revealed that under both high and low elaboration conditions, the effect of mood on attitudes was the same – positive mood was associated with significantly more agreement with the message than neutral mood. However, other results from the study indicated that these identical attitudinal outcomes were produced by different processes. Specifically, when the conditions favored elaboration (e.g. a high relevance message), positive mood influenced the favorableness of the students' thoughts about the message as well as their attitudes, and these positive thoughts induced by the mood were responsible for the positive attitudes. However, under low elaboration conditions (e.g. a low relevance message), positive mood did not have any impact on the favorableness of the students' thoughts. That is, their attitudes were more favorable when mood was positive, but their thoughts were not, suggesting a non-thoughtful process was responsible for the effect of positive mood on attitude change (e.g. classical conditioning or simply inferring they agreed with the message because they felt good; see Petty et al., 1991; Wegener & Petty, 1996, for additional discussion of the multiple processes by which mood influences attitudes).

Consequences of different processes

It is obvious why social psychologists care about predicting the effects of variables – we want to know if it is better to put somebody in a good or bad mood before attempting to persuade them. But, why do we care about the processes leading to the effect? To use our mood example, why do we care if good mood produced more persuasion by biasing the content of a person's thoughts about the message, or by invoking a simple "I feel good, so I must like it" heuristic? Of course, a sufficient conceptual justification is that we cannot really understand an outcome unless we know what produced it. However, sometimes there are important consequences of the process by which some effect is brought about. To take a simple example, someone can get a good grade on a test by cheating, or by studying. The outcome (i.e. a good grade) is identical, but the processes that brought the outcome about are different, and thus the consequences could vary. For example, the person who studied will probably be more likely to carry the substantive content of the course with him or her than the person who cheated. In a similar vein, if a person's attitude is changed because he or she generated many favorable thoughts about the topic, this change is more likely to endure over time, resist counter-persuasion, and direct the person's behavior than if the change was brought about with little thinking (see Petty, Haugtvedt, & Smith, 1995, for a review). That is, attitude changes brought about by thinking are stronger and more consequential than the *same* changes brought about with little thinking (see Petty & Krosnick, 1995, for additional discussion of attitude strength). This has important implications for many applications of persuasion research (e.g. producing favorable attitudes toward seat-belt usage, safe sex, etc.; see Petty, Gleicher, & Jarvis, 1993).

Multiple processes and the generations of research

Multi-outcome findings have been widely researched for one of the persuasion processes that we discussed. Specifically, when variables determine attitude change by influencing the extent of thinking, the outcome can be either more or less persuasion (e.g. see figures 17.1 and 17.2). In fact, research on relatively objective message processing is in its third generation of studies. However, the multiple outcomes of the other fundamental processes of persuasion have not received much empirical attention. For example, although it is clear that attractive sources can sometimes induce attitude change by serving as simple cues, the current assumption of investigators is that the cue value of attractive sources is positive. That is, when serving as a cue, attractive sources increase persuasion over unattractive sources – a first generation cue conclusion. However, it is reasonable that attractive sources (under some circumstances and/or for some individuals) can serve as negative cues as well and thereby reduce persuasion. The second generation of research on cue effects (yet to be conducted) will accommodate these divergent possibilities and produce insights into the psychological mechanisms by which cues have their impact.

In a similar vein, although research has focused on how some variables produce a positive (e.g. good mood) or a negative (e.g. forewarning of persuasive intent) bias to issue-relevant thinking, these first generation studies will inevitably yield to second generation research on biased message processing. Second generation research will examine circumstances under which forewarnings of persuasive intent can lead to enhanced persuasion by invoking favorable thoughts, and positive mood can lead to reduced persuasion by invoking negative thoughts, and will provide a conceptual framework to account for both effects.

Summary and Conclusions

In this chapter, I have used research on attitude change and persuasion to illustrate two key assumptions that have influenced research in social psychology – the single-effect assumption and the single-process assumption. The single-effect assumption typically dominates early research on a variable when investigators battle over what the effect of some variable is. A good case study is the voluminous literature on the effect of incentives on attitudes. First generation researchers asked: which is a more effective way to change attitudes – providing a person with a large (e.g. $20) incentive for engaging in a counterattitudinal action (e.g. writing an essay against your own point of view), or providing a small (e.g. $1) incentive? Consistent with learning theory, some work suggested that the large incentive was more effective in producing attitude change (e.g. Rosenberg, 1965). However, other work suggested the opposite – that small incentives can be more effective (e.g. Festinger & Carlsmith, 1959). After much debate in the literature in the 1960s about which effect was the correct one, social psychologists eventually abandoned the single-effect assumption and recognized that each effect could be produced reliably depending on the circumstances.

Once social psychologists agree on what the effect of some variable is and when this effect occurs, debate typically centers around the *process* that is responsible for the outcome. The single process assumption is that there is just one true process that is responsible for each effect. For example, social psychologists initially assumed that for the reverse incentive outcome (i.e. when low incentives produce more attitude change than high incentives), there was just one psychological process that was responsible, and the goal of researchers should be to uncover which process was the correct one. Considerable research and journal space in the 1970s centered around determining whether the reverse incentive effect was due to effortful cognitive reorganization stemming from the psychological tension induced by engaging in a discrepant action (as suggested by "dissonance theory," Festinger, 1957), or whether the effect was due to a relatively low effort cognitive inference process based on observation of one's own behavior (as suggested by "self-perception theory," Bem, 1972). Eventually, social psychologists recognized that each process could produce the same outcome (i.e. reverse incentive effect), but in different circumstances (see Fazio, Zanna, & Cooper, 1977).

Currently researchers in this area are wondering about those cases where psychological tension is produced by engaging in discrepant action, and cognitive reorganization takes place; what is the motivation behind the tension and the reorganization? Several alternative motivational frameworks have been proposed (e.g. Aronson, 1992; Cooper & Fazio, 1984; Steele, 1988), and theorists in the 1980s and early 1990s are currently engaged in battle over which is the *one* true motivation that is responsible for these tension/reorganization effects. Given the strong support for each of the motivational positions, however, it is likely that subsequent theorizing will attempt to accommodate multiple motivations by which these effects can be produced, and place these divergent motivations in an overarching framework.

In sum, the history of research in attitude change and persuasion may hold general lessons for the field of social psychology more generally and for any research enterprise. It is now clear that any given variable (e.g. source attractiveness, the mere presence of others) can produce different (even opposite) effects. The presence of many opposite effects in the attitude change domain led some investigators in the 1970s to see the area as a "reigning confusion" (Sherif, 1977, p. 370). These opposite effects for many variables contributed to the crisis in social psychology and the disillusionment with attitudes research in particular (see the editors' introduction to this volume). It *is* confusing when a variable that seems as simple as distraction or a positive mood is shown to both increase and decrease persuasion. Fortunately, this confusion was ended, in part, when researchers recognized that different (and opposite) effects can result from the same underlying process (see figures 17.1 and 17.2). The confusion was further clarified when it was realized that just as one process can be responsible for multiple outcomes, any one effect can be caused by different processes. Theories in social psychology tell us when these different processes operate. Although some investigators continue to cling to a single process model of attitudes (e.g. Fishbein & Middlestadt, 1995), the field in general has embraced multi-process models of persuasion (e.g. Chaiken, Liberman, & Eagly, 1989; Petty & Cacioppo, 1981, 1986) and many other social psychological phenomena (e.g. see Abelson, 1994; Smith, 1994).

Social-psychological work on attitude change has taught us that if we are interested in the effects of any variable, it is probably too simplistic to stop with the first generation question of whether the variable increases or decreases some outcome. It is likely that sometimes the variable increases and sometimes it decreases the outcome. The research enterprise is a quest to determine and understand when each effect occurs (i.e. one variable can have multiple effects, though these different effects can be a product of just one process). Second, however, it is critical to uncover all of the processes linking the variable to its outcomes. There probably isn't just one process involved (i.e. different processes can produce the same outcome). A coherent theory of the variable would account for multiple effects, would likely include multiple processes, and would specify the conditions under which these processes operate, and any differential consequences of these processes. Attitude change researchers have made great strides over the past century in identifying the building blocks of such a coherent theory, though much work remains to be done.

Further Reading

Baker, S. M., & Petty, R. E. (1994). Majority and minority influence: Source-position imbalance as a determinant of message scrutiny. *Journal of Personality and Social Psychology*, *67*, 5–19. The first published "third generation" study on how variables influence message processing.

McGuire, W. J. (1983). A contextualist theory of knowledge: Its implications for innovation and reform in psychological research. In L. Berkowitz (Ed.), *Advances in experimental social psychology* (Vol. 16, pp. 1–47). Orlando, FL: Academic Press. An interesting essay making the argument that opposite results are highly likely in social psychology.

Petty, R. E., & Cacioppo, J. T. (1986). The elaboration likelihood model of persuasion. In L. Berkowitz (Ed.), *Advances in experimental social psychology* (Vol. 19, pp. 123–205). New York: Academic Press. A presentation of the concepts of and research on the elaboration likelihood model of persuasion – a theory that follows the principles outlined in this essay.

References

Abelson, R. P. (1994). A personal perspective on social cognition. In P. G. Devine, D. L. Hamilton & T. M. Ostrom Eds.) *Social cognition: Impact on social psychology* (pp. 15–37). Hillsdale, NJ: Lawrence Erlbaum.

Allport, G. W. (1935). Attitudes. In C. Murchison (Ed.), *Handbook of social psychology* (pp. 798–884). Worcester, MA: Clark University Press.

Aronson, E. (1992). The return of the repressed: Dissonance theory makes a comeback. *Psychological Inquiry*, *3*, 303–311.

Asch, S. E. (1956). Studies of independence and conformity: I. A minority of one against a unanimous majority. *Psychological Monographs*, *70* (9, Whole No. 416).

Baker, S. M., & Petty, R. E. (1994). Majority and minority influence: Source-position imbalance as a determinant of message scrutiny. *Journal of Personality and Social Psychology*, *67*, 5–19.

Bem, D. J. (1972). Self-perception theory. In L. Berkowitz (Ed.), *Advances in experimental social psychology* (Vol. 6, pp. 1–62). New York: Academic Press.

Bornstein, R. F. (1989). Exposure and affect: Overview and meta-analysis of research, 1968–1987. *Psychological Bulletin*, *106*, 265–289.

Brehm, J. W. (1966). *A theory of psychological reactance*. San Diego, CA: Academic Press.

Cacioppo, J. T., Marshall-Goodell, B. S. Tassinary, L. G. & Petty, R. E. (1992) Rudimentary determinants of attitudes: classical conditioning is more effective when prior knowledge about the attitude stimulus is low than high. *Journal of Experimental Social Psychology, 28*, 207–233.

Cacioppo, J. T., & Petty, R. E. (1989). Effects of message repetition on argument processing, recall, and persuasion. *Basic and Applied Social Psychology*, *10*, 3–12.

Chaiken, S. (1987). The heuristic model of persuasion. In M. P. Zanna, J. M. Olson, & C. P. Herman (Eds.), *Social influence: The Ontario symposium* (Vol. 5, pp. 3–39). Hillsdale, NJ: Lawrence Erlbaum.

Chaiken, S., Liberman, A., & Eagly, A. H. (1989). Heuristic and systematic processing within and beyond the persuasion context. In J. S. Uleman & J. A. Bargh (Eds.), *Unintended thought* (pp. 212–252). New York: Guilford Press.

Cooper, J., & Fazio, R. H. (1984). A new look at dissonance theory. In L. Berkowitz (Ed.), *Advances in experimental social psychology* (Vol. 17, pp. 229–266). New York: Academic Press.

Ditto, P. H., & Lopez, D. F. (1992). Motivated skepticism: The use of differential decision criteria for preferred and nonpreferred conclusions. *Journal of Personality and Social Psychology*, *63*, 568–584.

Eagly, A. H., & Chaiken, S. (1993). *The psychology of attitudes*. Forth Worth, TX: Harcourt, Brace, Jovanovich.

Fazio, R. H., Zanna, M. P., & Cooper, J. (1977). Dissonance and self-perception: An integrative view of each theory's proper domain of application. *Journal of Experimental Social Psychology*, *13*, 464–479.

Festinger, L. (1957). *A theory of cognitive dissonance*. Evanston, IL: Row, Peterson.

Festinger, L., & Carlsmith, J. M. (1959). Cognitive consequences of forced compliance. *Journal of Abnormal and Social Psychology*, *58*, 203–210.

Festinger, L., & Maccoby, N. (1964). On resistance to persuasive communications. *Journal of Abnormal and Social Psychology*, *68*, 359–366.

Fishbein, M., & Middlestadt, S. (1995). Non-cognitive effects on attitude formation and change: Fact or artifact? *Journal of Consumer Psychology*, *4*, 181–202.

Friedreich, J., Fetherstonhaugh, D., Casey, S., & Gallagher, D. (1996). Argument integration and attitude change: Suppression effects in the integration of one-sided arguments that vary in persuasiveness. *Personality and Social Psychology Bulletin*, *22*, 179–191.

Greenwald, A. G. (1968). Cognitive learning, cognitive response to persuasion, and attitude change. In A. G. Greenwald, T. C. Brock, & T. M. Ostrom (Eds.), *Psychological foundations of attitudes* (pp. 147–170). New York: Academic Press.

Harkins, S. G., & Petty, R. E. (1981). Effects of source magnification of cognitive effort on attitudes: An information processing view. *Journal of Personality and Social Psychology*, *40*, 401–413.

Hovland, C. I., Janis, I. L., & Kelley, H. H. (1953). *Communication and persuasion: Psychological studies of opinion change*. New Haven, CT: Yale University Press.

Isen, A. (1993). Positive mood and decision making. In Haviland (Ed.), *Handbook of Emotion*, New York: Guilford Press.

Janis, I. L., Kaye, D., & Kirschner, P. (1965). Facilitating effects of "eating while reading" on responsiveness to persuasive communications. *Journal of Personality and Social Psychology*, *1*, 17–27.

Kelman, H. C. (1958). Compliance, identification, and internalization: Three processes of attitude change. *Journal of Conflict Resolution*, *2*, 51–60.

Knower, F. H. (1935). Experimental studies of change in attitude: I. A study of the effect of oral arguments on changes of attitudes. *Journal of Social Psychology*, *6*, 315–347.

Liberman, A., & Chaiken, S. (1992). Defensive processing of personally relevant health messages. *Personality and Social Psychology Bulletin*, *18*, 669–679.

Mackie, D. M., & Worth, L. T. (1991). Feeling good, but not thinking straight: The impact of positive mood on persuasion. In J. Forgas (Ed.), *Emotion and social judgment* (Oxford: Pergamon Press).

McGuire, W. J. (1983). A contextualist theory of knowledge: Its implications for innovation and reform in psychological research. In L. Berkowitz (Ed.), *Advances in experimental social psychology* (Vol. 16, pp. 1–47). Orlando, FL: Academic Press.

McGuire, W. J. (1985). Attitudes and attitude change. In G. Lindzey & E. Aronson (Eds.), *Handbook of social psychology* (Vol. 2, pp. 233–346). New York: Random House.

Meyerowitz, B. E., & Chaiken, S. (1987). The effect of message framing on breast self-examination attitudes, intentions, and behavior. *Journal of Personality and Social Psychology*, *52*, 500–510.

Moscovici, S. (1980). Toward a theory of conversion behavior. In L. Berkowitz (Ed.), *Advances in experimental social psychology* (Vol. 13, pp. 209–239). New York: Academic Press.

Olson, J. M., Roese, N. J., & Zanna, M. P. (in press). Expectancies. In E. T. Higgins & A. W. Kruglanski (Eds.), *Social psychology: Handbook of basic principles*. New York: Guilford.

Petty, R. E., & Brock, T. C. (1981). Thought disruption and persuasion: Assessing the validity of attitude change experiments. In R. E. Petty, T. M. Ostrom, & T. C. Brock (Eds.), *Cognitive responses in persuasion* (pp. 55–79). Hillsdale, NJ: Lawrence Erlbaum.

Petty, R. E., & Cacioppo, J. T. (1979a). Effects of forewarning of persuasive intent and involvement on cognitive responses. *Personality and Social Psychology Bulletin*, *5*, 173–176.

Petty, R. E., & Cacioppo, J. T. (1979b). Issue-involvement can increase or decrease persuasion by enhancing message-relevant cognitive responses. *Journal of Personality and Social Psychology*, *37*, 1915–1926.

Petty, R. E., & Cacioppo, J. T. (1981). *Attitudes and persuasion: Classic and contemporary approaches*. Dubuque, IA: Wm. C. Brown.

Petty, R. E., & Cacioppo, J. T. (1983). The role of bodily responses in attitude measurement and change. In J. T. Cacioppo & R. E. Petty (Eds.), *Social psychophysiology: A sourcebook* (pp. 51–101). New York: Guilford.

Petty, R. E., & Cacioppo, J. T. (1984). The effects of involvement on responses to argument quantity and quality: Central and peripheral routes to persuasion. *Journal of Personality and Social Psychology*, *46*, 69–81.

Petty, R. E., & Cacioppo, J. T. (1986). The elaboration likelihood model of persuasion. In L. Berkowitz (Ed.), *Advances in experimental social psychology* (Vol. 19, pp. 123–205). New York: Academic Press.

Petty, R. E., & Cacioppo, J. T. (1990). Involvement and persuasion: Tradition versus integration. *Psychological Bulletin*, *107*, 367–374.

Petty, R. E., Gleicher, F., & Baker, S. M. (1991). Multiple roles for affect in persuasion. In J. Forgas (Ed.), *Emotion and social judgments* (pp. 181–200). Oxford: Pergamon Press.

Petty, R. E., Gleicher, F. H., & Jarvis, B. (1993). Persuasion theory and AIDS prevention. In J. B. Pryor & G. Reeder (Eds.), *The social psychology of HIV infection* (pp. 155–182). Hillsdale, NJ: Lawrence Erlbaum.

Petty, R. E., Haugtvedt, C. P., & Smith, S. M. (1995). Elaboration as a determinant of attitude strength. In R. E. Petty & J. A. Krosnick (Eds.), *Attitude strength: Antecedents and consequences* (pp. 93–130). Mahwah, NJ: Lawrence Erlbaum.

Petty, R. E., & Krosnick, J. A. (Eds.) (1995). *Attitude strength: Antecedents and consequences*. Mahwah, NJ: Lawrence Erlbaum.

Petty, R. E., Ostrom, T. M., & Brock, T. C. (Eds.) (1981). *Cognitive responses in persuasion*. Hillsdale, NJ: Lawrence Erlbaum.

Petty, R. E., Priester, J. R., & Wegener, D. T. (1994). Cognitive processes in attitude change. In R. S. Wyer & T. K. Srull (Eds.), *Handbook of social cognition* (2nd ed., Vol. 2, pp. 69–142). Hillsdale, NJ: Lawrence Erlbaum.

Petty, R. E., Schumann, D. W., Richman, S. A., & Strathman, A. J. (1993). Positive mood and persuasion: Different roles for affect under high- and low-elaboration conditions. *Journal of Personality and Social Psychology*, *64*, 5–20.

Petty, R. E., Wells, G. L., & Brock, T. C. (1976). Distraction can enhance or reduce yielding to propaganda: Thought disruption versus effort justification. *Journal of Personality and Social Psychology*, *34*, 874–884.

Rosenberg, M. (1965). When dissonance fails: On eliminating evaluation apprehension from attitude measurement. *Journal of Personality and Social Psychology*, *1*, 28–42.

Ross, L., Greene, D., & House, P. (1977). The "false consensus effect": An egocentric bias in social perception and attribution processes. *Journal of Experimental Social Psychology*, *13*, 279–301.

Schwarz, N., Bless, H., & Bohner, G. (1991). Mood and persuasion: Affective states influence the processing of persuasive communications. In M. P. Zanna (Ed.), *Advances in experimental social psychology* (Vol. 24, pp. 161–201). San Diego: Academic Press.

Schwarz, N., & Clore, G. L. (1983). Mood, misattribution, and judgments of well-being: Informative and directive functions of affective states. *Journal of Personality and Social Psychology*, *45*, 513–523.

Sherif, M. (1977). Crisis in social psychology: Some remarks towards breaking through the crisis. *Personality and Social Psychology Bulletin*, *3*, 368–382.

Smith, E. R. (1994). Procedural knowledge and processing strategies in social cognition. In R. S. Wyer (Ed.), *Handbook of social cognition* (Vol. 1, pp. 99–152). Hillsdale, NJ: Lawrence Erlbaum.

Smith, S. M., & Petty, R. E. (1996). Message framing and persuasion: A message processing analysis. *Personality and Social Psychology Bulletin*, *22*, 257–268.

Staats, A. W., & Staats, C. K. (1958). Attitudes established by classical conditioning. *Journal of Abnormal and Social Psychology*, *57*, 37–40.

Steele, C. M. (1988). The psychology of self-affirmation: Sustaining the integrity of the self. In L. Berkowitz (Ed.), *Advances in experimental social psychology* (Vol. 21, pp. 261–302). New York: Academic Press.

Wegener, D. T., & Petty, R. E. (1994). Mood management across affective states: The hedonic contingency hypothesis. *Journal of Personality and Social Psychology*, *66*, 1034–1048.

Wegener, D. T., & Petty, R. E. (1996). Effects of mood on persuasion processes: Enhancing, reducing, and biasing scrutiny of attitude-relevant information. In L. L. Martin & A. Tesser (Eds.), *Striving and feeling: Interactions between goals and affect* (pp. 329–362). Mahwah, NJ: Lawrence Erlbaum.

Wegener, D. T., Petty, R. E., & Smith, S. M. (1995). Positive mood can increase or decrease message scrutiny: The hedonic contingency view of mood and message processing. *Journal of Personality and Social Psychology*, *69*, 5–15.

Worth, L. T., & Mackie, D. M. (1987). Cognitive mediation of positive affect in persuasion. *Social Cognition*, *5*, 76–94.

Zajonc, R. B. (1968). Attitudinal effects of mere exposure. *Journal of Personality and Social Psychology Monograph Supplements*, *9*, 1–27.

18

The relevance of language for social psychology

Gün R. Semin

Gün Semin was born in 1944, in Istanbul, Turkey. His first two degrees in psychology were at the Free University Berlin, 1968; he took his doctorate at the University of London, LSE, 1974. His first journal publications were in 1973. He was Research Fellow, University of London, LSE (1969–1972), and Lecturer and Reader at the University of Sussex from 1972 to 1990. Since 1990 he has been Professor and Chair, Department of Social Psychology, Free University Amsterdam. He is Scientific Director of the Kurt Lewin Graduate School for social psychology and its applications; Past President of the European Association of Experimental Social Psychology; and Fellow of the Alexander von Humboldt Foundation.

Of the numerous themes that straddle social psychology one has always struck me as a perennial intellectual challenge and problem. The challenge is simply the question of how one reconciles the individual and social levels of analyses. The tension between the individual and the social is not only a creative tension but it is also the source of an intellectual chasm within social psychology. It is a question that has been raised and addressed in many different historical contexts (see Semin, 1986). Early attempts to resolve this duality are to be found in the *Völkerpsychologie*-tradition that was established by Lazarus and Steinhal (1860) and others (Lazarus, 1861; Waitz, 1859; Wedewer, 1860). This then newly emerging "discipline" consisted of an attempt to introduce a level of analysis that would be more encompassing than that prevailing in the psychology of the mid-nineteenth century. More recently, this debate was

The writing of this paper was facilitated by an NWO Grant PGS 56-381. I would like to thank Craig McGarty and Alex Haslam for their helpful comments on an earlier draft of this paper.

the early and mid-1970s in social psychology (e.g. Israel & he intellectual chasm can be found in the fact that the very same heart of many of the debates that have led to major divisions contemporary social psychology – particularly European social is also at the core of some of the recent divisions that have retically and methodologically (Gergen, 1985; Harré & Secord, 1972, inter alia).

The question itself is relatively simple. How does one reconcile the individualist level of analysis in a branch of psychology that is expected, if not supposed, to address the "social," and not merely, individual functioning. The way this has been dealt with in mainstream social psychology is by retaining a type of dualism that is inherent in a methodological commitment to individual reductionism (cf. Moscovici, 1984; Tajfel, 1972; Sampson, 1981, inter alia). This commitment is accompanied by a tacit assumption about the existence of "society" outside of the individual.

In the following, I would like to start by drawing attention to a particular paradox that has emerged in social psychology as a consequence of this methodological commitment to individual and the absenting of the social. I single out this particular example, since it allows me to use language as an illustrative way out of the duality created by the individual and the social levels of analyses and it also allows me to elaborate on the important and central role that language has yet to come to play in an emergent social psychology.

The Paradox

Social psychology is often defined as the analysis and explanation of social behavior (cf. Kimble, 1990, p. 2; Sears, Peplau, & Taylor, 1991, p. 2; Sabini, 1992, p. 1, inter alia). And yet the prominent focus in mainstream social psychology is and has, for a long time been on the analysis and explanation of intrapsychological processes (cognitive and affective). As Markus and Zajonc (1985) have pointed out, "Social psychology and cognitive social psychology are today nearly synonymous. The cognitive approach is now clearly the dominant approach among social psychologists, having virtually no competitors" (1985, p. 137). Although this statement is over ten years old this situation has not changed dramatically. Even in the analysis of intergroup processes and self-categorization the focus is primarily on a tradition of cognitive processes, and one can argue, as some have, that central theories in this field are "a prime candidate for reduction to 'basic' information processing laws" (Tetlock, 1986, p. 255; Jahoda, 1986). The paradox comes about through the fact that while the goal is to explain social behavior, the persistent methodological commitment has been to the processes or properties of individual agents. In other words, *the methodological commitment has been to intrapsychological processes rather than social behavior* (interpsychological processes) *or even the interface between these two*. What is and has been missing is a conceptual loop that brings the two disparate chains into some coherent interface that is empirically examinable. Such a change also requires a shift in methodological commitment from that of the individual to that of the social.

It is in this context that one has to start thinking about what it is that enables social behavior and interaction. The answer is simple enough: symbolic communication which can take place by means of verbal or non-verbal symbols – G. H. Mead established this much some time ago (e.g. 1934). Indeed, Meadian social psychology treated forms of language as the mediators not only of cognition and consciousness but of the self and social interaction (cf. Rock, 1979, pp. 111 ff.); an issue that is beginning to attract renewed attention in the context of socio-cultural theory and semiotic mediation (e.g. Wertsch, 1991).

I would like to argue here that the absence of a fruitful link between interpsychological and intrapsychological processes has primarily been due to the fact that in contrast to the analysis of intrapsychological processes, to date, *we have not developed a handle on symbolic communication that allows us to make it amenable to systematic analysis.*

In principle, developing such a handle on social behavior is, first of all, to advance an approach to language and thus symbolic communication that could furnish the analysis of interpsychological processes with a privileged theoretical and empirical status. By privileged I mean a conceptual status that facilitates its analysis and empirical examination in a manner analogous to that afforded for intrapsychological processes. Not only that, I also mean a status that allows us to interface the interpsychological (social behavior) with the intrapsychological in a meaningful way so that the interactive relation between the two types of processes can be sensibly examined.

This argument is in itself not new. Pointing out the relevance of language for social psychology has been a fashionable argument in the social sciences and some of the more critical approaches to social psychology in particular and psychology in general (e.g. social constructionism, etc.). Unfortunately, these critical reflections upon the import of language to social psychological processes have remained policy statements without much, if any, systematic research ensuing from them. Most of the work has remained descriptive and has been unable to link the interpsychological with the intrapsychological. The difference between these approaches and the orientation represented here is that the current orientation proposes a link between the interpsychological and the intrapsychological (cf. Semin, 1995). This is not necessarily an easy argument since it requires some rethinking of the way we consider language and cognition.

The Centrality of Language for Symbolic Communication

Symbolic communication by which social interaction is maintained is a complex medium and its complexity has made it difficult to treat it in such a way that it is accessible to the systematic and objective analysis that is commonly regarded as the road to a science. It is no doubt the case that physical interactions without verbal exchange are a rarity. It would certainly appear to be correct if one were to say that the somewhat direct forms of physical interactions are increasingly being replaced by verbal and other relatively abstract forms of interaction and exchange, particularly in the emerging form of late twentieth-century society, which can be best described as an "*information culture*." It is primarily in the form of words that information about human interactions and other events is communicated and stored. We live in a world where words have in fact taken over from behaviors in terms of physical or non-verbal communication. Indeed, we were on the way to losing our reliance on non-verbal communication the moment humanity tripped over the fact that words can capture more complex forms of reality and abstract them in a more economical manner. Words have in the mean time become a weapon in an information society that is in fact increasingly becoming incapable of dealing with non-verbal action.[1] We plan, broker, initiate, guide, bully, love, terrorize, terminate, justify, or challenge through words. It is in words that we engage in social interaction and it is through a better *understanding of words and their use* that we can begin to appreciate social behavior. Much of our behavior essentially involves communication and is manifested in language use. Thus, studying language may contribute to unfolding interpsychological processes.

But if words are the means by which social behavior is realized, then an analysis of symbolic communication must begin with an approach that makes language accessible to an objective analysis. It is to this point that I now turn. This is relatively important since it constitutes a manner in which one can address the entire circle of social interaction taking into account the intra- as well as interpsychological processes in the analysis of social-psychological phenomena.

Symbolic Communication as Tool Use

The idea or metaphor that language is a tool upon which knowledge is mapped is critical to the development of this perspective. I use this analogy expressly to invite you to think about linguistic devices such as verbs, adjectives, and nouns very much in the way in which one would think about hammers, saws, and pliers. These tools, which are feats of centuries of engineering, are not only the *products* of experience and knowledge, they also *represent* this knowledge. There is no doubt that I can split a piece of wood into two with a hammer; but a saw is a more sophisticated tool engineered for this purpose. Indeed, I can push a nail into wood with the end of a saw, but a hammer is a more appropriate tool to do so. Yet certain hammers have other properties. They are also suitable for extracting nails, and so on. These special tools contain the distilled knowledge about the relationship between a task and the best fit between a task or goal and human propensities (in particular physical ones, namely, movement, handling, vision, etc.).

One task that the "language as a tool" metaphor entails is to examine and reveal the distinctive properties of such tools. In the case of interpersonal language, the *first* step for such a task is to identify the types of tools that are available. The second step is to determine the particular jobs for which such tools have been tailored. Obviously, these two steps are not independent from each other. We are able to identify properties of tools such as hammers, saws, and pliers more readily because the match between task, tool, and movement is more discernible. In contrast, the properties of linguistic tools are not so transparent. This is especially because language, in most of its facets (apart from its surface semantics), constitutes what Polanyi (1967) termed "tacit knowledge." Its properties are implicit.

The first type of research (examining the properties of tools) is, by definition, decontextualized in that it focuses on "language" in the abstract. Therefore, it does not constitute an investigation of "language in use," or "speech" (cf. de Saussure, 1914/1960; Ricoeur, 1955). "Language-in-use" is the medium of communication *par excellence*. This is the subject of the second type of research which I would like to use in order to illustrate different possibilities of interfacing the inter- and intrapsychological. In the latter case, the research questions are, among other things, about the strategic use of tools to communicate our intentions and goals in discourse; how such communication impacts others.

An Approach to the Tools of Interpersonal Language

The analysis of the tools of interpersonal language is in the first instance a decontextualized one. This approach is informed by a distinction that is widely shared and regarded as one of the central contributions by Ferdinant de Saussure and Louis Hjelmslev, namely the distinction between *langue* and *parole*, or language and speech. There exist a number of other distinctions that mimic the relationship between language as an abstract property of a linguistic community of speakers and its use, namely language and discourse, code and message (cf. Ricœur, 1955) or pragmatic and semantic meaning contexts (Meertz, 1985, *inter alia*). What is the relationship between language and speech? The answer to this question provides us a rationale for examining interpersonal tools separately from their use in everyday contexts. In order to be able to communicate an intention, experience, idea, wish, or desire, I have to access a medium that is "objective," namely shared and detached from each and every person. In Vygotsky's terms:

> In order to transmit some experience or content of consciousness to another person, there is no other path than to ascribe the content to a known class, to a known group of phenomena, and as we know this necessarily requires generalisation. Thus, it turns out that social interaction necessarily presupposes generalisation and the development of word meaning, i.e., generalisation becomes possible with the development of social interaction. (Vygotsky, 1956/1987, pp. 48–49)

Thus, if you were to read the sentence "The sun is rising" then you know what it "means." But consider different contexts in which the same sentence is uttered by (1) one of two spies in the process of bugging an embassy office; (2) a couple in bed, who are married to different people; or (3) a farmer's wife to her husband. The sentence acquires different rhetorical qualities as a function of context and conveys completely different meanings. For the spies: "We must get out soon"; (2) for the couple: "My spouse may be coming back any time now"; and (3) for the farmers: "It's time to feed the animals," etc. But the sentence also carries a power *in vacuo*, a certain invariance, which is how you understood in reading it the first time without a context, namely "*The sun is rising*" – full stop. This is the distinction that is referred to by some as the difference between the pragmatic and semantic value or meaning. "Pragmatic meaning is defined as meaning that is dependent on context, while the semantic value of a sign is the meaning, or notional core, that it has apart from contextual factors" (Meertz, 1985, p. 5). The decontextualized semantic value of words function as powerful invariant linguistic tools which in their variable strategic use convey what is referred to as indexical information (Garfinkel, 1967; Mehan & Wood, 1975). Thus, an analysis of the tools of interpersonal language acquires some importance, since without an understanding of their properties it is difficult to understand their significance in use contexts. Three questions arise in this context, namely (1) What are the features of the sentence "The sun is rising." in the abstract, in contrast to its utterance in the context of an embassy bugging, etc., in other words, between "language" and "speech?" (2) Related to (1), what are the features of the abstracted medium that I am accessing when I am communicating? And finally, (3) how is the sentence uttered "in vacuum" made meaningful in distinct and different ways from the sentence being uttered in a very specific context?

As Ricœur (1955) argues, *language* as a system is "virtual and outside of time" (p. 530); it has no subject. That is, the sentence "The sun is rising." on its own, does not evoke the question "Who is speaking?" the words and properties of such sentences can be understood with reference to language as a system; and what is more, *language as a system (e.g. syntax, semantics) is the "condition for communication*" (p. 531). That is, whereas *language* is timeless, without a subject and without a world, *speech* takes place in time; refers to its speakers (has subjectivity) and refers to a world and of course involves interlocutors. Thus, the knowledge represented in *language* is virtually "every person's," in that it is anonymous, "objective," and detached from contextual circumstances (i.e., personal, situational, etc.) and it facilitates the "reciprocity of perspectives through its detachment from the uniqueness of the individuals involved" (Semin & Manstead, 1979). In this context, it is important not to forget that language is the condition for speech and communication.[2]

The Tools of Interpersonal Communication

The analysis of the tools of interpersonal communication addresses the identification of the linguistic devices by which we characterize, describe, and classify social interaction and its actors. In principle, one can look at any communicative act in a number of different ways: its manifest content, its structural and mechanical characteristics; the types of tools that are used; the meta-semantic properties of such tools, etc. A research field that I have been engaged in for some time set out explicitly to identify categories of interpersonal terms as tools of communication about persons, their relationships, and interactions. The aim of such work is to then analyze the properties of such tools. Summarily, one can describe this research as comprising of getting a systematic handle upon interpersonal language by proceeding through the following three steps: (1) developing a taxonomy or classification of the tools of interpersonal language; (2) identifying the type of knowledge that is systematically mapped or coded in interpersonal language (e.g. the *types of cognitive inferences* that are systematically mediated by these tools); and, finally (3) identifying the uses that they can be put to.

Let me provide a brief overview of some of the work we have done to illustrate these points (cf. Semin & Greenslade, 1985; Semin & Fiedler, 1991; Semin & Marsman, 1994). Our aim was to develop a framework that would enable us to analyze how interpersonal language marks both the *features of social interaction* and the *properties of persons*. To this end, we began by identifying a number of convergent linguistic criteria by means of which it was possible to systematically differentiate between different types of interpersonal verbs and adjectives.[3]

Why is it relevant to analyze the properties of these linguistic devices or tools? Earlier on, when I gave the example of tools I referred to linguistic devices in much the same way as one would to saws, hammers, screw drivers, etc. There are particular purposes for which saws are suitable and others for which hammers are appropriate. The way in which these tools are designed represents the knowledge that has been accumulated and invested over centuries. One can therefore speak of the cognitive properties of such tools. Similarly, in using language, one makes (mostly unconsciously) strategic choices about the most suitable word or words to achieve or realize the goal or purpose one has in mind. Properties of tools refers to the types of things that one can do with such tools, that is *their* cognitive properties (cf. Semin, 1995) which define the range of things that are possible. Tools are not arbitrarily useable and are optimally suited for some tasks but not all.

For instance, if I find out that verbs depicting actions focus the origin of the action (help, cheat, amuse) upon the sentence subject and verbs depicting states (like, hate, admire) focus the origin of the event to the sentence object then I have an idea of a *systematic cognitive property of the tool* (Semin, 1995). Given a particular event, I can use different linguistic categories to depict it in a sentence (e.g. (a) John hit David; (b) John hurt David; (c) John hates David; or, (d) John is aggressive). If I know that the verbs in sentences (a) and (b) focus the origin of the depicted event to John and in sentence (c) to David, then I have a clear idea of what the different linguistic tools can do in symbolic communication. Such an analysis of the *cognitive properties of linguistic tools* reverses a persistent methodological commitment of psychological research. It entails a *shift of attention from processes or properties that are attributed to individual agents to the properties of the tools by which social communication and interaction are enabled.* Therefore, this step, namely analyzing the cognitive properties of tools (not individuals) constitutes an important step towards privileging the status of the interpsychological in social psychology.

Next, I shall illustrate how knowledge of such tools allows us to examine not only their strategic use in communicative contexts but also how knowledge of tool properties allows us to infer the cognitive processes that systematically mediate strategic communication. There are a few fields in which such strategic language use has been demonstrated (e.g. de Poot & Semin, 1995; Semin, Rubini, & Fiedler, 1995; Semin & de Poot, 1996), but I shall in the following focus on the work of Anne Maass and her colleagues to illustrate the point about strategic language use as tool use in the context of stereotypes and their communication.

The Strategic Use of Tools in Communicative Contexts – The Case of Stereotype Transmission

It is possible to investigate how people use language in a strategic manner to communicate stereotypes in a rather subtle and even subconscious manner (cf. Franco & Maass, 1996) only when one has a clear idea of the cognitive properties of the tools that are employed in the interpersonal domain. This is very much like deciphering the implicational meanings of a secret language. Such a deciphering reveals why particular tools are used in particular contexts and for what purpose. It is not only possible to examine why particular tools are used but also what types of cognitive implications they are expected to mediate and thus which types of effects or influence the produced verbal behavior is intended to have. This means that a systematic knowledge of the tools used in communication reveals three psychologically important aspects of interpsychological processes which are not necessarily revealed by a methodological commitment to the individual. These are: (1) What are the motives of the person communicating a stereotype? (2) What strategic decisions does such a person make in order to convey a particular intended content and goal? And finally, (3) what function does such a communicative composition have?

An added advantage of the precise understanding of the implications of interpersonal tools is the precise quantitative objectification of verbal behavior that is also a reliable method. The research on the transmission and maintenance of stereotyping is on a well-researched phenomenon, namely the so-called linguistic intergroup bias (LIB), introduced by Maass and her colleagues (Maass, Salvi, Arcuri, & Semin, 1989; Maass, Milesi, Zabbini, & Stahlberg, 1994; Fiedler, Semin, & Finkenauer, 1993; Rubini & Semin, 1994, inter alia).

This research question is about how positive perceptions of the ingroup and negative perceptions of an outgroup are not only maintained in the face of contradictory evidence, but how they are transmitted. The emphasis is on *transmitted* – namely, what are the types of verbal behaviors that are manifested in order to achieve or influence specific types of intrapsychological ends? The main argument that is used by the linguistic intergroup bias approach is that positive behaviors when they are performed by the ingroup lead to descriptions of such behaviors with more abstract predicates (e.g. "She is helpful and kind"). In contrast, if the same behavior is performed by an outgroup member, then it is described with concrete predicates (e.g. she held the door open for somebody). The reverse is the case with negative behaviors. When such a behavior is performed by an ingroup member, then concrete predicates are used to describe the behavior (e.g. "She insulted somebody"). However, if the same negative behavior is performed by an outgroup member then an abstract predicate is more likely to be used (e.g. "She is rude or aggressive").

In principle, any given event could be described at any level of predicate use identified in the linguistic category model (see Semin & Fielder, 1991). Thus, a particular event of aggression can be described as "John punched David," or "John hurts David," "John hates David," or "John is violent or aggressive." There are two points that are relevant given the choice that is available. The first one is that, as the research on this subject shows, predicate choice in describing such behaviors as a function of group membership is not random. More importantly, the choice of predicates conveys something more than the mere surface semantics. The more abstract predicate choice implies greater stability of the behavior in question and higher likelihood of the behavior being repeated in the future. Thus, if one is confronted with a positive behavior of an out-group member, then predicate choice in describing such behavior becomes critical. One does not wish to convey an impression of denying reality or denigrating it. Thus, the best possible choice is to use tools that convey the impression that the event was situated, particularistic, and temporary and not open to challenge. In contrast, the same behavior performed by an ingroup is conveyed with abstract predicates, conveying the impression of a positive feature that is a stable characteristic of the ingroup member.

The first set of experiments (Maass, Salvi, Arcuri, & Semin, 1989) used members of competing real-life groups in a horse race competition in Ferrara (Italy). In two critical experiments utilizing different dependent measures (including open-ended descriptions of positive and negative behaviors of in- and out-group members), it was shown that people use more abstract predicates when describing positive in-group and negative out-group behaviors and more concrete predicates when describing positive out-group and negative in-group behaviors.

This phenomenon has been demonstrated in a number of different contexts and settings such as sports teams, nations, political groups (Rubini & Semin, 1994) and in mass media reports (Maass, Corvino, & Arcuri, 1994). The more recent developments of this research have been concerned with making differential predictions about the types of intrapsychological processes that may be responsible for the generation of specific strategic tool choices in order to subtly transmit stereotypes (Maass et al., 1994). The contrasting models that have been examined are between an expectancy versus ingroup-protective motivational-based predictions. Thus, the question has become whether the particular verbal behaviors in question are driven by cognitive or motivational factors (cf. Rubini & Semin, 1994). The expectancy-based model predicts that expectancy congruent behavior, irrespective of whether the behavior in question is positive or negative and irrespective of whether or not it is performed by the in-group or the out-group, will be described in abstract terms. Thus, if Italians regard themselves as lazy (a negative property) then such behavior that is typically classifiable as lazy will be described with abstract predicates, although it is regarded as a negative characteristic. Similarly, if the outgroup performs a behavior that is regarded as positive but typical then this also will be communicated with the use of abstract predicates. In contrast, unexpected or surprising behavior will be described in concrete terms. The opposite predictions are derivable from a motivational perspective. One possible implication of Tajfel and Turner's (1979) social identity theory is that LIB reflects an in-group protective motivation. This perspective, in contrast to the differential expectancy model suggests that irrespective of expectancies, LIB will occur as a function of the valence of the behaviors in question. Indeed, Maass et al. (1994) in a series of three experiments find support for the expectancy hypothesis rather than the in-group protective motivation notion. However, more recently, Maass and Stahlberg (1993) have reported that under conditions where intergroup competition is high and salient one finds that the LIB is more pronounced than in the differential expectancies condition. Taken together, Maass and Stahlberg (1993) suggest that differential expectations are sufficient to produce the LIB. However, under heightened intergroup competition conditions the in-group-protective motivation increases this effect. They could show that there is a correlation between the degree to which the bias is manifested and self-esteem. More importantly, their research extends the applicability of this bias, with qualifications, from the intergroup context to interindividual relationships, namely verbal exchange about "friends" and "enemies."

These studies taken altogether constitute a programmatic attempt to investigate the processes that are involved in the translation of specific intrapsychological processes into a medium: namely, language and language use. Their aim and design is to demonstrate how particular intrapsychological processes lead to strategic tool use with the purpose of conveying preferences that can affect the recipient of the message. This step, namely the step of how and whether the strategic use of tools influence the recipient of the message has as yet not been analyzed empirically in the context of LIB. The process of strategic language use and its influence upon a recipient has also been analyzed systematically in a different context, namely how strategic word choice in the formulation of questions can influence a respondent's answers without their awareness (cf. Semin & de Poot, 1996; Semin, Rubini, & Fiedler, 1995, inter alia).

The Relevance of Language for Social Psychology: Conclusions

There is no doubt that the importance of language for social psychology was recognized relatively early on. Indeed, if one regards attribution theory as one of the most successful conceptual frameworks that has dominated social psychology for a considerable period of time, then one has to realize that this was based on Heider's (1958) original, careful, and insightful analyses of language in his volume on *The psychology of interpersonal relations*. His detailed analysis of a number of specific linguistic expressions that are highly relevant to the interpersonal domain were primarily interpreted in a *Zeitgeist* which had a methodological commitment to the individual and therefore had to disregard the analysis of powerful linguistic devices. If it is the case that the purpose of social psychology is to examine the establishment of a social reality and interpsychological processes, then an important task is to investigate the glue that holds persons together in communication. It is this persistent message, that has been signaled from the early nineteenth-century psychologists who were concerned with *Völkerpsychologie* to the inspirational work on language and interpersonal relations by Heider that we, in my view, have to take more seriously. Language and its strategic use is the paramount social reality within which all social psychological process take place, are manifested and managed. It is the pursuit of the subtle but fascinating properties of this medium which brings us together, by which we cheat or influence each other. It is the medium through which we gossip or prejudge others, argue, help, advise. Language is the most generally authorized artifact for which there are no individual authors. It is therefore one of the best instances of that aspect of our lives that is truly social and without which we would not be able to experience and communicate our subjective existences. It is words that are the most important glue of social behavior and it is the chemical composition of this glue that we have to understand better if we want to develop a social psychology that is attentive to an important aspect of what it means to be social.

Notes

1. Indeed, non-verbal action or non-representational behavior is the undoing of the information culture which we live in.
2. Indeed, to the extent that language is a condition for speech, discourse or communication, it is also *reproduced* in any speech event. As Giddens (1976) points out: "Language exists as a 'structure', syntactical and semantic, only in so far as there are some kind of traceable consistencies in what people say, in the speech acts which they perform. From this aspect to refer to rules of syntax, for example, is to refer to the reproduction of 'like elements'; on the other hand, such rules *generate* the totality of speech acts which is the spoken language. It is this dual aspect of structure, as both inferred from observations of human doings, and yet as also operating as a medium whereby these doings are made possible, that has to be grasped through the notions of structuration and reproduction" (pp. 121–122, emphasis in the original).
3. This procedure circumvents the problem of circularity in defining categories by psychological criteria alone.

Further Reading

Giles, H., & Robinson, W. P. (1990). *Handbook of language and social psychology.* Chichester: Wiley.

Semin, G. R., & Fiedler, K. (1992). *Language, interaction and social cognition.* London: Sage.

References

de Poot, C., & Semin, G. R. (1995). Pick your verbs with care when you formulate a question! *Journal of Language and Social Psychology*, *14*, 351–369

de Saussure, F. (1914/1960). *Course in general linguistics.* London: Peter Owen.

Fiedler, K., Semin, G. R., & Finkenauer, C. (1993). The battle of words between gender groups: A language-based approach to intergroup processes. *Human*

Communication Research, *19*, 409–441.

Fiedler, K., Semin, G. R., & Finkenauer, K. (1994). Welchen Spielraum läßt die Sprache für die Attribution? In F. Försterling & J. Stiensmeier-Pester (Eds.), *3. Bielefelder Symposium über Attribution*. Göttingen: Hogrefe.

Franco, F. M., & Maass, A. (1996). The linguistic intergroup bias: Is it under intentional control? Paper presented in the European Association of Experimental Social Psychology Meeting at Gmünden, Austria, July, 1996.

Garfinkel, H. (1967). *Studies in ethnomethodology*. New York: Prentice Hall.

Gergen, K. J. (1985). The social constructionist movement in modern psychology. *American Psychologist*, *40*, 266–275.

Giddens, A. (1976). *New rules of sociological method*. London: Hutchinson.

Harré, R., & Secord, P. F. (1972). *The explanation of social behaviour*. Oxford: Blackwell.

Heider, F. (1958). *The psychology of interpersonal relations*. New York: Wiley.

Higgins, E. T., & and Kruglanski, A. (in press). *Social psychology: Handbook of basic principles*. New York: Guilford.

Israel. J., & Tajfel, H. (1972). *The context of social psychology*. London: Academic Press.

Jahoda, M. (1986). Small selves in small groups. *British Journal of Social Psychology*, *25*, 253–254.

Kimble, C. E. (1990). *Social psychology: Studying social interaction*. Dubuque, IA: Wm. C. Brown.

Lazarus, M. (1861). Über das Verhältnis des Einzelnen zur Gesamtheit. *Zeitschrift für Völkerpsychologie und Sprachwissenschaft*, *2*, 393–453.

Lazarus, M., & Steinhal, H. (1860). Einleitende Gedanken über Völkerpsychologie als Einladung zu einer Zeitschrift für Völkerpsychologie und Sprachwissenschaft. *Zeitschrift für Völkerpsychologie und Sprachwissenschaft*, *1*, 1–73.

Maass, A., & Stahlberg, D. (1993). The linguistic intergroup bias: the role of differential expectancies and in-group protective motivation. Paper presented at the conference of the EAESP, Lisbon, September.

Maass, A., Corvino, G., & Arcuri, L. (1994). Linguistic intergroup bias and the mass media. *Revue de Psychologie Sociale*, *1*, 31–43.

Maass, A., Milesi, A., Zabbini, S., & Stahlberg, D. (1994). The linguistic intergroup bias: Differential expectancies or in-group-protection? *Journal of Personality and Social Psychology*, *68*, 116–126.

Maass, A., Salvi, D., Arcuri, L., & Semin, G. R. (1989). Language use in intergroup contexts: The linguistic intergroup bias. *Journal of Personality and Social Psychology*, *57*, 981–993.

Markus, H., & Zajonc, R. B. (1985). The cognitive perspective in social psychology. In G. Lindzey & E. Aronson (Eds.), *The handbook of social psychology* (3rd ed., Vol. 1, pp. 127–230). New York: Random House.

Mead, G. H. (1934). *The social psychology of George Herbert Mead*. Chicago, IL: University of Chicago Press.

Meertz, E. (1985). Beyond symbolic anthropology: Introducing semiotic mediation. In E. Meertz & R. J. Parmentier (Eds.), *Semiotic mediation* (pp. 1–22). New York: Academic Press.

Mehan, H., & Wood, H. J. (1975). *Studies in ethnomethodology*. New York: Wiley.

Moscovici, S. (1984). The phenomenon of social representations. In R. M. Farr & S. Moscovici (Eds.), *Social representations* (pp. 1–42). Cambridge: CUP.

Polanyi, M. (1967). *The tacit dimension*. London: Routledge.

Ricœur, P. (1955). The model of the text: Meaningful action considered as text. *Social Research*, *38*, 530–547.

Rock, P. (1979). *The making of symbolic interactionism*. London: Macmillan.

Rubini, M., & Semin, G. R. (1994). Language use in the context of congruent and incongruent in-group behaviours. *British Journal of Social Psychology*, *33*, 355–362.

Sabini, J. (1992). *Social psychology*. New York: W. W. Norton.

Sampson, E. E. (1981). Cognitive psychology as ideology. *American Psychologist*, *26*, 730–745.

Sears, D. O., Peplau, L. A., & Taylor, S. E. (1991). *Social psychology*. Englewood Cliffs, NJ: Prentice Hall.

Semin, G. R. (1986). The individual, the social and the social individual. *British Journal of Social Psychology*, *25*, 177–180.

Semin, G. R. (1989). On genetic social psychology: A rejoinder to Doise. *European Journal of Social Psychology*, *19*, 401–405.

Semin, G. R. (1995). Interfacing language and social cognition. *Journal of Language and Social Psychology*, *14*, 182–196.

Semin, G. R., & de Poot, C. J. (in press). You might regret it if you don't notice how a question is worded! *Journal of Personality and Social Psychology*.

Semin, G. R., & Fiedler, K. (1988). The cognitive functions of linguistic categories in describing persons: Social cognition and language. *Journal of Personality and Social Psychology*, *54*, 558–568.

Semin, G. R., & Fiedler, K. (1989). Relocating attributional phenomena within the language-cognition interface: The case of actor-observer perspectives. *European Journal of Social Psychology*, *19*, 491–508.

Semin, G. R., & Fiedler, K. (1991). The linguistic category model, its bases, applications and range. In W. Stroebe & M. Hewstone (Eds.), *European Review of Social Psychology* (Vol. 2, pp. 1–30). Chichester: Wiley.

Semin, G. R., & Fiedler, K. (1992a). Language, interaction and social cognition – introduction. In G. R. Semin & K. Fiedler (Eds.), *Language, interaction and social cognition*. London, California: Sage Publications.

Semin, G. R., & Fiedler, K. (1992b). The configuration of social interaction in interpersonal terms. In G. R. Semin & K. Fiedler (Eds.), *Language, interaction and social cognition*. London, California: Sage Publications.

Semin, G. R., & Greenslade, L. (1985). Differential contributions of linguistic factors to memory based ratings: Systematizing the systematic distortion hypothesis. *Journal of Personality and Social Psychology*, *49*, 1713–1723.

Semin, G. R., & Manstead, A. S. R. (1979). Social psychology: Social or psychological? *British Journal of Social and Clinical Psychology*, *18*, 191–202.

Semin, G. R., & Marsman, G. (1994). On the information mediated by interpersonal verbs: Event precipitation, dispositional inference and implicit causality. *Journal of Personality and Social Psychology*, *67*, 836–849.

Semin, G. R., Rubini, M., & Fiedler, K. (1995). The answer is in the question: The effect of verb causality upon locus of explanation. *Personality and Social Psychology Bulletin*, *21*, 834–841.

Tajfel, H. (1972). Experiments in a vacuum. In J. Israel & H. Tajfel (Eds.), *The context of social psychology* (pp. 69–122). London: Academic Press.

Tajfel, H. & Turner, J. C. (1979). An integrative theory of intergroup conflict. In W. G. Austin & S. Worchel (Eds.) *The social psychology of intergroup relations*. (pp. 33–47) Monterey, CA: Brooks/Cole.

Tetlock, P. E. (1986). Is self-categorization the solution to the level-of analysis problem? *British Journal of Social Psychology*, *25*, 255–256.

Tetlock, P. E., & Manstead, A. S. R. (1985). Impression management versus intrapsychic explanations in social psychology: A useful dichotomy. *Psychological Review*, *85*, 68–88.

Vygotsky, L. S. (1956/1987). *The collected works of L. S. Vygotsky. Vol. 1 Problems of general psychology*. New York & London: Plenum Press.

Waitz, T. (1859). Psychologische Anthropologie. *Zeitschrift für Völkerpsychologie und Sprachwissenschaft*, *1*, 387–412.

Wedewer, H. (1860). Über the Wichtigkiet und Bedeutung der Sprache. *Zeitschrift für Völkerpsychologie und Sprachwissenschaft*, *1*, 180.

Wertsch, J. V. (1991). *Voices of the mind*. London: Harvester Wheatsheaf.

19

Integrating the Psychological and the Social to Understand Human Behavior

Eliot R. Smith and
Diane M. Mackie

Eliot R. Smith (born in 1950) received his doctorate from Harvard University in 1975, the same year as his first social psychological publication. His dissertation was supervised by Thomas F. Pettigrew. He has taught at the University of California, Riverside and is currently Professor of Psychological Sciences at Purdue University. Dr Smith has served as a journal editor and has chaired a governmental grant review panel. He is the author of three books and over sixty chapters and scientific journal articles, most in the areas of his major research interests, social perception and social memory.

Diane M. Mackie was born in New Zealand in 1955 and received an undergraduate degree from the University of Auckland two years before her first research publication in 1979. Since receiving her doctorate (supervised by Joel Cooper) at Princeton University in 1984, Dr Mackie has served on the faculty at the University of California, Santa Barbara, where she is currently Professor of Psychology. Her research on social influence, persuasion, and intergroup perception has resulted in over fifty published articles and chapters. In addition to serving on several journal editorial boards, Dr Mackie has been active in both the Society of Personality and Social Psychology and the Society of Experimental Social Psychology.

From Topic-Specific Theories to Common Principles

To social psychologists, long familiarity makes the landscape of our discipline appear natural, even inevitable. Yet in reality the structure and emphases of our field are products of specific historical contingencies. Even more than most sciences, social psychology has been shaped by events and concerns external to the field itself. Reaction against the behaviorist movement in psychology in the 1920s and 1930s, the desire to contribute to the war effort and to understand Nazism in the 1940s and 1950s, and the continuing concern with intergroup conflict in the 1980s and 1990s, are just three examples of external forces that have profoundly shaped our field.

Social psychology responded to such forces by giving birth to new substantive research areas. In many cases, whether because of a particularly influential early contribution or because of the *Zeitgeist* in which an area emerged, specific theoretical approaches and research paradigms became associated with an area. The result is that our field is composed of a series of fairly specific pairings of topics and theoretical approaches. For example, since the early 1980s persuasion researchers have focused on the role of "cognitive responses" in mediating attitude change, but researchers studying the self-concept, group interaction, or stereotyping don't use this particular theoretical construct. Attraction researchers have often relied on equity or cost–benefit models, which have not been widely applied to persuasion or stereotyping. Attribution, altruism, and aggression are each explained with still other principles.

The scientific state of affairs in social psychology mirrors the conceptual landscape of psychology, and indeed of the social sciences in general. In contrast to the growing theoretical integration both within and across disciplines that has accompanied the remarkable recent progress in chemistry, physics, and biology, social science researchers have often argued that their disciplines must stand independent of the principles that govern the nonsocial world or even the principles that predominate in their sister disciplines. For example, mainstream economics has often dismissed evidence that human decision-making departs substantially from the "optimal" or "rational" ideal. Of course, diversity of theoretical and methodological approaches is important for the discovery of new knowledge. Still, progress in science is severely hampered when empirical observations are explained by an assortment of independent or even mutually contradictory middle-level theories, each unconnected to the knowledge being developed in neighboring disciplines. Unfortunately, as our earlier examples attest, exactly this state of affairs characterizes the development and current condition of social psychology.

In counterpoint to this fractionation, the social cognition movement emerged in the late 1970s. Its distinctive contribution was to stress the use of common explanatory principles across all areas of social psychology and even beyond – in clinical, personality, developmental, and cognitive psychology, for example. Because its earliest practitioners were particularly interested in the formation of impressions of other people, social cognition was sometimes viewed as just another instance of a research domain with its own favored topic and set of theoretical tools – focusing on how representations in memory are constructed and used (Hamilton et al., 1980; Hastie & Kumar, 1979). Even in those early days, however, the drive toward theoretical generality was evident in the conscious assumption that explanations for social psychological phenomena should be consistent with general principles of nonsocial cognition, as they were understood in that era (Anderson & Bower, 1973; Collins & Loftus, 1975).

Today, this commitment to theoretical generality means that more and more researchers interested in a diversity of social phenomena, extending far beyond person perception, draw on a common set of principles regarding the construction, representation, and use of social information. For example, Higgins's (in press) broad theory of mental accessibility and its effects is a major contribution to clinical, developmental, and personality psychology, as well as social psychology. It accounts, among other things, for emotional vulnerability arising from an accessible self-standard, for effects of recently encountered information on the interpretation of ambiguous stimuli, for shifts in the self-concept across times and situations, and for the activation of stereotypic information when a member of a stereotyped group is encountered. Thus the social cognition movement offered social psychology a strong impetus toward theoretical integration that still continues today.

Integrating the Psychological and the Social

Perhaps because principles involving the construction and processing of mental representations proved so powerful in explaining nonsocial cognition and many aspects of social behavior, social cognition in its infancy tended to adopt a decontextualized and individualistic approach. In fact, despite the recognition of the central importance of the social context in the seminal contributions of Sherif, Lewin, Milgram, and Asch, most of North American social psychology of the 1960s and 1970s shared this narrow focus. The need to incorporate the social into an overall integration was made particularly evident by the European development and elaboration of social identity theory and its relatives. These perspectives emphasized the importance of group membership and the intergroup context for social behavior. Although social cognition and social identity approaches have sometimes been cast as antagonists, their commonalities in our view make them natural allies. Like social cognition, the social identity approach is inherently integrative, offering broad explanatory principles that can be applied to an understanding of a variety of specific social behaviors, including attraction and cohesion, intergroup cooperation and competition, and feelings of heightened or lowered self-worth (Turner, Hogg, Oakes, Reicher, & Wetherell, 1987).

Most importantly, the social identity approach argues that social group membership is a central and indispensable aspect of the self, and thus that the self and the other – the psychological and the social – cannot be artificially detached from each other. These ideas were developed and formalized in self-categorization theory (Turner et al., 1987), which describes the process by which the group becomes part of the psychological self, so that group membership profoundly affects all forms of social perception and interaction. Moreover, its effects are mediated by the very same principles that social cognition researchers had already shown to have such explanatory power, such as the principle of accessibility. This conception of the nature of the social self provided an understanding of the interactive effects of the social and the cognitive on human behavior, and the integrative potential of this melding became evident as it was applied to a diversity of historically distinct research areas. Researchers could now understand why messages from some sources were influential while others were rejected out of hand (Mackie, Worth, & Asuncion, 1990; Turner, 1991); how intergroup and intragroup behavior were conceptually related (Turner et al., 1987); how socially shared and structured knowledge influenced the formation of the self-concept, impressions of other people, and stereotypes of groups (e.g. Macrae, Shepherd, & Milne, 1992; Moscovici, 1988; Ruscher & Hammer, 1994) and what parallels exist between membership in groups and participation in other forms of relationships (Smith & Henry, 1996).

These developments have set the stage for a new theoretical unification of the psychological and the social. We believe that social psychology is now ready to take advantage of its unique place as the science of the interface between the psychological and the social – between the "in here" of mental processes, perception, memory, emotion, and judgment, and the "out there" of social processes, interaction, group membership, and affiliation.

The Message of Social Psychology

A consensual conceptual framework for this new psychological and social integration has not yet emerged. Many in the field still identify themselves with one of the existing theoretical frameworks, and even (encouraged by some rhetoric) view alternative viewpoints as the enemy. We believe that, as the editors also suggest in their introduction to this book (pp. 6–7), social and psychological determinants of behavior are not competing alternatives, but inseparable complements. It is impossible to conceive of an individual having meaningful perceptions or thoughts in the absence of sociality, or of social interaction and relationships existing without extensive mental processing. Indeed, modern evolutionary psychology offers the insight that our mental abilities evolved in specific social situations and are therefore fundamentally shaped by the demands of social life. Equally, the forms of sociality that we find most natural and rewarding are reflections of our basic mental predispositions. To us, the essential message of social psychology is that a *small set of basic social and psychological processes operate – not separately but in an integrative and interactive fashion – to generate all forms of social perception, social influence, and social interaction.* Two processes are the most fundamental: the construction of reality through social and psychological processes, and pervasive social influence.

Psychological and social construction of reality

The reality we inhabit is not objectively given, but is constructed by each of us – and by all of us. The individual's own contribution to the world of experience has been a familiar theme in psychology since Freud, the *Gestalt* psychologists, and particularly the New Look in perception in the late 1940s. But social as well as psychological processes are inherently involved in this constructive process. We seek to validate our view of reality by checking our perceptions against others' – particularly others who share important relationships or group memberships with us. Thus, Muzafer Sherif (1936) wrote "Once a value is standardized and becomes the common property of a group . . . it acquires objective reality." And Leon Festinger (1954) commented "An opinion, a belief, an attitude is 'correct,' 'valid,' and 'proper' to the extent that it is anchored in a group of people with similar beliefs, opinions, and attitudes." For example, members of one Native American culture believed that the entire world is supported on the back of a giant turtle. Even without having personally seen the turtle, individuals accepted its reality without question. Many members of our own culture believe that the entire universe is composed of "quarks," "gluons," and other such entities. None of us has ever seen these particles, but we accept their existence nevertheless – because it is supported by a consensus of teachers and others who are socially defined as authoritative. In ways like these, socially shared consensus *creates* reality for us (Hardin & Higgins, in press; Mackie & Skelly, 1994).

Pervasive social influence

Our very need to reassure ourselves that our view of reality is shared with others opens us up to social influence when we discover that views differ. We may change our opinion because a consensus of fellow ingroup members seems likely to be correct. The more often noted reasons for conformity, the desire to reap the social rewards of agreement and acceptance as a "good group member," seem much less fundamental as well as less powerful by comparison. Social influence is at work in the familiar forms of persuasion, conformity, and obedience, but it is also far more pervasive. Socially constructed definitions of the self, the group, the situation, and the universe itself enter into our every thought, feeling, and action. This is true even when we are not consciously aware of pressure or attempted influence from others.

Social psychologists sometimes refer to this principle as the "power of the situation," but that language may lead us to think mistakenly of social influence as purely external or environmental. In fact, in the classic demonstrations of the "power of the situation" like Milgram's studies of obedience or Latané and Darley's work on bystander intervention, the influence is just as much internal as external. For example, the authority figure activates an internally represented norm of obedience, or the presence of others makes the individual reinterpret the situation in terms of what is appropriate behavior. Without internalized norms or reconstruals of appropriate behavior, no "situation" could have power. Social influence is pervasive because it operates through our thoughts and feelings as well as through the external social situation.

The construction of reality and the influence of social factors are mediated by several more specific principles of motivation and processing. Individual social psychologists may conceptualize these principles somewhat differently in terms of their specific identification and labeling; more important than disagreement at that level is a basic agreement that the principles are relatively few and of great generality across content domains. Each of these principles, like the two fundamental points, is both social and psychological in its operation.

Motivational principles

Three basic motivational principles include the desire for mastery (understanding the universe in order to obtain rewards), the desire for connectedness to other people and groups, and the desire to maintain and enhance a positive view of the socially extended self (the individual self as well as other persons or groups connected to the self). For example, people are susceptible to the illusion of mastery or control, are prone to falsely overestimate consensus for their opinions and beliefs, and are subject to many types of self-enhancing biases. Each principle also has a social aspect. We form and maintain groups and relationships to gain protection and concrete rewards, to solidify connections to valued others, and to magnify our ingroup's concrete outcomes, esteem, and value. These three motives, in both their psychological and social aspects, profoundly shape the way we construct reality and give and accept social influence. For example, we seek to construct a version of reality in which ourselves and our groups are positively valued, and (simultaneously) a version that is "valid" insofar as it guides veridical perception and rewarding actions.

Processing principles

Our construction of reality and social influence processes are also shaped by three basic processing principles. One is conservatism, the fact that mental representations and patterns of social action, once constructed, are slow to change. A second is accessibility, the extra impact of information that is cognitively or socially ready at hand. The third is depth of processing: sometimes we operate with simple heuristics, other times with extensive, effortful processing. Each of these processes is also both psychological and social in its operation. Conservatism means that both individual attitudes and social norms are difficult to change once formed. Accessibility operates at the level of our mental processes (Higgins, in press) and also in social situations: a social norm that is made accessible by someone else's action has increased power as a guide for action (Sherif, 1936; Cialdini, Reno, & Kallgren, 1990). The depth of processing principle is most familiar in the distinction between superficial and systematic mental processes, but also applies to groups, which sometimes adopt majority positions relatively unthinkingly and at other times, particularly when confronted with disagreement from a consistent minority, intensively evaluate the relevant evidence (Moscovici, 1980). Of course, these principles usually operate in combination rather than singly to generate social behavior. A few examples illustrate their inseparably interactive nature.

- We construct reality – our basic views of ourselves, other people, and the universe – partly in order to master the environment. In this process we offer and accept social influence because we want to construct an appropriate and correct version of reality, and other people help us do so. At the same time, exchanges of social influence help maintain connectedness with valued others, and enhance our views of the self and those connected to us.
- Our group membership influences the way we interact with other ingroup and outgroup members, so that we usually are more familiar with more members of the ingroup. Group membership also influences the way we think about ingroups and outgroups. Both these social and cognitive aspects of pervasive social influence combine to make outgroups seem more homogeneous than ingroups.
- Shared group membership or a close relationship can make us respond to other people's needs as to our own, producing cooperation and altruistic or even self-sacrificial helping. These types of social behavior are theoretically interesting because a purely individualistic perspective, focusing on individual rewards, has problems explaining them.
- We are influenced by ingroup members, whether in conformity or persuasion situations, because shared group membership defines them as appropriate sources of information about the world and also as valued connections.

Conclusion

Let us close with an analogy. In the medieval period one of the most popular types of books was the "bestiary" or "book of beasts." Such a work described, with detailed illustrations, strange and fantastic creatures from faraway lands – hippopotamuses, tigers, griffins – more often than not based on travellers' tales and other such "reliable" sources. Each chapter described a different beast, and of course one would not find much in common across the chapters. The explanation advanced in one chapter for how the camel got his hump had nothing to do with how the lion got his roar in another. But all the tales were fascinating.

Contrast the bestiary with a modern biology textbook. Instead of separate chapters devoted to an array of creatures, you will find a set of basic principles having to do with evolution, natural selection, adaptation to environment, and so on. These principles are understood to *generate* all the beasts that were celebrated in the medieval works, and to account for both their sameness and their diversity. The philosopher Alfred North Whitehead wrote "the scientific mentality . . . instinctively holds that all things great and small are conceivable as exemplifications of general principles which reign throughout the natural order" (1925/1967, p. 5). This attitude can give us new eyes with which to admire the beasts. We can even understand that, at a fundamental level, the very same principles account for the camel's hump and the lion's roar. It is this integrative theoretical understanding that underlies the great leaps that the biological sciences are currently experiencing.

In the past and sometimes still today, social psychology has been portrayed in a way that is rather like the bestiary: as a list of separate topics – stereotyping, group dynamics, persuasion, close relationships – and a separate set of *Just So Story* explanations for each topic. Each topic is fascinating in itself, both because of the way it reveals significant facets of human nature, and because of the concrete ways it touches our everyday lives. The time is now ripe for social psychologists to conceive of the incredible diversity of social life as stemming from the effects and interactions of a *common* set of principles that are both social and psychological. Theoretical integration is increasingly recognized as an important goal across all of psychology. According to Kurt Fischer, Tory Higgins, and Lawrence Pervin (1994, p. v),

> Increasingly, scholars in social, personality, developmental, cognitive, and other areas of psychology are moving away from investigating limited phenomena and issues constrained by disciplinary boundaries and toward the examination of basic psychological principles. This renewed interest in basic principles at multiple levels of analysis can serve to reunite the field of psychology.

We believe that this integration must rest on recognition of the inherent intertwining of the psychological and the social. Indeed, social psychology's sophisticated analyses of the ways that human behavior flows from a common set of principles that are both social and psychological may become a blueprint for greater integration in psychology as a whole.

Further Reading

Devine, P. G., Hamilton, D. L., & Ostrom, T. M. (Eds.) (1994). *Social cognition: Impact on social psychology*. Orlando, FL: Academic Press. Descriptions of trends toward theoretical integration, largely sparked by the social cognition movement, in many significant areas of social psychology.

Hardin, C., & Higgins, E. T. (in press). Shared reality: How social verification makes the subjective objective. In R. M. Sorrentino & E. T. Higgins (Eds.), *Handbook of motivation and cognition: Foundations of social behavior* (Vol. 3). New York: Guilford. An account of the role of social influences in the construction of reality.

Mackie, D. M., & Hamilton, D. L. (1995). *Affect, cognition, and stereotyping: Interactive processes in group perception*. Orlando, FL: Academic Press. A collection of chapters that integrate classic cognitive approaches to stereotyping and prejudice with contemporary theory and research about affect and emotion.

Smith, E. R., & Mackie, D. M. (1995). *Social psychology*. New York: Worth Publishers. An introductory social psychology textbook giving an integrative presentation of the entire field in terms of the basic principles outlined in this chapter.

Turner, J. C., Hogg, M. A., Oakes, P. J., Reicher, S. D., & Wetherell, M. S. (1987). *Rediscovering the social group: A self-categorization theory*. Oxford: Blackwell. A description of the basic theory of self-categorization and its many effects in social life.

References

Anderson, J. R., & Bower, G. H. (1973). *Human associative memory*. Washington: Winston & Sons.

Cialdini, R. B., Reno, R. R., & Kallgren, C. A. (1990). A focus theory of normative conduct: Recycling the concept of norms to reduce littering in public places. *Journal of Personality and Social Psychology*, *58*, 1015–1026.

Collins, A. M., & Loftus, E. F. (1975). A spreading-activation theory of semantic processing. *Psychological Review*, *83*, 407–428.

Festinger, L. (1954). A theory of social comparison processes. *Human Relations*, *7*, 117–140.

Fischer, K .W., Higgins, E. T., & Pervin, L. A. (1994). Series editors' note. In D. A. Kenny, *Interpersonal perception*. New York: Guilford.

Hamilton, D. L., Katz, L. B., & Leirer, V. (1980). Organizational processes in impression formation. In R. Hastie et al. (Eds.), *Person memory*. Hillsdale, NJ: Lawrence Erlbaum.

Hardin, C., & Higgins, E. T. (in press). Shared reality: How social verification makes the subjective objective. In R. M. Sorrentino & E. T. Higgins (Eds.), *Handbook of motivation and cognition: Foundations of social behavior* (Vol. 3). New York: Guilford.

Hastie, R., & Kumar, P. A. (1979). Person memory: Personality traits as organizing principles in memory for behaviors. *Journal of Personality and Social Psychology*, *37*, 25–38.

Higgins, E. T. (in press). Accessibility. To appear in: E. T. Higgins & A. W. Kruglanski (Eds.), *Social psychology: Handbook of basic principles*. New York: Guilford.

Mackie, D. M., Worth, L. T., & Asuncion, A. G. (1990). The processing of persuasive ingroup messages. *Journal of Personality and Social Psychology*, *58*, 812–822.

Mackie, D. M., & Skelly, J. J. (1994). The social cognition analysis of social influence: Contributions to the understanding of persuasion and conformity. In P. G. Devine, D. L. Hamilton, & T. M. Ostrom (Eds.), *Social cognition: Impact on social psychology* (pp. 259–289). Orlando, FL: Academic Press.

Macrae, C. N., Shepherd, J. W., & Milne, A. B. (1992). The effects of source credibility on the dilution of stereotype-based judgments. *Personality and Social Psychology Bulletin*, *18*, 765–775.

Moscovici, S. (1980). Toward a theory of conversion behavior. In L. Berkowitz (Ed.), *Advances in experimental social psychology* (Vol. 13, pp. 209–239). New York: Academic Press.

Moscovici, S. (1988). Notes toward a description of social representations. *European Journal of Social Psychology*, *18*, 211–250.

Ruscher, J. B., & Hammer, E. D. (1994). Revising disrupted impressions through conversation. *Journal of Personality and Social Psychology*, *66*, 530–541.

Sherif, M. (1936). *The psychology of social norms*. New York: Harper.

Smith, E. R., & Henry, S. M. (1996). An ingroup becomes part of the self: Response time evidence. *Personality and Social Psychology Bulletin, 22*, 635–642.

Turner, J. C. (1991). *Social influence*. Pacific Grove, CA: Brooks/Cole.

Turner, J. C., Hogg, M. A., Oakes, P. J., Reicher, S. D., & Wetherell, M. S. (1987). *Rediscovering the social group: A self-categorization theory*. Oxford: Blackwell.

Whitehead, A. N. (1925/1967). *Science and the modern world*. New York: Free Press.

20

"In the Beginning There is Society": Lessons from a Sociological Social Psychology

Sheldon Stryker

Sheldon Stryker, Distinguished Professor of Sociology, Indiana University, was born in 1924. He received a doctorate in Sociology, minoring in psychology, from the University of Minnesota in 1955. His major professor was Arnold M. Rose. His first publication in social psychology appeared in 1952. He has long-standing interests in symbolic interactionist theory, especially issues related to self and identity. Former editor of the *American Sociological Review*, *Sociometry* (now *Social Psychology Quarterly*) and the Rose Monograph Series, he is a past winner of the American Sociological Association Section on Social Psychology's Cooley-Mead Award for lifetime contributions to social psychology.

Introduction: The Meta-Theoretical Predilection of Sociological Social Psychology

Although not all psychologists share the awareness, there are "two social psychologies" (Stephan, Stephan, & Pettigrew, 1991; Stephan & Stephan, 1990; Stryker, 1977, 1987). The first – represented by the editors and almost all authors in this volume – is a social psychology produced by psychologists, the second a social psychology produced by sociologists. While there are a variety of theoretical, methodological and substantive differences between (*and* within) the two, the fundamental difference is meta-theoretical.

The predilection of psychologists is to approach social psychology from the standpoint of the individual ("in the beginning, there is the person"); the predilection of sociologists is to approach social psychology from the standpoint of units of interaction comprised of multiple persons ("in the beginning there is society"). I write as a sociologist, and I share the meta-theoretical predilection of my discipline.

What I take as the "message of social psychology," the principal lessons to be learned from it, derive from or relate to the meta-theoretical stance I begin with. To say this is not to say I rely on predilection in asserting my "message." There is certainly evidence, little of which can be cited here, giving force to the assertions; a recent start into that evidence is available in Cook, Fine, and House (1995). Given the sponsorship of this volume, and the likelihood that the vast majority of persons who read it are students of psychology, my emphasis is on how my lessons temper lessons available through the work of psychological social psychology.

"In the beginning there is society." The aphorism should not be construed literally, although it is not irrelevant that every human is born into, and cannot survive outside the context of, ongoing social relationships and interactions. These circumstances in part underlie the priority assigned to society. More pertinently at the moment, the aphorism is a sociologist's answer to the question: How can we best conceptualize the relation of "person" and "society," the constituent parts of social psychology? It asserts that social-psychological inquiry that takes the isolated individual as its starting point and *then* asks how the presence of others affects individual experience and behavior will fall short of a thorough understanding of many social psychological issues. Indeed, it asserts that treating the social as no more than setting for individual experience and behavior will be similarly deficient.

Intellectual Foundations: George Herbert Mead

The prime source of the views being presented is George Herbert Mead (1934), who, ironically (because his ideas influenced largely sociologists), was a psychologist as well as a pragmatic philosopher. Mead believed what was distinctive about human beings was that they developed "minds" and "selves" through the evolutionary process. That is, they could deal with problems (circumstances blocking ongoing behavior) by manipulating symbols internally to try out alternative solutions to those problems (mind); and they could respond reflexively to themselves and treat themselves as objects akin to other objects in the world (self). He argued that the source of mind and self was ongoing social process in which persons required others in order to construct their solutions to problematic situations. Requiring others implies that persons must take others into account through anticipating their responses to projected lines of action. This is made possible by communication, by developing in interaction symbols with reasonably common meanings among those implicated in the ongoing social process. Organized society is a never-ending process of routinization or institutionalization of solutions to repetitive problems, arrived at through interaction, and subject to continuous change as new problems emerge in interaction and are confronted by participants.

Both individuals – humans with minds and selves – and society are created in and through social process; each is *constitutive* of the other. There is no individuality outside society, and there is no society except through actions of individuals. The human is reflective, self-conscious and self-controlling, made possible by participation in interaction and through communication presupposed by interaction. The standpoint of others becomes part of self, representing the social control of individual conduct. At the same time, humans control their own behavior by selecting actions symbolically present in their experience. Social control makes possible self-control. Self plays back upon the society that shapes the self; thus, society is continuously being created and recreated. Change is an intrinsic part of the social process, as is emergence, the appearance of new, in principle unpredictable, experience requiring creative adaptations. That is, novel solutions to problems can arise as persons alter and adapt existing meanings and behavior to meet unforseen contingencies in social interaction – the social process – itself.

Derived and Related Lessons

For Mead, conceptualizing the relation of person and society involves recognizing the fundamental sense in which society is built into the individual, into mind and self. That recognition is entailed in beginning analyses of the individual with analyses of society. The question is: What lessons derive from or relate to this recognition? There are several.

The socially organized character of human experience

Perhaps the most basic lesson is: *Human experience is not random; it is, rather, socially organized.* Mead prepares us for this lesson by suggesting that interaction and resultant structure underlie and define individuality, that the content and organization of self reflect the participation of persons in society. What it requires beyond Mead is appreciating that contemporary "society" is not of one piece; persons have multiple location*s* within the social structure*s* of society.

The use of plurals is intended to imply the complexity of contemporary societies. Societies, today more than yesterday, are not invariably coherent. They are congeries of organized role relationships, social networks, groups, institutions, strata, some overlapping and some not, some conflicting and some not, some isolated from one another and some not. Further implied is that the experience of humans will be shaped in important respects by just what relationships, networks, groups, institutions, strata they enter or leave, as well as by how these structures relate to one another. Experience is normally not random; what happens to people will almost always be strongly impacted by their locations in social structures.

For present purposes, the significant property of social structures is that they define boundaries (Stryker, 1980), some relatively permeable, some relatively impermeable. As boundaries, they act as barriers to and facilitators of interaction. As barriers, they inhibit and can preclude interactions that cross the boundaries; as facilitators, they encourage and can require interactions with others within the boundaries. Structures serve (probabilistically not deterministically) to bring only certain people together to interact over certain topics with only certain instrumental and symbolic resources. Alternatively, social structures keep certain persons out of particular interactions, etc. If, then, as the social cognition perspective suggests (Markus & Zajonc, 1985), cognitions arise incrementally out of persons' experience, social structures importantly affect the probability of those persons having experiences that give rise to particular cognitions. Stated generally, involvement in role relationship, family, educational institution, ethnic group, social class, neighborhood – all social structures – makes it more or less probable that persons will "have" particular cognitions, cognitive schema, cognitive scripts, as well as that their cognitions will contain particular content. Illustratively, a long literature on occupational aspirations tells us that social class strongly impacts the likelihood that youth will know about and aspire to professional as compared with other kinds of occupations (e.g. Sewell & Orenstein, 1965). Another illustration: the meaning of the category "feminist" is likely to be quite different for black and white women of comparable class background (hooks, 1981).

Social life as constructed

A second lesson asserts that the forms and the content – roughly, the social structures and the culture – of social life are not given in nature and are not fixed. Rather, *the forms and content of social life are social constructions, the products of the collective activities of persons as they together develop solutions to problems met in their daily lives.* Thus, for example, Corsaro (1985, 1992) shows in detail how nursery school children take ill-formed or ambiguous information garnered from the adult world, then use their interaction with other children to explore the meaning of that information. Peer interaction becomes the vehicle through which children together construct a peer culture incorporating their collective understanding of the information, which peer culture then feeds back into and extends the adult culture. To take other examples, Thompson (1975) long ago noted that successive ethnic groups in Hawaii and elsewhere were characterized as inferior (lazy, dishonest, lacking in intelligence and motivation, etc.), as they moved into the position of plantation labor, and "lost" these negative traits as they moved out of this position; adolescence is a social invention that has been linked to a problem of surplus labor and the consequent need to remove significant numbers from the labor force (Kett, 1977); what "counts" as a family has expanded in recent years far beyond the so-called nuclear family consisting of husband, wife, and their immature children to which the term was more or less restricted one or two generations earlier (Baca Zinn & Eitzen, 1987); males and females are distinguished as much or more by social definition and resulting convention and socialization practice than they are by biology (West & Zimmerman, 1987).

It is important to understand what is – and what is not – entailed in this lesson. To say that social forms and content are constructions is indeed to say that these are the products of human action and interaction; and it is to say that their reconstruction and even radical change is always possible. It is not necessarily to claim, however, that there is nothing objective in the world that serves to limit or constrain the structures and cultures that are constructed. It is certainly not to claim that social constructions are invariably or even generally ephemeral, or that they do not, sometimes powerfully, limit the probability of reconstruction or radical change. Some (e.g. Gergen, 1982) assert that a social constructionist position implies that no objective social reality exists (or that objective reality cannot be known), then infer that only claims about the world exist and that the validity of varying claims cannot be differentiated objectively. I do not believe such implications and inferences are inherent in the lesson of social constructivism; and I certainly do not believe they are wise, if only because accepting them leaves little grounds other than raw power politics as the basis for adjudicating conflicting claims about the social world.

The human being as an active agent

Human beings have been portrayed, often only implicitly, by both sociologists and psychologists as completely the product of forces in an environment that is external to them. Thus, sociologists have sometimes presented a picture of individuals as socialized automatons, carrying out the obligations of social roles they are assigned to play in order to assure the stability of the social system of which they are members; and psychologists have conceptualized individuals as the resultant of classical or operant conditioning processes in which they react to environmental stimuli by producing the responses tied to the stimuli. Neither of these visualizations of individuals, each of which characterizes human beings as simply reactors, has proved adequate. Instead, a lesson that has emerged – in the social psychologies of both sociologist and psychologist, but perhaps more generally in the former – is that *the human being is an actor, an active agent who acts on and alters the (social and non-social) environment that impinges on her or him, who initiates transactions with that environment and responds selectively to it.* The lesson these words teach is foreshadowed in the writings of the Scottish moral philosophers (Bryson, 1945) and is made explicit in John Dewey's classic paper on what he termed the reflex arc concept in psychology (1896), a paper which it has been said also reflects Mead's ideas (Miller, 1973, p. xxvi). In that paper, Dewey observed that stimulus and response exist only in relation to one another, and that the couplet comes into being only in the context of action initiated by an actor in the process of seeking a solution to a problem that has disrupted her/his flow of activity. This kind of actor – one who acts with reference to the outside world rather than merely reacts to it, one who impacts that world through her/his actions rather than merely being impacted by it – is implied in the notion of social construction. Further, action that is produced at the initiative of the actor is made possible by the existence of mind and self, the symbolic and reflexive capacities of the human being. It is these which permit the actor to project alternative lines of action, examine the alternatives in terms of their likely outcomes, and select among them on the basis of their probable success, always retaining the possibility of revising the course of the selected action as evidence is returned in the course of the action itself. It is, I believe, important to understand that this view of the human as actor does not deny the fact or the power of conditioning, nor the fact or power of normative demands on persons to play out roles as scripted. It only (but not merely, for the point is not trivial in its implications for social psychology) asserts that humans can play a significant role in their own destiny. In general, it is reasonable to expect that all social behavior is likely to exhibit some blend of action and reaction. Stated in this way, the issue becomes just what the blend may be in a given instance under investigation, and when – under what conditions – do humans initiate actions that impinge significantly on their worlds and when do their behaviors largely, even totally, reflect prior conditioning and/or normative role demands. Parenthetically, the shift in focus contained in the lesson under discussion – that humans are actors as well as reactors – imposes on social psychology the task of investigating not only conformity, but autonomy, creativity, efficacy as well – not only social reproduction and stability but also social production and change.

The import of definitions and interpretations

"If men define situations as real, they are real in their consequences" (Thomas & Thomas, 1928). Likely the most quoted sentence in the literature of sociological social psychology, this sentence is a concise and straightforward assertion of the significance of the subjective and the symbolic in social life. The assertion implies both a substantive and a methodological lesson. The substantive lesson is that *the world to which humans react and on which they act is a symbolized world, a world specified by meanings attached to the objects comprising it rather than that which may in some sense exist independent of its being symbolized.* This lesson derives from the status of humans as active agents having mind and self, and from the constructed character of the social world in which they live out their lives. Humans, that is, live in physical and social environments that are symbolically represented in experience, that are defined and interpreted; and it is those environments as they are defined and interpreted with which they interact. Saying this does not imply either that there is no reality to the world outside of definitions and interpretations, or that undefined and uninterpreted aspects of the world can have no impact on persons. Certainly, by way of illustration, class location has important impacts on people whether or not they recognize the existence of classes and even if they deny that existence. What the lesson does imply is that actors' definitions and interpretations are consequential for how they construct their behavior, for the process in which their action is developed and elaborated, and ultimately for their collaborative social constructions. The methodological lesson that follows from this substantive lesson is: "*The point of view of the participants in social interaction must enter decisively into satisfactory accounts or explanations of that interaction*" (Stryker, 1980).

The significance of self

The concept of "self" has been introduced at various junctures above in ways that imply its central significance in the lessons that this chapter offers, but that significance has yet to be directly confronted. For Mead, to have a self is to respond reflexively to oneself, to respond to oneself as an object, which implies that persons can and do come to symbolize or define themselves as participants in social relationships and ongoing interaction. How they come to define themselves – the terms of definition, so to speak – will reflect responses of others to them, the others being co-participants in the relationships and ongoing interaction. However, once defined, an existing self can interact dialectically with others' responses to produce an emergent self to organize and to guide one's actions. There are, consequently, elements of both social control and self-control built into the concept of self; and there are means by which we can account theoretically for both the impact of society on person and the impact of person on society. The lesson is: *If the point of social psychology is to deal with the reciprocal relation of society and person, then social psychology must incorporate a concept of self, or the equivalent of self, to get very far; for it is the set of self-conceptions, or self-definitions that make up self, that mediate the relation of society to behavior and of behavior to society.*

The importance of self can be phrased in another way. The burden of the prior lesson was that persons' definitions and interpretations are critical in organizing their behavior. To act in an organized, coherent manner, one must define the "scene" (is this my home? a classroom? a contest? etc.), who the others in the scene may be (are these others family? students? opponents? etc.), and who one is himself or herself (am I a host? a teacher? an observer? etc.).

How an actor defines herself or himself – the actor's reflexive response to herself or himself as an object – is critical to ensuing behavior. Persons often behave in ways that simply reflect demands of situations they find themselves in. Sometimes they do not. Their self-conceptions contribute to making this difference.

Contemporary social psychology, in both its sociological and psychological varieties, is likely to conceptualize self in multiple terms, following William James's (1890) dictum that persons have as many social selves as there are groups of others who respond to them. Psychologists are wont, however, to view self as a constellation of behavioral traits, while sociologists are apt to view self as an organization of multiple identities, the identities being internalized expectations for behavior attached to the roles they play in discrete networks of social relationships (Stryker, 1980). More, in keeping with the implications of "In the beginning there is society," sociologists are likely to see the organization of self as reflecting the organization of societies, incorporating all of the latter's complexities. What difference this makes is the next lesson to be discussed.

The person as constrained and free

Clearly implied in what has been said is that much of any person's cognitive and other activity is highly constrained as a function of the person's status as a member of society. At the same time, however, the prior discussion has also implied that the person has some freedom of action, that it is possible for the person to be creative, cognitively and otherwise. The lesson, in brief, is that *there is both constraint and freedom in personal and social life*. The issue is how the apparent paradox asserted in this lesson can be resolved, how it is possible for the person to be both constrained and free at the same time.

Entailed in this lesson is a particular conception of "freedom" and of "constraint." In this conception, one is free in the degree to which one can exercise choice. Conversely, one is constrained in the degree to which choice cannot be exercised. However, we can choose only when options are realistically available to us. Thus, freedom can be measured by the range of realistic alternatives open to a person, constraint by limitations on that range. With this conception, the issue becomes: What expands or contracts the alternatives open to persons?

My answer to this question presumes a complex society, and a self, composed of multiple identities, to match. Adapted from an earlier statement (Stryker, 1994) the answer expands the meaning of this lesson. To exist and have reasonable chance of enactment, alternatives must be symbolically present in the person's reflection, since people cannot choose to do what they cannot or do not conceive of doing. To be viable, alternatives must link to self, since people are not likely to do what they cannot or do not conceive that *they* can or would do. To be likely, alternatives must link to salient identities, since if not they are unlikely to emerge in situations and be available for consideration. To be salient, identities must link to networks of social relationships to which persons are highly committed, since high levels of commitment to social roles leads to high levels of salience of identities associated with those roles. For alternatives to have a reasonable chance of being chosen, some networks of social relationships must be organized around norms underwriting those alternatives, otherwise the alternatives will have little or no social support and so little attraction. For networks of social relationships to support alternatives that are in opposition, the networks must be relatively independent of one another, since related networks are likely to evolve equivalent norms and so remove alternatives. To support oppositional alternatives, networks must be relatively open, since if they are not, persons' access to multiple identities with varying, oppositional alternatives will be restricted. For networks to be independent yet open, society must have cross-cutting boundaries and mobility across boundaries, otherwise networks will be restricted to persons with similar social characteristics or persons will be unable to resist conformity pressures from which they cannot escape.

The same elements account for constraint conceived as the contraction of alternatives. A society with few independent networks and little social mobility is unlikely to permit or support multiple independent identities that call for alterative, oppositional actions. If alternatives are not symbolically present, attached to salient identities, or supported by networks of relationships to which persons have high levels of commitment, alternatives are minimal or will have low likelihood of enactment.

The limits of determinism in accounts of social behavior

Since persons are social products and society is constructed, since persons have selves and are to some extent free as well as constrained, and since persons' definitions and interpretations impact their behavior, humans do not exist in a strictly deterministic world. Said differently, *there are limits to determinism as an underlying principle in social psychology*. For some (e.g. Gergen, 1982), this lesson implies that social psychology must forgo its claims and aspirations as a science. To my mind, this is not the case. The proper inference is that what is said in the name of social psychology must be probabilistic rather than deterministic in form. We will have to alter what is said to reflect emergent historical and social circumstance. The empirical generalizations we arrive at as well as the theoretical explanations constructed to account for generalizations we develop – we must be able to develop some, for otherwise organized social life would not exist – are subject to change. We cannot expect to arrive at general laws holding without exception for the duration of time. Accepting this limitation is a small price to pay for retaining models of science and scientific procedure aimed at producing objective knowledge of human behavior. The alternative is intellectual – and, probably, social – chaos.

The Lessons Applied

Applying the lessons offered above can bolster the claim that they serve to temper lessons available through psychological social psychology. I begin with two true stories, both set in meetings of an organization to which perhaps most active American researchers in psychological social psychology belong as do a few sociological social psychologists.

The first story involves a talk by a psychologist on developments in social cognition theory and research. The speaker celebrated the phenomenological turn in social cognition, endorsing and summarizing this turn with: "*All* there is, is phenomenology!" Earlier, this speaker reviewed his intellectual and professional evolution to ground his talk. He took his first post-doctorate job and remained at the same midwestern American institution. Doing this surprised him, for he assumed that on completing training he would return to home territory, but there were no jobs in New England when he entered the job market. Apparently, there is more than phenomenology. What more there is, is explicated below.

The second story: I was a discussant in a session on new directions in self theory containing four papers, one on self-verification and self-enhancement processes, another on self-discrepancy theory, a third on self-complexity theory, a last on sources of social and temporal comparisons through which persons arrive at their self-conceptions. Given the papers, it was clear I had to be in trouble. To explain: no presenter had given me a paper, if at all, until moments before the session. Thus, I could not prepare my discussion. In the terms of theories presented, I could not discuss the papers in a manner calculated to draw from the audience either verification of my self-cognitions as an able, articulate, responsible professional, or enhanced evaluations based on exemplary performance. More, without preparation, social comparisons with others who performed the discussant's role brilliantly and temporal comparisons with my own prior brilliant performances in that role had to lead to seeing myself as a failure. The predictable consequence was disaster: my audience would not love and respect me, so I could not love and respect myself. Still more, the situation had to engender self-discrepancies – disjuncts among my self-views, others' views of me, my ideal and normative self-guides, and others' ideal-based and norm-based expectations for my behavior, etc. – making me vulnerable to agitation and dejection. Finally, since my self-cognitions are not complex, the inability to perform my discussant role threatened performances in other roles – as spouse, parent, golfer. Taking the theories presented seriously, I had to be in trouble.

In fact, I was neither agitated nor depressed. I felt comfortable, even complacent. I slept well the night before, and felt no anxiety entering the session. I considered with equanimity announcing I had nothing to say about the papers.

I found it impossible to develop the sweat, sense of crisis, distress, the theories predicted I would have. Again, the moral in a moment.

Consider the first story. The contradiction between "*All* there is, is phenomenology" and the observation that no jobs were available in New England is patent. The assertion gives causal priority to cognitive processes in determining behavioral outcomes. That the outcome did not accord with prior cognition is not, however, the point to be made; after all, taking a position in the midwest institution could have resulted from a new cognitive construal – a belief that there were no jobs available in New England. The point, rather, is that a social structure – the job market – preempted any force cognition might have exerted had the job market been more benign. Stated differently, the behavioral outcome would not have changed had the original cognition been maintained.

The second story. Contemplating my lack of negative affect, I realized I did not care I was about to fail as a discussant. Then I realized I did not care because it did not matter to me. It did not matter to me because, while a member of the organization sponsoring the session, I am only peripherally attached to the world of psychologists. My prime identity is as a sociologist. I am a member of a department of sociology as well as a number of sociological organizations; my professional relations are largely with other sociologists; my pay and my prestige derive from my position as a sociologist. Why should I care if I came off badly as a discussant in the situation described? Unless one includes in one's thinking the kinds of structural matters just alluded to, one's understanding of social-psychological responses will be limited.

More generally, we will not understand the limits of the lessons of psychological social psychology without the tempering available through appreciating the major lessons available to us through sociological social psychology. If we seek to model social-psychological phenomena in purely individualistic terms we are likely to misinterpret findings of the research on those phenomena. For example, we may well accord too much influence to individuals' cognitions by failing to recognize that the cognitions are what is available to persons by virtue of their social locations. We may also misinterpret findings through a failure to appreciate the role of given social structures in activating particular cognitive structures or in activating conflicting cognitions. That is, many social-psychological theories – cognitive dissonance theory is an older example (Festinger, 1957), self-discrepancy theory (Higgins, 1987) is a more recent example – assert that persons will be distressed by holding conflicting cognitions, and that the distress will have one or another cognitive, emotional, or behavioral consequence. But there is little reason to expect either distress or its presumed consequences when the cognitions are effectively isolated from one another. While cognitions may conflict in the abstract, the conflicting cognitions will not be distressing unless they are simultaneously activated in the same situational context (Stryker & Macke, 1978). That there exists a variety of psychological defense mechanisms to keep that from happening is widely understood. Not so widely understood, but as any adolescent who keeps friends away from family intuitively knows, is that social structures are often constituted, sometimes but not necessarily deliberately, in order to prevent conflicting cognitions from being simultaneously activated (Stryker, 1993). Ideally, researchers will include social structural along with cognitive variables in their designs and analyses. In the nonideal case, however, researchers can still consider the implications of the point made and temper inferences drawn from their research.

All of this is not to deprecate in any way the import of psychological social psychology or the lessons learned from work done from that frame. It is simply to recognize that an individualistic perspective such as that underlying and deriving from classical sources of experimental social psychology, while useful for some purposes, is less than completely useful for many of the problems of social psychology. It has been the burden of this chapter to make a case for that message.

Further Reading

Gecas, V., & Burke, P. J. (1995). Self and identity. In K. S. Cook, G. A. Fine & J. H. House (Eds.), *Sociological perspectives on social psychology* (pp. 41–67). Boston, MA: Allyn & Bacon.

Mead, G. H. (1934). *Mind, self, and society*. Chicago, IL: University of Chicago Press.

Rosenberg, M. (1979). *Conceiving the self*. New York: Basic Books.

Stryker, S. (1980). *Symbolic interactionism: A social structural version*. Menlo Park, CA: Benjamin/Cummings.

Stryker, S. (1992). Identity theory. In E. F. Borgatta & M. L. Borgatta (Eds.), *Encyclopedia of sociology* (Vol. 2, pp. 871–876). New York: Macmillan.

Stryker, S., & Statham A. (1985). Symbolic interaction and role theory. In G. Lindzey & E. Aronson (Eds.), *Handbook of social psychology* (3rd ed., Vol. I, pp. 311–378). New York: Random House.

Turner, R. H. (1962). Role-taking: Process versus conformity. In A. M. Rose (Ed.), *Human behavior and social process* (pp. 20–40). Boston, MA: Houghton-Mifflin.

References

Baca Zinn, M., & Eitzen, D. S. (1987). *Diversity in American families*. New York: Harper and Row.

Bryson, G. (1945). *Man and society: The Scottish inquiry of the eighteenth century*. Princeton, NJ: Princeton University Press.

Cook, K. S., Fine, G. A., & House, J. S. (1995). *Sociological perspectives on social psychology*. Boston, MA: Allyn and Bacon.

Corsaro, W. (1985). *Friendship and peer culture in the early years*. Norwood, NJ: Ablex.

Corsaro, W. (1992). Interpretive reproduction in children's peer cultures. *Social Psychology Quarterly*, *55*, 160–177.

Dewey, J. (1896). The reflex arc concept in psychology. *Psychological Review*, *3*, 357–370.

Festinger, L. (1957). *A theory of cognitive dissonance*. Evanston, IL: Row-Peterson.

Gergen, K. J. (1982). *Toward transformation in social knowledge*. New York: Springer Verlag.

Higgins, E. T. (1987). Self-discrepancy: A theory relating self and affect. *Psychological Review*, *94*, 319–340.

hooks, B. (1981). *Ain't I a woman: Black women and feminism*. Boston, MA: South End Press.

James, W. (1890). *Principles of psychology*. New York: Holt.

Kett, J. F. (1977). *Rites of passage: Adolescence in America 1790 to the present*. New York: Basic Books.

Markus, H., & Zajonc, R. B. (1985). The cognitive perspective in social psychology. In G. Lindzey & E. Aronson (Eds.), *The handbook of social psychology* (3rd ed., Vol. I, pp. 137–230). New York: Random House.

Mead, G. H. (1934). *Mind, self, and society*. Chicago, IL: University of Chicago Press.

Miller, D. L. (1973). *George Herbert Mead: Self, language and the world*. Chicago, IL: University of Chicago Press.

Sewell, W. H. & Orenstein, A. M. (1965). Community residence and occupational choice. *American Journal of Sociology, 70*, 551–563.

Stephan, C. W., & Stephan, W. G. (1990). *Two social psychologies* (2nd ed.). Belmont, CA: Wadsworth.

Stephan, C. W., Stephan, W. G., & Pettigrew, T. F. (1991). *The future of social psychology: Defining the relationship between sociology and psychology*. New York: Springer Verlag.

Stryker, S. (1977). Developments in Two Social Psychologies: Toward an Appreciation of Mutual Relevance. *Sociometry*, *40*, 145–160.

Stryker, S. (1980). *Symbolic interactionism: A social structural approach*. Menlo Park, CA: Benjamin/Cummings.

Stryker, S. (1987). The two social psychologies: Additional thoughts. *Social Forces*, *68*, 45–54.

Stryker, S. (1993). Status inconsistency from an interactionist perspective. In R. W. Hodge & H. Strasser (Eds.), *Change and strain in social hierarchies: Theory and method in the study of status inconsistency* (pp. 114–132). Delhi: Ajanti Books International.

Stryker, S. (1994). Freedom and constraint in social and personal life: Toward resolving the paradox of self. In G. M. Platt & C. Gordon (Eds.), *Self, collective behavior and society: Essays honoring the contributions of Ralph H. Turner* (pp. 119–138). Greenwich, CT: JAI Press.

Stryker, S., & Macke, A. S. (1978). Status inconsistency and role conflict. *Annual Review of Sociology*, *4*, 57–90.

Thomas, W. I., & Thomas, D. S. (1928). *The child in America*. New York: Knopf.

Thompson, E. T. (1975). *Plantation societies, race relations, and the South: The regimentation of populations*. Durham, NC: Duke University Press.

West, C., & Zimmerman, D. H. (1987). Doing gender. *Gender and Society*, *1*, 125–151.

21 The Social Psychology of "Invictus": Conceptual and Methodological Approaches to Indomitability

Peter Suedfeld

Peter Suedfeld was born in Hungary in 1935, and survived the Holocaust as a hidden child in Budapest. He emigrated to the United States in 1948. After overseas service with the US Army, he obtained his B.A. from Queens College and his doctorate in 1963 from Princeton University, where he worked under the supervision of Harold M. Schroder and Jack A. Vernon. He has served as Head of the Department and Dean of Graduate Studies at the University of British Columbia, and currently chairs the Canadian Antarctic Research Program. His approximately 200 publications cover health, environmental, and political psychology as well as social psychology.

"Invictus" ("unbeaten" or "unconquerable"), by the nineteenth-century British poet William E. Henley, celebrates human courage and self-determination in the face of adversity. I have chosen the poem as the connecting thread in this essay because the attitudes that it expresses have been slighted in psychological research and theorizing.

Suffering is usually more dramatic than coping, and sufferers – deservedly – evoke sympathy and assistance. Psychologists and other helping professionals quite appropriately devote themselves to providing such assistance and to teaching their views of the effects of trauma.

Unfortunately, these humane reactions have led to a culture of pity and self-pity that exaggerates minor problems and thus trivializes serious ones, for example by treating casual criticism as though it were equivalent to physical assault. Research projects concentrate on the negative consequences of any identifiable adverse event: divorce, illness, poverty, unemployment, minority ethnic status, emigration, and so on without end. The one-sided emphasis leads to scientific inaccuracy, and may become a self-fulfilling prophecy: having been convinced that they cannot cope, the affected individuals and groups stop trying and become dependent on others.

Counteracting this trend, there has been a growing recognition by many psychologists of such positive facts of human life as moral and physical courage, self-sacrifice, altruism, resilience, successful coping, self-efficacy, hardiness, and "salutogenesis": the deeply meaningful, if badly named, ability that people have not only to survive extremely bad experiences but in fact to build upon them for greater strength, understanding, and purpose (Antonovsky, 1987). Stressful situations certainly have negative aspects and concomitants, but these can be balanced by positive reactions and outcomes, and most people can overcome the drawbacks that they pose. Without in any way neglecting the importance of helping those whose problems overwhelm them, this line of thought maintains that people can overcome unfavorable and even horrendous circumstances and contradicts the growing cult of victimhood that besets much of the discourse in Western cultures. Human strength is one of the important messages that psychologists must learn, understand, and teach.

> Out of the night that covers me,
> Black as the Pit from pole to pole,
> I thank whatever gods may be
> For my unconquerable soul.

The opening lines of "Invictus" evoke two of my areas of research on challenging environments. I first studied reactions to "sensory deprivation": prolonged periods of confinement in a small room under conditions of complete darkness ("black as the Pit," indeed!), profound silence, restricted movement, and minimal stimulation of taste and smell. As a graduate student in the early 1960s, I worked with Professor Jack Vernon, one of the pioneers of these studies.

At that time, the generally accepted view of sensory deprivation was that it was extremely unpleasant – most subjects quit the experiment – and caused hallucinations, emotional upheaval, intellectual deterioration, and "temporary psychosis." Some colleagues, journal editors, reviewers, granting agencies, and the mass media, viewed it as dangerous and verging on the unethical.

All of this seemed very strange to me. The period of confinement in most studies was between four and twenty-four hours; in a methodological variant, with the subject immersed in a tank of water, it was usually one to four hours. Most of us spend around eight hours a day lying fairly still, in darkness and silence. Why should a few extra hours have such dramatic negative effects? My wonder grew when, as a subject in such a study, I too got so anxious that I quit after only about four hours.

After pondering the matter, I tentatively concluded that we were producing a self-fulfilling prophecy. Participants in sensory deprivation studies were told in advance to expect bizarre, disturbing experiences; signed a legal release form to absolve the researchers in case the subject suffered mental damage; and were shown a prominent "panic button," clearly implying that panic was likely. In addition, a high level of uncertainty was evoked by not allowing subjects to see the chamber before the experiment began.

Research in social psychology tells us that high uncertainty makes one vulnerable to suggestion (Festinger, 1950, but see also Moscovici, 1976). Lacking complete information, people latch on to whatever cues are available as to what to expect and how to react. I thought that this might explain how the experimental procedure could have caused anxiety reactions, regardless of the effects of sensory deprivation itself. So I changed the procedures. Subjects were thoroughly familiarized with the chamber (with the lights on), the panic button and legal release form were scrapped, and the introduction to the experiment was low-key and reassuring.

Thirty years later, these procedures are standard, and both the scientific and popular views of what is now known as the restricted environmental stimulation technique, or REST (Suedfeld, 1980), have shown an amazing turnaround. REST, considered highly enjoyable and deeply relaxing, is used for stress management. It enhances intellectual processes such as learning, remembering, and creativity. It has been used successfully to treat chronic pain, insomnia, premenstrual syndrome, cigarette addiction, overeating, phobia, and compulsive self-injury, and to improve flying an airplane, playing basketball and tennis, throwing darts, and shooting at a target. The rate of REST participants who quit the session ahead of schedule is seldom more than 5 percent, and people in many cities around the world are willing to pay the equivalent of US$25–50 for the privilege of floating in a REST tank for an hour.

We can also extrapolate from REST to nonexperimental locations that involve confinement, monotony, reduced stimulation, and solitude. In the "real" world, such conditions tend to last for longer – sometimes much longer – periods. Nevertheless, their effects are frequently beneficial. In many cases, such periods are viewed as a chance to touch the infinite and to hone one's fortitude. Well-known examples, mixing spiritual epiphany with personal resourcefulness, include the lone "spirit quests" used by many cultures to mark the transition to adulthood and the self-imposed solitude of such religious leaders as Moses, Jesus, Mohammed, and the Buddha (Potter, 1958). In the contemporary world, the "solo" portion of Outward Bound teaches modern teenagers that they have the ingenuity and strength to survive alone in the wilderness; in retreats and hermitages, religious laypeople and monastic orders seek enlightenment through solitary meditation and study (Merton, 1957; Storr, 1988; Suedfeld, 1980).

Storr (1988) has pointed out that the life of many famous philosophers, artists, and political leaders was marked by experiences of low social and physical stimulation, and frequently by emotional coldness as well, both in childhood and later. In some cases, this experience could lead to lasting unhappiness and maladjustment; but creativity and productivity flourished in response to the challenge. This was often recognized and used by individuals who sought solitude as an aid to thought.

My second line of research related to the opening verse of "Invictus" is the study of how people adapt in the polar regions. Both the Arctic and the Antarctic are remote from the accustomed spaces of most human beings; their exploration has been marked by numerous disasters. The Antarctic is the coldest, driest, windiest, highest, and least fertile of the continents; it is the only one with no indigenous land fauna except for small insects; it is the only one that has never had an indigenous human population. The Arctic environment is more variable, with large stretches of livable areas including a variety of edible game and a long history of human habitation; but death by freezing, drowning, or starvation has been ever present, and the High Arctic environment is a frozen desert quite similar to Antarctica. Accordingly, much of the popular literature concentrates on horrors and dangers in these areas, while psychological studies focus on emotional hardships and how one might select people who will be able to withstand them.

These depictions are distorted. The diaries of polar sojourners refer to the beauty and grandeur of the landscape, comradeship and mutual help, and experiences of insight and increased sensitivity. Excitement and enjoyment are high during the first half-year on the ice, but continue to be reported throughout, even during times of darkness, cold, and deprivation (Mocellin & Suedfeld, 1991). Sailors on ships exploring or hunting whales in polar waters showed impressive levels of ingenuity, humor, zest, and problem-solving ability, and clearly had a considerable amount of fun (Johnson & Suedfeld, 1995).

Under modern conditions, much less dangerous than those faced by early explorers, there are negative reactions to the lack of privacy, boredom, remoteness from home and family. People may get irritable, anxious, depressed, and touchy; they may develop psychosomatic symptoms; their work efficiency and personal hygiene may deteriorate. At the same time, challenge also brings out fortitude, perseverance, ingenuity, and comradeship. Many polar workers form a strong emotional bond with the place, return as often as they can, and express great distress when asked to imagine if they could never go back again (Steel, 1994).

Perhaps the clearest evidence for a beneficial effect of the polar experience is in the work of E. K. E. Gunderson and Lawrence A. Palinkas (Palinkas, 1990). Naval personnel who had wintered over in Antarctica were compared with fellow sailors who were not assigned to the Antarctic. Both groups had passed the mental and physical tests for naval service, volunteered and been found qualified for wintering over, had similar training and occupational specialties, and had similar career paths.

The winter-over group had fewer hospitalizations overall, and reduced risk of various specific diseases, than the controls. They also showed lower short- and long-term rates of mental disorders and accidents. The conclusions were that "the lessons learned in coping with the stressful Antarctic environment may be utilized in coping with other stressful experiences as well" (Palinkas, 1990, p. 247), and that winter-over crew members learn behaviors that reinforce their feelings of being in control of themselves and their environment. This is definitely salutogenesis in Antonovsky's original definition, in that it shows "eustress" (that is, positive stress, rather than distress or negative stress): coping with or adjusting to the stressors did not merely prevent the Antarctic crew members from getting sick, but actually led them to become stronger and healthier.

Because the Antarctic is sometimes considered to be an earthly analog of space flight, it is interesting that the space program has suffered from a similarly one-sided approach. Psychological and psychiatric literature has exaggerated the behavioral problems of astronauts, to the point of predicting that no one would be able to cope mentally with long-duration missions – once again, overlooking the adaptiveness and resilience of the crews (Douglas, 1990).

In summary, REST has turned out not to be a stressor at all for most people; on the contrary, it may be a reducer of stress. Polar work, even the daunting winter-over version, can be both enjoyable and an enhancer of coping ability. But perhaps people can deal with these environments only because they are not sufficiently adverse. We shall next look at whether more severe stressors justify the pessimism of our discipline.

> In the fell clutch of circumstance,
>   I have not winced nor cried aloud.
> Under the bludgeonings of chance
>   My head is bloody, but unbowed.
>
> Beyond this place of wrath and tears
>   Looms but the Horror of the shade,
> And yet the menace of the years
>   Finds, and shall find, me unafraid.

These, the central verses of the poem, explicitly depict a situation of pain and impending death. What does scientific psychology, and especially social psychology, tell us about such environments?

When I consider the situations that could be characterized this way, I am struck by how many there are, and what this great number tells us about the human condition. Social psychologists have studied people who have suffered life-threatening diseases, crippling accidents, familial abuse, famine, war, natural disaster, torture, persecution, genocide, deep grief, impending execution – the list is virtually endless. Chance does indeed bludgeon us, and Henley was right: to a great extent, we stand unbowed. Perhaps more accurately, most of us stand fairly unbowed most of the time. One must look with awe upon the ability of people to endure and conquer misfortune (e.g. Gondolf, 1988; Higgins, 1994; Monat & Lazarus, 1977; Segal, 1986; Taylor, 1989; Wolin & Wolin, 1993).

I shall selectively touch upon a few of the topics that have especially interested me, personally and scientifically. Growing out of my research on REST, I was for some time concerned with the effects of solitary confinement on convicts. Historical evidence is highly selective, and mixed: while it is clear that many isolated prisoners deteriorate in mind and body, prisons and solitary cells have also been places where important works of philosophy, political theory, literature, and even scientific thought germinated (Davies, 1990; Suedfeld, 1980).

To examine the effects of solitary confinement in modern prisons, my research team for the first (and so far, only) time administered structured interviews and psychological tests to a broadly based sample of convict volunteers in five North American prisons (Suedfeld, Ramirez, Reaton, & Baker-Brown, 1982). Although prisoners fear negative effects when they first go into the isolation unit, we found no universally or uniformly adverse effects. In fact, solitary confinement was not rated as significantly more stressful than the general prison environment. Most prisoners reported that within a few days in the isolation cell, they had learned to cope satisfactorily by thinking about the future and through developing programs of physical and mental exercises. These findings contradict the clinical literature, which – using impressionistic data gathered from selected respondents – portrays solitary confinement as the willful destruction of the inmate's personality (e.g. Jackson, 1983).

A much more severe form of imprisonment, which had also been linked – completely mistakenly, as later evidence showed – with "sensory deprivation" is coercive persuasion, more commonly referred to as brainwashing. It was developed in China during the first few decades of the communist regime, and was applied to non- and anti-communist Chinese, foreign missionaries, teachers, and businessmen, and UN (mostly American) prisoners of war captured in Korea.

Social-behavioral studies (Lifton, 1963; Schein, 1961) have shown that many brainwashing victims never wavered in their resistance; others found ways to ridicule their captors or to appease them with superficial and minimal compliance (Hunter, 1956). Very few prisoners were really converted (Biderman, 1963; Lifton, 1963). After repatriation, 21 percent of ex-POWs said they had benefited from the experience (Schein, Colley, & Singer, 1960); and among civilians,

> Western subjects consistently reported a sense of having been benefited and emotionally strengthened, of having become more sensitive to their own and others' inner feelings, and more flexible and confident in human relationships. . . . Each had thus gone farther than ever before in realizing his human potential. (Lifton, 1963, p. 238)

Similar conclusions have been reached by and about American POWs in the Vietnam war, many of whom underwent years of torture, deprivation, solitary confinement, and brainwashing attempts. In all of these situations, prisoners survived by drawing upon support from each other, upon their religious, patriotic, and moral values, and upon self-discipline in setting daily routines, hygienic standards, and the like (Jones, 1980). Amazingly, in one interview study 61 percent of ex-Vietnam POWs reported having higher optimism and self-insight, and better social relationships than they had had previously (Sledge, Boydstun, & Rabe, 1980).

More ex-POWs than other combat veterans suffer from long-term medical problems and post-traumatic stress syndrome, and more die prematurely. Yet, combat soldiers – and therefore, POWs – are in vigorous youth or early middle age, trained, disciplined, used to rough conditions, and selected from among the mentally and physically healthy portion of the national population. What happens when the victims don't have these resources?

Our best data about civilian populations during the ravages of war come from World War II. The evidence indicates that

> the dire predictions made by many self-styled "experts" on mass behavior failed to take account of the psychological stamina of the average civilian. Bombing had little effect on the incidence of chronic mental disorder; outbreaks of mass panic were rare; behavioral morale was maintained at a relatively high level. Although emotional shock did occur on a sizeable scale, most cases recovered fairly rapidly. (Janis, 1951, p. 153)

Janis further reported "fairly rigid conformity to social norms and increased efforts to adhere to conventional morality," along with a preoccupation with maintaining normal activities (p. 170). Survivors of the atomic bombing of Hiroshima and Nagasaki showed general similarity to civilians bombed in Germany, Japan, or Britain. It is particularly noteworthy that there were no mass occurrences of depression or "survivor guilt." Adaptive mechanisms included increased communication of one's feelings, avoidance of social isolation, learning to recognize signs of danger and appropriate defensive responses, and a tendency to attribute outcomes to forces outside oneself (fate, God, superstitious rituals, or fetishes). Even in more dire circumstances, groups ranging from shipwrecked castaways (Leslie, 1988) to civilians brutally interned in wartime (Bloom & Halsema, 1983) have saved themselves from disaster through good leadership, ingenuity, and cooperation.

The most destructive large-scale persecution in recent history has been the Holocaust, and its survivors have been the subject of many publications. Despite early assumptions that most survivors suffered severe and permanent psychological damage, more recent scholars are concluding that the majority are in fact essentially normal people leading essentially normal lives (e.g. Antonovsky, 1987; Des Pres, 1976; Helmreich, 1992; Higgins, 1994; Krell, 1993). As in the case of solitary confinement, we have long known that some Holocaust survivors have built upon their experiences to create exceptional and admirable works, from the logotherapy of Viktor Frankl to the Nobel-winning literature of Elie Wiesel.

These eminent people exemplify a widespread phenomenon. Many less well-known survivors have worked productively, established happy families, and contributed to their communities through charitable and educational activities (not least in the area of education about the Holocaust, and ethnic relations in general). Their autobiographical narratives tell us that both during and since the Holocaust, they have tended to use planning and careful thinking to solve problems. They feel that their faith in God, or in their own luck, gave them strength to survive during the Holocaust itself. They placed less emphasis on help from other people than the POWs described above (perhaps because they were not sure whom they could trust not to betray them, or because unlike the POWs they had no pre-existing social framework such as military camaraderie). It is noteworthy that they did not rely on purely emotion-oriented ways of coping with stress, and also that they are not marked by survivor guilt, self-blame, or other negative self-perceptions (Suedfeld, Krell, Wiebe, & Steel, 1995). As we might expect by now, some consider that the Holocaust experience made them stronger and more sensitive to others (Lomranz, 1995).

Many of the coping resources that have enabled people to survive intact are related to social-psychological variables – broadly defined, as the scope of social psychology usually is. Leadership and intragroup cohesion, for example, are among the most prominent factors in minimizing the stresses of battle and of other life-endangering ventures such as exploration and captivity (Bartone & Kirkland, 1991; Fiedler & Garcia, 1987; Hunter, 1988; Suedfeld, 1987).

Social support is often crucial to survival. We tend to take it for granted that ingroup solidarity will lead to such support (experimental social psychology has shown this to be the case in even purely nominal groups: Billig & Tajfel, 1973), but in many cases rescue comes from outside, sometimes from surprising sources (e.g. Oliner & Oliner, 1988). Research has delineated the variables that enhance or diminish helping in everyday situations, such as coming to the aid of someone who may be injured: we know about diffusion of responsibility, clarity of need, and reinforcement variables such as time pressure and possible cost (Latané & Darley, 1970). But what can explain why some people risk everything, including their own and their family's lives, to assist strangers? Here, social psychology has so far let us down.

On one point, "Invictus" falls short. In extolling the virtue inherent in facing adversity, Henley ignored the advantages of not facing it. Modern psychologists, too, have treated denial, repression, and similar defense mechanisms as somehow wrong. However, the intriguing work of Taylor (1989) points out that exaggeratedly good opinions about one's own abilities, unrealistic optimism about one's outcomes, and an overestimate of one's ability to control events are related to good physical and mental health, professional success, and overcoming the effects of traumatic events. Obviously, these "positive illusions" must not be so extreme as to lose all touch with reality; but a positive outlook is a good foundation to build on.

It matters not how strait the gate,
  How charged with punishments the scroll,
I am the master of my fate;
  I am the captain of my soul

The last verse of the poem emphasizes what has become a central concern of psychologists: the perception of being in control. Social psychology and its offshoots – especially health and environmental psychology – have demonstrated the importance of this perception, and the deleterious effects that ensue when it is absent. Among the positive illusions discussed by Taylor (see above), the feeling of being in control is paramount. A much-studied concept, learned helplessness (Seligman, 1975), focuses on the non- and counter-productive behaviors people engage in when they feel that some outside force completely determines what happens to them. Everyday stressors become more tolerable if the individual views them as controllable even if not avoidable, and much of the behavior of prisoners of war, convicts, concentration camp inmates, hospitalized patients, and the like, is directed toward exerting what control they can given a generally non-responsive environment. Even the design of spacecraft was changed when astronauts complained about just being along for a ride that was mostly controlled by computers and instructions from the ground (Wolfe, 1973).

My own interest in this area, aside from the issue of control among the populations that I have already described (e.g. isolated prisoners, polar crews, and Holocaust survivors), has been on how people, especially national and international leaders, attempt to exercise control through decision-making. With a number of colleagues and students, we have developed a standardized method for scoring the degree to which speakers or writers recognize different aspects of a situation, or different points of view about it ("differentiation"), and the degree to which they perceive relations among these different aspects or points of view ("integration"). The resultant score indicates the individual's level of "integrative complexity", with higher scores representing higher complexity (Baker-Brown, Ballard, Bluck, de Vries, Suedfeld, & Tettock, 1992; Suedfeld, Tetlock, & Strenfert, 1992).

This research mostly falls within political psychology, another subdivision of social psychology. It also overlaps with the literature on cognition and decision-making, with its concern on how people use information in arriving at the best solution to a variety of problems. Many researchers in this field study only unsuccessful decisions, and argue that these are typical because of habitual reliance on cognitive short cuts that lead the person to overlook desirable decision strategies, such as searching for more information before deciding, calculating the mathematical probability of alternative possible outcomes, or reconsidering previously discarded options even when a change in the situation may make them more appropriate. Here, again, psychologists too often emphasize negative aspects of human behavior and ignore positive ones.

My own interpretation, the cognitive manager model (Suedfeld, 1992), argues that decision-making is like any other coping process: it calls upon psychological and material resources (time, mental and physical effort, energy, information, and so on), and these resources are provided to the extent that the problem requires them, is important enough, and enough resources are available to deal with it. Thus, short cuts are more likely to be used when they provide an acceptable solution, the problem is relatively unimportant (or many problems have to be addressed at the same time), or the decision-maker's coping resources are running short because of, e.g. insufficient or excessive information, stress, time pressure, fatigue, or emotional overarousal.

High levels of integrative complexity require the use of more resources than lower levels do. We would therefore expect that people under moderate levels of stress – e.g. trying to solve personal and professional problems – will show increased levels of complexity as they bring more resources to bear on solving the problem. We have in fact found this, particularly among men (one of the few instances of a sex difference in integrative complexity). By contrast, prolonged severe stress should lead to reduced complexity as resources are depleted; and this is indeed the pattern among, for example, political leaders trying to deal with crises so serious that they eventually resulted in war, national elites (such as eminent novelists and scientists) during wartime, military commanders in campaigns that were not going well, and individuals suffering through prolonged, eventually fatal, illnesses.

In addition, remember that not all problems require highly complex decision strategies. Being able to differentiate the ones that do from those that do not is an important aspect of being a good cognitive manager. For example, declaring war requires less complexity than negotiating to maintain the peace: nations launching surprise attacks such as Pearl Harbor show substantially reduced complexity several weeks or months before the attack occurs. Fighting a revolution requires less complexity than governing a country: the most successful revolutionary leaders are those who, like George Washington and Fidel Castro, evidence simple strategies (complete devotion to the cause, rejection of compromise, no concessions to enemies) during the phase of armed struggle but move to higher levels once they take over the government, when they must conciliate former opponents, convert former neutrals, and deal with the multiple problems of running a country. Those who cannot make this switch tend to lose their prominent positions. A similar phenomenon occurs in democratic countries. Tetlock (1981) has found that presidential speeches tend to be more complex than campaign speeches by the same person when he was a candidate, and those presidents who showed the least increase in complexity have been those generally considered the least successful or admired in recent times, such as Warren G. Harding and Herbert Hoover.

I think that the ability to recognize the best level of complexity for a given situation, and the ability to then work at that level, is a personality-related characteristic just like other coping factors such as hardiness and optimism. Some people have more ability as cognitive managers than others, so that a few international figures maintain their complexity even during the worst crises. These tend to be fairly successful, long-career statesmen, such as the Duke of Wellington and Andrei A. Gromyko. But in general, I believe that – contrary to social science critics (see Suedfeld & Tetlock, 1991) – most people are pretty good cognitive managers and that of the vast numbers of decisions that we all have to make, most are reasonably appropriate given the information, time, energy, and other resources available.

Conclusion

Most of my research has not been in the mainstream of social psychology, but rather in its offshoots and subdisciplines: environmental psychology, health psychology, and political psychology. Even within those, the studies I have pursued tend to be off the beaten path. Given my interests at the borders of the discipline, the message of social psychology that I want most to spread is that research must question current assumptions and orthodoxies to create surprising, novel, and valid knowledge. In the broad area of stress and coping, such an approach should integrate information not only from various areas of psychology, but from history, political science, literature, biography, medicine, etcetera; and should study both ordinary and unusual people. Such studies have demonstrated that human beings are tougher and more competent than social scientists believe, and have led large segments of society to believe. These characteristics deserve and need more detailed investigation and wider recognition.

Further Reading

Antonovsky, A. (1987). *Unraveling the mystery of health: How people manage stress and stay well.* San Francisco: Jossey-Bass. Presents and describes the concept of salutogenesis, the emphasis on successful and health-enhancing coping reactions to stress, and discusses research using the sense of coherence questionnaire, which measures a personality characteristic related to salutogenic capacity.

Apter, M. J. (1992). *The dangerous edge: The psychology of excitement*. New York: The Free Press. An examination of why people seek out challenging, exciting activities and environments even when these may be uncomfortable or even dangerous.

Helmreich, W. B. (1992). *Against all odds: Holocaust survivors and the successful lives they made in America*. New York: Simon & Schuster. Cases of Holocaust survivors who have settled in North America, analyzing the characteristics they evidence in speaking about the successful rebuilding of their lives.

Homer, *The Odyssey*. A prototypical example of adventurous, resourceful, and resilient coping with a series of severe and novel stressors. The reader may go on to any number of first-hand accounts of explorers and other travelers, sailors, soldiers, astronauts, ex-prisoners, etc.; but I don't think one can do much better than Odysseus.

Moos, R. H. (Ed.) (1976). *Human adaptation: Coping with life crises*. Lexington, MA: Heath. A compilation of studies of how both children and adults adapt to stressors that range from the first day of kindergarten through bereavement, life transitions, disasters, victimization, imprisonment, and so on.

Rosenbaum, M. (Ed.) (1990). *Learned resourcefulness: On coping skills, self-control, and adaptive behavior*. New York: Springer. Discusses theoretical constructs relevant to successful coping, such as hardiness, cognitive styles, and sense of coherence. Looks at resourceful coping in such areas as hazardous work, the hostage experience, and psychiatric illness.

Segal, J. (1986). *Winning life's toughest battles: Roots of human resilience*. New York: Ivy. One of the early professional examinations of successful adaptation, mostly through exercising control.

Wilson, J. P., Harel, Z., & Kahana, B. (Eds.) (1988). *Human adaptation to extreme stress: From the Holocaust to Vietnam*. New York: Plenum. Studies of the reactions of people who have survived such experiences as concentration camps, POW camps, combat in various wars, and the Cambodian auto-genocide.

Wolin, S. J., & Wolin, S. (1993). *The resilient self*. New York: Villard. A study of people who grew up in "dysfunctional" families and have adjusted well as adults. Proposes the "challenge model" of characteristics that contribute to their success: insight, independence, relationships, initiative, creativity, humour, and morality.

References

Antonovsky, A. (1987). *Unraveling the mystery of health: How people manage stress and stay well.* San Francisco: Jossey-Bass.

Baker-Brown, G., Ballard, E. J., Bluck, S., de Vries, B., Suedfeld, P., & Tetlock, P. E. (1992). The conceptual/integrative complexity scoring manual. In C. P. Smith (Ed.), *Motivation and personality: Handbook of thematic content analysis* (pp. 400–418). Cambridge: Cambridge University Press.

Bartone, P. T., & Kirkland, F. R. (1991). Optimal leadership in small Army units. In R. Gal & A. D. Mangelsdorff (Eds.), *Handbook of military psychology* (pp. 393–409). New York: Wiley.

Biderman, A. D. (1963). *March to calumny: The story of American POWs in the Korean War*. New York: Macmillan.

Billig, M., & Tajfel, H. (1973). Social categorization and similarity in intergroup behavior. *European Journal of Social Psychology*, *3*, 27–52.

Bloom, M., & Halsema, J. (1983). Survival in extreme conditions. *Suicide and Life-Threatening Behavior*, *13*, 195–206.

Davies, I. (1990). *Writers in prison*. Oxford: Basil Blackwell.

Des Pres, T. (1976). *The survivor: An anatomy of life in the death camps*. New York: Oxford University Press.

Douglas, W. K. (1990). Psychological and sociological aspects of manned spaceflight. In A. A. Harrison, Y. A. Clearwater, & C. P. McKay (Eds.), *From Antarctica to outer space: Life in isolation and confinement* (pp. 81–87). New York: Springer Verlag.

Festinger, L. (1950). Informal social communication. *Psychological Review*, *57*, 271–282.

Fiedler, F. E., & Garcia, J. E. (1987). *New approaches to effective leadership*. New York: Wiley.

Gondolf, E. W. with E. R. Fisher (1988). *Battered women as survivors: An alternative to treating learned helplessness*. Lexington, MA: Lexington Books.

Helmreich, W. B. (1992). *Against all odds: Holocaust survivors and the successful lives they made in America*. New York: Simon & Schuster.

Higgins, G. O'C. (1994). *Resilient adults: Overcoming a cruel past*. San Francisco: Jossey-Bass.

Hunter, E. (1956). *Brainwashing: The story of men who defied it*. New York: Pyramid.

Hunter, E. J. (1988). The psychological effects of being a prisoner of war. In J. P. Wilson, Z. Harel & B. Kahana (Eds.), *Human adaptation to extreme stress: From the Holocaust to Vietnam* (pp. 157–170). New York: Plenum.

Jackson, M. (1983). *Prisoners of isolation: Solitary confinement in Canada*. Toronto: University of Toronto Press.

Janis, I. L. (1951). *Air war and emotional stress: Psychological studies of bombing and civilian defense*. New York: McGraw Hill.

Johnson, P. J., & Suedfeld, P. (1995). *Nonwork activities of Arctic whalers and explorers: Coping with stress through creating microcosms of home and family*. Under editorial review.

Jones, D. R. (1980). What the repatriated prisoners of war wrote about themselves. *Aviation, Space, and Environmental Medicine*, *51*, 615–617.

Krell, R. (1993). Child survivors of the Holocaust: Strategies of adaptation. *Canadian Journal of Psychiatry*, *38*, 384–389.

Latané, B., & Darley, J. M. (1970). *The unresponsive bystander: Why doesn't he help?* New York: Appleton-Crofts.

Leslie, E. E. (1988). *Desperate journeys, abandoned souls: True stories of castaways and other survivors*. Boston, MA: Houghton Mifflin.

Lifton, R. J. (1963). *Thought reform and the psychology of totalism: A study of "brainwashing" in China*. New York: Norton.

Lomranz, J. (1995). Endurance and living: Long-term effects of the Holocaust. In S. E. Hobfoll & M. W. de Vries (Eds.), *Extreme stress and communities: Impact and intervention* (pp. 325–352). Netherlands: Kluwer.

Merton, T. (1957). *The silent life*. New York: Farrar, Straus & Giroux.

Mocellin, J. S. P., & Suedfeld, P. (1991). Voices from the ice: Diaries of polar explorers. *Environment and Behavior*, *23*, 704–722.

Monat, A., & Lazarus, R. S. (Eds.) (1977). *Stress and coping: An anthology*. New York: Columbia University Press.

Moscovici, S. (1976). *Social influence and social change*. London: Academic Press.

Oliner, S. B., & Oliner, P. (1988). *The altruistic personality: Rescuers of Jews in Nazi Germany*. New York: Free Press.

Palinkas, L. A. (1990). Group adaptation and individual adjustment in Antarctica: A summary of recent research. In A. A. Harrison, Y. A. Clearwater, & C. P. McKay (Eds.), *From Antarctica to outer space: Life in isolation and confinement* (pp. 239–251). New York: Springer Verlag.

Potter, C. F. (1958). *The great religious leaders*. New York: Simon & Schuster.

Schein, E. H. with I. Schneier & C. H. Barker (1961). *Coercive persuasion*. New York: Norton.

Schein, E. H., Colley, W. E., & Singer, M. T. (1960). *A psychological followup of former POWs of the Chinese Communists: I. Results of interview study*. Unpublished Technical Report, Massachusetts Institute of Technology.

Segal, J. (1986). *Winning life's toughest battles: Roots of human resilience*. New York: Ivy.

Seligman, M. E. P. (1975). *On depression, development, and death*. San Francisco: Freeman.

Sledge, W. H., Boydstun, J. A., & Rabe, A. J. (1980). Self-concept changes related to war captivity. *Archives of General Psychiatry*, *37*, 430–443.

Steel, G. D. (1994). *The structure of environmental relationships in polar regions*. Unpublished doctoral dissertation, University of British Columbia.

Storr, A. (1988). *Solitude: A return to the self*. New York: Free Press.

Suedfeld, P. (1980). *Restricted environmental stimulation: Research and clinical applications*. New York: Wiley.

Suedfeld, P. (1987). Extreme and unusual environments. In D. Stokols & I. Altman (Eds.), *Handbook of environmental psychology* (Vol. 1, pp. 863–887). New York: Wiley.

Suedfeld, P. (1992). Cognitive managers and their critics. *Political Psychology*, *13*, 435–453.

Suedfeld, P., & Tetlock, P. E. (1991). Psychological advice about foreign policy decision making: Heuristics, biases, and cognitive defects. In P. Suedfeld & P. E. Tetlock (Eds.), *Psychology and social policy* (pp. 51–70). New York: Hemisphere.

Suedfeld, P., Krell, R., Wiebe, R. E., & Steel, G. D. (1995). *Coping strategies in the narratives of Holocaust survivors*. Under editorial review.

Suedfeld, P., Ramirez, C., Deaton, J., & Baker-Brown, G. (1982). Reactions and attributes of prisoners in solitary confinement. *Criminal Justice and Behavior*, *9*, 303–340.

Suedfeld, P., Tetlock, P. E., & Streufert, S. (1992). Conceptual/integrative complexity. In C.P. Smith (Ed.), *Motivation and personality: Handbook of thematic content analysis* (pp. 393–400). Cambridge: Cambridge University Press.

Taylor, S. E. (1989). *Positive illusions: Creative self-deception and the healthy mind*. New York: Basic Books.

Tetlock, P. E. (1981). Pre- to post-election shifts in presidential rhetoric: Impression management or cognitive adjustment? *Journal of Personality and Social Psychology*, *41*, 207–212.

Wolfe, T. (1973). *The right stuff*. New York: Farrar, Straus & Giroux.

Wolin, S. J., & Wolin, S. (1993). *The resilient self*. New York: Villard.

22 A Cross-Cultural Perspective on Social Psychology

Harry C. Triandis

Harry Triandis was born in 1926 in Greece where, during World War II, he learned four foreign languages and developed a curiosity about cultural differences. He graduated from Cornell University (1958) with a doctorate in social psychology, supervised by William Lambert and W. F. Whyte. His first publication was in 1954. He has authored seven books and 200 chapters and papers. He was the general editor of the six-volume *Handbook of Cross-Cultural Psychology*. He has lectured on all inhabited continents. He has received awards from the Interamerican Society of Psychology, and the American Psychological Association (the Distinguished Contributions to the International Advancement of Psychology Award), an honorary degree from the University of Athens, and the Klineberg Award.

Historically, social psychology has been a European–North American product. As social psychologists who had been exposed to other cultural traditions began their research, dissatisfaction with traditional social psychology began. Among the pioneers in this movement was Otto Klineberg, who provided a cross-cultural social psychology text (1954) as well as a historical perspective on the field (1980).

All humans are ethnocentric, at least to some extent. This observation can be analyzed in two parts. (1) Most people do not know that they have a culture, because they believe that the way they see the world and act is universal; and (2) when they discover that those on the other side of the mountain or across the

I thank John Adamopoulos, John Berry, Darm Bhawuk, Jim Davis, and Michele Gelfand for critical comments on an earlier version of this paper.

sea look upon their environment or act differently, they judge them harshly. Specifically, people see their own culture as the standard and evaluate other cultures according to their similarity to their own culture. This is an aspect of the human condition (Triandis, 1994b) comparable in importance to having two legs and a large brain. It has a profound influence on social psychology, because we social psychologists think that what is true in our culture must be a universal truth. In short, "social psychology" can be used in two senses: as a scientific discipline and as a socially mediated account of the way humans think about social behavior. These two "social psychologies" are related, but they are not identical.

Cross-cultural studies indicate that our theories often need to be modified. Dimensions of cultural variation become parameters of the universal social psychology. That is, for instance, when a culture is high on a dimension a particular phenomenon occurs; when it is low on that dimension a reversal of the phenomenon may occur. More commonly, when a culture is high on a dimension of cultural variation a social psychological finding may be accentuated and when it is low it may disappear.

Illustrative of this point, Richard Shweder has studied judgments of the appropriateness of social behaviors in Bhubaneshwar, India and Chicago, Illinois (see a summary in Triandis, 1994b). He found, for example, that in the Indian sample most people think that it is a sin for widows to eat chicken. When asked if that should be considered a sin in all cultures, the Indian respondents answer with an unqualified "yes." When the same question is asked in Chicago the answer is "No." In Chicago people see the widow as an independent agent, and "if she wants to eat chicken she can eat chicken." Furthermore, they think that *universally* people believe that widows may eat chicken, and in all ideal societies widows should be able to eat whatever they, as free and independent individuals, would like to eat.

The underlying cosmology of the two cultures is different, and we can understand this only if we realize that the Indians see people as interdependent, and the Americans see them as independent. In India they see widows linked with their husbands for eternity. If they eat chicken, they believe, they will become sexually aroused, have sex with someone, and break the eternal bond with their husbands. They also think that this is the way things are and should be *universally*, and those who do not see it that way are misguided, or insufficiently educated in the "truths of everyday life." The Americans see widows as autonomous agents, and thus as able to eat what they like to eat. In short, the naive social psychologies of each culture are different and reflect the dimensions of cultural variation, in this case the relative emphasis on individualism and collectivism.

Notice the interesting similarity between the "ethnocentric universalism," just described, and a phenomenon that social psychologists call the "false consensus effect" (Mullen, Atkins, Champion, Edwards, Handy, Story, &

Vanderlok, 1985). People who agree with a position believe that a large percentage of the population agrees with that position; people who disagree with a position believe that a very small percentage of the population agrees with the position. For example, if people think that smoking is dangerous, they think that almost everybody thinks that smoking is dangerous; if they think that smoking is not dangerous they think that only a few "extremists" think that smoking is dangerous. The effect is strong (Mullen et al., 1985, report effect sizes of 0.3 to 1.3), extraordinarily statistically significant ($p < 0.0000000001$); and several attempts to eliminate it have proved ineffective (Krueger & Clement, 1994).

In this chapter I will first provide some definitions of important constructs. Then I will argue that traditional social psychology is really Western social psychology which is a special case of the universal social psychology we hope to develop in the future. I will then examine how we can sort out what are universal from culture-specific aspects of social psychological phenomena. To do that we need a universal framework for social psychology, within which the various indigenous social psychologies can be situated as special cases. I will describe four ways of thinking about social-psychological phenomena that need to be considered in order to predict social behavior, and will end by discussing the determinants of social behavior in different cultural settings.

Definitions

Culture is to society what memory is to individuals (Kluckhohn, 1954). It includes all that "has worked" in the past, and became a *shared* perspective, transmitted from generation to generation. More generally, culture can be defined as all that is human made (Herskovits, 1955). However, this definition is too broad, and thus it is useful to distinguish its objective aspects (e.g. roads, tools) from its subjective aspects (e.g. categories, associations, beliefs, attitudes, norms, role-definitions, self-definitions, values, and so on), described in detail by Triandis (1972, 1989). Cultures differ in innumerable ways. In the present discussion I will mention only two types of culture: individualist and collectivist.

In cultures that emphasize *individualism* people think of individuals as independent of groups, i.e. as autonomous entities whose social behavior can be traced to internal processes like attitudes. In such cultures people place their personal goals ahead of the goals of their groups, and keep score on how much they "profit" from a social relationship relative to the cost of the relationship, and stay in the relationship only if it is clearly "profitable," i.e. they get more out of it than they put into it.

In *collectivist cultures* people think of individuals as interdependent, as representatives of groups who act according to the norms of these groups

(Davidson, Jaccard, Triandis, Morales, & Diaz-Guerrero, 1976), who place the goals of their groups ahead of their personal goals, and pay attention to the needs of the members of these groups, so that they are likely to stay in a relationship that is not "profitable" if it satisfies the needs of the group.

Sorting Out what is Universal and Culture Specific: The Universal Framework

A universal framework (Triandis, 1978) is required to situate the culture-specific social psychologies. This framework is as follows:

- Level 4: Behaviors that show strong individual differences, determined by a complex interaction of genetic, situational and cultural factors. To make predictions here we keep culture and situation constant and study individual differences. The field is covered by personality psychology.
- Level 3: Culture-specific manifestations of the fundamental dimensions of cultural variation. To make predictions here we must specify the culture and the situation. Indigenous social psychologies belong here. Most of social psychology is a Western indigenous psychology, and belongs at this level.
- Level 2: The study of the fundamental dimensions of cultural variation (see text for definitions), such as cultural complexity, tightness, individualism, and collectivism. This is one of the domains of cross-cultural psychology.
- Level 1: Universal psychological laws, that reflect biological-genetic influences. Phenomena that are found among all humans and many mammals (e.g. that behavior is a function of its consequences). This is the domain of general and comparative (animal) as well as neuro-physiological psychology.

It defines four levels of analysis. A level of analysis specifies the generality of phenomena. Level 1 deals with phenomena that are found among all humans and many other animals; level 2 deals with phenomena that are common among large groups of humans such as Europeans or East Asians; level 3 deals with phenomena that only occur in specific cultures; level 4 with personality differences that may occur regardless of culture.

Level 1: Universal psychologies

Humans have much in common with other animals, especially pack-hunting primates (Lee & DeVore, 1968), lions, wolves, and hunting dogs. In those animals we see strong evidence of territoriality, in which the defense of the territory is accomplished by attacking intruders, while in-group members are protected. The corresponding human dimension was called association versus dissociation (Triandis, 1978). It is reflected in behaviors such as to love, support, admire versus to fight with, avoid, and attack. Studies of social distance (Bogardus, 1925) provide a more differentiated dimension from extreme association (to marry) to extreme dissociation (to kill). These basic behaviors can also be seen in animals. For example, Hebb and Thompson (1954) describe thirty-six specific acts that were identified among chimpanzees at the Yerkes laboratory. They called them "first-order categories of behavior." These basic acts were combined into "second-order categories of behavior," such as the animal is "friendly," "aggressive," or "shows avoidance." This contrast corresponds to association vs dissociation. A "third-order level" includes behavior sequences, such as friendly and then aggressive (deceit).

Pecking orders are also widely found in animals, and the human dimension that corresponds to them is superordination versus subordination (Triandis, 1978). Behaviors such as to give orders to, to instruct, to criticize, to supervise versus to obey, to ask for help, to accept advice of, and to submit work for approval of, provide examples along this contrasting dimension. Animals have definable social structures, e.g. roe deer and baboons are "patriarchal" and sheep are "matriarchal" (Hebb & Thompson, 1954, p. 541).

Many animals also show division of labor, such as one animal doing the hunting and the other taking care of the newborn. This corresponds to role differentiation in humans. Role differentiation increases the predictability of social behavior. Humans often seek predictability and control over their social environment and culture is one of the ways in which they control their social environment (Hebb & Thompson, 1954). When most humans were hunters, they often were subject to attacks by wild animals, and were in constant fear of such attacks. As "civilization" evolved, more structure, predictability, and control of the environment became possible. A number of norms, taboos, and standard operating procedures developed that increased the predictability of events. For example, institutions that regulate disputes (e.g. the courts), that decide how to distribute resources (e.g. political systems), or how to regulate behavior (e.g. laws, salary schedules) develop in such "civilizations." More specifically, people who work "on salary" (a specific cultural element) often expect to be paid at *regular* intervals. But people who have never had that experience often show "ecosystem distrust" (Triandis, 1976), that is, they distrust their environment and do not believe that they can predict it. The environment appears to them to be chaotic, characterized by dog-eat-dog relationships.

Level 2: Psychologies that include cultural differentiation

Humans live in different ecologies, and the variations in these ecologies result in the development of cultural differences (see Berry, Poortinga, Segall, &

Dasen, 1992). Social behavior became differentiated (Adamopoulos, 1984), as one historical period succeeded another, and reflected some of the structures present in level 1, but over time resulted in more complex, differentiated structures, including dimensions of cultural variation.

Among the most important dimensions of ecological variation are three dimensions: homogeneity of the population, extent to which economic activities require interdependent actions, and population density.

The more homogeneous the culture the more norms are clear and deviation from norms is likely to be punished. When slight deviations from norms are punished we call this culture "tight." Conversely, when deviation from norms is unpunished, unless it reaches very high magnitudes, we have a "loose" culture. The greater the density of the society, the more norms are needed to avoid friction and thus tightness is often high where density is high. When survival depends on cooperation and coordination of effort, people who do not follow norms are punished, and the culture is tighter. Conversely, in environments that are heterogeneous, with different norms specifying what one is to do, it is difficult to be very tight. Also, in environments that are sparsely populated (e.g. deserts, the Arctic), people can allow others to deviate from norms. In cities people create distance by using walls, and that allows them to be loose. When people can do their own thing and still survive, looseness is likely.

As humans master their environments they develop different levels of affluence. A complex set of factors is responsible for economic development (Triandis, 1984) and affluence is associated with cultural complexity.

Cultures that are very tight and also simple tend to be collectivistic; cultures that are loose and complex tend to be individualistic (Triandis, 1994b, 1995).

Individualism, collectivism, tightness, and cultural complexity are cultural syndromes. Cultural syndromes are detected when beliefs, attitudes, norms, roles, and values are widely shared, and organized around a central theme, among those who speak a particular language, live in a specific historic period, and in a definable geographic region (Triandis, 1993). The central theme of individualism is the autonomy of the individual; the central theme of collectivism is the importance of the collective; the central themes of tightness is the rejection of even minor deviation from norms; the central theme of complexity is the *large number* of different social structures, political systems, religious beliefs, and aesthetic standards found in a society.

A large literature reviewed by Triandis (1995) suggests that collectivists define themselves as interdependent members of groups; individualists define themselves as autonomous individuals (Markus & Kitayama, 1991). Table 22.1 summarizes some of the differences between individualism and collectivism

When role differentiation emphasizes differences in power, and such differences are functional in a particular ecology – for example, as occurs when outside threat requires coordination of action under the leadership of some

Table 22.1 The main differences between collectivism and individualism

Collectivists	*Individualists*
Define the self independently	Person is independent of groups
Give priority to group goals	Give priority to personal goals
Behavior is strongly influenced by norms, secondarily by attitudes	Behavior is strongly determined by attitudes, secondarily by norms
Have communal relationships	Have social exchanges

authority, or a major public work requires coordinated action to increase survival – the boss is very different from the followers. The coordinators are at the top and are high in the social dominance orientation (Pratto, Sidanius, Stallworth, & Malle, 1994); the coordinated are at the bottom of the hierarchy. When people are hierarchically differentiated we call this a vertical culture. We can have either vertical collectivism (VC) or vertical individualism (VI).

When role differentiation is not especially functional, and people can best make a living by working cooperatively and by emphasizing equality, we have horizontal collectivism (HC) or horizontal individualism (HI).

Triandis (1995) has reviewed evidence that suggests that in every culture people use all four of these patterns, but with different probabilities across the situations that commonly occur in their culture. For example, across situations, one individual may be VC 50 percent of the time, HC 10 percent of the time, VI 20 percent of the time and HI 20 percent of the time. A culture that includes many such individuals would be called a VC culture. Traditional India, China, Africa, and Latin America are good examples of such cultures. On the other hand, when the modal pattern is HC (e.g. the Israeli kibbutz) or VI (e.g. the USA, England, France, Germany) or HI (e.g. Sweden, Australia) we would have quite different cultural patterns.

In level 2, the universal variables of level 1 acquire specific meanings in each culture. For example, while social distance is a universal dimension, the exact form it will take depends on ecology, history, and culture. For example, in one culture it may be manifested by accepting or rejecting another person from one's golf club. Clearly golf clubs are not universal; they can be found in only a few countries. In another culture, e.g. India, social distance takes the form of avoidance of physical contact, because the idea of ritual pollution is important. In that case, to measure social distance, instead of asking if the subject accepts another person to a golf club one would ask if the subject allows the other person to touch his kitchen utensils.

In sum, the social psychologies of each culture will emphasize different determinants of the social phenomena that they describe, but if we know the location of a culture on the individualism and collectivism dimensions we will be able to make predictions concerning how phenomena will occur in each culture. We can also examine how applications of differing psychologies might become manifested in specific settings, such as work settings (Triandis, 1994a).

Level 3: Indigenous psychologies

While in all cultures people favor in-group members, the exact way they do it and what they emphasize is different. For example, in Japan *amai* (Doi, 1986) reflects the strong interdependence (Markus & Kitayama, 1991) that characterizes that culture, and people presume that they can be dependent on another person; in traditional Greece self-descriptions emphasized that the respondents viewed themselves as high in *philotimo* (Triandis & Vassiliou, 1972), that is, they implied that they generally do what their ingroup expects them to do; among Hispanics *simpatia* is an especially important cultural script that specifies that people must behave positively and avoid negative behaviors (Triandis, Marin, Lisansky, & Betancourt, 1984) more than is the case among non-Hispanics. This cultural script is an indigenous version of the way collectivists deal with other people. Similarly, "Confucian dynamism" (Chinese Cultural Connection) is an indigenous Chinese dimension of values.

Most theories about social behavior that were developed by social psychologists reflected what is known as "naive psychology" (Heider, 1958) and were largely reflections of the culture of these social psychologists. Culture envelops humans to such an extent that it is very difficult to become aware of the extent that the social psychological theories developed in that culture are products of that culture.

Traditional social psychology is largely Western, and reflects cultures that are relatively high in individualism and relatively low on collectivism. It is an "indigenous" social psychology that applies to Western cultures. An indigenous social psychology is one that is applicable to only one culture. Cultural anthropologists identify culture regions, such as Africa South of the Sahara, East Asia, and so on. Traditional social psychology is an indigenous social psychology (Berry, 1983; Kim & Berry, 1993) because most of it is applicable only to the West. It is estimated that about 30 percent of humankind lives in Western, individualist cultures; about 70 percent live in collectivist cultures (Triandis, 1995).

Triandis, Vassiliou, and Nassiakou (1968) and Triandis and Vassiliou (1972) found social behavior, in traditional societies such as Greece of the 1960s, to be a consequence of norms and roles much more than a consequence of attitudes, and very different when people interact with ingroup as opposed to outgroup members. In short, the most important determinants of behavior in traditional cultures are norms and roles; in individualistic cultures the most important determinants of behavior are usually attitudes and beliefs. That does not mean that attitudes and belief are unimportant in collectivist cultures. They are just not as important as norms and roles. Thus, the determinants of social behavior are "weighted" differently in each society.

For example, when a person in most (but not all) collectivist cultures meets another person, she asks first "what is my relationship with that person?" In some relationships the collectivist has many duties and obligations; in other relationships he or she can behave as he or she pleases. In fact, collectivists behave toward ingroups in extremely helpful and cooperative ways and toward outgroups by taking advantage of them (if they can). In other words, the "weight" that is given to the "in-group–out-group" factor as a determinant of social behavior is very large in collectivist cultures and not as large in individualist cultures.

To put it differently, the social psychology of the individualistic cultures of the West differs from the social psychology of the collectivist cultures of the East, and the traditional cultures of Africa and Latin America (Triandis, 1988, 1989, 1990, 1994b, 1995; Triandis, Brislin, & Hui, 1988; Triandis, McCusker, & Hui, 1990; Triandis, Bontempo, Villareal, Asai, & Lucca, 1988). While the general links between individualism and collectivism belong to level 2, the specific social psychological manifestations of different kinds of collectivism and individualism belong to level 3.

Level 4: Individual differences in behavior

Personality emerges at this level. For example there are extroverted and introverted people (relative to the cultural standard) in all cultures. But the cultural standard may be different, reflecting the differences in the ecology and history of the group.

Culturally Sensitive Methodologies

To measure social psychological phenomena at levels 2 and 3 we need measurements that reflect local conditions, i.e. are culturally sensitive. To compare cultures we need measurements that have the same meaning in each culture. These needs resulted in methodologies that used both universal and culture-specific ideas in each culture. For example, attitude items derived from *many* cultures were standardized separately in *each* culture (e.g. Triandis, Davis, & Takezawa, 1965; Triandis, 1992). Consideration of how to measure both universal and culture-specific factors became the standard for the evaluation of cross-cultural studies (Triandis & Berry, 1980). Sophisticated cross-cultural research required the use of theory to eliminate plausible rival hypotheses (Malpass, 1977). Taking seriously the definition of culture as *shared* attitudes, beliefs, norms, role definitions and values, Triandis, Bontempo, Leung, and

Hui (1990) measured the time it takes for three people (a triad) to agree that an element of culture is desirable or important. When 90 percent of the triads agreed in less than two seconds that an item is important or desirable, it was considered an element of culture. Similarly when 90 percent of a sample of individuals gave the same response to an attitude item, this suggested the that item is an element of culture. Since each method of getting information about a culture is interpreted differently in each culture, multimethod approaches were advocated (Triandis et al., 1990) in which the various measurements converged. Thus, cross-cultural psychology emerged as a multifaceted enterprise (Berry et al., 1992).

Social behavior

The influence of culture on social behavior can be studied by using models. Triandis (1971, 1977, 1980) has presented such a model that specifies how elements of culture, such as shared attitudes and values, guide and shape social behavior. Rewarded repetitions of this behavior become habits and later customs. Thus, in a pattern of circular causation, culture influences social behavior and social behavior shapes culture. Associated with this model is a methodology to obtain culture-sensitive measurements (e.g. Triandis, 1992).

In addition to the cultural factors described above, demographic factors such as age, gender, social class and the like increase, when they are similar, and decrease, when they are different, the rate of interaction among individuals, and thus the sharing of the elements of culture. This means that similarities in culture emerge under the influence of demographic factors (Latané, 1994), as well as similarities in ecology and history.

Concluding Comment

Social psychology emerged in the West and under the influence of cross-cultural psychology it is broadening to develop an integrated framework for placing indigenous social psychologies, including the indigenous social psychology that was developed in the West, into a coherent theory. This theory is held together by universal patterns of social behavior, but allows each indigenous social psychology to develop in its own way. The major contributions of cross-cultural social psychology, from at least one perspective, are two: the development of culture-sensitive methodologies that allow the identification of indigenous social psychologies (Kim & Berry, 1993; Triandis & Berry, 1980) and the comparison of these social psychologies, and the development of a better understanding of cultural syndromes (Triandis, 1993, 1995) and the way they mediate among the indigenous social psychologies.

The realization that ethnocentrism is a consequence of the total immersion of humans in their own culture, which makes their own culture the standard against which other cultures are judged, is perhaps the most important insight of cross-cultural social psychology. It also leads to a hopeful future, that will permit the reduction of ethnocentrism. Such reduction occurs as humans are exposed to other cultures and see strengths in these cultures that their own culture does not have. Similarly, the ethnocentric universalism of social psychology can be reduced by studying social psychological phenomena in different cultures.

Ethnocentrism can be reduced also by teaching people to see the world the way people in other cultures see the world (Triandis, 1975). For example, a person from a no-contact culture (people who keep their bodies far from the bodies of others in social relationships, do not touch much, do not look others into the eye) such as Japan, who meets a person from a contact culture (people who keep small distances between bodies in social interaction, touch, hold hands, look into the eye, like to feel the other's breath when talking) such as Mexico, must learn that when a Mexican holds their hand for a long time he is simply "friendly." If you ask the Mexican "why are you holding this person's hand?" he might say "I like that person." But if you ask a member of a no-contact culture to make an attribution about the Mexican's behavior if he says that Mexicans are pushy or even homosexual he is clearly misunderstanding the behavior of members of the other culture.

Misunderstandings across cultures occur when people make very different attributions to explain a specific behavior. One example is what happened in Geneva when the Iraqis met the Americans, just before the Gulf War of 1991 (see Triandis, 1994b, for details). The Americans told the Iraqis that they would attack if they did not get out of Kuwait, but they said it without anger, and the Iraqis did not believe them. In Iraqi culture if you are sincere you exaggerate your statements. The Americans were not understood, and that cost the Iraqis about 100,000 lives and four billion dollars! In cross-cultural interactions myriads of misunderstandings occur every day. Cross-cultural training can help us avoid such misunderstandings.

References

(Those marked * are recommended for further reading.)

Adamopoulos, J. (1984). The differentiation of social behavior. *Journal of Cross Cultural Psychology*, *15*, 487–508.

Berry, J. W. (1983). The sociogenesis of social science: An analysis of the cultural relativity of social psychology. In B. Bain (Ed.), *The sociogenesis of language and human thought*. New York: Plenum Press.

Berry, J. W., Poortinga, Y., Segall, M., & Dasen, P. (1992). *Cross-cultural psychology*. New York: Cambridge University Press.

Bogardus, E. S. (1925). Measuring social distance. *Journal of Applied Sociology*, *9*, 299–308.

Davidson, A. R., Jaccard, J., Triandis, H. C., Morales, M. L., & Diaz-Guerrero, R. (1976). Cross-cultural model testing: Toward a solution of the emic-etic dilemma.

International Journal of Psychology, *11*, 1–13.

Doi, T. (1986). *The anatomy of conformity: The individual versus society*. Tokyo: Kadansha.

Hebb, D. O., & Thompson, W. R. (1954). The significance of animal studies. In G. Lindzey (Ed.), *Handbook of social psychology* (pp. 532–562). Cambridge, MA: Addison-Wesley.

Heider, F. (1958). *The psychology of interpersonal relations*. New York: Wiley.

Herskovits, M. J. (1955). *Cultural anthropology*. New York: Knopf.

Kim, U., & Berry, J. W. (Eds.) (1993). *Indigenous psychologies*. Thousand Oaks, CA: Sage.

Klineberg, O. (1954). *Social psychology*. New York: Holt.

Klineberg, O. (1980). Historical perspectives: Cross-cultural psychology before 1960. In H. C. Triandis & W. W. Lambert (Eds.), *Handbook of Cross-Cultural Psychology* (Vol. 1, pp. 31–68). Boston: Allyn & Bacon.

Kluckhohn, C. (1954). Culture and behavior. In G. Lindzey (Ed.), *Handbook of social psychology* (Vol. 2, pp. 921–976). Cambridge, MA: Addison-Wesley.

Krueger, J., & Clement, R. W. (1994). The truly false consensus effect: An ineradicable egocentric bias in social perception. *Journal of Personality and Social Psychology*, *67*, 596–610.

Latané, B. (1994). Theory of culture. Paper presented at the Regional Congress of the International Association of Cross-Cultural Psychology, Merida, Mexico, October 25.

Lee, R. B., & DeVore, I. (Eds.) (1976). *Kalahari hunter-gatherers: Studies of !Kung San and their neighbors*. Cambridge, MA: Harvard Press.

Malpass, R. S. (1977). Theory and method in cross-cultural psychology. *American Psychologist*, *32*, 1069–1079.

Markus, H., & Kitayama, S. (1991). Culture and self: Implications for cognition, emotion and motivation. *Psychological Review*, *98*, 224–253.

Mullen, B., Atkins, J. L., Champion, D. S., Edwards, C., Handy, D., Story, J. E., & Vanderlok, M. (1985). The false consensus effect: A meta-analysis of 115 hypothesis tests. *Journal of Experimental Social Psychology*, *21*, 262–283.

Pratto, F., Sidanius, J., Stallworth, L. M., & Malle, B. F. (1994). Social dominance orientation: A personality variable predicting social and political attitudes. *Journal of Personality and Social Psychology*, *67*, 741–763.

*Schwartz, S. (1994). Beyond individualism/collectivism: New dimensions of values. In U. Kim, H. C. Triandis, S. Choi, C. Kagitcibasi, & G. Yoon (Eds.), *Individualism and collectivism: Theory, method, and applications* (pp. 85–122). Thousand Oaks, CA: Sage.

Triandis, H. C. (1971). *Attitudes and attitude change*. New York: Wiley.

Triandis, H. C. (1972). *The analysis of subjective culture*. New York: Wiley.

*Triandis, H. C. (1975). Cultural training, cognitive complexity, and interpersonal attitudes. In R. W. Brislin, S. Bochner, & W. J. Lonner (Eds.), *Cross-cultural perspectives on learning* (pp. 39–78). Beverly Hills, CA: Sage.

Triandis, H. C. (1976). *Variations in black and white perceptions of the social environment*. Urbana: University of Illinois Press.

Triandis, H. C. (1977). *Interpersonal behavior*. Monterey, CA: Brooks/Cole.

*Triandis, H. C. (1978). Some universals of social behavior. *Personality and Social Psychology Bulletin*, *4*, 1–16.

Triandis, H. C. (1980). Values, attitudes and interpersonal behavior. In H. E. Howe & M. M. Page (Eds.), *Nebraska Symposium on motivation, 1979* (pp. 195–260), Lincoln, NE: University of Nebraska Press.

Triandis, H. C. (1984). Toward a psychological theory of economic growth.

International Journal of Psychology, *19*, 79–95.

Triandis, H. C. (1988). Collectivism and individualism: A reconceptualization of a basic concept in cross cultural psychology. In G. K. Verma & C. Bagley (Eds.), *Personality, attitudes, and cognitions* (pp. 60–95). London: Macmillan.

*Triandis, H. C. (1989). Self and social behavior in differing cultural contexts. *Psychological Review*, *96*, 269–289.

*Triandis, H. C. (1990). Cross-cultural studies of individualism and collectivism. In J. Berman (Ed.), *Nebraska Symposium on motivation, 1989* (pp. 41–133). Lincoln, NE: University of Nebraska Press.

Triandis, H. C. (1992). Cross-cultural research in social psychology. In D. Granberg & G. Sarup (Eds.), *Social judgment and intergroup relations: Essays in honor of Muzafer Sherif* (pp. 229–244). New York: Springer Verlag.

*Triandis, H. C. (1993). Collectivism and individualism as cultural syndromes. *Cross-Cultural Research*, *24*, 155–180.

Triandis, H. C. (1994a). Cross-cultural industrial and organizational psychology. In H. C. Triandis, M. Dunnette, & L. Hough (Eds.), *Handbook of industrial-organizational psychology* (Vol. 4). Palo Alto, CA: Consulting Psychologists Press.

*Triandis, H. C. (1994b). *Culture and social behavior*. New York: McGraw-Hill.

*Triandis, H. C. (1995). *Individualism and collectivism*. Boulder, CO: Westview Press.

Triandis, H. C. (1996). The psychological measurement of cultural syndromes. *American Psychologist, 51*, 407–415.

Triandis H. C., & Berry, J. W. (Eds.) (1980). *Handbook of cross-cultural psychology* (Vol. 2). Boston, MA: Allyn and Bacon.

Triandis, H. C., & Vassiliou, V. (1972). Comparative analysis of subjective culture. In H. C. Triandis (Ed.), *The analysis of subjective culture* (pp. 299–338). New York: Wiley.

Triandis, H. C., Bontempo, R., Leung, K., & Hui, C. H. (1990). A method for determining cultural, demographic, and personal constructs. *Journal of Cross-Cultural Psychology*, *21*, 302–318.

Triandis, H. C., Bontempo, R., Villareal, M. J., Asai, M., & Lucca, N. (1988). Individualism and collectivism: Cross-cultural perspectives on self-ingroup relationships. *Journal of Personality and Social Psychology*, *54*, 323–338.

Triandis, H. C., Brislin, R., & Hui, C. H. (1988). Cross-cultural training across the individualism-collectivism divide. *International Journal of Intercultural Relations*, *12*, 269–289.

Triandis, H. C., Davis, E. E., & Takezawa, S. (1965). Some determinants of social distance among Americans, German, and Japanese students. *Journal of Personality and Social Psychology*, *2*, 540–551.

Triandis, H. C., Marin, G., Lisansky, J., & Betancourt, H. (1984). Simpatia as a cultural script of Hispanics. *Journal of Personality and Social Psychology*, *47*, 1363–1375.

Triandis, H. C., McCusker, C., & Hui, C. H. (1990). Multimethod probes of individualism and collectivism. *Journal of Personality and Social Psychology*, *59*, 1006–1020.

Triandis, H. C., Vassiliou, V., & Nassiakou, M. (1968). Three cross-cultural studies of subjective culture. *Journal of Personality and Social Psychology*, Monograph Supplement, 8, No. 4, 1–42.

23 The Socially Structured Mind

John C. Turner and Penelope J. Oakes

John C. Turner obtained his B. A. Hons and doctorate in social psychology in the UK at the Universities of Sussex and Bristol in 1971 and 1975 respectively. His doctorate on social categorization, social comparison and intergroup relations was supervised by Henri Tajfel. From 1974 to 1977 he was research associate then co-director at Bristol with Henri Tajfel and Howard Giles of a major research program developing and testing social identity theory. He joined the teaching staff of the Department of Psychology at Bristol in 1976. In 1982–83 he spent a year as Visiting Member of the Institute For Advanced Study, Princeton, NJ, and in 1983 he joined the staff of Macquarie University, Sydney, Australia. In 1990 he took up the position of Chair of Psychology at the Australian National University, Canberra, subsequently becoming Head of Department and Dean of Science for separate periods. His interests are in social identity and self-categorization, intergroup relations, group processes, and social cognition.

Penelope J. Oakes obtained her B.Sc. Hons in psychology and doctorate in social psychology at the University of Bristol, UK, in 1978 and 1983 respectively. Her doctorate was on factors determining the salience of social group memberships in social perception. She was a member of the psychology staff of Macquarie University in Sydney, Australia, from 1984 to 1990 and in 1991 joined the Division of Psychology of the Australian National University, Canberra, where she is currently senior lecturer. Her interests are in social categorization and social cognition, particularly stereotyping, perceived group homogeneity, and the psychological salience of social categories.

Introduction: Interactionism Versus Individualism

We are asked to state our view of the message of social psychology. We take it we are being invited to be thought-provoking and that a statement of platitudes is not what is wanted. We do have a view and we shall state it as straightforwardly as possible. In the space available and given the task we are bound to put things more baldly, with less elaboration and qualification, than would be appropriate in other contexts, but much of what needs to be elaborated is already available in earlier publications.

Social psychology is a branch of psychology. It is not part of sociology (there is a sociological social psychology, but this is not the field we are discussing) and nor is it an interdisciplinary field. It is the branch of psychology which explores mental phenomena in their relationship to human social interaction and society at large (Turner, 1994). Since its inception in the early decades of this century it has studied crowds and social groups, social influence and persuasion, attitudes and attitude change, intergroup relations, stereotypes and prejudice, interpersonal relationships, motives, emotions, and social cognition, to name only the best known topics. There are as many "messages" to be drawn from this great array of research as there have been questions asked. But there is also one general message, one which appears in different forms in the major areas. This message has to do with social psychology's *raison d'être*, with the vindication of its role as a unique branch of psychology without which we would be unable to make sense of the special properties of human social interaction.

The message of social psychology is that the human mind is not a purely individual process or product. *The mind is socially structured, not individualistic.* Minds belong to individuals – there is no group or collective mind in the literal sense – but their content, structure, and functioning are nevertheless socially shaped and interdependent with society.

Importantly, it is not simply that the *contents* of the mind are assimilated from society. It is also that psychological *functioning*, the way the mind works, presupposes an interaction with social context and social processes. The corollary is that general or individual psychology, abstracted from these social influences, is no more able than biology or neuroscience to explain adequately the realities of human social conduct or to provide more than a partial account of mental life. The principles of general (individual) psychology will not and cannot do the job of social psychology (Tajfel, 1981, Chapter 2).

Sherif, Asch, and Lewin, and before them LeBon, McDougall, Freud, Durkheim, and others, all pointed to the fact that the group, society, is *more than the sum of its parts*. Further, the "parts" – individuals – are changed through their involvement in the "whole." Social interaction gives rise to emergent *psychological* properties, not merely emergent *behavioral* properties. We can find examples of this point in Sherif's (1936) analysis of social norms as internalized shared frames of reference, in Asch's (1952) discussion of psychological group formation and joint action as taking place within a shared field of mutual reference, and in Lewin's (1948, 1952) field theory of individual behavior shaped by complex, holistic patterns of social forces, and of group life as a product of common fate and interdependence.

The same argument was put in a new form by Henri Tajfel in discussing prejudice and intergroup relations as well as the specific character of social psychology (see Turner, in press). Social psychological phenomena, he argued, do not arise simply from intraindividual processes; they also have an origin in society. His development of the concept of social identity illustrates what he meant by this point. He saw social categories as representations of social structure, representations that define an individual in terms of a common social location and that are shared with others in that location. They can be internalized to change the psychology and conduct of the individual, producing a qualitative shift to a collective psychology:

> Any society which contains power, status, prestige and social group differentials (and they all do), places each of us in a number of *social* categories which become an important part of our *self*-definition. In situations which relate to those aspects of our self-definition that we think we share with others, we shall behave very much as they do . . . They acted together, but it was not because of any *individual* facts of their personal psychology. (Tajfel, 1977, p. 66)

Similarly, Tajfel saw intergroup relations – the very opposite of individual behavior – as a quintessential problem of social psychology. The task was to find out "why so many people behave in unison – which they often do" (Tajfel, 1977, p. 66). Social psychology is not about individual differences or the individual exception, he argued, but about the socially shared, the collective aspects of conduct, and the social forces that shape the many.

To phrase our argument in a slightly different way, we are suggesting that *society is psychologically creative*: the mind is characterized by emergent psychological properties which are socially produced and reciprocally affect social behavior. This is the message of social psychology, and we believe that it is both scientifically and socially important and still radical in its implications. Nearly all social psychologists would probably agree with this general statement phrased in the abstract, but in practice many seem to embrace a different view of the relationship between psychology and society, a view we shall refer to as the thesis of *individualism*.

The idea of the mind–society interaction, which we shall refer to as the thesis of *interactionism* (Turner & Oakes, 1986; Turner, Hogg, Oakes, Reicher, & Wetherell, 1987), is one of the two major views that have continually opposed and debated each other during the development of the subject. The alternative view is *reductionism*, or, in the context of social psychology, as we have said, *individualism*. This view seeks, in one form or another, to deny the socially structured mind, and to reduce social psychology to no more than the application of the principles of general psychology to behavior within the "social environment." Thus, general principles of learning theory have been used to explain both how rats run mazes and how individuals in a crowd influence each other (e.g. Allport, 1924). The concept of "limited information-processing capacity" is used to explain aspects of the character of short-term memory and to account for the perception of individuals as group members (e.g. Macrae, Milne, & Bodenhausen, 1994). The subject matter of cognitive and social psychology may be different but some assume that, in principle at least, the fundamental explanatory principles can be the same.

It can be argued that progress in social psychology has been bound up with the conflict between interactionism and individualism and that each has had to deal with the ideas, data, and criticisms of the other. We think this must be true in some sense. Certainly, the conflict seems to be present whenever real theoretical progress is being made. However, the weight of ideological pressure from general psychology and Western culture seems to favor the individualistic perspective. The tendency, particularly recently, seems to be for individualism to become the orthodoxy and interactionism the minority stance. Yet paradoxically in our view it is the interactionist message which is specifically social psychological. In the following pages we shall elaborate the idea of the socially structured mind by tracing the conflict between individualism and interactionism as it has unfolded in major areas where we have conducted research. It is this conflict which gives the notion of the socially structured mind its developing meaning. The conflict, we stress, is between ideas, not researchers, for it commonly occurs within the theoretical output of individual researchers. Our brief summary of complex issues is as accurate as we can make it in the circumstances, but there is no pretence of neutrality.

Social Influence: The Divorce of Cognition From the Group

Social influence is the study of how people's attitudes and behaviors are affected by others. The major theories assume that two distinguishable processes account for such influence (e.g. Deutsch & Gerard, 1955; Petty & Cacioppo, 1986; see Turner, 1991). One (normative) process is conformity to others' expectations to avoid rejection and gain approval. This is compliance as a result of group pressure, leading to outward behavioral change but not private cognitive change. The other (informational) process is cognitively motivated conformity in which, in order to reduce uncertainty and perceive the world correctly, others' behavior is accepted as evidence about reality.

The dual-process model is almost prototypically individualistic in conception. The normative process describes public conformity to the group for purely instrumental reasons related to the desire to satisfy individual needs. It suggests that group-based influence only affects the public and not the private self and does not provide valid information about the world. The group exercises constraining power but not "influence" in the true sense, implying that people adhere to norms blindly, and that accurate cognition has no social basis. Inherent in the very concept of (sheep-like) "conformity" is a model of cognition as "naturally" individual, and of social influences as behavioral distortions of the true, private self. The related concept of "group pressure" takes for granted that the group is psychologically external to the person.

The informational process, as Moscovici (1976) points out, presupposes that individual cognitive functioning is primary and that society is a substandard, secondary source of information, a substitute process. This assumed primacy of the individual process of cognition is inherent in Festinger's (1950) distinction between physical and social reality testing. The idea is that social reality testing (consensual validation of information) only takes place to the degree that physical reality testing (investigating the world through "physical, objective, nonsocial" means) is difficult and the individual is uncertain. In other words, normally and firstly, the individual sees the world as it is, directly and correctly, through his or her own individual efforts. There is no need to turn to others except where this purely individual process of perception is unavailable or difficult. Only then, as a substitute, is there a role for ingroup norms in the definition of accurate perception and appropriate behavior. The implication is that accurate cognition is primarily/usually private, asocial and uninformed by values and norms, that social influence is not inherent in normal cognitive activity, and indeed that truth established by social influence is inferior.

In fact, this model is quite implausible (see Turner, 1985, 1991). Uncertainty leading to acceptance of influence does not arise from an asocial interaction between the individual perceiver and the ambiguous attributes of the stimulus world. It is social reality testing that both produces uncertainty and resolves it. There is no evidence for physical reality testing in isolation from social reality testing (Turner, 1985, 1991). The individual always acts as a member of a group, society or culture, applying established norms even when physically alone, interpreting the physical world in light of how similar others in the same situation would be expected to respond, and achieving subjective validity through the perceived or assumed agreement of others.

The original experimental paradigms devised by Sherif (1936) and Asch (1952) to examine social influence provide evidence for this argument. In both paradigms we find that the standard accounts of the findings in terms of versions of the dual-process model do not hold up. In Sherif's "autokinetic" situation, where subjects make judgments about the apparent movement of a point of light in a darkened room, people are influenced by others not because reality is ambiguous but, on the contrary, because they *assume* it to be objectively unambiguous and shared by similar perceivers (see Turner, 1991, p. 84). Otherwise, what motive for mutual influence could there be? Agreement about an idiosyncratic illusion would be arbitrary and futile. In the Asch paradigm, where subjects are exposed to the obviously incorrect judgments of the lengths of lines by other subjects (really confederates of the experimenter), people do not remain confident of the outcome of their supposedly straightforward physical reality testing, but nevertheless conform to the group knowing that it is wrong. They become uncertain, *despite* the ease of individual testing, because a group of people similar to themselves makes different judgments. As Asch (1952) pointed out, similar people judging the same stimulus array *ought to agree* – this is a natural requirement of the psychological context.

To make sense of both sets of results we must suppose that people never function as isolated perceivers. Rather, they take for granted a social and psychological similarity, a shared awareness of a common reality and common social identity. Perceivers' socially shared expectations about themselves and about stimulus reality are *basic to*, and always a part of the normal functioning of physical perception. Recognition of this point reverses the direction of the traditional relationship between the group and social influence: the individualistic conception supposes that an individual state of uncertainty produces a need for influence, as a substitute for physical reality testing, and mutual influence leads to group formation and structure. Our argument, developed in detail elsewhere (Turner et al., 1987), is that a social bond, in the form of shared group membership, is a precondition for the experience of uncertainty and the validation of cognition through mutual social influence.

In the social influence field, then, the idea of a socially structured mind translates into a rejection of the dominant model in which cognition is defined as a purely individual process and social influence as a form of public coercion. The role of social relationships and reference group norms is not to constrain and compel as if society were alien and external to the self. Mutual influence and shared norms validate "information," and private cognitive change is an interdependent product of individual testing and group-based influence. Thus, *information processing* is socially as much as psychologically mediated. Cognitive states (such as uncertainty) and cognitive processes (such as cognitive change) of a special human form are made possible and generated by social relationships.

Social Conflict and Intergroup Relations

What are the causes of social conflict? There are many relevant perspectives, but social psychologists have naturally focused on the psychological aspects of conflict. In doing so, however, they have tended to psychologize conflict, to look for causes in the psychology of the individual. Thus they have defined the problem of social conflict as primarily one of *prejudice*, to do with individual attitudes, stereotypes and opinions founded on cognitive and emotional distortions and biases.

An alternative perspective is provided by Sherif, by Tajfel, and by our own work on social identity and stereotyping. Sherif (1967) showed that negative outgroup attitudes and behavior followed rationally from the structure of the functional relationships between groups in terms of their collective goals. Personal attitudes and relationships could be seen as epiphenomena of intergroup relations, rather than vice versa. To understand intergroup relations one needed to analyze the cooperative or competitive nature of goal relations, members' identification with groups, and the social norms that groups developed in the course of their relationships. In this view, "prejudice" is normative, anchored in group structure and processes, operating in specific intergroup relationships. Sherif demonstrated that outgroup hostility and negative stereotypes could be reversed as a function of the influence of superordinate goals and intergroup cooperation. The individual attitude is secondary to group relations, not primary, and only appears irrational if one denies the social context within which the individual actually lives. At the group level social conflict may be fully rational.

Tajfel and Turner (1979) identified other group-level processes that come into play where individuals perceive themselves in terms of their intergroup relationships. They pointed out that people define themselves in terms of *social identity* as well as *personal identity* (Turner, 1982), and that self-evaluation in terms of social identity depends upon and has consequences for intergroup behavior. People seek positive distinctiveness for their own groups compared to others under certain conditions where social identity is salient. That is, when acting as group members, people want their own group to be better than others, as this has positive psychological implications for their self-definition. Hence there are ethnocentric motivations inherent in intergroup relations producing (social) competition between groups independent of their goal relationships (see Turner & Bourhis, in press).

Properly understood, social identity theory helps us to see that experimental manifestations of ingroup "bias" (in the "minimal group" paradigm of Tajfel, Flament, Billig, & Bundy, 1971, for example) are not unreasonable or irrational. Of course, within a deliberately artificial and controlled experimental setting a general process may be persuaded, for theoretical reasons, to produce an odd, "unreasonable" outcome, but such settings are by definition not normal. The real issue is whether the general processes identified are in themselves irrational.

Interestingly, social identity theory has itself tended to be psychologized, reduced to an irrational intrapsychic cause, an individual need for self-esteem that produces ingroup bias without regard for reality and social structure (e.g. Rabbie, Schot, & Visser, 1989). Having psychologized the theory, the critics then blame it for a reductionism which they have imposed upon it. Turner and Bourhis (in press) have rebutted this false picture. Social identity theory does not postulate a quasi-biological "drive" towards prejudice, and nothing in the theory implies that positive self-evaluation is achieved through an ego-defensive distortion of reality. The minimal group data are irrational only from the limited perspective of purely individual self-definition and self-interest. In contrast, social identity theory offers an analysis of the complex processes at work at the interface between self-definition, social comparison, social values, and perceived social structure. It seeks to accommodate the impact of social forces which influence the varying relative salience of social versus personal identity, the degree to which people define themselves as group members rather than as individuals in particular circumstances. The theory draws our attention to the fact that we seek to evaluate our collective selves positively in terms of our social values, in terms of "the implicit and explicit ideologies" of our sub-group, group, society, or culture (see Tajfel, 1981, p. 36). A social value is a dynamic human meaning that requires action. It is not irrational to hold values, and given that we hold them it would be irrational not to employ them and seek to live up to them.

It is in answer to the tendency to reduce intergroup conflict to interpersonal and intrapersonal causes that social identity and self-categorization theories (see below) make important distinctions between *interpersonal and intergroup* behavior and between *personal and social identity*. These distinctions have helped to show the qualitative complexity of human social interaction, and the consequent futility of extrapolating from the individual to the social level, as if that complexity did not exist. One major implication is that it has become possible to see stereotypes as cognitively veridical representations of the group-level properties of self and others.

A popular contemporary view is that stereotyping is the result of an information-processing error, a tendency to overgeneralize and oversimplify people's individual attributes in order to cope with limitations in information-processing capacity. Social categorization of self and others, leading to the perceptual accentuation of intragroup similarities and intergroup differences between people, is regarded as distortion of people's true (individual) character. We have argued in contrast that stereotyping is in fact cognitively veridical, a representation of group-level realities that is flexible and context-dependent (Oakes, Haslam, & Turner, 1994). It is no more false in principle to see people as group members than as differing individuals. The fallacy of distortion arises from the assumption that social reality is purely individual.

In our attempts to understand large-scale human conflict the pervasive tendency has been to look for individual-level psychological causes. But we are not a collection of random, undifferentiated particles floating in a homogeneous, socially unstructured medium, governed by basic laws of individual psychology (see Tajfel, 1979, pp. 187–188). Personality, individual differences, personal relationships, and attitudes can explain *heterogeneity* within and between groups, but social conflict involves the collective reactions of people sharing *common* social identities and acting in terms of those identities. It is social forces and social organization which give form and substance to the social categorizations, norms and values, social comparisons, collective goals, and so on that mediate individual behavior in social conflict. Our minds and our selves are socially structured, and social identity provides the psychological link between social structure and large-scale collective behavior.

The Psychological Reality of the Group

Implicit in the distinction between interpersonal and intergroup behavior is a more fundamental point about the psychological reality of the group. A basic conflict in social psychology has been between those who believe that people are only individual persons and those who accept the psychological reality of the group. The former do not deny the fact of group interaction – the impact of group life on individual perception and conduct is one of social psychology's most important and undeniable findings – but they reduce it theoretically to interaction between individual persons following the laws of basic, general, asocial psychology, acting and reacting to each other as social stimuli, no different in kind to any other stimuli in the environment. According to this view, there are no novel qualitative processes which emerge in the group – the group is only the sum of its parts, an aggregation of individual actions and reactions (see Turner et al., 1987).

Much of our work has employed the concept of social identity to show that the group is a distinct psychological process, not merely a summation of personal relationships. Specifically, we have developed self-categorization theory (Turner, 1982, 1985; Turner et al., 1987) to elaborate the argument that human beings are psychological group members and not only individual persons. We agree with Asch (1952) that individual and group are the twin fundamental poles of social existence. In fact, we have argued that the very perception of personality derives from social comparison and interpersonal differentiation within a group context.

During the 1960s and 1970s group theory emphasizing personal self-interest and "interdependence" produced an impasse in the study of group processes. In focussing on *personal* interdependence (i.e. a relationship between "parts" which were not changed qualitatively by their membership of the "whole") it gradually moved away from a distinctive theoretical concept of the group and became more and more inconsistent with data showing that the group is an active *determinant* of the character of social relationships. A range of data (reviewed in Turner et al., 1987) showed that, far from arising from interpersonal relationships of attraction, influence and cooperation, the group was a precondition for such processes to develop, and that some concept of group as a psychological process was necessary to explain these phenomena. Social identification with fellow group members seemed able to create mutual attraction, influence, and cooperation without the intervention of personal contact, interdependence, or knowledge. As Turner and Bourhis (in press) have recently demonstrated in some detail, interdependence theory and personal self-interest cannot explain some basic and easily observed facts about group formation and ingroup favoritism.

In self-categorization theory, we argue that self-conception varies in level of inclusiveness from personal to social identity, and that salient social identity both reflects and makes possible emergent group phenomena. A "salient" identity is one that is currently psychologically active, determining self-perception at a given moment and created out of an interaction between the perceiver's motives, expectations and theories and the social relationships and actions being represented. Individuals acting in terms of shared social identity are, in effect, *not* individuals, but depersonalized. They are the subjectively interchangeable members of a social group, able to act and react collectively. Thus, it is the subjective equivalence of perceivers, salient shared identity, that (1) creates shared expectations of agreement in face of the same stimulus entity, gives rise to uncertainty where similar others disagree and engenders mutual influence to reduce uncertainty; (2) produces cohesiveness between people mutually perceived as similar to and part of a higher-order self; and (3) enables joint cooperation for collective self-interest deriving from the we-group. All these hypotheses have been subjected to empirical study in one form or another and generated supportive data (e.g. Bourhis, Turner, & Gagnon, in press; David & Turner, 1992; Hogg, 1992; Caporael, Dawes, Orbell, & van de Kragt, 1989; Gaertner, Mann, Dovidio, Murrell, & Pomare, 1990; Turner & Bourhis, in press).

From this perspective, the concept of group is far from being a nominal fallacy, a convenient fiction. It is a pervasive, ever-present psychological mechanism which creates social cohesion and collective action and makes possible certain higher-order, emergent forms of social life. These forms are evidenced by phenomena which have proved difficult to explain in reductionist terms. How does minimal social categorization produce psychological group formation? Why do negative group outcomes sometimes increase group cohesiveness? Why are people seemingly unable to cooperate even when it is in their joint interests to do so? How and under what conditions do group norms become polarized? Why do we stereotype ourselves? These questions arise directly from important research findings. Reductionist accounts have not done well in answering them, whereas we have derived novel, plausible and testable answers to them from self-categorization theory. The advantage of the theory is that it takes for granted the indissoluble psychological connection between individual and group, grounded in the variable nature of the self. The idea of social group membership as defining and transforming of the self is critical to understanding how the mind is socially structured and how new psychological processes emerge in consequence.

Self and Cognition

The nature of self and its relationship to cognition is at the theoretical core of social psychology. Explicit research on the self-concept has never dominated social psychology in the way that research on group dynamics, attitude change, or social cognition has. Yet in fact virtually all the phenomena and theories of social psychology touch on the self-process in one way or another. This is not accidental. The message that the mind is social psychological can be rephrased as the idea that the human mind cannot be understood by theories which leave out the self and its activities. It is the fact of self which makes human cognition social cognition. It is the self-process which is the dynamic principle which acts to internalize society as part of cognitive functioning. In the words of a recent paper, the self is "a mechanism for the social determination of cognition, for translating variation in one's 'social place' into relevant 'cognitive choice'" (Turner, Oakes, Haslam, & McGarty, 1994, p. 462). What we mean by "cognitive choice" is *the selective representation of phenomena from the vantage point of the perceiver*.

Recent work on the self, however, has tended to borrow theories and concepts from individual cognitive psychology in order to devise models of self which reduce it to a cognitive structure which processes information just like other cognitive structures (e.g. Kihlstrom & Cantor, 1984). The self is seen as a relatively fixed, separate mental structure that is activated according to the situation and that defines one's personality (or personality core). The "true" self is personal, unique and private and stored as an organized system of interrelated self-concepts. The public self is what one presents to and is perceived by others, though it is not a self that one *shares* with others in the sense of social identity. In its cognitive aspects, therefore, the self-structure is strangely asocial, a set of cognitive generalizations largely built up from one's past experience, from observations of one's past behavior. It comprises core self-schemata reflecting past experience and providing stability of interpretation and resistance to change.

This idea of self as a fixed cognitive structure or system that processes information raises some fundamental and difficult theoretical questions. For example, does the self-concept process all incoming information or only self-relevant information? How does one distinguish between self-relevant and self-irrelevant information? Isn't all experience in some way relevant to the perceiver? If this is accepted, then how can the self-concept exist as a separate structure? What distinguishes cognitive structures which are self-concepts from those which are not? What exactly creates the boundary between them in the cognitive system? Surely any piece of information is potentially self-defining and the same information can be used to define both self and others? Is the same information stored in two or more different places in the cognitive system, as self and not-self?

Moreover, this model must face the empirical fact that there is great variability in self-perception. The idea of an underlying mental structure sits awkwardly with this fact and complicates the task of explaining such variability. Understanding the fluidity of self-perception has thus become a matter of explaining when, why, and how some specific subset of cognitive structures is activated. The idea of structure itself makes no direct contribution to the answer. It simply puts the question of variability at second remove: not why does self-perception vary, but why does some (completely hypothetical) mental structure (which is supposed to produce self-perception) get activated? The real point of structure is to answer a different question: why is there stability?

Our research suggests a different approach (see Turner et al., 1994). It argues that self-categorizing varies lawfully and systematically (in level of inclusiveness, specific kind of self-category at each level, comparative attributes, and relative prototypicality of instances) so as to express the varying social comparative properties of the perceiver. The self is a varying, reflexive representation of the perceiver which is inherently fluid and flexible because it is a *comparative, relational judgment*. It defines the individual in a social context or, if one prefers, it defines the individual in social relational terms. To define the self as male is to represent it in terms of similarities with other males and differences from females, reflecting the perceiver's goals, theories and knowledge, and employing particular relevant dimensions of comparison in a given situation. This is the outcome of an active process of judgment in which the self-category of male is given a specific meaning and form as a function of the particular set of relations being represented. It is not the activation of some stored, invariant generic concept of "maleness" (see Oakes et al., 1994).

The argument we have made is that self-categorizing provides a varying social definition of the perceiver, and that *the varying, socially defined self actively shapes and determines cognition by directing its functioning from the specific vantage point of a given self.* Changing one's self-definition can, in turn, change values, self-relevance, goals, knowledge, the boundaries of social influence, the perception of agreement and disagreement, and so on. Are we Australians very similar to each other, or very diverse? Do I share the values of radical feminists, do I agree or disagree with them? Is my discussion partner creative and tolerant, or is she systematic and logical? Our research has shown that these judgments vary as salient *self*-categorization is affected by the demands of different comparative contexts. The answers will vary depending on whether one is comparing Australians with other nationalities, whether there are anti-feminists around or not, and whether one is taking part in this discussion as a science student or as a woman (see David & Turner, in press; Haslam, Oakes, Turner, & McGarty, 1995; Oakes, in press; Reynolds, 1996). All cognition, including basic processes such as categorization, takes place from a specific vantage point, a singular perspective: that of the self currently salient. Perception and thought are not neutral or disinterested, but actively involved in representing and understanding the world from the point of view of the participating perceiver. Hence cognition varies as the socially defined self varies. Hence there is socially mediated cognitive variation within and between individuals.

These are complex arguments which cannot be fully elaborated here. In essence, we are suggesting that the self is indissolubly social and that all cognition is social because of the impact of self. *It is the fact of self that transforms cognition into social psychology*. Cognitive principles can only provide an adequate account of human perception if they involve the self, and in so doing they become social psychological. This is what Tajfel (1981) meant when he described cognitive dissonance theory as social psychological because it used concepts such as "commitment" and "justification," concepts which invoke the self. Far from being able to reduce the self to a cognitive structure, it is the socially variable self that transforms cognition into social psychology.

The Relativity of Perception and the Problem of Bias

Major inferences we would like to draw from the discussion so far have to do with the relativity of human perception and the determining role of the self in this relativity. The active role of the perceiver in perception is well established. Almost all the data of social psychology could be cited in one way or another as relevant evidence, from the study of attitudes, through the "New Look" in perception to current studies in social cognition. They show that human perception is characterized by relativity, that it varies not only with the objective characteristics of the stimulus field but also with the perceiver, and with the social and psychological states of the perceiver. What a person perceives is a function of an interaction between the person doing the perceiving and the object being perceived. Perception is active, selective, constructive, elaborative, evaluative, motivated, and always takes place from the particular vantage point of the perceiving self. Our discussion suggests that it varies not only with the perceiver but also with the salient self-category for a given perceiver – different people see the same thing differently, and the "same" perceiver sees the same thing differently as the varying self changes.

The relativity of perception means that it is selective, relevant, interpretative and evaluative, but it does not imply that it must be invalid. Given our own goals, needs, values, perspectives, the self provides perception that is valid from one's own premises rather than someone else's. It functions to ensure that we see the world veridically, but in a way that is useful and relevant to our goals and needs and stamped by our values and theories. Perception that was not relative to self would be pointless, futile, unimaginable and meaningless. It would not be human. The ideal of human perception is not that of an omniscient being who sees all things at all times from all perspectives, nor of a neutral computer that analyses exhaustively and mechanically with no social purpose or emotional investment. What would be the point of perceiving from another's point of view? Why would one want judgments that evaluated and described reality from the standpoint of others' values and self-interest? It is hard to imagine how or why any biological (or other) system would evolve a capacity for perception unaffected by the functions, aims, properties, and location of the perceiver.

As human beings we often take for granted what is most revealing about our psychology. In social life, we disagree about, argue with, dissent from, rebel against, discuss and reject each others' views, just as much as we agree, accept and conform. Variety and heterogeneity are the spice of our cognitive life both within and between groups and even within the same individual. This is perceptual relativity in action. It is evidence for the variability of self-definitions which express people's varying social relationships. It is a sign that human cognition is social psychological.

If the human self were not socially determined and variable, if it were a biologically or sociologically given universal, fixed and common to all, then our reality would appear as an absolute. Human cognition would be fully constrained by the stimulus world, and all differences of judgment would reflect no more than differences in the object of judgment. There could be no disagreement, conflict, or negotiation over reality, in terms of our subjective premises and perspectives. It is social and psychological variation in the perceiver that ensures that all our judgments of the world are relative.

Social psychology has had no choice but to accept the contribution of the perceiver to perception. But it has chosen to define this contribution as error, bias, distortion, prejudice. The assumption seems to be that disagreement must be a symptom of inaccuracy, as if there were some absolute identity of the human perceiver which should produce identical appraisals of stimulus reality. But human beings are social agents, we inhabit different social locations, belong to different groups, societies, and cultures and hence appraise the world from different perspectives. It seems absurd to cry "bias" and "prejudice" because the indefensible model of the "standard," fixed perceiver is falsified. Surely it is more realistic to recognize that human accuracy demands relativity because "we," our social locations and our specific perspectives, differ.

Importantly, none of the points that we have made about the effects of the self contradict the fact, or the role of stimulus *reality*. It is simply that representation of reality is active and interpretative and is informed by one's own perspective, values and goals. Perception is an interactive product of the perceiver and reality, but not a distortion of the latter by the former. The political, ideological, and social contents of cognitions are selective, relative and partisan but not psychologically inaccurate. They are appraisals from a partial set of premises and their validity is partial and relative to those premises, but they still have a form of validity. Others making judgments from different premises will produce different judgments, also psychologically valid (see Oakes et al., 1994, chapter 8; Oakes & Reynolds, in press). As Sherif noted in 1967, it is the very fact that stereotypes, for example, represent groups from a "singular point of view" which renders the search for some absolute validity "unrewarding" (p. 37).

We are arguing for *relativity* but not for the idea that all views are equally valid or equally meaningless. The latter idea, usually described as *relativism*, is one that we strongly reject. We are suggesting that the same processes operating on different perceivers in different social locations will produce different judgments which are nevertheless equally accurate psychologically. *But* that is not the end of the story. The very same socially structured self that produces relativity provides the possibility of rising above it. The same processes of varying self-categorization that produce heterogeneity of views also make possible group formation, social influence and the coordination of differing views. The differentiation of personal identities within the group produces differing individual views, but salient social identity transforms difference into uncertainty and generates a search for a consensual, more accurate view in terms of the higher-order self defined by shared group membership. In appropriate circumstances a shared group identity comes into being which requires that group members agree, if they are to be correct from their own shared perspective. Perception may always be relative, but relative judgments may nevertheless be shared and consensual at a higher level. Such judgments are rationally more likely to reflect a deeper truth about the world, not because agreement always indicates accuracy, but because they have emerged from, and survived processes of discussion, argument, and collective testing.

Relativity is therefore not relativism. Far from precluding the search for higher-level truths, it is an outcome of the same processes which motivate us to seek such truths. In fact, relativity at the different levels of the socially defined self is a creative process, actively producing a multiplicity of information, uncertainty and cognitive conflict which feed into a collective process of physical and social reality testing. To see relativity as a sign of cognitive deficit, prejudice or subjective bias is to fail to see that human understanding is not given in a one-off percept but arises from a *process*, stimulated by a creative tension between the individual and the group, personal and social identity, physical and social reality testing. The issue of the veridicality of cognition must be unravelled in the context of these interconnections and tensions.

Conclusion

In this chapter we have argued that the human mind is socially structured and that therefore a proper understanding of the mind is impossible without the distinctive contribution of specifically social-psychological theory. Social psychology cannot be reduced to some kind of asocial general psychology or to some kind of psychology-free biology or social analysis. It is indispensable because it reflects the actual nature of the subject matter.

In trying to explain what we mean by the idea that the human mind is socially structured, we have traversed a number of contrasts between individualistic and interactionist analyses. In the area of social influence, where we began, the dominant dual-process theory splits off human cognition from social influence, implying that group processes either only affect outward behavior or provide an inferior, secondary source of information about the world. In fact, normal cognitive activity, we suggest, is mediated as much by social as physical reality testing. Private cognitive activity is socially influenced by the norms and values of one's group *as a matter of course*. This is a basic fact about human information processing which changes its qualitative nature.

Next, we pointed to and criticized the long-standing tendency to seek the causes of social conflict within the psychology of the individual. By definition, social conflict is not about the actions of individuals as individuals. It is about the large-scale, collective behavior of masses of people, acting in common, as members of social groups, in terms of shared perceptions of their intergroup rather than interpersonal relationships. The large-scale social uniformities of intergroup behavior show the impact of social structure. We need psychological concepts which explain how people behave in unison in relation to the social structure. Such concepts, of reference group membership, group norms and values, social identity, perceived intergroup relations, etc., developed in the intergroup tradition of Sherif and Tajfel, show how society produces socially shared action through transforming, socially organizing, the so-called individual mind.

Further, the concept of social identity not only contributes to explaining certain kinds of intergroup processes, it also provides a general account of the psychological reality of the group. Where people act in terms of a collective self rather than a personal self, there is an emergent shift in the kinds of psychological and behavioral interrelations that become possible between people. People are not merely individuals, they are at varying times and in varying ways both individual persons and psychological group members. This enhancement of the complexity of human social interaction reflects the social structuring of the mind through the internalization of representations of shared social locations (i.e. social categorizations) to define and modify the self. Developing this theme, we then argued that a variable, socially defined self is the basic means whereby cognition is socialized. All cognition takes place from the vantage point of a reflexively defined perceiver, where self-definition is in inherently social terms. Social identities and group memberships, and their related products and processes, are one instance of the general point that the mind is socially structured by means of the self.

Pulling these points together, we finally tried to show that the issue of the relationship between social and cognitive processes is closely tied up with the problem of "bias" in cognition. The idea that human perceptions, attitudes, and actions are prejudiced and irrational is a pervasive theme in reductionist accounts of social cognition and intergroup relations. We have suggested that there is a different way of looking at the problem of "bias." Human perception is characterized by relativity and relativity is evidence for the role of the self in cognition. The self is socially defined and variable and hence relativity is evidence that cognition is *social* psychological. Relativity is not a sign of cognitive deficit, prejudice or subjective bias, but of a rational, selective, purposeful representation of the world from a specific vantage point. The same social variability of the self which underlies the variety of human experience also requires that it be consensually tested within relevant groups before it is accepted as a valid reflection of reality.

This last point is important and, briefly elaborated, will serve as our conclusion. There is no process, social, psychological or scientific, which, if followed, will insure in advance that any particular cognition must reflect the world accurately. One can aspire only to processes which are rational, adaptive and probabilistically likely to enhance accuracy. The interdependence of individual and social reality testing is one such process. Individual and collective testing both build on each other's strengths and correct for each other's limitations. The strength of individual testing lies in the multiplicity of different views and judgments generated within the group, the mass of new information, the capacity of one person to challenge established orthodoxy and produce uncertainty. The weakness is found in the limited, partial and possibly idiosyncratic character of purely individual perspectives. The strength of collective testing lies in the detection of higher-order patterns and invariances in the welter of individual judgments, the uncovering of shared, consensual reactions which imply that the group response is a reaction to the objective, public features of the world. A response shared with similar others is a response which is likely, accurately, to reflect the real world, not one's personal biases. The limitation of collective testing is the tendency for success to produce blind conformity, for established norms to ossify into dogma, for complacency to eliminate and prohibit new thought, the very conditions challenged by the relativity of personal judgment. The tendency of reductionist accounts is to define the active role of the self in cognition as a source of bias, distortion and error. The reality, in our view, is that the social structuring of the mind through the self represents a major expansion of its behavioral and cognitive capacities, including the capacity for accurate, valid cognition.

References

(Those marked * are recommended for further reading.)

Allport, F. H. (1924). *Social psychology*. New York: Houghton, Mifflin.

*Asch, S. E. (1952). *Social psychology*. Englewood Cliffs, NJ: Prentice-Hall.

Bourhis, R. Y., Turner, J. C., & Gagnon, A. (in press). Interdependence, social identity and discrimination: Some empirical considerations. In R. Spears, P. J. Oakes, N. Ellemers, & S. A. Haslam (Eds.), *The social psychology of stereotyping and group life*. Oxford, UK and Cambridge, MA: Blackwell.

Caporael, L. R., Dawes, R. M., Orbell, J. M., & van de Kragt, A. J. C. (1989). Selfishness examined: Cooperation in the absence of egoistic incentives. *Behavioral and Brain Sciences*, *12*, 683–699.

David, B., & Turner, J. C. (1992). *Studies in self-categorization and minority conversion*. Paper presented to the Symposium on Minority Influence at the Joint EAESP/SESP Meeting Leuven/Louvain-la-Neuve, Belgium, 15–18 July.

David, B., & Turner, J. C. (1996). Studies in self-categorization and minority conversion: Is being a member of the out-group an advantage? *British Journal of Social Psychology*. Special issue on Minorities: Influence, processes and outcomes, *35*, 179–199.

Deutsch, M., & Gerard, H. B. (1955). A study of normative and informational social influences upon individual judgment. *Journal of Abnormal and Social Psychology*, *51*, 629–636.

Festinger, L. (1950). Informal social communication. *Psychological Review*, *57*, 271–282.

Gaertner, S. L., Mann, J., Dovidio, J., Murrell, A. & Pomare, M. (1990). How does cooperation reduce intergroup bias? *Journal of Personality and Social Psychology*, *59*, 692–704.

Haslam, S. A., Oakes, P. J., Turner, J. C., & McGarty, C. (1995). Social categorization and group homogeneity: Changes in the perceived applicability of stereotype content as a function of comparative context and trait favourableness. *British Journal of Social Psychology*, *34*, 139–160.

Hogg, M. A. (1992). *The social psychology of group cohesiveness*. Hemel Hempstead: Harvester Wheatsheaf.

Kihlstrom, J. F., & Cantor, N. (1984). Mental representations of the self. *Advances in Experimental Social Psychology*, *17*, 1–47.

Lewin, K. (1948). *Resolving social conflicts*. New York: Harper & Brothers.

Lewin, K. (1952). *Field theory in social science*. London: Tavistock.

Macrae, C. N., Milne, A. B., & Bodenhausen, G. V. (1994). Stereotypes as energy-saving devices: A peek inside the cognitive toolbox. *Journal of Personality and Social Psychology*, *66*, 37–47.

*Moscovici, S. (1976). *Social influence and social change*. London: Academic Press.

Oakes, P. J. (in press). The categorization process: Cognition and the group in the social psychology of stereotyping. In W. P. Robinson (Ed.), *Social groups and identity: Developing the Legacy of Henri Tajfel*. Oxford: Butterworth Heinemann.

*Oakes, P. J., Haslam, S. A., & Turner, J. C. (1994). *Stereotyping and social reality*. Oxford, UK and Cambridge, MA: Blackwell.

Oakes, P. J., & Reynolds, K. J. (in press). Asking the accuracy question: Is measurement the answer? In R. Spears, P. J. Oakes, N. Ellemers, & S. A. Haslam (Eds.), *The social psychology of stereotyping and group life*. Oxford, UK and Cambridge, MA: Blackwell.

Petty, R. E., & Cacioppo, J. T. (1986). The elaboration likelihood model in persuasion. *Advances in Experimental Social Psychology*, *19*, 123–205.

Rabbie, J. M., Schot, J. C., & Visser, L. (1989). Social identity theory: A conceptual and empirical critique from the perspective of a behavioural interaction model. *European Journal of Social Psychology*, *19*, 171–202.

Reynolds, K. J. (1996). Categorization and impression formation in interpersonal and intergroup contexts. Paper presented at the General Meeting of the European Association of Experimental Social Psychology, Gmunden, Austria, 13–18 July.

Sherif, M. (1936). *The psychology of social norms*. New York: Harper.

Sherif, M. (1967). *Group conflict and cooperation: Their social psychology*. London: Routledge & Kegan Paul.

Tajfel, H. (1977). Social psychology and social reality. *New Society*, *39*, 65–66.

Tajfel, H. (1979). Individuals and groups in social psychology. *British Journal of Social and Clinical Psychology*, *18*, 183–190.

Tajfel, H. (1981). *Human groups and social categories*. Cambridge: Cambridge University Press.

Tajfel, H., Flament, C., Billig, M. G., & Bundy, R. F. (1971). Social categorization and intergroup behaviour. *European Journal of Social Psychology*, *1*, 149–177.

Tajfel, H., & Turner, J. C. (1979). An integrative theory of intergroup conflict. In W. G. Austin & S. Worchel (Eds.), *The social psychology of intergroup relations* (pp. 33–47). Monterey, CA: Brooks/Cole.

Turner, J. C. (1982). Towards a cognitive redefinition of the social group. In H. Tajfel (Ed.), *Social identity and intergroup relations* (pp. 15–40). Cambridge: Cambridge University Press and Paris: Editions de la Maison des Sciences de l'Homme.

Turner, J. C. (1985). Social categorization and the self-concept: A social cognitive theory of group behaviour. In E. J. Lawler (Ed.), *Advances in Group Processes* (Vol. 2, pp. 77–122). Greenwich, CT: JAI Press.

Turner, J. C. (1991). *Social influence*. Milton Keynes, England: Open University Press and Pacific Grove, CA: Brooks/Cole.

Turner, J. C. (1994). El campo de la psicologia social (The field of social psychology). In J. F. Morales (Ed.), *Psicologia social* (pp. 3–21). Madrid, Spain: McGraw Hill/Interamericana de Espana.

*Turner, J. C. (in press). Henri Tajfel: An introduction. In W. P. Robinson (Ed.), *Social groups and identity: Developing the Legacy of Henri Tajfel*. Oxford: Butterworth Heinemann.

Turner, J. C., & Bourhis, R. Y. (in press). Social identity, interdependence and the social group: A reply to Rabbie et al. In W. P. Robinson (Ed.), *Social groups and identity: Developing the legacy of Henri Tajfel*. Oxford: Butterworth Heinemann.

Turner, J. C., Hogg, M. A., Oakes, P. J., Reicher, S. D. & Wetherell, M. S. (1987). *Rediscovering the social group: A self-categorization theory*. Oxford and New York: Blackwell.

Turner, J. C., & Oakes, P. J. (1986). The significance of the social identity concept for social psychology with reference to individualism, interactionism and social influence. *British Journal of Social Psychology*, *25*, 237–252. Special issue on the Individual/Society Interface.

*Turner, J. C., Oakes, P. J., Haslam, S. A., & McGarty, C. A. (1994). Self and collective: Cognition and social context. *Personality and Social Psychology Bulletin*, *20*, 454–463. Special issue on *The Self and the Collective*.

Author Index

Subject Index

(numbers in **bold** refer to glossary entries at the end of Chapter 1)